Richard Hollis

Swiss Graphic Design

The Origins and Growth of an International Style

1920-1965

Laurence King
Publishing

Published in 2006
by Laurence King Publishing Ltd
71 Great Russell Street
London WC1B 3BP
United Kingdom
Tel: +44 20 7430 8850
Fax: +44 20 7430 8880
e-mail: enquiries@laurenceking.co.uk
www.laurenceking.co.uk

A catalogue record for this book
is available from the British Library.

ISBN-13: 978-1-85669-475-9
ISBN-10: 1-85669-475-5

Printed in China

PR●HELVETIA
■Γ
Arts Council of Switzerland

Preface

Getting off the train in Zurich in 1958 was like walking into an exhibition of avant-garde design. In the main station, above the platforms, and across their combined width, was a single strip of billboard advertising cigarettes. Black-and-white photographs – smokers' heads and shoulders and smiling cropped faces – alternated with black panels carrying the brand name Turmac in huge red 'oriental' capitals, the rest of the smaller lettering in plain sanserif.

The same style of sanserif lettering appeared on a ten-metre-high wall in the centre of the city, recording the changing statistics of the city's traffic accidents – last year's, this year's, last week's. This wall formed one of the intersecting planes of a coloured geometrical structure, a Mondrian painting taken into three dimensions – a shelter for streetcar passengers. Here design and art, in as pure an example as could be found of the International Style, were shown as not entirely separate activities.

This book is an account, from an outsider, of how this style came into being.

I had arrived in Zurich in the summer of 1958 after visiting the World Exhibition in Brussels, looking at design. In Switzerland artists had integrated the practice of art and graphic design. Curiosity about their ideas then, in the early 1960s and again more recently, led me to meet several of the artist-designers and graphic designers who appear in the following pages. At one of these encounters, in 1958, Richard Paul Lohse, a painter and designer in mid-career, emptied a box of matches onto a table and exclaimed, 'Abstract Expressionism!' – meaning Jackson Pollock – then rearranged the matches in a perfect rectangular pattern to the approving shout of 'Mondrian!' He was expressing an excitement with the idea of clarity and order that typified both his own art and design, and that of his colleagues. At the time, their confidence in the value of their work and the importance of design was as unusual as the assurance of the work itself. This confidence has been justified. The result of their persistence was an attitude to design and a style recognized across the world as 'Swiss', and acknowledged also as the International Style.

▲ Public information presented as Abstract, geometrical art. The construction is linked to a bus shelter in the centre of Zurich and shows traffic accident statistics. Graphic design by Josef Müller-Brockmann; architect: Beppo Bivio, 1953.

◄ Zurich main railway station, Summer 1958. Cigarette advertisement designed by Josef Müller-Brockmann. To use black-and-white photography for billboards at this time was as much a novelty as the plain lettering, an almost standardized feature of the Swiss graphic design.

▲ As the chief stereotype of Swiss culture, the cuckoo-clock has been replaced by the Swiss Railways station clock, designed in its final form in 1955 by Hans Hilfiker. The red second hand takes its form from the disc waved by the guard to signal a train's departure. Hans Hilfiker (1901-1993), an electrical engineer and industrial designer, was later director of the Therma kitchen appliance firm, one of the few important instances of 'total design', linking the product to every aspect of its graphics (see pp. 236-7).

Note on the design of the book
Images and captions in the margins are additions to the continuous text, and often independent of it. Where possible the colour of the original and its print process is given. Sizes, unless of a standardized dimension (e.g., A4), must be inferred by the reader from a general description (e.g., brochure). Unless specified otherwise, posters are Weltformat (128 × 90.5 cm / 50.4 × 35.6 in.). Where titles and texts had done without capitals in the original German, they appear in capitals and lowercase to follow the conventional English style.

Introduction

The Swiss people's finest work of art is their free federation of twenty-two sovereign states, each protective of its own special character. No two states are alike: where one is Catholic, the other is Protestant; one is a modern town, the other an Alpine valley; here they speak a German dialect, here French, and there Italian, or Romansch, or Ladin. Taking these differences into account, as well as the three factors of canton, language and religious tradition – in a variety of combinations – makes a total of no fewer than 52 quite distinct cultural types!
– Denis de Rougemont,
Les Arts dans la Vie en Suisse,
brochure 22b/1,
Swiss National Exhibition,
Lausanne, 1964.

▲ Flag of the Uri canton, 15th century.

◄ Wall of district flags at the Swiss National Exhibition, 1964: the popular graphic tradition of powerful emblems and geometry.

This book traces the growth of a style. It tells the story of those who formed the style, the ideas that influenced them and the successive generations who were attracted to a radical, progressive movement. It is not concerned with the whole of graphic design in twentieth-century Switzerland but with the 'Swiss' style that had its origins in the 1920s and was exported in the 1960s to become an international style.

At least three factors account for the 'Swiss' style. First was the country's position and its neutrality at the centre of Europe. Second was language. The north of Switzerland (with the two largest cities, Basel and Zurich) shares a language with Germany, where progressive ideas were proposed, attacked and defended in the 1920s. Third was a number of cultural factors: the Swiss interest in precision, in craft skills; its widely admired system of education and technical training, and the enlightened attitudes in its museums; and the Swiss enjoyment of a 'graphic culture'. They like flags, for instance. Each town and district, as a reminder of its identity within the canton, has its own banner; so has each of the twenty-two cantons in the Swiss Federation. They also have coats of arms which appear on official documents, on the sides of streetcars, on uniforms. The flags' emblems and colours, dating from the battlefields of the Middle Ages, today accompany festive occasions. All are boldly graphic.

A heraldic quality; a care for detail; clear, refined and inventive lettering and typography, and a high standard of printing have added to the appeal and efficiency of Swiss business and industry, exemplified not only in the technical and promotional print of the large pharmaceutical and engineering industries but also in that of smaller enterprises, and by the tourist industry's posters, brochures and timetables. In the twentieth century the volume and variety of printing throughout the country was huge. The larger cities of Basel, Berne, Lausanne and Geneva, for example, still have their own broadsheet daily newspaper; Zurich has two.

Federal authorities have acknowledged the importance of graphic design: Switzerland was the first country to have its passport professionally designed. Public commissions, such as for the state's banknotes, postage stamps and Swiss charities, are in general the result of competition, as are posters for national events – and for several decades the Ministry of the Interior promoted an interest in design by selecting and exhibiting the 'Best Posters of the Year'.

Design and Social Action
Among national flags, Switzerland's white cross on a red background is one of the most easily recognized. With its colours reversed the red cross identifies the best known of many Swiss charitable organizations. Posters, leaflets and exhibitions for the Red Cross have been produced by leading designers.

Das Schweizerische Rote Kreuz braucht Rotkreuz-Spitalhelferinnen Wenn wir in Notzeiten wirklich helfen wollen, müssen wir uns heute vorbereiten. Wir rufen alle Schweizerinnen auf: Melden Sie sich jetzt! Schweiz. Rotes Kreuz, Sektion Zürich Hirschengraben 60 Telefon 34 82 22

▲ 'The Swiss Red Cross Needs Assistants in Red Cross Hospitals', an appeal to women in a poster designed by Paul Trauffer, 1961.
▼ Poster designed by Carlo Vivarelli, 1949, for 'Help the Aged', the national charity which makes annual appeals through poster advertising. The design was selected as one of the 'Best Posters of the Year'.

Posters such as these had to allow for slogans in at least three of the national languages. For Vivarelli's design in German, see p. 134.

Economics, Politics and Design
Dependent on trade for more than half its food and raw material, Switzerland is not isolated economically.
▼ Display panels at the Swiss National Exhibition in Zurich, 1939.

▲ Economic facts presented in a mural graph. The export-import balance graphically shows Swiss economic activity at a peak in 1920, levelling off in the 1920s, and in a deep trough after the world economic crisis of 1929-30. During the 1930s the decline of confidence in Modernism went parallel with the fall in trade.
▼ Switzerland's position: to the north and east, Nazi Germany and Austria; to the south, Fascist Italy; and to the West, France, soon to be overrun and occupied.

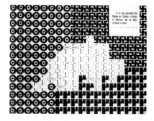

This book is divided into five parts. Part One traces the origin of the 'Swiss' style in the revolutionary political and cultural upheaval of Europe following the First World War. Russia, the source of the most radical aesthetic innovations, was taken over by the Bolshevik dictatorship, suffering civil war and famine. Germany, where the Modern Movement was pioneered, endured a series of attempted coups and assassinations, mass unemployment, hyperinflation and violent political confrontations between left and right.

Switzerland too was gripped by social unrest. As a neutral country, it had looked after the exchange of wounded and prisoners of war; it had given sanctuary to political refugees, pacifists and deserters. Emigrés who embraced anti-militarism and class struggle encouraged lasting antagonisms between the bourgeoisie and the avant-garde.

Between the two wars the comfortable and confident section of society revelled in modern life, in its pace and the industrial possibilities that new technology could bring; the less fortunate were marching and fighting in the streets. Intellectuals fought with manifestoes; artists made startling revolutionary art. The demand for change and the search for a new aesthetic created groups of like-minded creative people – Modernists. The progressive graphic designers among them shared with architects a modern aesthetic – an abstract, geometrical style – and joined them in calling for reform.[1] They set about making a 'new world'.

While these efforts were underway, in 1929 the New York stock market crashed and a world economic crisis followed. Currencies, including the Swiss franc, were devalued. The uneasy liberal democracy of the interwar years in Germany ended in dictatorship. By the mid-thirties, Switzerland was bordered by Hitler's National Socialist regime in the north and in the south by Mussolini's Fascist Italy. In this period too, within Switzerland's own borders, tension increased and continued into the years of the Second World War.

Part Two describes how Modernism survived the war, largely thanks to the artist-designers. The convergence of Abstract painting and graphic design, unique to Switzerland, is a persistent theme of the book. In Part One, painters are seen leaving their easels to work as graphic designers, realizing an aim both of nineteenth-

Politics and Design
Modernist designers were most likely to be supporters of progressive or radical political movements. Their designs broke new ground in style and technique.

▲ 'United Front against Lower Wages', poster designed by Theo Ballmer, 1933. The innovation typical of Modernist work is the use of all-lowercase lettering.
▼ 'Social Democrats: Against Crisis and Poverty, for Work and Food', poster by the photographer Paul Senn, 1931. An early example of a photographic poster, the image echoes Soviet Social Realism, rather than following the avant-garde exemplified by Lissitzky in his 1929 poster for the Russian Exhibition in Zurich. (See p.57.)

---

1. The later 'international style' of graphic design, unlike the International Style in architecture (known originally as 'Neues Bauen': New Building), did not propagate an obvious aesthetic. It was a simple means of carrying information. This accounts for its success in such contexts as highway signs and pharmaceutical labelling.

Art and Design

Several painters with a reputation as artists worked as poster designers. Their painting style was often distinct from their commercial art. The most celebrated artist-designer was Niklaus Stoecklin (1896-1982), whose posters became increasingly photorealistic in the 1930s and 1940s (see below and p.75).

▲ Poster by Niklaus Stoecklin, 1930. The design uses the simplified forms of Abstract painting to make a picture. Printed in black, blue-grey and yellow by lithography. More usually flat colours would be printed from linocut blocks.
▼ 'Enjoy your Meal!', poster by Niklaus Stoecklin, 1961. Stoecklin's full-colour painted image, printed lithographically, exploits the apparent objectivity of photography – the Modernists' only medium for illustration.

century thinkers and of the avant-garde Modernists: to unite art and industry. In Switzerland poster designers and most illustrators were traditionally artists: their prime activity was painting pictures. Throughout the book there are references to Constructivism and Concrete art. Constructivism was the foundation for many of the principles of the Modern Movement in architecture and design. As a movement, Constructivism originated in Soviet Russia alongside the country's political revolution; its influence extended across central and northern Europe. Though it had declared 'uncompromising war on art', its appeal was more aesthetic than political. This was expressed in a clear use of geometry – with an emphasis on the structure of a design – a use of flat colours, of layouts on a diagonal axis, of asymmetry, and of photography rather than drawn illustration.

Concrete art extended the Constructivist aesthetic by adding mathematical thinking. Since Concrete artists were in many cases also graphic designers, their use of mathematics provided a model for the geometrical organization of space in two-dimensional design.

Equally influential was the Constructivists' practice of photography. Photography was intrinsic to realizing the aim of objectivity ('Sachlichkeit') – the straightforward, impersonal recording of objects and events – a feature which runs through the book. Such an interest, and the avant-garde's insistence on standardization and precision, found a natural response in the Swiss temperament.

The preference for photography over drawn illustration helped to replace the idea of commercial art and the commercial artist ('Gebrauchsgraphik' and 'Gebrauchsgraphiker'). These terms gave way to graphic design and the graphic designer ('Graphik' and 'Graphiker').[2] The German word 'Typographie' embraces both typography and graphic design. There is a chronological sequence to its changing use: 'elemental' in 'elementare Typographie' and 'new' in 'neue Typographie', both connected with Jan Tschichold in the 1920s; 'functional' in 'funktionale Typographie', associated in the 1930s with Max Bill in particular; and 'integral' in 'integrale typographie', introduced by Karl Gerstner in the early 1960s.

In Parts One and Two the terms 'progressive' and 'Modernist' are used almost interchangeably. Modernist

Concrete Art and Design

Painters who were also progressive designers and typographers practised Concrete art: abstract, geometrical, computational, flat-coloured. They carried their mathematical methods of spatial organization directly into their graphic work.

▲ Page from *Kalte Kunst?*, a book by the designer-artist Karl Gerstner, 1957. The typical Concrete painting illustrated is by Richard Paul Lohse. Lohse and Gerstner were leading figures as both artists and designers.
▼ Page from the architectural magazine *Bauen+Wohnen* (Building+Home), designed by Lohse, 1948. Like the painting above, the layout has an underlying modular grid of squares.

2. The 'ph' in 'Typographie' and 'Graphik' (and in 'Photographie') could become 'f', usually to give a more up-to-date connotation. Hence 'Typografie', 'Grafik', 'Photografie'. Alternative German words for commercial art – without aesthetic aspiration – are 'Werbegraphik' or 'Werbegestaltung' ('werben' meaning 'to advertise').

◀ 'Cartography in Switzerland: Kümmerly and Frey Centenary', exhibition poster designed by Richard Paul Lohse, 1952. As a 'Concrete' artist, Lohse employed the same simple geometry and permutation of elements in his design work as he used in his paintings. In this poster the squares are made up of prints at different stages of the production and proofing process in map printing.

▼ Emblem for the photoengraving firm Schwitter, designed by Karl Gerstner, 1958. The design is based on the process of the halftone reproduction of images: the way that dark and light tones are broken into larger or smaller dots or squares when passed through a screen. The emblem appeared in black on all the company's stationery; a series of improvisations on the forms were used in colour over several years in advertisements (see p.180). As in the case of Lohse, the geometrical forms have an affinity with those used by the Concrete artists, of which Gerstner was one.

Geometry and minimalism

The spare geometry of the Concrete painters was also economical in both the design and printing of posters.

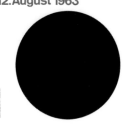

Eidg. Schützenfest
Zürich
24. Juli bis
12. August 1963

▲ 'National Shooting Fair', poster designed by Fridolin Müller, 1963. Although the circle could derive from a target or the bore of a rifle, it is a geometrical abstraction. Printed letterpress in black and red from linocut and poster type.

implies a designer who shared the outlook of Modern Movement architects. In Part Three, in the 1950s, the Modernists are given a group identification as 'Anonymous', before then being given the label 'Constructive' – an acknowledgement of their Constructivist antecedents.

In Part Four a further link with the Modernist tradition appears with the introduction of the grid as a tool in typographic design – a development alongside the New Architecture's geometry and standardization. And when a magazine was launched at the end of the 1950s to represent Modernist attitudes, taking as its title *Neue Grafik*, 'Constructive' graphic design was identified as 'Neue Graphik' (New Graphic Design). This later became known as 'Swiss Graphic Design', or simply 'Swiss style'. Its most obvious features – sanserif type arranged within a grid – were widely imitated across the world and, with the Swiss-designed typefaces Helvetica and Univers, its influence has survived into the digital age.

Part Five shows the Swiss style being dismantled in its home country, while in much of the rest of the world it had become part of a common visual language: on the one hand as the style of large corporate design and, on the other, of public service information: forms, booklets, the signs on highways, the labelling of medicines. Swiss design magazines found an international market and inspired widespread imitation. Swiss designers were invited to schools in the United States; they helped to establish courses in Asia; and they were welcomed in other European countries. For all these reasons 'Swiss' has also been described as the 'International Style'.

Information Design and Signage

An enduring Swiss influence has been in 'information design'. The clear typography and the Swiss sanserif typefaces have been used for all kinds of information design and public transport systems in cities around the world.

▲ Signage for Zurich public transport, designed by Ernst Hiestand, 1980s. The Zurich city emblem on the streetcar was designed by Helmuth Kurtz, one of the most progressive designers of the 1930s (see also p. 261).

▼ Proposal for signing in the subway system in Washington D.C., designed by Unimark under the direction of Massimo Vignelli and Peter van Delft, 1970. The figure is included to show the height of a column whose four sides carry the lettering.

Massimo Vignelli, a Milanese designer, emigrated to New York in 1965. In his long, successful career he was consistently Modernist and exemplified the Swiss style as the foundation of an international style (see also p. 255).

kunsthaus zürich
abstrakte und
surrealistische malerei
und plastik

6. oktober bis 3. november 1929 täglich geöffnet 10-12 und 2-5 montags geschlossen

▲ The origin of the Swiss Modernist
graphic style was in Abstract painting.
This poster for the 1929 exhibition
'Abstract and Surrealist Painting
and Sculpture', designed by Hans Arp
and Walter Cyliax, has two ingredients
common in later Swiss design –
simple geometrical elements and
lowercase lettering.

1

The New Typography:
Towards a New Graphic Design
1920-1938

I am convinced that in one or two generations architecture and the world
of design . . . will have been transformed with a universality of style, the style
of logical form and purity of idea.

Henry van de Velde, *Le Nouveau: Son Apport à l'architecture et aux industries d'art*, Brussels 1929, p.104.

At every moment of the past all variations of the past were 'new'.
But it was not 'THE' new. We should not forget that we stand at the end of a culture,
at the end of everything old.

Piet Mondrian, epigraph in Jan Tschichold, *Die neue Typographie*, Berlin 1928, p.6.

The 'New', the Arts and Crafts Tradition, and the Werkbund Idea

The 'New'
Suggesting innovation and a fresh start, 'new' was a term adopted by many of the avant-garde movements of the 20th century. In the Netherlands there had been Mondrian's 'New Plastic Art'; in France, Le Corbusier's *L'Esprit nouveau* (The New Spirit); and in Germany, *neue Sachlichkeit* (new objectivity), the New Architecture, the New Typography and the New Photography.

▲ 'The New Home', catalogue cover for an exhibition at the Zurich Kunstgewerbemuseum (Museum of Applied Arts), 1926. Designed by Ernst Keller, 'the father of Swiss graphic design'.
Keller used the same lettering on the exhibition poster and again for a second exhibition of 'Das neue Heim' two years later.
'Das neue Heim' was part of a longstanding mission of design reformers to liberate the domestic interior from stifling conventions.
The exhibition was one of a series in Switzerland which helped the general public to an awareness of progressive attitudes.

Modern design began in the nineteenth century with artists looking for a new role in an industrialized society. Their efforts intensified in the twentieth century. After the First World War in Europe these artists brought about a revolution in the design of print. This was introduced as the New Typography. Out went symmetry, ornament and drawn illustration; in came white space, plain letterforms and photographs. The New Typography evolved in the 1920s and 1930s. It is in this tradition and in this period that what became the Swiss graphic style has its roots.

Henry van de Velde was a leading figure among the artists who aimed to bring art to industry. Already well known in the 1890s, first as a painter, then as an architect and theorist, Van de Velde was a pioneer of modern design: not so much for the masterpieces of craft objects or the fine buildings that he designed, but rather for the practical and ideological attitudes which he represented. His aim was to make a new style, but one based on a principle which connected with

> that chain which has extended across the centuries which in the end shows just *one* family, *one single* family of *pure* form and pure decoration, a *unique* *style*: one that is rationally conceived, consisting of *pure* forms *determined by their function*.[1]

Although the publicity and packaging work which Van de Velde designed in the early 1900s was carried out in a version of Art Nouveau – abstract in decoration, its style far removed from later Swiss design – it was nonetheless important as an early instance of an artist working for industry, producing 'commercial art'.

Van de Velde was inspired by John Ruskin and William Morris, the nineteenth-century social critics and writers on art, and by the English Arts and Crafts Movement. In 1890 he concluded, 'There will be no place in the society of the future for anything which is not of use to everyone.'[2] Abandoning his easel on the grounds that painting had no socially useful function, he created a precedent for those artists in the 1920s who gave up painting to become graphic designers.

The debate initiated by Ruskin and Morris – the social role of the artist and the impact of machine production – continued long into the twentieth century. It engaged Italian Futurists, Constructivists in Russia and Central Europe, the De Stijl Movement in Holland and the Bauhaus school in Germany. Progressive architects,

Henry van de Velde 1863-1957
Belgian painter, architect, designer and theorist. Distinguished survivor of an earlier tradition of the 'new'. In 1947 retired to Switzerland. Until his death in Zurich ten years later he remained a magisterial presence and guiding spirit to younger Swiss colleagues.

▲ Pages of the play *Prométhée* by H.H. Dubois, designed by Van de Velde in 1929. Then in his mid-sixties, Van de Velde showed himself to be still in the avant-garde. Aligning the text right and left on a dual axis was itself an innovation, and the geometrically based Futura font had only recently become available.

---

1. Henry van de Velde, Lecture to the Swiss Werkbund, Langenthal, 16 November 1947, in *Das Werk*, January 1948, pp.34-42.
2. Quoted in introduction to 'Henry van de Velde: Extracts from His Memoirs', *Architectural Review*, September 1952, p.144.

▲ Poster designed by Josef
Müller-Brockmann for a memorial
exhibition of Van de Velde's life
and work at the Zurich
Kunstgewerbemuseum (Museum
of Applied Arts) in 1958, the year
following his death.
Printed in black on brown.
The last ten years of Van de
Velde's life were spent writing his
not always reliable autobiography,
Geschichte meines Lebens
(Story of My Life), Munich, 1962.

artists and designers committed their practical and
intellectual energies to finding a new formal and visual
language, and at the same time a means for the artist
of engaging in the cultural and industrial life of the new
mass society.

For half a century Van de Velde produced a stream of
essays embodying a single principle: that of logic applied
to every kind of design. He took his lead from engineers
and bridge builders, admiring them for their employment
of reason and calculation. In 1929 he published a long
essay on 'The New'.

> We want to create a durable new, one which renews
> itself, not a series of new 'new's. . . . From now on, the
> style imposed by the machine will be marked by its
> clarity, by that precision which spontaneously endows
> each clear and precise design with mechanical
> perfection.[3]

Van de Velde was not alone in wanting reform. In 1907
a group of German industrialists, architects and designers
had formed the Deutscher Werkbund, an association
aimed at bringing together art and industry. Van de Velde
had been one of the founding members. Called to
Germany at the turn of the century as the Grand Duchy of
Saxony-Weimar's artistic adviser for industry, his job was
'to raise the level of arts and crafts production'. This, and
the hope of increasing the appeal of German goods in
an international market, was also the stated aim of
the Werkbund.

Van de Velde's sermons on the obligation to make
an entirely new, rational style were welcomed by some
and rejected by others. In Germany, immediately before
the First World War, Van de Velde and his supporters, who
believed in the individual work produced by the artist-
craftsman, were vigorously opposed by those who
favoured a limited number of standardized 'types',
principally of furniture. Such discussions continued in
postwar Germany.

The Werkbund was the chief forum for discussion and
the means of publicizing avant-garde ideas. Its journal,
Die Form, reported on the new advertising design and
typography, and the Werkbund arranged exhibitions to
demonstrate the use of new materials and techniques:
in building, the use of concrete, glass and more open
functional planning; in graphics, the use of photography
and montage. In the 1920s and 1930s several of these
Werkbund exhibitions travelled to Switzerland. Their

The Werkbund
In Germany and Switzerland the
Werkbund organizations debated
the role of artists, craftsmen, architects
and designers in an industrial society.
And they helped make common ground
between the professions.

▲ This 1926 cover of *Die Form*,
the journal of the German Werkbund,
was designed by the Bauhaus master
Joost Schmidt.
In common with Swiss designers,
Schmidt used a geometrical
construction for his letterforms,
a style that belonged more to the
engineer than to the traditional
lettering artist.

---

3. Henry van de Velde, *Le Nouveau*, Brussels: Amis de l'Institut Supérieur des Arts
Décoratifs, Abbaye de la Cambre 1929, reprinted in Henry van de Velde, *Déblaiement
d'art*, Archives d'Architecture Moderne, Brussels 1979, pp.98-99.

18

▲ Cover for the Swiss Werkbund
monthly, *Das Werk*, in 1928, redesigned
by Walter Cyliax, a young German art
director working for the magazine's
Zurich printers.
In this early stage of the New
Typography, headings are in capitals.
Like Schmidt's lettering for the cover of
Die Form, Cyliax's is plainly designed
with ruler and compasses.

ideas were matched by equally radical posters, which
familiarized a generally conservative public with
progressive design.

The Swiss Werkbund was founded in 1913, with
the same aims as its German counterpart. Members
came from all professions in the visual arts; a handful
represented industry. Through meetings and lectures,
and in its monthly journal, *Das Werk*, the Werkbund
organizations provided common ground for architects
and artists, designers and crafts workers. Like the German
Werkbund, it arranged exhibitions, some of which
toured abroad.

An immediate Werkbund interest was standardization.
In mechanized industry standardization was essential:
for parts of buildings, such as windows and fittings; in
engineering; and in the industries in which Switzerland
had an international reputation. In the advertisements
and catalogues required for marketing such standardized
items can be found the origins of the objective, rational
manner of presentation that became a commonplace
achievement of Swiss graphic designers. One of them
later described what they then saw as

> ... a new field that called for new media of expression.
> It was at once clear to me that in industrial graphics
> the main accent has to be placed on information and
> documentation ... and requires a more factual graphic
> treatment.[4]

And he had no doubt that industrial graphics were the
seedbed of graphic design.

Standardization (norms) and 'Types'

These two ideas were essential
to Modernism. Although concerned
with the economy of production and
assembly, such concepts had an
effect on graphic style, encouraging
a tendency towards austere geometry.
The standardization of paper sizes was
incorporated in the Deutsche Industrie-
Normen (German Industrial Standards)
DIN system. This was adopted by
Switzerland in 1924 but was not to
become generally common in Europe
until the 1960s.
A standard size for Swiss posters,
the Weltformat (world format – 128 x
90.5 cm) had been in use since 1914:
special structures in the street were
designed to take posters in this size.
Like the German standards for paper
sizes, it was based on the 1:√2
rectangle (in the proportion 1:1.414)
which, when folded or cut in half
across, gives two rectangles of the
same proportion (see p.56). Small
horizontal posters were sometimes
produced in the half size.

▲ Poster designed by the Basel
architect Ernst Mumenthaler (1901-
1978) for the exhibition 'Typenmöbel'
(standard furniture), 1929.
Typenmöbel were rational,
undecorated, industrially produced
furnishings intended to replace items
made individually.
The message of rational rather than
decorative design is emphasized by
presenting the wardrobe in a severe
axonometric drawing rather than in
a pictorial illustration.

---

4. Hans Neuburg, 'Graphic Design or Commercial Art', inaugural address,
Icograda conference, Zurich 1964, typescript.

▶ Poster by Ernst Mumenthaler for
a touring exhibition on standardization
in industry and trade at the Zurich
Museum of Applied Arts in 1928.

Exhibitions at the museums of
applied arts in Basel and Zurich
(the Gewerbemuseum in Basel and
the Kunstgewerbemuseum in Zurich)
introduced the public to new ideas.
Their posters, often designed by
teachers at the related applied arts
schools (in Basel, the Allgemeine
Gewerbeschule and in Zurich, the
Kunstgewerbeschule), helped to make
the progressive graphic styles more
familiar.

The division of the surface area by
squares was one of the most popular
devices of Swiss designers.

The Bauhaus and Switzerland

In 1907, the same year as the inauguration of the Deutscher Werkbund, the School of Arts and Crafts opened in Weimar. Van de Velde designed the building, and became the School's first director. During the First World War, however, his status as an enemy alien prevented him from continuing as principal, and he suggested an architect, Walter Gropius, as his successor. In 1919 the School, combined with the Weimar Art Academy, became the Bauhaus, the most famous school of art and design in the twentieth century.

Gropius, a long-time member of the Werkbund, extended the Arts and Crafts aims at the school. The Bauhaus would provide 'a thorough, practical, manual training in workshops actively engaged in production, coupled with sound theoretical instruction in the laws of design'. And, 'Teaching of a craft is meant to prepare for designing for mass production.'[1] In August 1923, when the Bauhaus held its first public exhibition to show what it had achieved after nearly four years, Gropius inscribed its aims in the slogan: 'Art and technology, a new unity'.

The Bauhaus, first in Weimar and then in Dessau, was hundreds of miles to the north of Switzerland, nearly as distant as Berlin. But German-speaking northern Switzerland was especially open to German culture; Swiss interest in the school lasted until its closure in 1933, and its influence continued for several decades.

The 1923 Bauhaus exhibition was widely reported. The Swiss Werkbund's monthly, *Das Werk*, carried an enthusiastic account. The art historian Sigfried Giedion wrote that the objectives of the Bauhaus

> are to discover the new principles of form which are essential if the creative forces of the individual are to be reconciled with industrial production. . . . For the past ten years all the arts have been dependent on painting. . . . The creative work of the Bauhaus is likewise based upon the principles of contemporary painting.[2]

To many readers the Bauhaus was a challenge. The President of the Swiss Werkbund sounded the alarm in the next issue of *Das Werk*.

> Not only political and economic circles but also artistic and above all intellectual circles are caught up in this mad frenzy of revolution . . . promoted with an uncanny intelligence and sense of opportunism, without doubt largely induced and fostered by alien elements.[3]

1. *Idee und Aufbau des Staatlichen Bauhauses in Weimar*, 1923, translated as 'The Theory and Organisation of the Bauhaus', in Herbert Bayer *et al.* (ed.), *Bauhaus 1919-1928*, New York 1938, pp.22, 29.
2. *Das Werk*, Zurich, September 1923, pp.232-33. Quoted in Sigfried Giedion, *Walter Gropius: Work and Teamwork*, New York / London 1954, pp.31-35.
3. *Das Werk*, Zurich, October 1923, p.288. Quoted, *ibid.*, pp.35-36.

The 1923 Bauhaus Exhibition
The exhibition's publicity, under Constructivist influence, was evidence of a new, mechanical aesthetic.
▶ Above the doorway in the former Weimar art school building, designed by Van de Velde, the exhibition poster shows how far the school had come from an Arts and Crafts style. So does the advertisement in the local newspaper. ▼

In Switzerland the Bauhaus exhibition was reported in *Das Werk* by one of the central figures of Swiss and international Modernism, Sigfried Giedion.

▲ Giedion's review was reprinted in a 1924 booklet, *Pressestimmen für das Staatliche Bauhaus Weimar* (Press Support for the Weimar Bauhaus), designed by the Bauhaus teacher László Moholy-Nagy. The booklet's mannerisms are typical of early Bauhaus typography: extreme contrasts of type, the use of printer's 'rules' (black strips or bars) and the huge size of page numbers.

From Expressionism to Constructivism

Gropius followed Van de Velde in his belief that the individual artist and crafts worker would be the leader in design reform. Crafts were the basis of the Bauhaus curriculum, and the workshops were run by artists. After the First World War, the prevailing avant-garde style was the graphically violent Expressionism. The first painters at the Bauhaus – Lyonel Feininger, Johannes Itten and Gerhard Marcks, followed by Paul Klee, Georg Muche and Wassily Kandinsky – were not radical Expressionists, but were concerned with personal expression. The change in direction at the Bauhaus after its first three years was brought about by two artists, Theo van Doesburg and László Moholy-Nagy, who represented aspects of Constructivism. Their interest was in structure and form connected naturally to design. Both practised graphic design. Van Doesburg did not teach at the Bauhaus, but welcomed students to his Weimar studio where he filled them with the Dutch, De Stijl version of Constructivism.

▼ Max Burchartz, not a Bauhaus student but resident in Weimar, attended a short course at Van Doesburg's studio in the town. His move from Expressionism is exemplified by two works.

▲ In 1919 Burchartz made this lithographed design for Dostoevsky's *Die Dämonen* (The Devils) in a Cubist-Expressionist style. By 1923 he had turned to Constructivism.
▼ Advertisement for a department store, designed by Burchartz in 1924, after he had established his graphic design studio where he produced some of the earliest commercial examples of the New Typography.

It was true that the Bauhaus had attracted radical ideas from abroad, Giedion correctly identifying its driving force: Abstract art of the kind imported from the Dutch De Stijl movement and from Russia, in the form of Constructivism. For the majority, Soviet Russia represented a threat to the established order; the President was justified in connecting aesthetic revolution with social upheaval, since a great many progressive designers shared the view associated with the Bauhaus – that their work could help to construct a new society.

The early Bauhaus reflected the turbulent artistic and political atmosphere of post-First World War Germany. Elements of Cubism, Dadaism and Expressionism combined with radical or utopian aspirations to form a new community of artists and crafts workers. Among the teachers were painters such as the Russian, Wassily Kandinsky, and the Swiss, Paul Klee. Another Swiss artist, Johannes Itten, later Director of the Zurich Kunstgewerbeschule, ran the preliminary course.

Itten made strikingly original typographic experiments at the Bauhaus. Taking a different path from that taken by the Modernist graphic designers, he overrode centuries-old conventions, opening the way for the crude, powerful innovations of the Hungarian painter László Moholy-Nagy, who arrived at the school in 1923, the year Itten left. Proposing that 'typography is a tool of communication' – a revolutionary idea – Moholy-Nagy developed 'typofoto', a new form of expression using type and photographic images.

> We want a new language of typography whose flexibility, variability and freshness of typographic composition is exclusively dictated by the inner law of expression and optical effect.[4]

Moholy-Nagy stressed the importance of photographic illustration 'set within the text where formerly we used inexact, subjective interpretations of ideas'.

It was some years before the Bauhaus had its own printing workshop and taught advertising design. Young Swiss designers relied on Bauhaus publications for an indication of the school's approach to typography. There was little graphic work to be seen in the Bauhaus exhibitions in Basel and Zurich in 1929, at the time when two of the school's Swiss students returned home – Max Bill to Zurich and Theo Ballmer to Basel. Their influence was lasting. Bill – artist, architect, teacher, theorist and designer, as wide-ranging in his activities as Van de Velde

4. *Staatliches Bauhaus in Weimar 1919-23*, Munich 1923, p.141. This large, square book was published to coincide with the Bauhaus public exhibition. Its text pages were designed by László Moholy-Nagy.

Sigfried Giedion 1893-1968

Swiss architectural historian, trained as an engineer. Friendly with many Bauhaus figures, especially Gropius and László Moholy-Nagy. From 1929 intimately connected with the Modern Movement as Secretary General of the International Congresses of Modern Architecture (CIAM). Co-founder in 1931 of Wohnbedarf furniture store in Zurich and Basel, and associated with manufacturers. Commissioned brochures and advertising from leading Swiss designers and from former Bauhaus graphic designer Herbert Bayer. Later Professor of Architectural History at Harvard. His best known books are *Space, Time and Architecture* (1941) and *Mechanization Takes Command* (1948).

Johannes Itten 1888-1967
Swiss painter, teacher and theorist. Planner and supervisor of first Bauhaus foundation course, 1919-23. Forced to resign when his mystical attitudes ran contrary to the school's move away from individual expression. Replaced by Moholy-Nagy. Ran his own 'Itten-Schule' in Berlin, 1926-34. Director of the Kunstgewerbeschule and Kunstgewerbemuseum (School and Museum of Applied Arts) in Zurich, where he remained from 1938 to 1956.

22

Theo Ballmer 1902-1965
Basel designer, photographer and teacher. Bauhaus student, 1928-29. Apprenticed to Basel lithographic printer and studied at Kunstgewerbeschule in Zurich. Worked for pharmaceutical company Hoffmann-La Roche. Best known for his exhibition and political posters using only simple images in silhouette with his own powerful lettering (see facing page). Also a pioneer of the New Photography. Taught photography and design at the Basel Allgemeine Gewerbeschule, 1931-65.

Max Bill 1908-1994
See p.54

– was the key personality in Zurich. His graphic design introduced the later, functionalist attitudes of the Bauhaus, whereas Ballmer's posters shared the formal, geometrical aspects of Bauhaus graphics. Ballmer at the same time absorbed the new German attitudes to photography, which he taught at the Basel Allgemeine Gewerbeschule (Trades School) from 1931 until his death in 1965.

A third Swiss graphic designer who studied at the Bauhaus was Xanti Schawinsky. Although he did no significant graphic work in Switzerland, Schawinsky left his mark on graphic design history. In Germany he collaborated with Gropius on exhibitions, was graphic designer for the city of Magdeburg and, when the Nazis took power, left for Italy. In Milan Schawinsky helped make the reputation of Studio Boggeri, where a succession of the most able Swiss designers worked in the 1940s and 1950s.[5]

That Bauhaus ideas survived in Switzerland was largely due to Sigfried Giedion; he maintained links with several figures from the Bauhaus (including Gropius); he identified with their aims, and he commissioned and collaborated with Bauhaus designers (see pp.109-111). He was connected to the leading architects of the Modern Movement through his work for CIAM and was an historian of technology as well as architecture.[6] And he had been trained in the profession of the Modernists' heroic figure – the engineer.

Xanti Schawinsky 1904-1979
Born in Basel. Graphic designer, painter, and exhibition and stage designer. Leading personality among students at the Weimar Bauhaus. Important historical link between Switzerland, the Bauhaus, and Milanese design. Successful career as designer in Germany until Nazi seizure of power, 1933. Emigrated to Milan, designing, among other graphics, famous publicity for Olivetti. Left to teach (with Josef Albers, also a refugee from the Bauhaus) at Black Mountain College in North Carolina, USA, 1936. Returned to Switzerland, 1961.

▲ After he left Germany in 1933, Schawinsky was photographed by Lucia Moholy-Nagy for the cover of Basel's weekly picture magazine. Although Basel was Schawinsky's home town, by the end of the year he had left for Italy, .

5. Studio Boggeri was founded in Milan in 1933. Xanti Schawinsky worked there throughout 1934 and accompanied its founder, Antonio Boggeri, to Zurich in 1935, where he introduced him to the photographer Hans Finsler. In addition to Schawinsky, the Swiss designer Max Huber was a crucial figure in assuring the place of the studio in graphic design history. In a tradition which continued into the 1970s, a number of Swiss designers followed Huber at Studio Boggeri (see pp.138, 255).
6. Congrès Internationaux d'Architecture Moderne (International Congresses of Modern Architecture) founded in 1928 at the Chateau de La Sarraz in French Switzerland. At the annual meetings progressive architects and planners exchanged ideas. Sigfried Giedion remained Secretary General until CIAM's end in 1956. Throughout CIAM's life, the typography of its publications exemplified the current state of Swiss graphic design and typography. There were several Swiss members, including Max Bill. In 1951 Giedion edited *CIAM: A Decade of New Architecture*, designed by Richard Paul Lohse, an important figure in Swiss graphic design and co-editor and designer in the 1950s of the architectural magazine *Bauen+Wohnen* (see p.178).

Bauhaus Exhibitions in Switzerland

As well as the school's publications, travelling exhibitions were organized to promote Bauhaus ideas and to attract students.

▲ In 1929, two exhibitions were held in Basel. Just visible at the top of the advertising column is the poster for the exhibition at the Gewerbemuseum (Trades Museum). Printed in red and black on yellow paper, it was designed at the Bauhaus by the student Franz Ehrlich, based on a sketch by Joost Schmidt, the master in charge of the school's advertising and printing workshop.

Typical of Bauhaus practice is the use of all-lowercase lettering. Tilting type at an angle and the reversal of lettering out of solid black were graphic devices that became part of the Modernist visual language. The poster at the base of the column, for the Bauhaus painters' exhibition, was overprinted – again all in lowercase – on the standard Kunsthalle design by Karl Hindenlang, which was all in capitals.

▲ When the Bauhaus exhibition came to Zurich the following year, the catalogue cover gave little idea of Bauhaus typography, apart from the use of lowercase lettering.

▲ Poster by Theo Ballmer for 'Neues Bauen' (New Building), a travelling exhibition organized by the German Werkbund in 1928.

Apart from the geometrically drawn lettering, the design is not typical of Bauhaus graphics: it is uniquely Swiss in the skill of its drawn lettering, whose geometrical forms it shares with the New Architecture.

Artists as Designers

24

Bauhaus Typographic Influence

Typical Bauhaus typography used 19th-century sanserif typefaces known as grotesque. This style in Germany was in general known as Akzidenz Grotesk (Akzidenz meaning everyday jobbing or commercial printing). It was made with slight variations and different names by several typefounders. Capital letters were often fitted into rectangles, with type material such as rules (lines) and bullets (small solid circles) used as ornament.

▲ This card, designed by Herbert Bayer in 1925 for the Fagus factory, is a stereotype of 'Bauhaus typography'. The factory, which made tools for footwear production, was designed by Walter Gropius. In a true collaboration of art and industry, the firm was an example of Werkbund principles in action. Its stationery and advertisements were designed at the Bauhaus and also by other Modernist designers, including Van Doesburg. ▶

▲ The style of Bauhaus typography such as Bayer's was soon taken up in Switzerland. This quarter-page advertisement for binders for the year's issues appeared in Das Werk, where display advertisements were laid out at the printers under the design direction of Walter Cyliax. The predominance of capitals soon gave way to an exclusive use of lowercase – in keeping with the urge towards rationalization and economy. One of the Bauhaus letterheads asked, 'Why use two alphabets, when one will do?' The New Typography demanded function above form, 'truth to material', both in terms of typographic means and construction of the message.

Theo van Doesburg 1883-1931

Dutch painter, writer and architect. Leader of the De Stijl (The Style) group, whose best-known early associate was the painter Piet Mondrian. Gave courses on De Stijl ideas in Weimar, home town of the Bauhaus, 1922. Critical of school's artist-teachers' failure to confront issues of industrial production.

De Stijl's emphasis on the organization of planes in two-dimensional and three-dimensional space (a principle adopted by Swiss Modernist designers), was soon evident in Bauhaus work. Van Doesburg's use of Akzidenz Grotesk typeface in De Stijl magazine (early 1920s) was the protoype for Herbert Bayer's typography at the Bauhaus. Van Doesburg explained De Stijl principles in his Bauhaus Book Grundbegriffe der neuen gestaltenden Kunst (Principles of the New Plastic Art) and edited the only issue of his journal Art Concret, 1930. He died in southern Switzerland in 1931.

▲ Van Doesburg's advertising designs for Fagus products used exclusively Grotesk type – the sanserif, so-called grotesque or Akzidenz type; illustrations were photographs rather than drawn illustrations. This example from 1925 is a clear forerunner of the later Swiss style.

Gropius believed that modern painting 'has thrown up countless propositions which are still waiting to be used by the practical world'.[1] But when he talked of a new unity of art and technology, what kind of art was he thinking of? The highly personal work of the first artists on the Bauhaus staff, such as Paul Klee, did not seem a promising source of ideas for industrial production. And after 1921, the school's individualistic crafts-based Expressionist style gave way to Constructivism.

Constructivism originated in Soviet Russia, as an ideology rather than a style. Its aims radically extended Arts and Crafts ideas. Van de Velde had wanted to make art socially useful. Constructivists aimed to integrate art and society so that art would disappear. Artists were to function in collective activity, working in industry and, like scientists in a laboratory, developing new forms to construct a new world.

Constructivism spread across Europe, from Moscow to Rotterdam, mainly via Berlin.[2] The movement consisted of a small group of artists whose work, favouring pure colour and geometric form, was based on science and rationality. Constructivist artists exchanged ideas through visits and lectures and in confrontational exhibitions. They argued with each other at conferences and published their own magazines and each others' manifestoes.

The Bauhaus came to share the Constructivists' outlook. That it did so is attributed to the presence in Weimar of Theo van Doesburg, leader of the Dutch De Stijl group and editor of its journal. In 1921 he had moved to Weimar, where the Congress of Constructivists and Dadaists took place the following year. Although both the Constructivists and the Dadaists were devoted to destroying the old attitudes to art, they represented opposing positions: the one emphasized rationality; the other, spontaneity and chance. The anarchistic Dada movement, launched by émigrés in Zurich during the First World War, followed the Futurists in typographic innovation. Announcements and programmes for Dada meetings disregarded printing conventions; unlikely typefaces, often positioned at an angle, were thrown together with bits and pieces found at the printer.

Van Doesburg belonged to both camps: to the Dadaists as a writer (under the pseudonym I.K. Bonset); to the Constructivists as a De Stijl painter and theorist,

1. 'Idee und Aufbau des Staatlichen Bauhauses', translated as 'The Theory and Organization of the Bauhaus', in Herbert Bayer et al., Bauhaus 1919-28, New York 1938, p.29.
2. Russian émigré artists congregated in Berlin, where 'The First Russian Art Exhibition' took place in 1922.

Typography and Dada

Zurich had been a centre of revolutionary cultural and political activity during the First World War. Dadaists, mostly émigrés, followed the Italian Futurists in their violation of printing conventions.

▲ In this announcement of a Dada event in Zurich in 1919, visual anarchy replaces the usual vertical-horizontal symmetrical arrangement, and exclamation marks, asterisks and printer's rules are used as expressive devices. Dada typography had little direct influence. But several of the avant-garde who were associated with the movement later, mainly in Berlin, helped to found the New Typography.

▲ Van Doesburg played a part in Dadaism. The typography of this 'Bauhaus Balance Sheet' is part Dada, part Constructivist. The design, from Van Doesburg's magazine *Mécano*, no.4/5, 1923, celebrates the triumph of the Dutch De Stijl square over the folksy attitude at the school, represented by the circle. At the bottom it reads, 'Already many are using the □, but only a few understand it.' The square, crucial to Van Doesburg, became a much-repeated element and constructional motif in the work of Swiss designers. (See also pp.171-3.)

sharing their views on collective activity and their spatial aesthetic of geometrical planes. His typography and his geometrical lettering, even before 1920, was a forerunner of Bauhaus design and of the coming typographic revolution. But it was the Constructivists, many of them former Dadaists and Expressionists, who founded the New Typography. Their innovations were consolidated by a few young designers who were trained in a craft-based printing industry, which greeted the new forms of art with either outraged hostility or puzzled indifference.

Some progressive painters abandoned their easels altogether, as Van de Velde had done, to become full-time designers; others continued painting and considered graphic design work not merely as a source of income, but as an extension of their artistic activity. These artists were, to begin with, as important for formulating Modernist principles as for the typography they produced. The first to do so was Moholy-Nagy in the book accompanying the 1923 Bauhaus exhibition. The title of his essay, 'Die neue Typographie', initiated an assortment of articles and manifestoes on the New Typography. Although written by painters, these pronouncements were concerned not with art but with the design of print as part of a wider culture. Indeed, a year earlier, Moholy-Nagy had defined Constructivism as

> not confined to the picture frame or the sculptor's plinth. It expands into industrial design, into houses, objects, forms. It is the socialism of vision, the common property of all men.[3]

The Congress of Constructivists and Dadaists in Weimar had been attended by almost all the artists who contributed to the birth of the New Typography. These included, as well as Van Doesburg and Moholy-Nagy, Lissitzky, the former Dadaist Kurt Schwitters, the artist-poet Hans Arp, Max Burchartz and Werner Graeff.

Lissitzky had suggested to Schwitters that he collaborate on a book explaining modern art. Schwitters declined the invitation; Arp accepted. Work went ahead while Lissitzky was being treated for tuberculosis in the south of Switzerland in 1924, and the resulting book, *Die Kunstismen* (The Isms of Art), was published simultaneously in Zurich, Munich and Leipzig the following year.[4] With its German, French and English text set in bold Grotesk type, this book was revolutionary, both in its layout and in the dogmatic, aggressive

---

3. *Sibyl Moholy-Nagy, Moholy Nagy: Experiment in Totality*, 2nd edition, Cambridge, Mass. 1969, p 21.
4. Hans Arp and El Lissitzky, *Die Kunstismen*, Erlenbach/Zurich 1925. Reprint, Baden 1994.

László Moholy-Nagy 1895-1946
Hungarian artist, designer, teacher, photographer and writer. Member of avant-garde circle in Berlin which included Dadaists and Lissitzky, 1920-22. Signed Elementalist manifesto in Van Doesburg's *De Stijl* journal, 1922. Invited by Gropius to Bauhaus, 1923. Taught preliminary course and edited Bauhaus Books with Gropius, including his own *Malerei, Photographie, Film* (Painting, Photography, Film), 1925, and *Von Material zu Architektur*, 1929 (translated as *The New Vision*). Left Bauhaus to work as artist and in various fields of design in Berlin, 1928-33. Emigrated to Holland, then England. Opened New Bauhaus in Chicago, 1937. His views were elaborated in the book *Vision in Motion*, published in 1947 in Chicago, where he had died the previous year.

Kurt Schwitters 1887-1948
German artist, poet and graphic designer. Friend and collaborator of Van Doesburg. Famous as 'Merz' artist, for the Merzbau construction in his home and for his *Merz* magazine. Typographer for the city of Hanover, 1929-31. Organizer of the Ring neuer Werbegestalter, an international association of avant-garde graphic designers, and arranged exhibitions of work by Ring members, including 'Neue Werbegraphik', Basel, 1930 (see p.60). Emigrated to Norway, 1937, and England, 1940. Died in Ambleside, Cumbria.

Werner Graeff 1901-1978
German designer, writer and photographer. Studied at the Bauhaus under Johannes Itten. Co-editor of *G□*, and collaborator of Van Doesburg. Member of the Werkbund. Press officer for the Werkbund's Weissenhof-siedlung housing development near Stuttgart, 1926-27. Advanced avant-garde ideas in several books, including *Es kommt der neue Fotograf!* (Here Comes the New Photographer!) for the Werkbund 'Film und Foto' exhibition, 1929. Invited by Swiss Werkbund to give Zurich lecture on the New Photography, 1931. Taught photography at the Reimann school in Berlin. Emigrated to Spain, 1934. Moved to Switzerland, 1937. During the Second World War taught photography in Locarno (see p.151), and published instructional books in Switzerland including *Kamera und Auge* (Camera and Eye), 1942, and *Prospekte wirksam machen* (Making Effective Brochures), 1950. In the layout of his books, integrating text and image, he was an important innovator. After the war returned to painting. Died in USA.

▲ ▼ Two double-page spreads of Hans Arp and El Lissitzky's *Die Kunstismen* (The Isms of Art), 1925.
▲ The list of art movements continues over several pages in a layout as aggressive as the book's language. The heavy printer's rules, although they became a mannerism, helped to suggest a radical urgency. Their even weight was echoed in the bold Grotesk type. Three columns for tri-lingual books later became standard practice in Switzerland.

The 'isms' are defined mainly by artists representing each tendency. Each 'ism' is illustrated by an example.
▼ Sometimes, as here in the case of Malevich, this is accompanied by a portrait of the artist.

Geometrical elements, generous white space, Grotesk type, asymmetry, these ingredients of *Die Kunstismen* belonged to the New Typography. This was the earliest example originating in Switzerland.

▲ In *Die Form* Van Doesburg contrasted the decorative weakness of Lissitzky's *Die Kunstismen* cover, at the top left of the page, with the objective purposefulness of a leaflet designed by Max Burchartz for an iron foundry. Burchartz's studio in the Ruhr has been identified as the stylistic origin of the later Swiss style of graphic design.

Kasimir Malevich 1878-1935
Russian painter, architectural designer and theorist. Originator of Suprematism, a 'new realism' – Abstract painting of geometrical forms in primary colours on a white ground. Famously exhibited a black square in 1915, the square symbolizing the triumph of the human mind over nature. Visited the Bauhaus, which published his book *The Non-Objective World*, 1927.

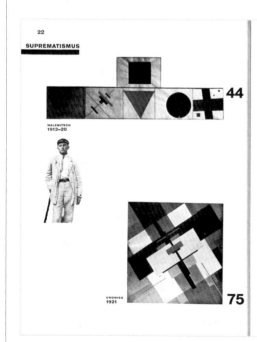

El Lissitzky 1890-1941

Russian painter and designer, trained as an architect in Germany. Best-known early design work is the poster, *Beat the Whites with the Red Wedge*, 1919. Head of the architecture section of Vkhutemas, the 'Moscow Bauhaus', 1921. Active in Berlin before coming to Switzerland, 1924. Although he came as an invalid and stayed little over a year, Lissitzky's activities in Switzerland were intense and influential. In Germany he made famously innovative designs for Soviet sections of international exhibitions, such as Pressa in Cologne, 1926, and for *USSR in Construction* magazine after his return to Russia, 1926. Died in Moscow.
▼ Lissitzky's double-exposure portrait of Hans Arp, made in Switzerland at the time that they were working on *Die Kunstismen*.

Hans (Jean) Arp 1886-1966

Artist and poet, born in Alsace. Took refuge in Switzerland to avoid conscription into the German army, 1915. Painted murals for the Cabaret Voltaire, venue for Dada events in Zurich. In Berlin after First World War, friendly with many avant-garde artists, Lissitzky and Schwitters among them. Set up studio in Paris, 1921. Married to the Swiss artist Sophie Taeuber (1889-1943), but was refused Swiss citizenship. Withdrew to Paris, 1925.

language of the editors and the quotations from the artistic innovators: 'From Cubism and Futurism has been chopped the minced meat, the German beefsteak: Expressionism.'

Advertisements for *Die Kunstismen* proclaimed the cosmopolitan origins of the new art: '15 isms, 13 countries, 60 artists'. Lissitzky's emphatic, original typography and spatial layout make it one of the earliest examples of the New Typography in Switzerland. The book's style is that of Constructivism, the 'ism' which underlay what became the Swiss style.

Lissitzky spent only a little over a year in Switzerland, from February 1924 to March 1925. To pay for his treatment, he not only prepared advertisements for the German firm of Günther Wagner, producers of Pelikan office supplies and art materials, but also wrote articles, and a small book on his fellow Russian, the painter Malevich. It was in Switzerland that Lissitzky made his photographic experiments, including a portrait of Arp and the famous self-portrait known as *The Constructor*. Lissitzky also finished co-editing and designing issue 8/9 of Schwitters's *Merz* magazine, produced in Hanover. Like *Die Kunstismen*, this double issue was set entirely in Grotesk type.

It was not only the avant-garde magazines such as *Merz* which carried the progressive message to Switzerland. *Die Form*, the Werkbund journal, was another. Among contributors on graphic design, Johannes Molzahn was the most significant avant-garde theorist. Both living in Weimar and designing for the Fagus shoe-last factory brought him into working contact with Gropius. Molzahn's 1926 essay, 'Economics of Advertising Mechanics', was an aggressively argued plea that advertising should be recognized not only as the engine of manufacturing turnover, but also as a machine, in its functions and manner of operation.

Among other propagandists writing in *Die Form* were Max Burchartz and Werner Graeff, who played their parts in introducing Modernism to Switzerland. Burchartz was an Expressionist painter turned Constructivist. In 1923 he was joint editor of a German edition of Van Doesburg's *De Stijl* magazine. The following year he opened a design studio in Weimar, known as Neue Reklame Gestaltung (New Publicity Design). Burchartz soon replaced this by a new enterprise, Werbe-bau (literally, Advertising-Construction), set up with Johannes Canis in the manufacturing centre of Bochum in the Ruhr.

In July 1924 Burchartz produced an A4 leaflet setting

▲ Stationery for the Fagus factory, manufacturers of shoemaking equipment, designed by Johannes Molzahn, 1924. The design shares its style with Herbert Bayer's – typical of so-called Bauhaus typography. As well as the red-printed dots (or 'bullets'), the right-angled black rules help the typist align the left margin, the black dot on the right marks the position for the date and the short lines on the left edge indicate folds across the page, dividing in half or into thirds. The identifying credit 'Molzahn design' appears within the rule on the lower margin; on the right is the note on paper standardization: 'DIN 476 A4.'
▼ One of the illustrations in Molzahn's article on trademarks in *Die Form* was his design for the engineering firm of Wilmking. Molzahn described the trademark as the essential link between production and consumption, predicting that 'the half-tone photographic image and the logo will govern the future of the advertisement'. Even in 1926, with the avant-garde, this was already true.

Johannes Molzahn 1892-1965

German painter, graphic designer and teacher. Studied in Weimar, taught in Magdeburg and Breslau. Emigrated to USA, 1938. Taught at Moholy-Nagy's School of Design in Chicago, 1943-47. Returned to Germany, 1959. Resident in Weimar, a painter moving away from Expressionism in the early 1920s, Molzahn's development ran parallel with that of the Bauhaus towards a Constructivist aesthetic.

28

Max Burchartz 1887-1961
German painter, designer, teacher and writer. Taught at Folkwangschule, Essen (a building designed by Van de Velde), 1926-33. Friendly with Schwitters and Lissitzky, and with Van Doesburg, who gave lectures in Burchartz's Weimar studio. Translated Mondrian's and Van Doesburg's Bauhaus Books. Member of De Stijl group. Returned to painting, writing and teaching at the Folkwangschule after Second World War.

▲Postcard for Max Burchartz's Werbe-bau design office, 1926. The square identifies Burchartz as a Constructivist. Not only does it dominate the logo but the type on the left-hand side of the card is also arranged within square limits. To configure information as a list within a box of printer's rules was a common device of early Modernist typography.
Burchartz's studio in the Ruhr was the stylistic source of *Industrie-Werbung*, the graphic design for industry later developed by the Swiss.

▲Inside page from an A4 leaflet advertising a system of rail joints, one of a series for the Bochum iron foundry, designed by Burchartz in 1925. These met not only with Van Doesburg's approval of their objectivity, but were also reproduced in Tschichold's *Die neue Typographie* and more than once in *Die Form* magazine. The technique of cut-out and montaged photographs originated with the collages of Dadaist and Constructivist artists.

out a programme for Werbe-bau. It is headed 'Publicity Design'. 'Advertising is the handwriting of every enterprise! Like handwriting, it shows up a firm's character, its strength and potential.' The leaflet then lays down, following its own recipe for straightforwardness, the requirements of a good advertisement. It must '1. be objective / 2. be clear and concise / 3. use modern means / 4. have a punchy design / 5. be cheap.'

Burchartz's leaflet is emblazoned with an orange square: 'Watch out for every leaflet with a coloured square.' Burchartz planned more, announcing that the leaflets would 'contain articles [mostly illustrated] by artists and specialists about general and specific questions of culture and organization, on building design, industrial product design and about publicity'. And he promised that 'they will bring in profits, if you follow their advice'. In the event, Burchartz carried on his campaign in the pages of *Die Form*.

The avant-garde's socialist tendencies did not preclude an interest in market economics. In 1926, when *Das Werk* first gave an account of the New Typography, the article carried the bald heading, 'Advertising'. Written by the painter Lajos Kassák, it included Werbe-bau's work. With the slogan 'Advertising is *constructive* art', the article concluded with typically Constructivist rhetoric: 'To design advertising means to be a *social artist*.'[5] As a Hungarian, imprisoned and then exiled after the collapse of a revolutionary government, Kassák pointed admiringly to Russia's achievement in transforming advertising both in its social purpose and aesthetically. Yet for Kassák, an advertisement should be judged not as beautiful or as ugly, but as to whether or not it is effective.

> The good advertisement does not analyze or define, it synthesizes – a unity of time, content and subject matter. Its basic [elemental] simplicity and purity makes us stop in the street and go into a shop which we had not thought about until a minute ago, puts a book in our hands by a writer we had never heard of, wakes us from our usual blindness and deafness and, *through its 'elemental' colours and its dynamic structure, first excites our curiosity and then forces us into a decision.*[6]

Here Kassák seems to be referring specifically to one of the illustrations included in his article, namely Otto Baumberger's poster for the PKZ clothing store. This design, which appears in many publications of the 1920s, is reproduced in the book that offers the most informative

Advertising, alongside the new buildings, was regarded as a means of disseminating the new culture, and reflecting the sense of functional organization. The modern image of the United States, of its industrial efficiency and of its glamorous cities, as portrayed in the cinema, were seen as models.
▼ Invitation designed by Max Burchartz to a talk on 'Advertising in America' by his partner, Johannes Canis, to be followed by a film, *America, Land of Unlimited Opportunity*, 1927.

Lajos Kassák 1887-1967
Hungarian artist, writer and designer. Co-edited the journal *Ma*, 1920-25. Collaborated with Lissitzky and Moholy-Nagy. Member of Kurt Schwitters's avant-garde organization, the Ring neuer Werbegestalter (Circle of New Advertising Designers). Introduced the New Typography to Switzerland in *Das Werk*, where he wrote, 'Advertising is *constructive* art', 1926.
Kassák was among the Hungarian avant-garde artists who had been the first to adopt the Russian Constructivists' simple geometry. They gave their works the title 'Picture Architecture'. Kassák reproduced one example, in black only, in the French magazine *Manomètre* in 1923.▼

---

5. Lajos Kassák, 'Die Reklame', in *Das Werk*, July 1926, pp.226-28.
6. *Ibid.*, pp.227-28.

B

Sachlichkeit

Baumberger's overcoat poster is an example of *Sachlichkeit* (objectivity). The word 'sachlich' recurs throughout writings on design in the 1920s and 1930s. The term originated in painting, where 'neue Sachlichkeit' (New Objectivity) signified the opposite of Expressionism. In the context of graphic design it usefully refers to the style of industrial and advertising graphics which is plain, undecorated, straightforward, factual, realistic. 'Sachlich' contains the idea of factual reportage, and also of being functional – what Van de Velde described as 'neutral'.

When it was possible to use photography at the scale of posters, the image was seen as an undistorted, factual representation. That 'the camera never lies' was an accepted notion at the time. The advertiser appealed to the public, not with emotional suggestions or promises, but with only essential information – what the product is and what it looks like.

▼ In 1934 PKZ reworked Baumberger's hyperrealism in a photograph. Though equally 'sachlich', this magazine advertisement lacks the seductive appeal of Baumberger's original.

Otto Baumberger 1889-1961
Poster designer, painter and illustrator. Apprenticed in Zurich lithographic printer's studio. Studied in Munich, Paris and London. Lithographic draughtsman and art director for Zurich printers Wolfensberger, 1911-13. In Berlin (theatre designs for leading director, Max Reinhardt), 1920-22. Returned to Zurich. Assistant teacher at the Kunstgewerbeschule until 1933. Lectured in architectural department, Eidgenössische Technische Hochschule (Federal Technical Institute), 1931-59. Designed more than 230 posters in a wide range of styles. Half a dozen of Baumberger's works of the 1920s and 1930s are pioneering examples of Modernist style. (See pp.30, 35 and 58).

▲ Otto Baumberger advertises the PKZ clothing store, 1923. This full-colour poster, entirely untypical of the artist's free style, was the most often cited Swiss work in manifestoes of the New Typography.
It was remarkable not so much for the skill of the photorealistic drawing as for its absolute objectivity, its lack of obvious aesthetic intention, and its economy – the name of the advertiser integrated into the image.

30

Gefesselter Blick
(Captured Glance)

The earliest comprehensive compendium of Modernist graphic design was published in Stuttgart in 1930. The 112-page book had the support of the advertising section of the Swiss Werkbund, although only two of the designers listed on the cover were Swiss: Otto Baumberger and Max Bill. Walter Cyliax, who worked in Zurich, was also among them.

▶ Under the clear plastic cover on the front of the book, on a flap of red paper, is a list of the 25 (in fact, 26) contributors, almost all of them artists as well as designers.

▲ Images are by Willi Baumeister (top) and by El Lissitzky.

▲ The first of Otto Baumberger's two pages in *Gefesselter Blick*, where he shows only his 'sachlich' manner, just one in a variety of his painterly styles.

▲ The first of Max Bill's three pages shows his letterhead. When folded, it becomes its own envelope, with the postmark adding proof of posting date.

▲ Walter Cyliax was adventurously dependent on the styles of other designers. One of the pages representing his work shows an imitation of a John Heartfield collage. Others show him as an imitator of Burchartz and also as a good run-of-the-mill commercial designer.

▲ One of two pages in *Gefesselter Blick* by Johannes Canis, Burchartz's partner as a specialist in graphic design for industry. They show him as the clearest forerunner of the later 'Swiss' style.
'The photographic representation of the product', Canis wrote, 'must be composed in such a way (angle of vision, cutting, etc.) as to "reveal" not only the technical form of the product but its "inner being", its retail value for both dealer and buyer and its use for the consumer.'

account of Modernist graphic design, *Gefesselter Blick* (Captured Glance).[7] Published in 1930 in Stuttgart but sponsored by the Swiss Werkbund's Advertising Designers Circle, *Gefesselter Blick* was edited by two brothers, the architects Heinz and Bodo Rasch. Their introduction to its 112 pages is one of the earliest, clearest statements made about graphic design, which it describes as a more or less dense grid of images, like film.

> Film is function interpreted by images. . . Text is simply a film made up of symbolic signs. . . . Images are supported by text; text is supported by images. This mixture of image and word is graphic design's chief field of activity.

The Rasch brothers collected a statement and examples of work from twenty-six artists and designers: a virtual directory of the avant-garde. Of these most were German. They included the virtuoso intellectual Werner Graeff, who later taught and published in Switzerland. Two contributors were Dutch – Paul Schuitema and Piet Zwart. From Moscow there was Lissitzky and from Prague, Karel Teige. Three designers from Switzerland were included: Otto Baumberger, Max Bill and Walter Cyliax.

What does the work of these twenty-six have in common with the later 'Swiss' style?

With few exceptions, the designs are not symmetrical; the type is sanserif; the illustrations are photographs, not drawings. There are fewer of the bands, lines and dots typical of early Bauhaus work, and printer's rules are used for a purpose, especially in tabular lists, to separate one category from another. These were the features that survived into Swiss design. Technical innovations were later refined: the crude collage of photographs, for example, was transformed into the type of montage where one image dissolved into another. The most common stylistic feature to reappear in Basel and Zurich was the diagonal. Inspired by Van Doesburg, it was a device frequently employed by the Dutch designers Paul Schuitema and Piet Zwart.

Gefesselter Blick's letterpress printing, in black and a single colour, was the standard, restricted medium for most small-scale graphic work until well into the 1960s. The most striking difference between the work in *Gefesselter Blick* and Swiss typography twenty years later is the use of capital letters. Although nearly half the designers had their names and text set in lowercase, most

7. Heinz Rasch and Bodo Rasch (eds.), *Gefesselter Blick*, Stuttgart 1930; reprint, Baden 1996. The Rasch brothers were architects, furniture designers and manufacturers in Stuttgart. Their graphic work was an extension of their architectural and interior design interests.

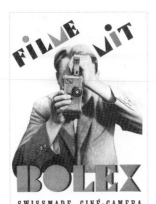

▲ Poster for Bolex film cameras, designed by Walter Cyliax, 1928. Printed in red and black, the poster was reproduced in the special Swiss issue of the German trade magazine *Archiv für Buchgewerbe und Gebrauchsgraphik* (Book Design and Commercial Art Record) in 1929 and also included in *Gefesselter Blick*. The technical facilities of Fretz allowed Cyliax to pioneer the use of photographs in posters.

of the headings in their designs – again, like the early work of the Bauhaus – were set entirely in capitals.

The most often repeated word in the statements is 'clarity'. Otto Baumberger notes that his work ranges from the objective to the impressionistic (for tourist posters), but here he is represented by his most 'sachlich', most photographic, manner. About his poster for the PKZ store showing part of an overcoat, the caption comments: 'The thing advertises itself. A fleecy, snug, double-breasted topcoat.' And it adds that, just as we want to turn a fine china cup upside down to see the maker's mark, the poster encourages the same impulse in the viewer – to look for the manufacturer's name. When word and image are integrated, it continues, the result is 'the simplest and most effective type of *Sachreklame* [objective advertising]'.

The realism of such illustrations as Baumberger's depended on the remarkable skill of Swiss printing technicians in tonal draughtsmanship. The images of many Swiss posters until the 1950s can be mistaken for photographs, when they are more often drawings by lithographic artists. A designer's skilled craftsmanship was taken for granted: in *Gefesselter Blick* Baumberger claims that, with no typographic training, he draws all his lettering.

The hand-drawn, geometrically constructed lettering in Max Bill's contribution to *Gefesselter Blick* is as typical of the Bauhaus as his writing paper, folded to form its own envelope, an impeccable illustration for his functionalist statement, which emphasized 'the greatest possible economy'. And Bill comments on the avant-garde's preoccupations. Standardization of printed material is necessary, he says, but has to be flexible, to deal with the needs of different types of consumer. The use of lower-case, he argues, is justified not only on the grounds of simplicity, but aesthetically, because its forms are richer than those of the capitals.

A similar personal philosophy was put forward by Walter Cyliax, a German printing executive working in Zurich as an art director and typographer.

> Principles are a useful intellectual tool as long as they are alive. Dead principles correspond to intellectual laziness. My basic principle is above all: clarity and flexibility, fresh adaptability to the pace and demands of industry. . . . In typography as elsewhere, that which is most effective [as communication] is also the most beautiful.[8]

Walter Cyliax 1899-1945
German print manager, art director, designer, photographer, writer. Came to Switzerland in the early 1920s. As art director of the large Zurich printers, Fretz Brothers, one of the first designers in Switzerland to adopt the 'New Typography', and co-founder of *Typographische Monatsblätter* (Typographic Monthly), 1933. After returning briefly to Germany in 1936, moved to Austria. Cyliax managed an 'Aryanized' printing firm in Vienna, where he died in a bombing raid.

31

---

8. *Gefesselter Blick*, p.38.

32

► Poster announcing the opening of
the Simmen furniture store, designed
by Walter Cyliax, 1930.
Cyliax borrowed lowercase lettering,
obvious asymmetry and overprinting
from the avant-garde. The image of
the building is drawn to simulate a
photograph. Printed by lithography in
two colours.
▼ 'Simmen Furniture', poster designed
by Walter Cyliax, 1930. One
of the earliest uses of photography
in a commercial poster, printed by
photogravure. Although the illustration
of the sideboard is 'sachlich', its sharp
perspective is at variance with the
Modernist insistence on emphasizing
the flatness of the graphic surface.

▶ Poster for PKZ men's outfitters, designed by Alex Diggelmann, 1930. Diggelmann has combined the flat planes of colour and the geometry typical of Modernism with a 'sachlich', almost photographic, presentation. It is the same graphic technique as Baumberger's earlier poster showing an overcoat. But the half-open box excites curiosity. The image links the half-revealed garment and its PKZ label, and further identifies the company by giving its full name on the box. Printed by lithography.

Alex Diggelmann 1902-1987
Teacher, graphic designer and artist. Trained in Berne as an art teacher, in Paris and then as a book designer in Leipzig. Best known for his sports posters, he won a gold medal for his Berlin Olympics design, 1936. Drawing teacher in Zurich, 1938-67.

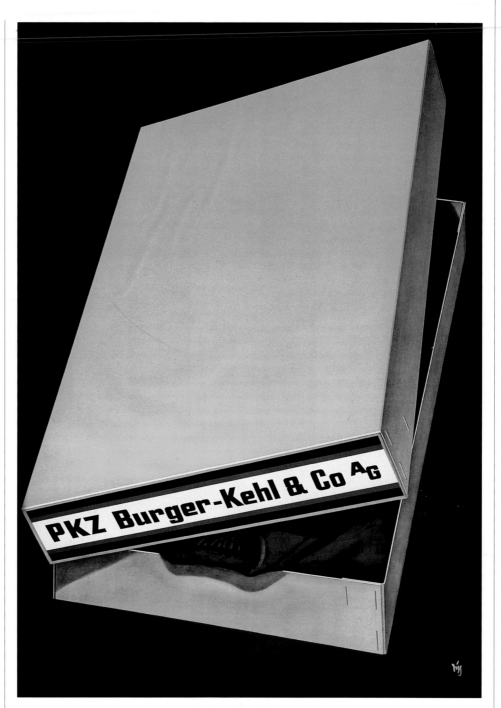

34 ▶ 'International Office Equipment
Exhibition' at the Basel Trade Fair
Building, 1928. Poster by Theo Ballmer.
The drawn lettering, typical of Ballmer,
makes an image which implies
the precise order and efficiency
of a modern office.

▶ Poster for a sale of carpet remnants, designed by Otto Baumberger, 1930. Baumberger, master of every style, including the latest, here adopted the cleanest Modernism.
The rectangle defined by a heavy line, placed obliquely and cropped, is both an echo of Van Doesburg's paintings of the same time and a precursor of the most minimal 'Swiss' style of 30 years later (see p. 52).

Art and the New Typography

Constructivism and Design

'*Elementare Typographie*' (Elemental Typography), edited by Jan Tschichold, published in 1925, was a special issue of the printing trade magazine *Typographische Mitteilungen*. In only 24 large-format pages, printed in red and black, readers were introduced to the New Typography.
Tschichold says that the New Typography will be built on 'Russian Suprematism, Dutch Neo-Plasticism [Mondrian and De Stijl] and especially Constructivism'.

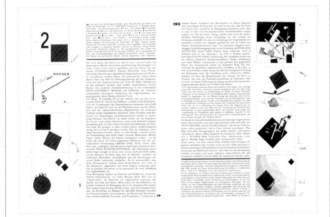

The first double-page spread is bordered by the pages of El Lissitzky's fairytale, *The Story of Two Squares*, designed in 1920 and reprinted in Holland. This is followed by Tschichold's adaptation of a Russian Constructivist programme. This omitted the demand in the original that 'the Constructivist must be a Marxist who has outlived art', but proposed that Constructivism would play its part in helping to create a new society.
Seven of the 24 illustrations are by Lissitzky; others are by Herbert Bayer, Burchartz, Molzahn and Schwitters. Only one and a monogram are by Tschichold himself. Baumberger's overcoat appears as an illustration to an article on posters by Mart Stam and Lissitzky, reprinted from the Basel architectural magazine *ABC* (see pp.29, 56).

Painter-designers such as Max Burchartz, Lajos Kassák and László Moholy-Nagy practised the new Abstract art. But in graphic design they considered aesthetics to be less important than making the message clear to the reader. Meanwhile, young designers such as Jan Tschichold, trained not in an art school but in the printing industry, recognized the gulf between the antiquated traditions of their trade and the progressive outlook of modern artists. Overwhelmed by a visit to the 1923 Bauhaus exhibition, Tschichold identified the new Abstract painting as the basis for the new visual thinking.

Tschichold was to become its most ardent propagandist. A teacher at the Leipzig printing school, a brilliant and scholarly calligrapher, he persistently stressed, in books, articles and lectures, the importance of art to design. From the mid-1920s, after a conversion to the brash but developing Bauhaus version of the New Typography, he codified its principles in his writings and brilliantly exemplified them in his own typography. In 1933 he left Germany for Switzerland, where he remained an important figure for three decades.

Among Tschichold's many writings in the 1920s and 1930s were three landmarks in the developing principles of the Swiss style. The first was '*Elementare Typographie*' (Elemental Typography) – a special issue of the German trade monthly, *Typographische Mitteilungen* (Typographic News) – published in 1925.[1] The second, in 1928, was his most important book, *Die neue Typographie* (The New Typography).[2] In a small, A5 format, with illustrations and diagrams on almost all of its 240 pages, this became the progressive designers' textbook. *Typographische Gestaltung* (Typographic Design), published in Basel in 1935, was the third.[3]

'*Elementare Typographie*', which appeared in the same year as *Die Kunstismen*, opens as follows:

The New Typography, the subject of this special issue, is based on what is shown in the logically consistent work of Russian Suprematism, Dutch Neo-Plasticism and especially Constructivism.

Tschichold then gives a brief account of the new movement's antecedents – Impressionism, Cubism, Futurism, Expressionism and Dada. The word '*elementare*' (elemental) in the title '*Elementare Typographie*' was taken from Van Doesburg, who had

1. Special issue of *Typographische Mitteilungen*, Leipzig, October 1925.
2. *Die neue Typographie*, Berlin 1928; reprint 1987; *The New Typography*, English edition, trans. Ruari McLean, Berkeley and Los Angeles 1995.
3. *Typographische Gestaltung*, Basel 1935; English trans. Ruari McLean as *Asymmetric Typography*, London 1967.

Jan Tschichold 1902-1974

German (later Swiss citizen) calligrapher, typographer, writer, teacher and type designer, born in Dresden. Trained as calligrapher, letterer and print designer in Leipzig and Dresden. Assistant teacher at Leipzig Academy, 1921-23. Freelance in Leipzig, 1923-25, and in Berlin, 1926. Teacher at the Meisterschule für Deutschlands Buchdrucker (Advanced College for German Printers) in Munich, 1926-33. Designed influential series of film posters, beginning 1927. Founder-member of the Ring neuer Werbegestalter (New Advertising Designers Circle), 1927. After arrest by Nazis, emigrated to Switzerland, 1933. In Basel employed by Benno Schwabe publishers, taught at the Allgemeine Gewerbeschule, gave lectures, worked as freelance designer and was regular contributor to *Typographische Monatsblätter*, 1933-46. Worked as designer for Penguin Books in London, 1947-49. From 1950 freelance in Basel, including work for pharmaceutical company Hoffmann-La Roche, writing and lecturing. Died in Locarno, Switzerland.

For Tschichold's books, which were crucial to the New Typography and to the origins of Swiss graphic design, see bibliography.

adopted it from a manifesto for an anti-individualistic art that appeared in his own *De Stijl* journal in 1921.[4] Its message was stirring but vague: 'We pledge ourselves to Elementalist art. It is elemental because it does not philosophize, because it is built exclusively of its own elements. . . . Down with the reactionary in art!'

Elementalism gave a theoretical basis for Tschichold's practical ideas. Van Doesburg returned to Elementalism in the first issue of the magazine *G* □ two years later. His statement is prefaced by an editorial demanding 'a clean relationship between strength and economy. This relies on elemental means, complete single mastery of elemental means, elemental arrangement, regularity.' This is followed by Van Doesburg's exposition of *elementare Gestaltung* (elemental design), where he repeats the demand for precision issued by Van de Velde.[5] After stating emphatically that 'THE ERA OF DECORATIVE TASTE HAS VANISHED', he insists that the modern artist 'must establish laws creating a system, that is to say, he has to master his elemental means of expression in a conscious manner'.[6]

Tschichold emphasized the basic geometric forms, the square and the circle, which the Russian painter Kasimir Malevich had seen as the 'fundamental Suprematist elements'. Squares and circles appear in more than half the illustrations of '*Elementare Typographie*'; its first double-page spread is bordered by the eight pages of Lissitzky's Constructivist fairytale, *The Story of Two Squares*. Lissitzky, describing the upheavals at the time of the First World War, wrote, 'Into this chaos came Suprematism, extolling the square as the very source of all creative expression.'[7] When Van Doesburg proclaimed, 'Already many people are using the square', he was stating a fact. Hans Arp wrote that his wife, Sophie Taeuber, had 'discovered' the square in 1916. In Switzerland after the First World War, when they saw the rectangles in foreign magazines such as *De Stijl*, they thought it was 'a joke, as if everyone who had drawn a square had been forced to yell with ecstasy and excitement'. True to the spirit of Dada, 'We still decided to register our own squares at the Patent Office'.[8]

Taking his cue from Malevich and Lissitzky, Van Doesburg extended Elementalist ideas by advocating diagonal compositions that would contrast with the

Elementalism, *G* □ and Geometry
The term 'elemental' derived from Van Doesburg, who contributed to the first issue in 1923 of the Berlin magazine, *G* □. The title '*G*' was for 'Gestaltung', followed by a square, in honour of Van Doesburg. ('Gestaltung' is here translated as 'design', but has a more complex meaning that implies the act of creating a structure.) The magazine was intended to represent 'Constructivism in Europe'. El Lissitzky and Werner Graeff were on the editorial board of *G* □, which folded before it could publish no. 7-8, planned as a double issue on typography.

▲ The editorial on the front of the 4-page issue no.1 proposed that, 'The basic demand of elemental design is economy: a clear relationship between strength and material. This requires elemental means, complete mastery of means, elemental order, rules.' Below the editors' statement is the start of Van Doesburg's essay on 'Elemental Design', intended as a basic method for use internationally. The word 'elementare' (elemental) was adopted in 1925 by Jan Tschichold to identify his idea of the New Typography. *G* □ was the model for the Basel magazine *ABC*, launched in 1924.

▼ *G* □ no.4, 1925, carries a drawing by the French Purist painter Amédée Ozenfant with a slogan from Van de Velde: 'The line is a force!', to which Werner Graeff adds 'The line – not the object!' Graeff is making it clear that an abstraction is independent of what is represented.

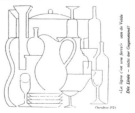

---

4. *De Stijl*, vol.4, no.10, 1921. Hans Arp and Moholy-Nagy were among those artists who signed the manifesto.
5. 'Zur elementaren Gestaltung', *G* □, no.1, Berlin 1923, p.1.
6. *Ibid.*, p.2.
7. 'Suprematism in World Reconstruction', Lissitzky archive, quoted in Sophie Lissitzky-Küppers, *El Lissitzky*, London 1968, p.327.
8. Hans Arp, *Unsern täglichen Traum . . .* , Zurich 1955, pp.19, 73.

horizontal-vertical balance in the natural and architectural world and so would excite a new revolutionary spirit.

In *Die neue Typographie*, Tschichold points to the aspect of Cubism that became central to Modernism. This was the disappearance of perspective: with Cubism, '"background" and picture suface are identical'.[9] The most recent Abstract art becomes a point of departure for both design and architecture. The form of geometrical Abstract painting and sculpture that was crucial to Swiss graphic design was Concrete art, a concept that also originated with Van Doesburg. Tschichold used 'concrete' as a term in '*Elementare Typographie*'. In *Typographische Gestaltung*, he defined it:

> Most people call a non-representational painting abstract. Yet it is not a question of abstractions, but of the concrete: in this type of painting the meaning of a line, or a circle, or a flat plane is just its individual, actual self, whereas in representational painting it would stand for something else.[10]

Some of the leading Swiss designers after the Second World War were also Concrete artists – Max Bill, Richard Paul Lohse and Karl Gerstner being the best known. For others, the discipline of Concrete art lay behind the formal, geometrical organization of their graphic work.

Tschichold had seen the new art as a metaphor of a new world, as well as a model for graphic design. 'Painting now', he says,

> strives towards a new and elementary harmony of surface, colour, form and their relationships, which are subject to certain laws . . . its aim is utmost clarity and purity. It makes use of exact geometric forms and so achieves an aesthetic paraphrase of our technical-industrial times.[11]

This is as far as he goes in applying any principles derived from the painting he describes. As a professional in the printing trade, he was obliged to remind his readers of 'the factors which really control design, such as demand, purpose, raw materials and manufacturing methods'. It was Tschichold who acted as a guide to a typographic practice which followed the demand for a new unity of art and technology.

Art and *Die neue Typographie*
▼ Tschichold's book, the first bible of Modernist graphic design, embodies the Bauhaus link between art and technology. After quoting Mondrian ('We are at the end of everything old'), Tschichold first pays tribute to the constructions of the engineer, then deals with the old before he turns to the artist. 'In order to fully understand the new typography,' he says, 'it will help to study the most recent developments in painting and photography.' Almost all the Abstract works illustrated are by painters who were also graphic designers, such as Rodchenko and Kassák.
Of the graphic design, apart from Tschichold's own work, and several by Lissitzky, almost all the examples are by German artist-designers, with Burchartz the most represented.

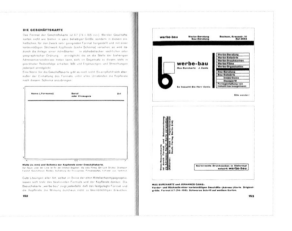

9. *Die neue Typographie*, Berlin 1928, p.34; *The New Typography*, trans. McLean, London 1987, p.33.
10. *Typographische Gestaltung*, Basel 1935, p.83. In the English translation, *Asymmetric Typography*, London 1967, p.80, Tschichold has slightly amended this passage, and states that the term 'concrete' is 'not suitable in the English language'.
11. An echo of Van de Velde's call for clarity. *Die neue Typographie*, pp.46-47; *The New Typography*, trans. McLean, London 1987, p.45.

Technology, Business and *Die neue Typographie*

Many pages of Tschichold's book are used to explain practical matters, especially the recommended formats for stationery published in Germany as DIN (Deutsche Industrie-Normen). These dealt not only with paper sizes but also with the disposition of the printed elements.

▼ The official instructions for the standardized layout of the A4 letterhead. Spaces are given for the addressee (on the left), for a date-of-receipt endorsement or 'action taken' note (on the right). There is a sequence and position for: your ref., your letter of, our ref., date, and for the sender's name, address, telephone, etc.

▼ The standardized letterhead sheet shown in *Die neue Typogaphie* is designed as a form to be filled in by the typewriter. Envelopes, also standardized, affect the letterhead's layout. The position of the window demands that the paper be folded so that the address will show. Marks are placed on the edge of the sheet to show where the folds should be. Tschichold suggested that the sheet could be pre-punched for filing, that there should be a printed dot at the bottom to indicate where the typing

should stop, and also that printed type should avoid the folds. This gave a clear structure in which countless variations were made in the next half century.

Geschäftsbrief
Format A 4 (210×297)
DIN 676

Firma
Erzeugnisse Abbildungen usw

des Absenders Postanschrift · Drahtwort · Fernruf · Geschäftzeit · Banken

Anschrift des Empfängers

Eingang- u. Bearbeitungsvermerke

Ihre Zeichen · Ihre Nachricht vom · Unsere Zeichen · Tag

Betreff

Leitsätze für den Briefvordruck

1 Die Linien deuten lediglich die Abgrenzung der einzelnen Felder an; auf dem Geschäftsbrief selbst sollen nur der Heftrand (möglichst auch auf der Rückseite, dort rechts), Schluß-, Falt- und Lochmarken sowie das Anschriftfeld durch feine Linien, Eckzeichen, Punkte usw kenntlich gemacht werden.

2 Unbedingt einzuhalten sind
ein Heftrand von mindestens 20 mm
Lage und Abmessungen der Felder für Anschrift des Empfängers, für Eingangsvermerke und für des Absenders Postanschrift
die Reihenfolge der Post- und Geschäftangaben (Fernruf, Banken)
die Reihenfolge der Zeichen- und Tagangaben.

3 Nur die unterstrichenen Inschriften sollen wörtlich oder sinngemäß abgedruckt werden. Die anderen Inschriften haben lediglich erläuternden Zweck.

4 In der Zeile für Post- und Geschäftangaben (Fernruf, Banken) können einzelne Angaben weggelassen und neue zugefügt werden.

5 Es ist empfehlenswert, die Leitworte für Zeichen- und Tagangaben so zu setzen, daß die zugehörigen Eintragungen nicht daneben, sondern darunter erfolgen, um wiederholtes genaues Einstellen der Schreibmaschine zu vermeiden. Aus demselben Grunde sollte die Jahreszahl bei der Tagangabe nicht vorgedruckt werden. Unter „Ihre Zeichen" und „Unsere Zeichen" sind Akten- und Ansage- (Diktier) Zeichen zusammenzufassen.

6 (siehe Fortsetzungsblatt)

Dinformat A 4 (210×297)   Geschäftsbriefvordruck nach DIN 676

¹) Zweckmäßig wird der Schriftwechsel nach den Einheits ABC-Regeln abgelegt.
Lochabstand 80 mm (nach Beschluß der Briefordnerkonvention).
Geschäftsbriefe, Halbbriefe Format A 5 siehe DIN 677.
Briefhüllen siehe DIN 678. Fensterbriefhüllen siehe DIN 680

Ausschuß für wirtschaftliche Verwaltung (AWV)
Fachausschuß für Bürowesen

Mai 1924   Fortsetzung Seite 2

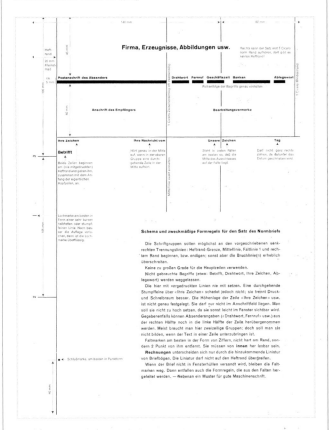

Firma, Erzeugnisse, Abbildungen usw.

◀ Tschichold reproduced this bookseller's letterhead in *Typographische Entwurfstechnik* (Making Typographic Layouts), a 24-page guide for compositors and designers published in 1932. The letterhead is an elegant example of the standardized DIN A4 format. 'Your reference', 'Your communication dated', 'Our reference' and 'Date' are run in a single line. Each piece of typewritten information aligns on the left (on pre-set tab settings) below the printed words.

◀ Even for industrial companies, it was possible to make standardized stationery informal and appealing. In Zurich, Burchartz's student Anton Stankowski framed the space left for the address, which would show through the envelope window, with photographs of machine parts made by the company, c.1933. The printing is in black and grey.

Principles of the New Typography

The new set of rules to replace the conventions of traditional typography were laid down between 1923 and 1928, mainly by artists, and chiefly in Germany. As we have noted, although they owed something to the graphic excesses of the Futurists and the Dadaists, their concern was with function rather than aesthetics.

The first significant statement was by El Lissitzky, whose 'Topography of Typography' appeared in Schwitters's *Merz* magazine in July 1923.[1] It is a series of declamatory assertions of first principles, beginning, 'In communicating, the printed word is seen, not heard.' Lissitzky was followed a few months later by Moholy-Nagy. His essay, 'The New Typography', was published at the Bauhaus.[2] Both statements give priority to photographic illustration and a more dynamic typography. Moholy-Nagy echoes Lissitzky's reminder that typography is a visual medium, that 'words on the printed page are taken in by seeing them, not hearing them'. And whereas the New Typography later took the opposite view, restricting choice, he says that 'we use all typefaces, type sizes, geometric forms, colours, etc.' In fact, Moholy-Nagy's ideas on typography, which he shared with his fellow Hungarian artist-designers, were derived from contacts with Soviet Russia, from Russian artists and from former Dadaists in Berlin, and sharpened by Van Doesburg's presence in Weimar.

Moholy-Nagy's attitude to graphic design became visionary. By 1925 he was writing, 'The printer's work is part of the foundation on which the NEW world will be built.' He concluded that this new world would find its expression by means of 'typophoto'. And typophoto is another name for what became the central medium of graphic design.

What is typography? What is photography? What is typophoto? –

Typography is the communication of ideas through printed design.

Photography is the visual representation of the thing seen.

Typophoto is the most precise visual communication.[3]

The techniques and technology were there: machine typesetting, photo-engraved halftones, photogravure, printing on rotary presses – they were the means for mass-producing illustrated books, magazines and newspapers.

At the same time as typophoto, Moholy-Nagy introduced the idea of the photograph not only as illustration but, alternatively, as 'phototext', 'replacing words, as an unambiguous form of representation, which in its objectivity [*Sachlichkeit*] leaves no room for personal-accidental interpretation'. He had been impressed by Le Corbusier's *Vers une architecture*, published in 1923, whose arguments depend on the images which interrupt or preface the text on almost every page. Two superlative examples of typophoto in books, where photographic illustrations either reinforce or substitute for the text, appeared in 1929. These were Werner Graeff's *Es kommt der neue Fotograf!* (Here Comes the New Photographer!), published to accompany the Werkbund 'Film und Foto' exhibition, and John Heartfield's visual editing of the book *Deutschland, Deutschland über alles* by Kurt Tucholsky.

Kurt Schwitters's 'Theses on Typography', published a year after Lissitzky's in *Merz*, showed surviving Dadaist tendencies: 'Countless laws can be made for typography. The most important is: Don't do it like anyone has before.' This was not necessarily anti-functional: the rationalizing Tschichold was also opposed to standard solutions. And Schwitters's other suggestions could equally have been made by Tschichold. For example,

The textually negative parts, the unprinted areas of the sheet, are typographically positive. The smallest piece of type matter has typographic value: letter, word, piece of typesetting, punctuation mark.[4]

Many of the principles set out by Tschichold in '*Elementare Typographie*' are less easy to follow than the lessons of the illustrations. But he defines elemental typography in any design as, 'the creation of the logical and visual relationship between the given letters, words and text'.[5] He excludes any typographical ornament but admits, 'to increase the sense of urgency', the use of printer's rules (lines) vertically and diagonally as well as the essentially elemental forms (squares, circles, triangles), which were also standard printer's items.

By 1960 such pronouncements were a description of

---

1. Lissitzky's 'Topography' was reprinted in Tschichold's *Die neue Typographie*, p.61. McLean, English translation, p.60. 'Merz' was the name Schwitters gave to much of his activity, and was the title of his magazine, which appeared irregularly in almost 20 issues from 1923 to 1927. *Merz* was important for its typographic experiments, especially issue 8/9, designed by Lissitzky in Switzerland, and no.11, devoted to advertising design for Pelikan office supplies and artists' materials.
2. In *Staatliches Bauhaus in Weimar 1919-23*, 1923. English translation in Richard Kostelanetz (ed.), *Moholy-Nagy*, New York / London 1970, pp.75-76.
3. From 'Typo-photo', in '*Elementare Typographie*', 1925, pp.202-204. The essay appeared in a slightly different form in Moholy-Nagy's Bauhaus Book, *Malerei, Photographie, Film*, Munich 1925; English translation: *Painting, Photography, Film*, London 1969, pp.38-40.

4. *Merz* 11, 1924, p.91.
5. '*Elementare Typographie*', p.200. Useful translations of Tschichold's text and other contemporary statements appear in Robin Kinross, *Modern Typography*, London 1992; second edition, London 2004.

Le Corbusier

(Charles-Edouard Jeanneret) 1887-1965
Architect, town planner, painter, writer.
Born in French Switzerland. Studied
Arts and Crafts Movement in Germany,
then worked in Switzerland and in
Germany (in the studio of Peter
Behrens, whose work as architect and
designer for the electrical company
AEG is considered the origin of the
concept of 'corporate identity') before
settling in Paris.
Le Corbusier was the best known of
International Style architects. Like Van
de Velde, he was an admirer of
engineers, expressed in his *Vers une
Architecture* (Towards a [New]
Architecture), 1923. His theoretical
books, although symmetrical in layout,
are early examples of integrated text
and illustration. Volumes of his
complete architectural works were
published in Zurich, designed by
Max Bill.

LES TRACES REGULATEURS

▲ Chapter title in Le Corbusier's book
Vers une Architecture, 1923. This early
concern with proportion led to his
Modulor system in the 1940s
(see p. 176).

everyday practice in Switzerland. But at the time, in
the 1920s, the printing trade gave the New Typography
a hostile reception. In January 1926 the *Schweizer
Graphische Mitteilungen* (Swiss Graphic News) described
Tschichold's '*Elementare Typographie*' as 'the new
Moscow Trend', which 'we are tempted to speak of as the
communist style', dismissing it as fashionable folly. Yet an
exhibition at the Gewerbemuseum in Basel at the close of
1927 gave a serious response to the new movement. 'To
see the new direction as the fashion of the day', said the
catalogue to the 'Exhibition of New Typography',

> ignores the fact that it is connected to the tendencies
> which pervade architecture, indeed all the applied arts,
> as well as much of the fine arts. Like the modern trend
> in architecture, the new graphic style aims to be
> functional, to be objective [*sachlich*] and minimal in
> its means; it rejects symmetry as too solemn for
> advertising, sets material at different angles, and
> contrasts points of emphasis with spatial voids
> according to the meaning of the text.[6]

Visitors to the exhibition were able to form a more
complete picture of the radical tendencies and the ideas
behind them later the same year, when *Die neue
Typographie* was published.

With the larger 1930 exhibition in Basel, 'Neue
Werbegraphik' (New Advertising Design), the catalogue,
designed by Tschichold and set entirely in lowercase,
established some general principles. Writing on poster
design, Tschichold paraphrases what he said in *Die neue
Typographie* the previous year. Discussing first the poster
with type only, Tschichold compares the extravagant
Victorian typefaces and the artistic lettering often used on
lithographic posters with clear, plain poster types cut from
wood. He maintains his enthusiasm for the simplicity of
nineteenth-century 'grotesque' typefaces; he stresses the
importance of contrasts – of horizontal and vertical, large
and small type, closed and open groupings, positive and
negative, colour and black-and-white. And in the same
way as he chooses an impersonal typeface, so the new
designer will use an 'objective' means of illustration: the
photograph.

The illustrations in the essay are taken from
Tschichold's next book, given the title *Einfache
Druckgestaltung* (Simple Print Design), and soon to
appear as *Eine Stunde Druckgestaltung* (One Hour of
Typographic Design).[7] Among the works reproduced is
Lissitzky's photogram advertising Pelikan ink, made when

---

6. *Ausstellung neue Typographie*, catalogue, Gewerbemuseum Basel, 1928, n.p.
7. *Eine Stunde Druckgestaltung*, Stuttgart 1930.

Exhibitions in Switzerland

▼ The first exhibition of the New
Typography was in Basel in 1927-28.
There were more German than
Swiss contributors. Among the
schools represented, as well as the
Gewerbeschulen in Basel and Zurich,
were several from Germany, including
the Bauhaus and the Munich Printing
School where Tschichold taught.
The catalogue cover, designed at the
Basel Gewerbeschule, follows the early
Bauhaus practice of using only capital
letters in headings.

GEWERBEMUSEUM BASEL

AUSSTELLUNG
NEUE
TYPOGRAPHIE

GEÖFFNET VOM 28. DEZEMBER 1927 BIS
29. JANUAR 1928

Tschichold Teaching

After his arrival in Switzerland, Tschichold set exacting standards. ▼ Designs for 'a simple invitation card' by printing students taught by Tschichold at the Allgemeine Gewerbeschule (General Trades School) in Basel were published in *Typographische Monatsblätter* in 1936.

The reduced-size illustrations, typeset following the students' original designs in A6 postcard format, were accompanied by Tschichold's critical comments.

Der neue Montag
Werkbund und Studentenschaft
bringt **Montag, den 12. Februar,** den neuen russischen Tonfilm
Goldene Berge von Yutkewitsch
Der Film wurde im Mai 1933 fertiggestellt und ist seit dem «Weg ins Leben» der erste russische Tonfilm, der in die Schweiz kommt
Vorführungen 3, 5, 7, 9 Uhr im **Eldoradokino**

1. The first line is overemphatic. Type justified in a box at the top should be avoided. The lower part is weak and unsure in its placing.

Der neue Montag Werkbund und Studentenschaft
bringt Montag, den 12. Februar,
den neuen russischen Tonfilm **Goldene Berge** von Yutkewitsch
Der Film wurde im Mai 1933 fertiggestellt und ist seit dem «Weg ins Leben» der erste russische Tonfilm, der in die Schweiz kommt. Vorführungen 3, 5, 7, 9 Uhr im Eldoradokino

2. Type in the original too big.

Der neue Montag Werkbund und Studentenschaft
bringt
Montag, den 12. Februar,
den neuen russischen Tonfilm **Goldene Berge** von Yutkewitsch
Der Film wurde im Mai 1933 fertiggestellt und ist seit dem «Weg ins Leben» der erste russische Tonfilm, der in die Schweiz kommt.
Vorführungen 3, 5, 7, 9 Uhr im Eldoradokino

3. 'Der neue Montag' too big. 'Goldene Berge' too small. Upper two groups too wide on the left; above on the right too empty.

Der neue Montag Werkbund und Studentenschaft
bringt
Montag, den 12. Februar,
den neuen russischen Tonfilm **Goldene Berge** von Yutkewitsch
Der Film wurde im Mai 1933 fertiggestellt und ist seit dem «Weg ins Leben» der erste russische Tonfilm, der in die Schweiz kommt
Vorführungen 3, 5, 7, 9 Uhr im Eldoradokino

4. The three lines at the bottom must have less leading [space between the lines] to make them into a group. The lower and right-hand margin must be wider.

Der neue Montag Werkbund und Studentenschaft
bringt
Montag, den 12. Februar,
den neuen russischen Tonfilm **Goldene Berge** von Yutkewitsch
Der Film wurde im Mai 1933 fertiggestellt und ist seit dem «Weg ins Leben» der erste russische Tonfilm, der in die Schweiz kommt.
Vorführungen 3, 5, 7, 9 Uhr im Eldoradokino

5. The word 'bringt' does not need a line to itself.

Der neue Montag Werkbund und Studentenschaft
bringt **Montag, den 12. Februar,**
den neuen russischen Tonfilm **Goldene Berge** von Yutkewitsch
Der Film wurde im Mai 1933 fertiggestellt und ist seit dem «Weg ins Leben» der erste russische Tonfilm, der in die Schweiz kommt.
Vorführungen 3, 5, 7, 9 Uhr im Eldoradokino

6. Makes sense of the message, visually correct sizes of type, breaking of lines follows the sense and the groups are made clearly and elegantly distinct.

he was in Switzerland, and Tschichold refers to Lissitzky's poster for the recent Russian Exhibition in Zurich (see p.57).

Kurt Schwitters's contribution to the catalogue of 'Neue Werbegraphik' was a note on the Ring neuer Werbegestalter and a definition of *Werbegestaltung* (advertising design): a theoretical statement, but without Tschichold's dry dogmatism (see p.145-7). Schwitters's provocative statements were tempered by his five years' experience as a professional graphic designer.

> To advertise means to draw attention to something. And the advertising designer draws the viewer's attention to what he is advertising not by means of words, phrases or artificial artistic additions but simply by designing the printed matter as a unified whole. Design is the creation of a consciously unified gestalt, and the designer can do this using accepted conventions – rather like the musician. This is basically because we human beings are all the same and function in the same way.[8]

This unity, Schwitters explains, is made by balancing the varied elements of a design, holding them in a state of tension, 'in such a way that, when they are added to or subtracted from, the result is zero'.

> Design consists not of the forces themselves, but of putting them in equilibrium. In printed matter, the forces are image, lettering, the typographic material used, printed and unprinted areas, etc., in a state of tension with one another. Everything [in the design] is equally important.[9]

Schwitters concludes with an aside directed at those who have not understood. 'We don't believe, as our imitators do, that design means a kind of decoration using printer's metal rules.'

Such fundamental Modernist typographic ideas as these had a long life. Schwitters's concept of a 'unified gestalt' was echoed two decades later by Karl Gerstner, whose 'integral typography' superseded Tschichold's 'elemental typography'. 'Integral', said Gerstner in 1959, 'means shaped into a whole.'

8. 'Der Ring neue Werbegestalter', *Neue Werbegraphik,* Gewerbemuseum Basel, 1930, n.p.
9. *Ibid.*

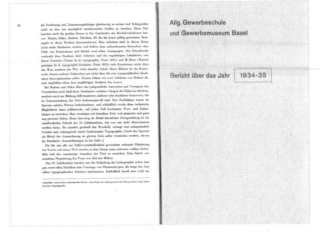

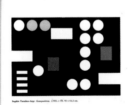

Tschichold's third important book, *Typographische Gestaltung* (Typographic Design), was a Swiss production, published in Basel in 1935. Typeset in Bodoni in an A5 format, it includes some work reproduced in facsimile, in two colours, and on different papers.

The 'new typography' is alternatively described as 'functional typography'. The dramatic avant-garde typography of the 1920s, which Tschichold showed in '*Elementare Typographie*' ten years earlier, has been replaced, mainly by his own work, more refined and delicate.

Art has moved from the front to the back of the book, under the heading 'Concrete Art'. Tschichold is loyal to Lissitzky, reproducing four works, but apart from a prospectus cover by Herbert Bayer, the Bauhaus is represented only by its painters, Josef Albers and Moholy-Nagy.

Typefaces and Lettering

Capitals, lowercase and typestyle

In the German language all nouns begin with capital letters. Many books and newspapers were printed in the traditional German Fraktur typeface. The Bauhaus followed other reformers in abandoning these conventions.

▼ In 1929, Franz Roh shared the editing of the photographic book *foto-auge (Photo-Eye)* with Jan Tschichold. To explain why the book was typeset in a grotesque typeface there was an insert which put the question, 'Why Four Alphabets?'

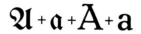

Roh said that the capitals and lowercase both of the German (Fraktur) and of the seriffed roman letterform 'each represent the same sound'. They can be replaced by lowercase in a single typeface, which Roh represents by the sanserif lowercase 'a'.

The Akzidenz Grotesk typeface became the most frequently used in the New Typography and almost the norm in later Swiss graphic design.

To clinch his argument against 'gothic' type, Roh asks ironically if German music should have its own four types of musical notation.

For several years the New Typography followed the old in using capital letters for titles and headings. But the rationalizing spirit of New Typography questioned the normal practice in German text of using capitals for the initial letters of nouns. From 1925 the Bauhaus answer was to use only lowercase type. At the foot of the Director's letterhead was the message:

> we write everything in lower case to save time. and besides, why two alphabets, where one will do? why use capital letters if we don't use them when we speak?

The lowercase alphabet, it was argued, was easier to learn and to read. It took less space, and was more economical – typesetting was easier and composing machinery (and typewriters) could be simplified.

Upper and lower case was not the only issue. In the 1920s most German text, including newspapers, was set in 'gothic' (Fraktur) type. There was the choice of either this German style of letterform or seriffed roman (confusingly described as 'Mediäval' or 'Antiqua'). In *Die neue Typographie* Tschichold wrote that 'sanserif is always and absolutely better'. Speaking to the Zurich branch of the Swiss Werkbund in 1929, he identified Grotesk, for its clarity and precision, as the 'elemental' typeface. 'It corresponds', he said, 'to the spare, straightforward attitude that is required of today's forms.'[1] Grotesque (nineteenth-century sanserif) letters, with an even thickness of line, showed fewer traces of the antiquated letterforms which originated in writing by hand with a reed or quill pen; it was more suited to a machine age, more 'sachlich'. The grotesque Tschichold was referring to, known as Akzidenz, became the standard text typeface of the designers in Switzerland who embraced the New Typography.

Later, Tschichold revised his views, announcing that it was juvenile to consider the sanserif as the most suitable or even the most contemporary typeface. It remains curious that the Modernists (Schwitters was an exception), particularly when many of them were drawing geometrical letters, were not more inclined to the geometrical sanserif typefaces, such as Erbar and Futura, which came onto the market before the end of the 1930s.

The designers who adopted the New Typography did not exclude the use of serif types, especially for continuous text, most often choosing neo-classical designs such as Bodoni.

▼ When Walter Dexel, one of the pioneer propagandists, introduced readers of the *Frankfurter Zeitung* to the New Typography in 1927, his text remained in the normal newspaper typesetting of Fraktur typeface with centred headings.

▼ Detail from Wassily Kandinsky's prose-poems, *Die Klänge*, 1913. A rare use of the Akzidenz Grotesk typeface, intended for commercial printing, but chosen here to counterbalance the weight of the woodcut illustrations.

OFFEN

Bald im grünen Gras langsam verschwindend.
Bald im grauen Kot steckend.
Bald im weißen Schnee langsam verschwindend.
Bald im grauen Kot steckend.
Lagen lange: dicke lange schwarze Rohre.
Lagen lange.
Lange Rohre.
Rohre.
Rohre.

Swiss designers in the 1950s used Monotype Grotesque (series 215 and bold 216) for machine-set text, since the German 19th-century style Akzidenz Grotesk was not available for composing machines until well after the Second World War.

---

1. 'Schweizer Werkbund', report in *Das Werk*, January 1930, p.xv.

Typefaces

Grotesk

▲ Because it fitted the concept of 'Sachlichkeit' with no obvious aesthetic to its design, Grotesk became the most common typeface of the New Typography, and later of Swiss graphic design. The 19th-century grotesque, also known as Akzidenz (jobbing), was made in slightly varying forms. When used in England and the US in the 1960s it was known as Standard.

Futura

▲ New sanserif designs such as the geometrical Futura appeared during the late 1920s for typesetting by machine. Futura was used in Germany by *Die Form*, for example, and in Switzerland *Typographische Monatsblätter* used a similar typeface, Erbar. For long texts many designers accepted that serif typefaces were more easily read

Antiqua

▲ Of serif designs, the neo-classical, late 18th-century, so-called modern (in German, jüngere Antiqua), such as Bodoni, were preferred by Modernist designers.
In posters printed from type the most common form of lettering was a condensed version of Grotesk. This made it easier to include more words and make them as large as possible. Condensed letters also made a satisfying visual echo of the vertical proportion of the poster.
▼ For an exhibition of posters by Basel designers, Hermann Eidenbenz drew typical poster lettering which was printed in black from linocut letters. The lettering in BA-PLA-KU – an abbreviation of *Basler Plakat Kunst* (Basel Poster Art) – shows the condensed Grotesk. Detailed information was added with a printed stuck-on label.

▲ Wooden type used for letterpress posters was often set without space between the letters. Such close spacing became commonplace in Swiss graphic design. Here the lettering was enlarged from a type proof, and printed offset in red. The economical technique of this 1934 poster by Hermann Eidenbenz emphasizes the message 'I am not rich enough to buy cheaply'.

Lettering

Fine lettering is a distinguished element in Swiss culture and its townscape. Posters by designers such as Theo Ballmer depended on the effectiveness of the lettering alone to attract the eye and convey the message. The modern styles of Swiss lettering were born out of a tradition of exacting craftsmanship and the most inspiring teachers. Of these the most celebrated was Ernst Keller at the Zurich Kunstgewerbeschule.

▲ A virtuoso calligrapher, in 1924 Keller produced a rare example of informal lettering for a Zurich department store. The slogan 'Jelmoli good and cheap' is as objective a statement as could be made, and its apparently artless, economical graphic expression underlines the straightforward message.

The lettering most fitted to the machine age was geometrical, constructed with ruler and compasses.
▼ For established virtuoso designers such as Otto Baumberger, it could be used when it fitted the subject, as it did in his poster for the 1932 Zurich Motor Fair.

▼ The lettering course at the Bauhaus under Joost Schmidt was rigorous in applying ruler and compasses. All the lowercase letters could be made from a set of fixed elements. No optical adjustments were included.

▼ By contrast with the Bauhaus course, the Swiss designer Hermann Eidenbenz, teaching in Magdeburg from 1926 to 1932, presented his classes with sanserif letters based on the proportions and refinements of the capital letters of Roman inscriptions.

▼ The Bauhaus circle and line construction of letters was used imaginatively in Max Bill's name style drawn for the interior design store Wohnbedarf in 1932. Circular 'counters' (internal spaces) run through the centre of the lowercase letters.

wohnbedarf

▼ Ernst Keller used a more or less square form of capitals on the Zurich Kunstgewerbemuseum in 1932. The word is broken by the city's coat of arms, also in relief.

▼ The following year, 1933, Keller's lettering for the Zurich Landscape Gardening Exhibition, Züga, was a lowercase version of the architectural lettering above. There was no precedent for numerals the same height as the lowercase.

züga
zürcher
gartenbau
ausstellung
24. juni
17. sept.

▼ Apprentices from the Fretz printing company who attended the Kunstgewerbeschule in 1937, as well as learning traditional seriffed forms, followed Keller's squarish geometrical style.

abcdefgiml
hknopqrst
uvwxyz
otto fischer
elektrisch

New Technology, Politics and Social Issues

Since the First World War, leading poster artists had designed for elections and for referenda on policy decisions.

Between the two world wars, Switzerland was not isolated from the political struggles of Europe or the ideological pressures of Fascism and Communism. The sympathies of progressive designers were most often engaged to the left of the political centre.

Ernst Keller 1891-1968

Graphic designer, lettering artist and teacher. Trained as lithographic draughtsman in Aarau in northwest Switzerland, midway between Basel and Zurich, 1906-10. Studied lettering in Leipzig, centre of the German printing trade, 1911-14. Returned to Switzerland for military service, 1914. Joined Swiss Werkbund, 1915. Started teaching at Zurich Kunstgewerbeschule (School of Applied Arts), 1918. As a teacher over a long period, Keller was the most important single influence on the development of Swiss graphic design. As well as posters, logotypes and lettering on buildings, he designed postage stamps and a variety of heraldic devices for civic authorities. The economically drawn images and inventive lettering of his posters designed in the 1920s and early 1930s made an important contribution to Modernism.

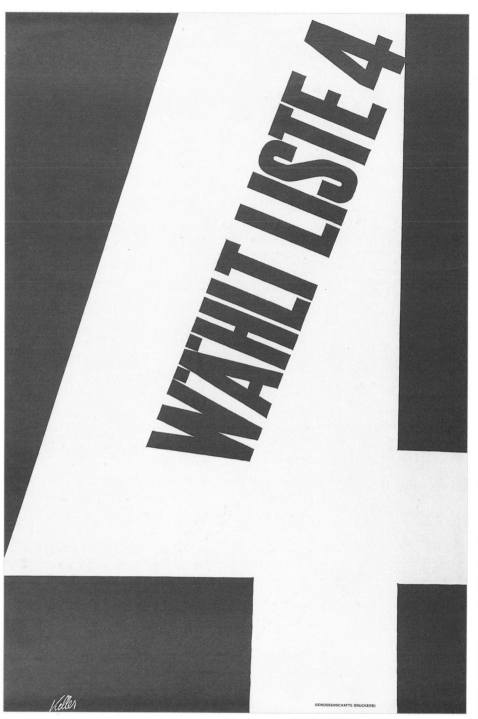

▲ 'Vote List 4.'
The litho-printed election poster for the Social Democrats in 1935 was drawn by Ernst Keller.
Although geometrical, the design has none of the constructional devices, nor the underlying mathematical structure used by the younger Constructivist designers such as Max Bill (see p.59).

▲ At the start of Tschichold's *Die neue Typographie* he acknowledges the truly contemporary, truly modern is created 'without reference to the aesthetics of the past by a new kind of man: **the engineer!**'

The avant-garde's heroes belonged to the machine age, the final phase of the industrial revolution. In the early years of the century Van de Velde had singled out the engineer, whose 'employment of reason and calculation can lead to the purest beauty!'[1] In 1929, Van de Velde could claim that 'From today, the style imposed by the machine distinguishes itself by that clarity, by that constant precision which endows every clear and precise design with mechanical perfection.'[2] This so-called machine aesthetic was fundamental to Modernist graphic design. In a similar vein to Van de Velde, Le Corbusier was quoted in *Das Werk*, saying, 'The mechanization of life has made our eyes more perfect', and also, 'Our senses and our minds have become more demanding. They demand an art that is absolutely precise.'[3]

Moholy-Nagy too saw that 'the reality of our century is technology – the invention, construction and maintenance of the machine . . .'. And the use of the machine implied changes in society. 'There is no tradition in technology, no consciousness of class or status. . . . This is our century – technology, machine, socialism. . . . Shoulder the task.'[4] Moholy-Nagy, like Kassák a member of the Hungarian avant-garde which had been uprooted after the failure of their country's socialist revolution, understood the radical social and political aims of the Russian Constructivists. Even the middle-aged Van de Velde was optimistic about the Russian initiatives. So was the young Tschichold, who also makes the connection with technology in 'Elementare Typographie'. He quotes from Trotsky's *Literature and Revolution*, published in Berlin in 1924:

> The wall dividing art and industry will come down. The great style of the future will not decorate, it will organize. It would be wrong to think that this means the destruction of art as giving way to technology.[5]

In Tschichold's view, the way to ensure the survival of art and to give it a new social purpose was to integrate it with graphic design. His explanation of modern art movements ends by saying that 'our objective, impersonal collective work intended for everyone is the decisive guarantee of this being brought about'.

▲ In 'Elementare Typographie' Jan Tschichold showed his sympathy for the Soviet revolution by substituting the Russian forename Ivan (or Iwan) for his own. His personal logo derives from Lissitzky's letterhead (just visible in the photomontage on p.56).

▲ Small poster for exhibition of industrialized building at the Winterthur Gewerbemuseum, designed by Heiri Steiner, 1929.

Heiri (Heinrich) Steiner 1906-1983 Graphic designer, photographer. Studied under Ernst Keller, later with Hans Finsler at Zurich Kunstgewerbeschule and in Berlin. Taught at the Zurich School, 1931-35. Freelance designer from 1930, and with the photographer Ernst A. Heiniger, 1934-39. One of most committed young designers of the avant-garde, with Heiniger he produced some of the most radical designs of the 1930s (see pp.79, 80). Steiner abandoned photography and later worked in an illustrative style.

---

1. 'The Role of the Engineer in Modern Architecture', quoted in Tim Benton *et al.*, *Form and Function*, London 1975, pp.32-33.
2. 'Le Nouveau', 1929, reprinted in Henry van de Velde, *Déblaiement d'art*, Brussels 1979, pp.98-99.
3. *Das Werk*, January 1926, p.228. Le Corbusier's statements are printed in their original French: 'La vie avec son machinisme a perfectionné notre oeil.' And, 'Notre sens et notre esprit sont devenus plus exigeants. Ils exigent un art intense de précision.'
4. From 'Constructivism and the Proletariat', *Ma*, Budapest, May 1922, quoted in Richard Kostelanetz (ed.), *Moholy-Nagy*, New York 1970/London 1971, p.185.
5. 'Elementare Typographie', special issue of *Typographische Mitteilungen*, Leipzig, October 1925, p.195.

The most conspicuous graphic examples of political commitment were posters by the Basel teacher and designer Theo Ballmer. The hammer and sickle and the Soviet Union's five-pointed star made an immediate identification with Communism; they were invaluable emblems for designers and cartoonists, whether hostile or sympathetic.

◄ 'Working People Choose Communists', designed in 1935, Ballmer's most direct poster in its image and lettering, both printed from linocut blocks.

▼ 'Make a United Front against the Wage Cut. On 28 May Vote No!', 1933.

Some people realize that the only things that are absolutely convincing in this chaos, that are really 'live' and which belong to the present, are the works of engineers and technicians, the engineering structures and machines. One tries to take on the relevance and mathematical logic of these *objects*.[6]

Such idealism was typical of many of the progressive designers who identified with left-wing groups and looked to the example of the Soviet Union. Theo Ballmer was the most conspicuous. Some were members of the Communist party, which was banned in certain Swiss cantons, and outlawed by 1940.

For Modernist designers in the West, mainly architects, the Soviet Union had seemed a promised land. Even Le Corbusier's failure to win the competition for the Palace of the Soviets – evidence of a growing hostility in Russia towards the avant-garde – did not undermine the optimism of those such as Hannes Meyer. After the Bauhaus he left for Moscow, where he worked from 1930 until 1936.

The visual excitement of the new Soviet cinema, with films such as Eisenstein's *Strike* and *Battleship Potemkin*, reinforced the interest in unexpected camera angles and in montage. In 1929 *Das Werk* included, in the same issue as its history of photography, a summary of *Kino-Eye*, a manifesto by the Russian documentary filmmaker Dziga Vertov. This was the year of the 'Russische Ausstellung' (Russian Exhibition), held in Zurich. Although there was a good deal of aesthetically conservative work in the exhibition, the propaganda posters in a Constructivist style reinforced the public association of Modernism with socialism.

In the political uncertainty that followed the world trade crisis and the stock market crash in 1929, unemployment rose and continued rising. The polarization between left and right was reflected in the conflicting styles of progressive graphic design and typography and the traditional styles of commercial art.

▶ Max Bill was a student at the Bauhaus when the school was dominated by left-wing politics. In 1932, back in Zurich, he designed the small monthly journal *Information*. The topics listed on the cover were 'business, science, education, technology and art'. *Information* viewed them from a socialist position. The geometrically based lettering in the red flag-like masthead is typical of Bill's graphics of the 1930s. The cover type is Grotesk, the text is Bodoni. The official endorsement – the crossbow and the slogan 'This sign is the guarantee of Swiss goods' – is used ironically to remind readers of the national armaments industry.

▲ The gas-masked soldier is captioned 'A Free Swiss, 1932'. The 'Soldier's Letter' on the right-hand page makes the satirical suggestion that the photograph could be sent on a postcard home as a 'picture of war'.

▼ Bill also designed the independent anti-fascist weekly *Die Nation*, founded in 1931. The centred sanserif 'N' matches the column width. The rest of the title, like the text, is in Bodoni, the Modernists' preferred serif face in the 1930s.

6. '*Elementare Typographie*', p.195.

50

▼ 'To the Military Moloch, War and Fascism, Say No!' By this time, 1935, Theo Ballmer had developed this economical letterpress technique of linocut images and poster type, printed in red and black.

◄ Lithographed posters allowed Ballmer a new approach. 'Fight or Impoverishment. Vote for the Communists', 1931. The hammer and sickle become 'sachlich', documentary. Their effect is doubled: both symbolic and actual, the real tools of real workers, not merely the emblem within the star.

This and the poster below are half the standard vertical format.

◄ Ballmer uses a map to emphasize the verbal message, '14 Years of Social Democracy's Betrayal: 14 Years of Development in the Soviet Union. Vote Communist', 1931.

The poster is also dependent on text, arranged in an appropriately dialectical manner of 'us' and 'them'. At the top right are exaggerated statements. 'In spite of the social democrats' and capitalists' lies, we know today that: The USSR is the only crisis-free country

The USSR is the only country with no unemployed

The USSR is the only country with an economic plan

The USSR is the only country' and so on.

These are contrasted, below left, with the ills of the social democratic states – financial crisis, unemployment, fascism, etc.

▶ 'Out with the Enemies of the People, the Majority in the National Assembly! Vote Communist, List 6.' Poster by Hans Trommer (using the pseudonym 'Pollux'), 1935.

Graphic design was only one of Trommer's activities. He had studied theatre in Berlin, and the poster shows photomontage used in a way similar to the German political artist John Heartfield. In Zurich, after a short time at the Dalang agency, Trommer opened a studio with Richard Paul Lohse in 1931. He later became celebrated as a director of mainly documentary films.

Graphics and Architecture

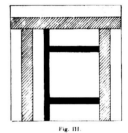

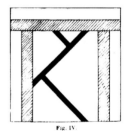

The Diagonal
Placing text and images at an angle attracted the eye by creating a tension with the vertical-horizontal axis of a printed sheet.
▼ Van Doesburg supplied a theoretical basis. He demonstrated that the horizontal-vertical structure of architecture could be opposed in painting by diagonal 'counter-composition', which he saw as part of a new spiritual anti-bourgeois movement.
De Stijl VII, 1926, pp.73-74.

▲ 'Walter Gropius, Rational Building Construction', poster by Ernst Keller for two exhibitions at the Zurich Kunstgewerbemuseum, 1931.

This poster uses the diagonal to attract the eye and to suggest dynamic activity. This was a common device by this time, but Ernst Keller's poster is entirely original in its control of space, masterly drawing and integration of text.

The printing of the image is by letterpress from linocut blocks overprinted from type in opaque grey. The fingers gripping the handle of the trowel turn the hand into a fist, a commonplace symbol in political propaganda to suggest the acclamation and solidarity of a crowd.

The New Typography and the New Architecture had much in common: asymmetry and an enjoyment of undecorated flat surfaces.

▲ Students on a balcony of the Dessau Bauhaus building designed by Gropius. Photo: *c.*1931.
The uninhibited use of the camera produced the typical Modernist snapshot with oblique angles.

The ideological foundations which underlay the New Typography had their counterpart in the New Architecture, easily identified by its flat roofs, horizontal expanses of glass and white-painted concrete. Tschichold commented:

> The old typography is much more closely related to the facade architecture of the Renaissance and its associated styles than it is to the painting of the period. . . . Yet there is a connection between typography and the new architecture. That is not to say that typography is dependent on architecture, but that both have relied on the new painting, which has brought with it forms that serve as a model.[1]

Architecture was the medium in which progressive ideas were focused. Central to Modernist thinking, it linked art and life, the aesthetic with the practical and social.

In Switzerland the main forum for discussing new ideas was the Werkbund journal, *Das Werk*. In 1930, three years after Giedion had confronted readers with Bauhaus ideas, came a further challenge. In a special issue, the Basel architect Hannes Meyer announced: 'It is our mission to give our world a new shape with the means of today.' The layout of *Das Werk* took on a new shape, to match Meyer's long, illustrated hymn to mechanization, 'Die neue Welt' (The New World), in which he attacked the old art and applied arts. Each paragraph ends with a rallying cry. 'We are becoming citizens of the world.' 'The community governs the individual.' 'Every age demands its own form.' And so on. As a preliminary to Modernist graphic design, Meyer's text is important.

> Today every phase of our culture of expression is constructive . . . . in the means of advertising, in mechanical typesetting, in the cinema, in photographic processes. The new poster presents lettering and product or trademark in a meaningful, functional arrangement. The poster is not done to be art, but to make a strong visual impact.[2]

In 1927 Meyer had been appointed Architecture Master at the Bauhaus. The following year he succeeded Gropius as the school's Director. Meyer took an interest in graphic design and photography. His functionalist ideas and typographic style – his practice of breaking texts into lines as units of meaning was followed by several typographers – were a crucial influence on Max Bill: each job appears as a fresh task with an unpredictable solution.

---

1. *Typographische Gestaltung*, 1935, p.82; *Asymmetric Typography*, 1967, p.78.
2. *Das Werk*, July 1926. Reprinted with English translation in Claude Schnaidt, *Hannes Meyer*, Teufen/London 1965, p.93.

Born in Basel, architect and theorist. Architecture Master at Dessau Bauhaus, 1927-28. Followed Gropius as Director, 1928-30. Architect and town planner in Soviet Union, 1930-36, and in Mexico, 1939-49. Returned to Switzerland, 1949.
At the Bauhaus Meyer introduced a less aesthetic, more scientific and socially engaged programme. By the time of the school's Zurich exhibition in 1930, Meyer was losing support and was soon obliged to resign.

junge menschen
kommt ans bauhaus!

▲ 'Young People – Come to the Bauhaus!' Back cover and inside page of a 44-page A5 prospectus designed by Hannes Meyer in 1928. The inside page shows a breakdown of the school's 170 students by nationality, gender, financial needs, and their subject of study. The eight Swiss make up the largest national contingent after the Germans, who represent more than half the student body. The publicity and printing workshop has 27 students.

54

▲ Max Bill's 1931 poster showing the Neubühl estate as an exhibition of design for the home. This housing development was the Swiss Werkbund's demonstration of 'Modern Architecture and Modern Living', presented as 'single-family show houses and other kinds of home fitted out with the newest furniture'. Bill himself designed the 'Painter's and Draughtsman's Studio' and a 'Studio for a Married Painter and Draughtsman' for the exhibition. The lettering 'neubühl', overprinted in red on a plan of the estate's layout, follows the forms of the logo for Wohnbedarf, the firm which supplied the exhibition's furniture. The poster is printed letterpress from linoblocks and type in red, pink, green and black.

Mart Stam 1899-1986
Dutch architect, designer and writer. Occasional poster designer, and famous as maker of first tubular-metal cantilevered chair. Helped organize display of modern architecture for the 1923 Bauhaus exhibition. Like his associates in the ABC group, Hannes Meyer and Hans Schmidt, he worked in Soviet Russia in the 1930s. Taught in East Germany after the Second World War and retired to Switzerland in 1966.

Hannes Meyer was only one of the architects whose activities, practical and theoretical, influenced the course of Swiss graphics. Alfred Roth, like Meyer, spent much of his early career abroad. Painter and writer as well as architect, Roth was later president of the Swiss Werkbund. For a crucial twelve years beginning during the Second World War, he was joint editor of *Das Werk*. 'Architecture and graphic design', he stated, 'have one thing in common: they are obliged to consider practical questions of use and, unlike painting and sculpture, their scope for artistic expression is limited.'[3]

Roth had been an assistant to Le Corbusier in Paris. Like his master, he was a follower and friend of Mondrian.[4] He had supervised the construction of the houses designed by Le Corbusier and Pierre Jeanneret at the Weissenhofsiedlung near Stuttgart in 1927. This development was the German Werkbund's demonstration of New Architecture – the International Style – linked to a housing exhibition.[5] A similar prototype development was completed four years later by the Swiss Werkbund. For this, the Neubühl estate in the Zurich suburbs, Max Bill designed a poster encouraging the public to visit. The interiors were later fitted with modern furnishings supplied by the Zurich firm Wohnbedarf (see p.109).

Avant-garde visitors to Switzerland made a lasting impact. In 1924, when Lissitzky had stopped on the way to his sanatorium in Locarno, he was met at Zurich station by Hans Arp and by the Dutch architect he had known in Berlin, Mart Stam. The eventual outcome for Arp was work on the book *Die Kunstismen*, and for Stam, the launch of a new magazine inspired by Lissitzky.

The magazine, named *ABC* and subtitled 'Beiträge zum Bauen' (Contributions to Building) and laid out by Stam and his fellow architect, Hans Schmidt, made no typographic innovations. But it was the first Modernist journal in Switzerland to include statements on graphic design. The second issue looked at two aspects of graphics. First, the architect Paul Artaria called for a new standardization of paper sizes. Already used by the Swiss engineering industry, the system of German Industrial Standards (DIN) was adopted by the Swiss government in 1924. Artaria proposed retaining only one aspect of the

As a co-founder of the interior design store Wohnbedarf, Sigfried Giedion kept his faith in friends with Bauhaus connections. When the store in Zurich was to open new showrooms in January 1933, he commissioned Marcel Breuer to design the interior.

▲ Wohnbedarf's reopening was announced in *Information* with an advertisement designed by Max Bill, January 1933.

Max Bill 1908-1994

Designer, artist, architect, writer and teacher. Trained as silversmith at Zurich Kunstgewerbeschule, 1924-27. Studied at Bauhaus, 1927-29. Freelance in Zurich in many fields of art and design from 1929. Joined Swiss Werkbund, 1930. Designed Swiss pavilion, Milan Triennale (Gold Medal), 1936. As well as the Bauhaus artists, came to know many of the leading figures in 20th-century art, including Hans Arp, Max Ernst, Marcel Duchamp, Piet Mondrian and Henry van de Velde. Joined Allianz, modern Swiss artists' group, 1937. Organized 'Konkrete Kunst' exhibition, Basel, 1946; 'Die gute Form' exhibition, 1948. Designed Swiss pavilion, Milan Triennale; Grand Prix for Sculpture, Sao Paulo Biennale, 1951. Architect and first rector of Hochschule für Gestaltung at Ulm (successor to the Bauhaus), 1951-56. Monument to the Unknown Political Prisoner Competition, 3rd prize, 1956. Joined German Werkbund, 1956, and Association of Swiss Architects, 1959. Architect, Cinevox cinema, Neuhausen. Zurich district councillor, 1961-68. Member, Federal Art Commission, 1961-69. Architect, 'Education and Creation' section, Swiss National Exhibition, Lausanne 1964. Numerous international honours and awards. Died on visit to Berlin.

3. 'Grafische Einflüsse in der Gegenswartsarchitektur', *Werk*, August 1943, p.242.
4. The story of Roth's relationship to Mondrian is recorded in *Correspondance/Piet Mondrian, Alfred Roth*, Paris 1999.
5. The 'International Style' was a term coined by Alfred Barr for an exhibition of Modern Movement architecture at New York's Museum of Modern Art in 1932. As the architect and writer Peter Blake put it: 'The Modern Movement, in our view, was a politically radical commitment to enhancing the human condition . . . .', *No Place like Utopia*, New York 1993, p.147.

Zett-Haus (Z-House)

This development, begun in 1928 in the centre of Zurich, was almost a district of the city in itself.
The building, with underground parking, contained flats, offices, shops, a cinema, bar and restaurant.
An example of the New Architecture, the building used the most up-to-date technology. The Zett-Haus was explained in a series of full-page advertisements in the *Neue Zürcher Zeitung*, designed by Max Bill.
They represent a type of informal functionalism rather than neo-Constructivist aestheticism.

◄ The first advertisement, in December 1931, showed what the Zett-Haus looked like, where it was, its facilities, and what was available for rent.
The aerial view, which included street names, made it easy for the reader to identify the location of this new arrival within their familiar environment.
Bill's early ambition to practise as an architect was only fully realized many years later.
► For the Zett-Haus he designed painted lettering on the facade.

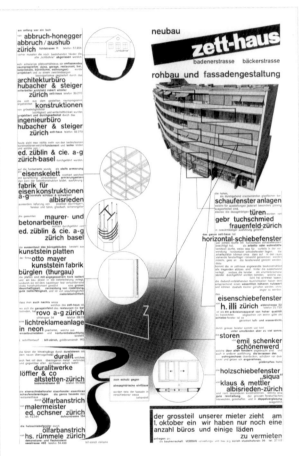

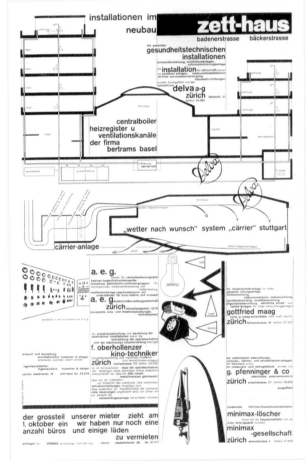

▲ As the Zett-Haus was completed, the contractors and suppliers responsible for its novel techniques, services and fittings were listed in the advertisements, starting with the demolition contractors, followed by the architects, engineers and the firms responsible for the steelwork, the reinforced concrete, artificial stone cladding, illuminated signing and different types of paintwork.

The black 'bracket' on the left leads to a panel explaining that the exterior has more than one type of finish.
On the right of the advertisement, under the photograph of the building, are names of suppliers of metal and wooden windows and blinds.
The firms' names are connected to explanatory drawings and in some cases to related parts of the building.
The airbrushed 'cloud' gives Bill a background for a white line to represent neon.

Bill's typography is eccentrically informal: lines justified, ranged left and ranged right, but limited to two sizes of Grotesk, all lowercase.
The advertisement on the left was followed two days later by another (not shown), which added more suppliers of Zett-Haus services: insulating materials, and seating and cloakroom fittings for the bar and cinema.

▲ Within a few days a further page of the *Neue Zürcher Zeitung* describes the heating and air-conditioning system, and lists the electrical engineers (light, power and telephone) and the suppliers of cinema equipment and fire extinguishers. Where a drawing or diagram is useful, Bill includes it.

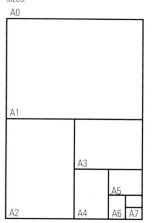

Beiträge zum Bauen Serie 2 No. 3
Adm. Augustinergasse 5 ÷ Basel

▲ The Basel architectural magazine *ABC*, with Lissitzky as its inspiration and support, edited by Hans Schmidt, Mart Stam and Hannes Meyer, was published from 1924 to 1928.
The standard cover design contrasts with the amateurish layout and typography of the inside pages.
▼ Lissitzky, the inspirer of *ABC*, was represented in the magazine by a cropped version of his self-portrait, *The Constructor*. The multiple-printed image was made in Switzerland, where Lissitzky was being treated for tuberculosis. It is here trimmed to a square, and has a pasted-on label reading 'Brit.Pat.169434'. The headline reads 'Atelier Lichtbilder Lissitzky', (Lissitzky Photo Studio).

JEDER Künstler, der sich auf ABC abonniert, hat das Recht, seine Photographie gratis zu veröffentlichen. (Mit der Garantie, sofort berühmt zu werden). JEDE Dame, die sich auf ABC abonniert, hat das Recht, ihre Photographie gratis zu veröffentlichen. (ohne Garantie).
JEDER abonniere sich auf ABC

The caption is in an ironical Dadaistic spirit. 'EVERY artist who subscribes to *ABC* has the right to publish his own photograph free. (With the guarantee that he will be famous instantly.) EVERY woman subscriber to *ABC* has the right to publish her photograph free. (Without guarantee.) EVERYONE subscribe to *ABC*.'

DIN system – halving or doubling a sheet to provide the next size – but he proposed a length of one meter for the basic size.[6]

The following article was on advertising, written by Lissitzky and Mart Stam.[7] They begin with a general statement: 'Advertising has become a necessary part of the present social fabric, a result of commercial competition.' Advertising in general is not discussed – only posters, for which they lay down strict rules. First they emphasize the text: 'Everything that is unimportant or beside the point should be omitted.' Nothing should be there for aesthetic reasons, as it will 'do nothing but harm', and 'the individual element (the artist's individual touch) is entirely out of place. It is of prime importance that the product itself should be shown, not merely its name.'

Two illustrations were included with the article: a design by Stam for Bruijnzeel flooring and Otto Baumberger's poster with the overcoat. Each demonstrates an aspect of the later Swiss style: geometrically organized drawn letterforms in Stam, and 'sachlich' representation in Baumberger's hyperrealist overcoat, whose prominent PKZ label supplied the only text.

Stam and Lissitzky make fun of the common view that poster art is the prostitution of painting: it is the same as saying that journalism is a prostitution of literature and film a prostitution of the theatre. Such concern with the professional or cultural status of graphic design runs through the history of graphic design in Switzerland.

The example of Soviet Russia was crucial to *ABC*. If the magazine's design showed little Constructivist influence, its attitudes were nonetheless revolutionary. 'We felt like a league of conspirators,' said Schmidt, its co-editor. This attitude was important for Swiss designers, and when Lissitzky left Switzerland, the radicalism remained.

6. Readers were invited to test Artaria's proposals by folding up their copies of *ABC*.
7. *ABC*, no.2, 1924. Tschichold reprinted this article in *'Elementare Typographie'*. As *ABC*'s guest editor in 1926, Hannes Meyer reciprocated, reprinting Tschichold's article 'Die neue Gestaltung' from *'Elementare Typographie'*. The original first paragraph, connecting typography with art, is omitted and, given Swiss political sensibilities, the contribution stops short of the quotation from Trotsky (see p. 47).

Paper Standardization
Architects saw standardization as a means of rationalizing their reference to technical specifications, and information supplied by manufacturers. This could be helped by adopting the German DIN sizes (see p.7, 18). Based on a sheet with sides in the ratio of 1:√2 (1:1.414), folding or cutting the sheet in half across the width produces smaller sheets that retain the same proportion. The basic sheet, with an area of one square meter, is designated A0. The smaller sizes are described by the number of times the basic sheet is folded or cut. Hence, A4, the most common size for letters and catalogues, derives from the sheet of one square metre, cut or folded in half four times. The Swiss Weltformat poster size (128 × 90.5cm) is in the same proportion, but not in the range of A sizes.

A0		
A1		
A2	A3	A5 A6 A7
	A4	

▼ In an unpublished document the *ABC* co-editor Hans Schmidt calls for the standardization of catalogues and brochures. 'Why not 1 standard size?' Looking at 50 catalogues, he finds 26 different formats, and writes that, with only slight adjustments to the margins, 31 of these could be A4. He ends with the slogan, 'Clear layout (Uebersicht) saves work.'

▶ Poster by El Lissitzky for the Russian Exhibition in Zurich in 1929 (see p. 60). Lissitzky sent the design, a double-exposed photograph and montage, heavily retouched, from Moscow. Outlandish, breaking with every convention, the poster has a political message. The word 'Russische' (Russian) is overwhelmed by branding the couple's foreheads with the initials of the Union of Soviet Socialist Republics in red and making a link with the word 'Ausstellung', also in red. That is, it is a Soviet exhibition, rather than merely Russian. Although they dominate the design, the couple appear as backdrop to the image in the lower half, apparently the model of an exhibition design.

Such disturbing novelties, which included arranging lettering vertically, on the red band at the left, did not deter the more than 8,000 visitors to the exhibition.

Printing, in red by lithography and in black by gravure, was by Fretz, where its production was supervised by Walter Cyliax.

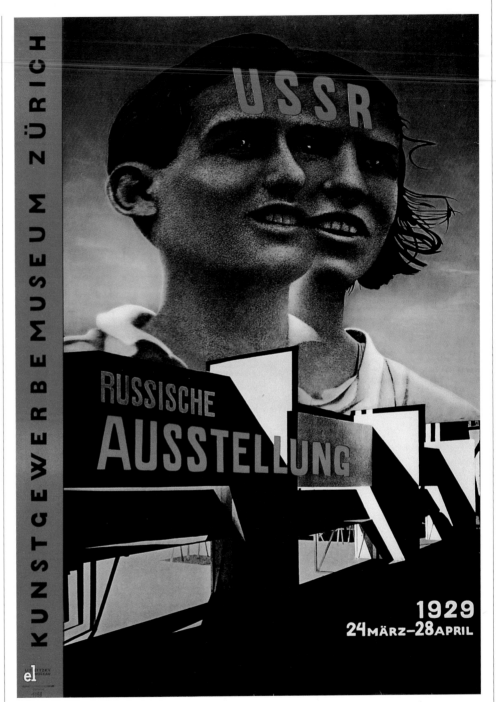

Geometry

58

In their demand for precision and their admiration of the machine, designers such as Lissitzky and the former Dadaist Kurt Schwitters saw 'every technology, indeed, the entire world' dependent on the 'basic technical forms of the universe' – 'crystal, cone, plane, bar, ribbon or strip, spiral, sphere' (*Merz* 8/9, 1924, p.75).

Van Doesburg and the Western Constructivists had aesthetic motives in borrowing the 'elemental' forms – the circle, square and triangle – from the Russian painters, notably Malevich. These forms, seen as the basis of two-dimensional art and design, were also reminders of the renewal of visual art from first principles. The square and circle in particular were adopted by the Swiss Modernists. The square was used as a basic division of the design area and as a modular unit, and later became popular as a book format. Geometry can be used by graphic designers in two ways. First, it supplies 'elemental' forms. Second, it is a means of relating the graphic components to each other and to the surface area of their designs. This has been especially the case with posters; in the design of books it is a centuries-old tradition. During the 1920s leading architects and designers of the Modern Movement, typified by Le Corbusier and Tschichold, buttressed their working practice by investigating the mathematical principles underlying works of the past. (See pp. 77, 155)

▲ Geometry in a winter sports resort in the early 1930s: the designer-photographer Herbert Matter's sign for his parents' restaurant.

AMTLICH BEWILLIGT

AB 15. JAN. BIS 13. FEBR.

TEIL FORSTER AUSVERKAUF

NEBEN CORSO THEATERSTR: 12

J.C. MÜLLER. ZÜRICH 8.

B

▲ A sale by the carpet firm Forster, poster designed by Otto Baumberger, 1928. The public was familiar with Baumberger's style of painted illustrations and the geometric forms he uses here are a naturalistic representation – the end view of a roll of floor covering and the rectangle of a rug. In this way the geometry is not 'concrete'.

Baumberger's use of a Modernist compositional device – the square – is unexpected: the lower edge of the rectangle is at the base of a square which begins at the top of the poster. There is a striking similarity between this and the poster on p.14 by Walter Cyliax and Hans Arp.

The use of abstract form rather than an illustration of the subject typifies the Modernist Swiss poster.

▶ The graphic image of Max Bill's 1931 'Negerkunst' exhibition poster derives from Bill's artistic interests at the time. The connection to the subjects of the exhibition, 'Negro Art and Prehistoric Rock Paintings of South Africa', is made specific only by the words in the label at the bottom right of the poster.

The design is not only made up of geometrical forms but is also constructed on a geometrical basis.

▲ Bill's *Well-Relief* (Wave Relief) construction, produced at the same time as the poster, uses the same forms, in different proportions.

▼ The same circle within a symmetrical elipse reappears in Bill's lettering for the Neubühl poster and the 'o' of the Wohnbedarf logo.

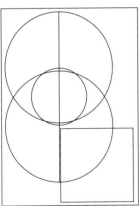

▲ The structure of Max Bill's 'Negerkunst' poster.

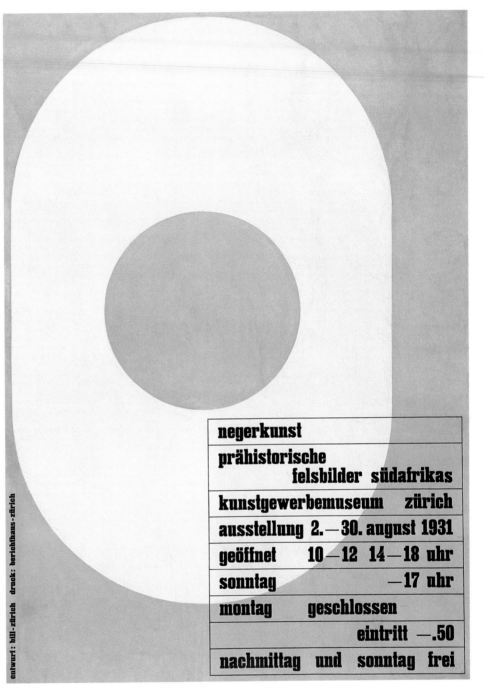

entwurf : bill · zürich   druck : berichthaus · zürich

| negerkunst |
| prähistorische felsbilder südafrikas |
| kunstgewerbemuseum   zürich |
| ausstellung 2.—30. august 1931 |
| geöffnet   10—12 14—18 uhr |
| sonntag   —17 uhr |
| montag   geschlossen |
| eintritt —.50 |
| nachmittag und sonntag frei |

Exhibitions and Their Posters

▼ Catalogue cover for the second exhibition of progressive graphic design at the Basel Gewerbemuseum, 1930. Jan Tschichold, although he was working in Germany, lent posters from his collection, designed the catalogue – entirely in lowercase – and provided an essay on poster design.

gewerbemuseum basel

neue werbegraphik

30. märz bis 27. april 1930

Exhibitions at the applied arts museums in Zurich and Basel showed mainly contemporary, often avant-garde, ideas and work. The exhibitions were didactic. With such themes as *Form ohne Ornament* (Design without Decoration), they challenged conventional ideas. And in such exhibitions as 'Die praktische Küche' (The Practical Kitchen) they presented radical solutions to domestic planning.

The museums were linked to the schools of arts and crafts, and the exhibition posters, often designed by the teachers, made Modernism familiar – Ernst Keller's for 'Das neue Heim' (The New Home) in 1928, for example, and Theo Ballmer's for 'Neues Bauen' (New Building) the same year. Ballmer had the year before made the astonishingly original poster for '100 Jahre Lichtbild '(100 Years of Photography), which inaugurated a succession of geometrical posters advertising exhibitions (see p.72).

An extreme example of the new, dauntingly rational presentation was Helen Haasbauer-Wallrath's 1930 design for 'Die praktische Küche' (The Practical Kitchen), which illustrated the centre of the Swiss housewife's world with a bleak, efficient isometric drawing. By contrast, Lissitzky's poster for the 'Russian Exhibition' – one of the most famous images of modern design – had no stylistic successors in Switzerland: first, on account of its technique – the photomontage is symbolic, not 'sachlich'; second, because its formal design, where deep perspective breaks the surface of the sheet, belonged to an outdated pictorial tradition.

In fact the 'Russian Exhibition' was far from entirely Constructivist. The catalogue makes much of the woodcut illustrations, explaining that this was an economical means of reproduction, replacing the half-tone block at a time when photomechanical materials were in short supply in the Soviet Union. The exhibition nonetheless exposed the Swiss to the Soviet avant-garde: among a long list of artists is the October Group, which included Alexander Deineka, Gustav Klutzis, Sergei Senkin and Solomon Telingater – all more or less Constructivist and connected with the state Vkhutemas school, the 'Moscow Bauhaus'.

The 'Russian Exhibition' was followed immediately in Zurich by the travelling display of Bauhaus work, first seen in Basel. This indicates remarkable commitment to progressive ideas by the museums, which also provided direct introductions to the New Typography and Modernist graphic design, exemplified by the two important exhibitions, in 1927 and 1930, at the Basel Gewerbemuseum (see also p.41).

▲ 'Art of the Soviet Union Exhibition', poster by the Russian designer, Valentina Kulagina, 1932.
As with Lissitzky's 'Russian Exhibition' poster, the design, sent from Moscow, was printed in Zurich. Kulagina's design is hand drawn and printed in colour by lithography. The stylized realistic elements are overlaid on a geometrical background, echoed in such posters as Helmuth Kurtz's 'Autophon Radio' design (p.94) and Theo Ballmer's '5000 Years of Lettering' (p.95).

► Poster by Helene Haasbauer-Wallrath for 'The Practical Kitchen' exhibition in Basel, 1930. The axonometric drawing of this piece of domestic planning, like Ernst Mumenthaler's poster for standardized furniture on p.18, makes it clear that the exhibition is about rational planning, not about interior decoration. Lithograph.

62 ▶ 'New Sports Buildings', exhibition
poster by Ernst Mumenthaler, 1931.
The exhibition was a survey of
stadiums, sports complexes and
swimming pools in Northern Europe
built on Modernist principles.
In common with posters of the same
time by Theo Ballmer and Max Bill, the
text is all lowercase, with the opening
times in a ruled grid.
Lithoprinted.

▶ Poster for the 'International Poster Exhibition' in Zurich, designed by Walter Käch, 1933.
Käch has played with perspective and depth, illustrating the poster as a rectangle in space. Both the rectangle in the top left corner – outlined with white-on-black and black-on-white lines and lettering – and the exhibition dates at the bottom, parallel with the edges of the sheet, emphasize the plane of the paper. At the same time, the rectangle implies depth, as though it is floating in front of the wedge-shaped light area on which the words 'plakat' and 'ausstellung' appear to recede in space.

Walter Käch 1901-1970
Graphic designer, lettering artist, teacher. Apprenticed to a lithographic printer and student of Ernst Keller, 1919-21. Assistant to F.H. Ehmcke at the Munich Kunstgewerbeschule, 1921-22. Freelance designer, 1929-40. Taught printmaking at Zurich Kunstgewerbeschule, 1925-29, and later taught lettering at the school, 1940-67.
Käch was responsible for some of the clearest demonstrations of avant-garde design in the 1930s. He was to become more traditional in outlook, best known and influential for his teaching and writing about lettering.

64

gewerbemuseum basel

ausstellung

die frühzeit des plakats

6.–27. oktober 1935

▲ Catalogue title page for 'The Early Years of the Poster' exhibition, 1935. The catalogue explains that the exhibition ended with Art Nouveau, a turning point. Since then the artist has disappeared behind the 'sachlich' pursuit of the advertising aim, and the poster has become 'simpler, more impersonal, more sober'.
The efforts of the Basel Gewerbemuseum to present the history of design, and also to show the practical application of Modernist ideas, were well served by the simple and sober style of its catalogues and posters.
▼ Exhibition posters at the Basel Museum were printed from type, to standardized layouts prepared by Tschichold. The designs were slowly refined over the second half of the 1930s, when upper- and lowercase type replaced the out-and-out Modernist lowercase-only. Ranging type flush left on two axes became a common layout method in the 1960s.

Gewerbemuseum Basel

Ausstellung

Amtliche Drucksachen

in Vergangenheit und Gegenwart

28. August bis 25. Sept. 1938

	Werktags	14-19	
Eintritt frei	Mittwochs	14-19	19-21
	Sonntags	10-12	14-19

The first, 'Die neue Typographie', showed mainly Swiss and German work. *Das Werk* took note of the exhibition by reproducing eight cinema posters on a single page. Seven were by Tschichold. The remaining odd poster was by Cyliax, in a style that in no way suggested film, being merely a strangely Cubistic Art-Deco background on which smaller typographic handbills would be pasted.

The larger Basel exhibition in 1930, 'Neue Werbegraphik' (New Advertising Design), organized by Tschichold, was arranged in three parts. The first section consisted of members of Schwitters's international Ring neuer Werbegestalter; the second was 'The New Poster' and the third, French posters. The everyday use of graphic design was the focus of two further Basel exhibitions. In 1934 the Werkbund helped to organize 'Planvolles Werben' (Advertising with a Purpose), with the subtitle 'From Letterhead to Advertising Film'. Four years later, 'Amtliche Drucksachen in Vergangenheit und Gegenwart' (Official Printed Matter Yesterday and Today) showed the long history of notices and decrees, forms, legal documents, passports, certificates, tickets, visiting cards, invitations, letterheads and envelopes. Alongside earlier examples was work by contemporary typographers, among them Theo Ballmer, Hermann Eidenbenz and, of course, Tschichold, who had standardized and refined the letterheads, forms, certificates and catalogues for the School and the Museum of Applied Arts in Basel.

Such shows of small-scale typography presented the layman with a less exciting aspect of graphic design than the exhibition of Basel Poster Art held in 1933, the same year as an International Poster Exhibition in Zurich. Both were advertised with posters in the style of the New Typography; one by Hermann Eidenbenz (BA-PLA-KU, see p.45), the other by Walter Käch (see p.63).

Commercial fairs were usually, as they have remained, specific to individual trades and industries. The first and second occasions of the 'Graphische Fachausstellung' (Printing Trades Exhibition) – 'Grafa' – were in Zurich in 1934 and 1935. At the first, the public, when asked to vote for their favourite poster, chose the famous Gaba throat lozenge poster by Niklaus Stoecklin.

The third Grafa took place in 1936 in the building of the Basel Trade Fair, organized with the help of the Werkbund. As well as work by Swiss designers, foreign work was included, arranged by Tschichold. Political considerations must have weighed with Tschichold, now an émigré: no Russian work was on display, and none by designers such as Schwitters, whose painting had been denounced by the Nazis as 'degenerate'.

▲ Poster for Gaba throat pastilles, designed by Niklaus Stoecklin, 1927. Printed from linocut blocks, it shares its economy of means with the geometrical, abstract posters of the Modernist designers. The logo was replaced by GABA in capital letters for later versions of the poster.

Niklaus Stoecklin 1896-1982
Painter and designer. Trained in Basel. Studied at Munich Kunstgewerbeschule, 1912-14, and with Burkhard Mangold, a leading designer of the previous generation at the Allgemeine Gewerbeschule in Basel, 1914-15. Painter and freelance poster artist in Basel from 1917. Represented with one-man exhibitions, Kunstmuseum Winterthur, 1927; Kunsthalle Basel, 1928 and 1940; Gewerbemuseum Basel, 1966. Died in Riehen, Basel.
Like Baumberger, Stoecklin showed a brilliant virtuosity. Although the various styles of his work were typical of the range of graphic idiom in Switzerland, he is most celebrated as a hyperrealist: a practitioner of 'Sachlichkeit'.

▶ Poster design for the second
'Graphische Fachausstellung' (Printing
Trades Exhibition) – Grafa – by Gérard
Miedinger, 1934.
Miedinger's unused design followed
the example of Walter Käch's 1933
design for the International Poster
Exhibition.

Gérard Miedinger 1912-1995
Studied with Ernst Keller, 1932-34,
then in Paris, 1934-35. Employed at the
Zurich printer-publishers Orell Füssli
and in an advertising agency before
becoming freelance in 1938. Developed
progressive 1930s style in one of the
most successful design practices in
Zurich. Responsible for large part of
Swiss pavilions at World Exhibitions
in Brussels, 1958, and Montreal, 1967.
President of the Verband
Schweizerischer Grafiker (VSG):
Association of Swiss Graphic
Designers, 1968-72.

▲ The black-and-white poster used for
the second Grafa exhibition, designed
by Alex Diggelmann, 1934.

Miedinger has suggested the three-
dimensional space of the exhibition by
using perspective, a graphic device
generally avoided by adherents to the
New Typography since it broke the
surface plane of the paper, which they
were keen to emphasize. Miedinger
has resolved this by the large areas of
colour which create tension: they
remain flat yet they help in the illusion
of space.

66 ▶ Cover of the special Grafa issue
of *Typographische Monatsblätter*,
(Typographic Monthly), May 1936,
designed by Hermann Eidenbenz.
The photograph shows printer's ink
being mixed by hand. The words of
the subtitles which appeared on the
cover of every issue, 'typo, foto, graphik,
druck' (typography, photography,
graphics, printing) are distinguished
by their letterforms – bold grotesque,
Bodoni bold condensed, script (hand-
drawn by Eidenbenz), and Bodoni
extra bold.

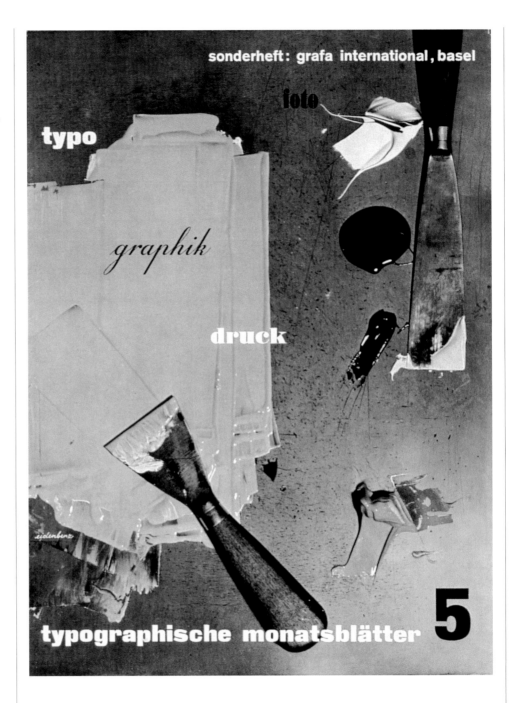

grafa
international

Graphische Fachausstellung
Basel, im Mustermeßgebäude
13.–29. Juni 1936

Prospekt beim Sekretariat Peters-
graben 47, Telephon Nr. 24.934

▲ Single-column advertisement in *Das Werk* for the Grafa exhibition in 1936. Publicity for this, the third Grafa, was in the hands of Hermann Eidenbenz. The logotype in bold Akzidenz Grotesk was applied in all the printed material for the exhibition.

◄ Poster (also adapted as the exhibition catalogue cover) designed by Hermann Eidenbenz for the third Grafa.

Hermann Eidenbenz 1902-1993 Graphic designer, lettering artist, type designer and art director. Apprenticed with printers Orell Füssli in Zurich. Student of Ernst Keller at Kunstgewerbeschule, 1922-23. Worked in Berlin in the studios of leading commercial designers, with Wilhelm Deffke, 1923-25, and Oskar Hadank, 1925-26. Teacher at Magdeburg Kunstgewerbe- und Handwerkschule, 1926-32. Opened studio in Basel with brothers Reinhold and Willi, 1932. Teacher at Werkkunstschule, Brunswick (Braunschweig), 1953-55. Art director Reemstma tobacco company, Hamburg, 1956-67. A prolific and virtuoso designer and craftsman in every graphic medium throughout his career. A leader of the pioneering Modernists in the 1930s and 1940s.

The single repeated figure, increasing in size, suggests events taking place in time and space. The circular silhouettes illustrate a rotary press and the process of printing. The cut-out photographs of the newspaper boy make the link to the final outcome of the process – the newspaper or magazine on the street.

The variety of effect with only a two-colour litho printing is typical of Swiss design before the widespread use of colour nearly three decades later.

▲ Herbert Matter used the same photograph of the paper seller in a booklet promoting newspapers as an advertising medium, 1936. The image is printed red, the type black.

Designers were employed to put across information as clearly as possible. Pre-prepared exhibitions were often made up of flat panels – book pages in space.
▼ The Swiss section at the German Building Exhibition in Berlin, 1930. The graphics, designed by Max Bill, presented Zurich's town planning in maps, aerial photographs and printed statistics.

▲ Part of the Swiss Tourist Board display at the Brussels World Exhibition, 1935. Max Bill's design is an unusually symmetrical arrangement: photographs cut-out above, on rectangular and square panels below, and the text on square white panels.

The Swiss government understood the value of exhibitions for public information, and recognized the value of progressive designers. An early example was the dramatic use of photography and lettering on a large scale in the first of the annual Health and Sport Exhibitions (HYSPA) held in Berne in 1931.

Exhibitions abroad advertised Switzerland's industries, achievements and tourist attractions. In 1928 the Swiss contributed to the _Pressa_ printing and publishing exhibition in Cologne, dominated by Lissitzky's spectacular displays of photomontage and dramatic effects of light and movement. Such a demonstration indicated an impressive confidence in the most radical design for publicity and propaganda. Whereas Lissitzky's energetic improvisations represented the hectic optimism of post-revolutionary Russia, Swiss architects and exhibition designers were effective by the restraint of elegant, modern structures and by their clear graphics.

Max Bill attracted a series of public commissions. In 1930 he designed the graphics for a tourist exhibition in Poland. The following year, when the Bund Schweizer Architekten (Association of Swiss Architects) (BSA) took part in the German Building Exhibition in Berlin, he contributed a display of town planning, using all-lowercase captioning on square graphic panels. He was again commissioned, with Walter Käch, for the Swiss Tourist Board's display in the national pavilion at the 1935 Brussels World Exhibition. The following year, the award of the Gold Medal to Bill's pavilion for the 1936 Milan Triennale consolidated the international reputation of Swiss design.

The Trades Union display at the first Health and Sport Exhibition (HYSPA) in Berne, 1931. The visitor is dwarfed by photographic enlargements demanding an emotional response. The design is credited to two Zurich designers, Walter Käch and Heini Fischer.

▲ Giant strides in the growth of trades union membership.
▼ 'Made Redundant. Who's Helping?'

Milan Triennale 1936

The Triennale was the only regular
international exhibition devoted to
contemporary design, architecture
and planning. The commission to
design the country's pavilion was
the result of a competition organized
by the Werkbund. The reputation of
Swiss exhibition design was confirmed
when Max Bill's design won the
Triennale's Gold Medal.

◄ On entering the main exhibition
space, visitors passed the country's
name, 'svizzera' – made of three-
dimensional tubular letters mounted
in a curved red-painted panel – and
were faced with a mountainscape
panorama of square photographic
panels. Beyond this to the left was a
curved wall displaying a selection of
posters: Hermann Eidenbenz's Grafa
poster and Heiri Steiner and Ernst
Heiniger's poster for Bally shoes (see
p.79) are easily identifiable.

▼ Looking back, the reverse sides of
the square photographic panels are
filled with an elemental 'concrete'
design of blue-grey painted discs sized
in arithmetical progression. In front of
this screen are two sculptures by Bill,
one each side of the poster wall, which
includes his 'Negerkunst' design.
Typographical work was also displayed.
Pottery, jewellery and glass were
confined to a long display case, its end
visible as a black rectangle at the left
of the photograph.

▶ 'Light in Home, Office, Workshop', poster for an exhibition at the Zurich Kunstgewerbemuseum, designed by Alfred Willimann, 1932.
▼ Entrance to the exhibition with lettering and signs designed by Max Bill.

▼ The poster for the Basel version of the exhibition, by Theo Ballmer. The limitation of letterpress determined the crudely geometricized lettering (cut from lino). The black printing is on two sheets, white for the top half, yellow for the bottom – perhaps to suggest daylight and artificial light. The result, a much weaker graphic expression of the exhibition theme, emphasizes the imagination and craftsmanship of Willimann's design.

Alfred Willimann 1900-1957
Graphic designer, photographer, lettering artist and teacher. Studied at the Zurich Kunstgewerbeschule, 1917-18. Active as sculptor and freelance graphic designer, 1919-21. Studied at Akademie der Bildenden Künste (Academy of Fine Arts), Berlin, 1921-23. Teacher of drawing and lettercutting (later typographic design in the photographic class) at the Zurich Kunstgewerbeschule from 1929.

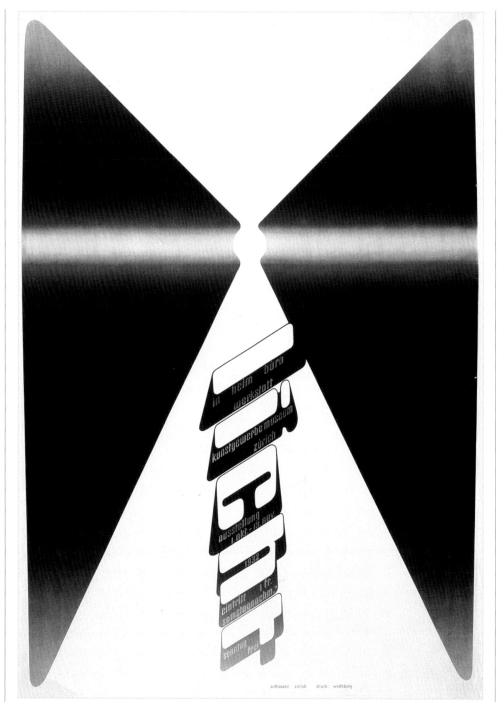

▶ Poster for the 'Exhibition of the Fourth International Radiologists' Congress', at the Zurich Kunstgewerbemuseum, designed by Walter Käch, 1934.

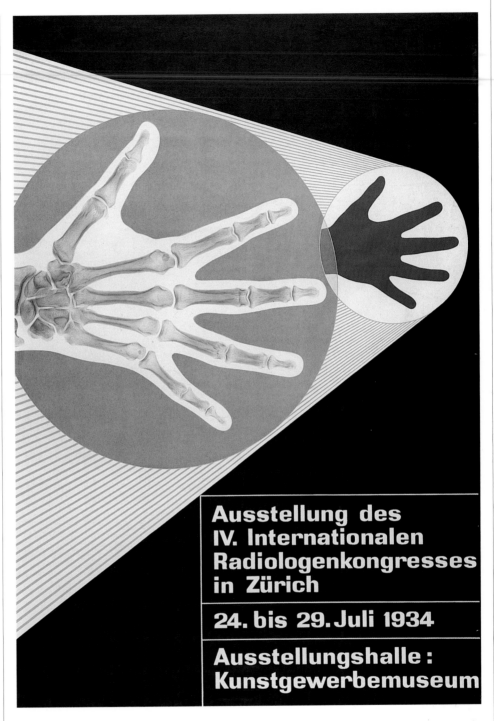

Ausstellung des
IV. Internationalen
Radiologenkongresses
in Zürich

24. bis 29. Juli 1934

Ausstellungshalle :
Kunstgewerbemuseum

In 1925 Moholy-Nagy's comment on the examples of X-ray photographs in his book *Malerei, Photographie, Film* was: 'Penetration of the body with light is one of the greatest visual experiences.' It was in the spirit of the time that the Kunstgewerbemuseum should take the opportunity to demonstrate the aesthetic interest of scientific images as part of a new vision of the world.

Käch has made a literal illustration of the process of radiation: the rays pass through the flesh to show the position of the bones (which have absorbed the rays) within a negative silhouette of the hand.

The New Photography and Photo-Graphic Design

72 ▶ '100 Years of Photography', exhibition poster designed by Theo Ballmer, 1927.

Ballmer, himself a pioneering photographer, makes an image from the lens and the leaves of its shutter. The gradation of tone in the designer's hand-drawn lettering suggests the tonal range of a photograph. The angling of the lines has depended on the length of each part of the text.

The aspiration of progressive artists and designers to build a new world did not spring only from hatred of the old. It was also determined by technology. The camera was included in their enthusiasm for the machine. When Hannes Meyer announced the arrival of a 'new world' in the special issue of *Das Werk* in 1930, he stated that its 'reality' would be recorded by photography. This was a medium, he claimed, that was untainted by historical precedent.

The Swiss Werkbund's general secretary, F.T. Gubler, pointed out that, while every photograph relies on the same physics and chemistry, its effect depends on the person behind the camera. Among the painters behind the camera in the 1920s, many were also graphic designers. The best-known examples are, in Russia, Alexander Rodchenko and, of course, Lissitzky; in Germany, Moholy-Nagy. Not only a pioneer of New Typography, Moholy-Nagy was also a practitioner and propagandist for what became known as the New Photography. One of the Bauhaus Books, *Malerei, Photographie, Film* (Painting, Photography, Film), published in 1925, was his manifesto for new ways of seeing.[1] The camera, he said, extends the range of 'our own optical instrument, the eye'. And it

> reproduces the purely optical image and therefore shows the optically true distortions, deformations, foreshortenings, etc., whereas the eye, together with our intellectual experience, supplements perceived optical phenomena by means of association and formally and spatially conceives a conceptual image. Thus in the photographic camera we have the most reliable aid to a beginning of objective vision.[2]

Photography was by no means a new medium. In 1927 the Basel Gewerbemuseum presented its history in '100 Jahre Lichtbild' (100 Years of Photography). For the huge German Werkbund exhibition, 'Film und Foto' (Fifo), held in Stuttgart in 1929, Moholy-Nagy arranged a historical section. *Das Werk* adapted this as the basis of a long illustrated article, 'The Most Important Periods in the History of Photography'. The essay was laid out (presumably by Walter Cyliax) in the clear, informal manner of Werner Graeff's *Es kommt der neue Fotograf!* (Here Comes the New Photographer!), a book produced to coincide with the exhibition. The significance of

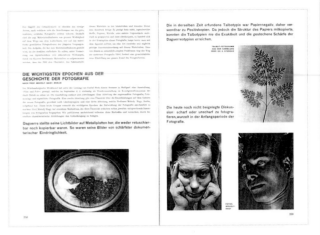

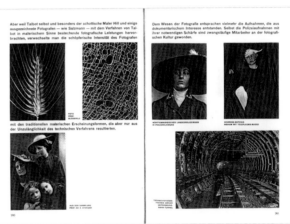

▲ *Das Werk* abandoned the magazine's usual conventional layout in 1929 for a ten-page version of Moholy-Nagy's 'The Most Important Periods in the History of Photography'. The article was based on material prepared for the German Werkbund's 'Film und Foto' exhibition, which was shown in an abridged form at the Zurich Kunstgewerbemuseum later that year. The layout loosely followed Werner Graeff's method in the book which accompanied the exhibition, *Es kommt der neue Fotograf!*, where text and image are both closely related and have the same visual weight. Graeff was given the opportunity to introduce the New Photography in Zurich when the Swiss Werkbund invited him to lecture in 1931.

Moholy-Nagy demonstrates that contemporary discussions, practical and theoretical, between the photograph's aesthetic and its documentary value, are part of the medium's history. And he finishes by saying, 'It is not a question of making photography into an art in the old sense, but it is the profound social responsibility of the photographer who strives, with the given basic photographic means, to do what cannot be done with any other. This work must be the undistorted document of contemporary reality.'

1. Bauhaus Books, edited by Walter Gropius and Moholy-Nagy, were planned as a series to include 50 titles, but only 14 were published between 1925 and 1931. They were available in Switzerland: the first 8 were discussed on a whole page of *Das Werk* (July 1926, p.234). Gropius and Moholy-Nagy each wrote two books; other authors included Van Doesburg, Paul Klee, Malevich and Mondrian.
2. *Malerei, Photographie, Film*, Munich 1925; reprint Mainz 1967; translated as *Painting, Photography, Film*, London 1969, p.28.

▲ Small poster by Heiri Steiner for an exhibition of 'Photographs of Nature and Technology by Renger-Patsch', 1928. At this time photography for posters was, due to its expense, restricted to small tourist posters. Albert Renger-Patsch was a German photographer, a member of the Deutscher Werkbund, whose book *Die Welt ist schön* (The World Is Beautiful) was published the same year. That Renger-Patsch's preferred title was *Die Dinge* (Things) reveals his commitment to 'Sachlichkeit'. With a studio at the Folkwang Museum in Essen, Renger-Patsch was a colleague of Burchartz, who taught at the adjoining school.

▲ 'Made-to-measure Still the Best.' Poster by Walter Käch, 1928. The photograph is printed by gravure in black and pasted on the blue background to the lettering, printed in lithography. Photography was slow to compete with drawing for the images in posters. This is one of the earliest posters to include a photograph.

photography for designers was demonstrated by the activity of typographers in the organization of Fifo. Tschichold co-edited and designed *Foto-Auge* (Photo-Eye), a book reproducing key works from the show, and was on the exhibition committee; Moholy-Nagy selected the German work, Piet Zwart the Dutch, and Lissitzky the Russian. Moholy-Nagy showed almost one hundred of his own photographs, including photograms and montages, and there were twenty-six photographs by the former Bauhaus teacher, Herbert Bayer.

The small Swiss contribution to Fifo, arranged by Sigfried Giedion and F.T. Gubler, included photographic posters by Cyliax, Walter Käch and Ernst Keller. Gubler claimed to identify a recognizable style in each country's photography. 'In Russia,' he wrote,

> with the same technical means, there are signs that a different ideology changes the meaning of the image. It is not the subject of the photograph that changes. An American photograph of a factory is distinct from a Russian photograph of basically the same subject.[3]

A travelling version of 'Film und Foto' was shown in Basel and Zurich, where it was followed by the Russian Exhibition. Although the New Photography advanced in Russia at the same time as in Germany, the photographs on show in Zurich followed the pictorial conventions of painting. There were none by, for instance, Alexander Rodchenko or Lissitzky.

So, rather than the Russians, it was Moholy-Nagy's editing and layout of the series of Bauhaus Books that had the most immediate and lasting influence on the progressive Swiss designers. The Bauhaus view of the camera as a mechanical eye is most obviously expressed in the angling of horizontals and verticals in the viewfinder, transforming the natural image into a pictorial abstraction; indeed, they resembled Moholy-Nagy's Abstract paintings and those of Van Doesburg and Lissitzky. Moholy-Nagy anticipated Herbert Matter's Swiss tourist posters by ten years when he wrote,

> An equally decisive change in the typographic image will occur in poster design as soon as they are produced by photography rather than by painting. . . . An immense area is opened up by expert use of the camera and the whole range of photographic techniques, such as retouching, blocking out, superimposition, distortion, enlargement, etc.[4]

---

3. 'Es wird Fotografiert', *Das Werk*, September 1929, p.257.
4. 'Die neue Typographie,' in *Staatliches Bauhaus in Weimar 1919-23*, 1923, p.141; reprinted in an approximate English translation in Richard Kostelanetz (ed.), *Moholy-Nagy*, New York / London 1970, p.76.

gewerbemuseum basel
11. januar
8. februar
1931

die neue fotografie

werktags
14-19
sonntags
10-12 u. 14-19
eintritt frei

gewerbemuseum basel

ausstellung

die neue fotografie

in der schweiz

eintritt frei			
werktags		14-19	
mittwochs		14-19	19-21
sonntags	10-12	14-19	

12. märz
- 9. april

▲ Posters for the pioneering Modernist exhibitions 'The New Photography' (1931) and 'The New Photography in Switzerland' (1933). Both designed at the Basel Gewerbeschule and printed letterpress. The first is all in red type with a diagonal band in yellow; the second in black only.
In Gewerbemuseum posters the setting of the opening hours within a tabular grid became slowly more refined during the 1930s.

▲ Photograph by Hans Finsler reproduced by photogravure in the special Swiss issue of *Archiv für Buchgewerbe und Gebrauchsgraphik* (Book Design and Commercial Art Record), 1929.

Hans Finsler 1891-1972
Photographer and teacher. Studied architecture and art history in Munich. Friendly with Sigfried Giedion and Franz Roh. Art history teacher and librarian at Kunstgewerbeschule near Halle, Germany, 1922. Contacts with Bauhaus. Taught photography in Germany, 1928-32. Photographs exhibited by Werkbund, 1927; in 'Film und Foto', Stuttgart, 1929; 'Die neue Fotografie', Basel, 1931. In 1932 organized new photographic department at the Kunstgewerbeschule in Zurich, where he taught until 1958.
Finsler specialized in photographing objects and is recognized as an exponent of 'Sachfotografie'. His methodical technique influenced generations of Swiss photographers and designers.

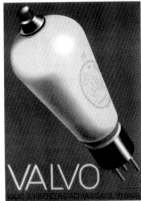

▲ Full-colour hand-drawn lithographic poster for radio valves by Niklaus Stoecklin, 1931. Although photographs offered a means of representing an object without artistic distortion, it was at this time technically and economically impossible to reproduce photographs to the size of a poster. Drawing by hand in imitation of a photograph, especially in colour, made a new, dramatic impression.

In *Das Werk*, Georg Schmidt suggested that

the photographic poster has shared the same fate as the flat roof: it is now taken for granted. It no longer calls attention to itself. But the aim of the flat roof is not to stand out, whereas this is precisely what a poster is designed to do.[5]

Schmidt, too, seems to have been referring here to the work of Herbert Matter.

Curiously, the use of photomontage remains relatively new, relatively uncommon in posters. And yet, with the dramatic contrasts it can provide, with its surprising and exciting juxtapositions, and with its ability to fuse together images that come from entirely different times and places, photomontage might have been invented for the purpose of making posters.[6]

Matter had learned photography in Paris. There he had acquired a Purist compositional style of flat colour and simplified outline which he now replaced in his designs with a fluid three-dimensionality. His mastery of the camera, his skill with the airbrush for retouching and his understanding of reproduction techniques allowed him to make images which are both powerful and elegant. Matter, who did not return from a visit to the United States in 1935, left a large body of inventive work, a few imitators, but no lasting influence.

Large-scale photographs were used extensively in exhibitions, where the Swiss were impressive innovators. But for Schmidt photomontage was no longer a novelty and Lissitzky, he notes,

has already taken up new tools for working on the photographic plate . . . so the old airbrush – looked down on for so long – now suddenly has a new life, producing startling effects. Witness the poster for the Russian Exhibition at the Zurich Kunstgewerbemuseum. 'Photopainting' is what I believe Lissitzky calls this process.[7]

In Switzerland there were no photographic classes before 1932, but when they began they were in the hands of distinguished innovators, Ballmer's in Basel and Hans Finsler's in Zurich. Finsler's approach was known as 'Sachfotografie'. In a Finsler photograph, what appears as a straightforward record of what was placed in front of the lens was the result of hours in the studio, achieved by meticulous control of lighting and in studied compositions, which often, like the New Typography, showed the clear influence of Abstract painting.

5. Georg Schmidt, 'Foto und Plakat', *Das Werk*, September 1930, p.273.
6. *Ibid.*
7. *Ibid.*

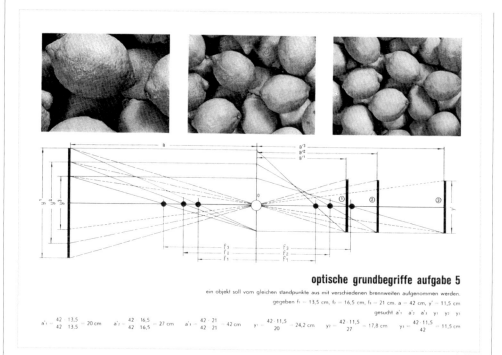

optische grundbegriffe aufgabe 5

ein objekt soll vom gleichen standpunkte aus mit verschiedenen brennweiten aufgenommen werden.

gegeben $f_1 = 13,5$ cm, $f_2 = 16,5$ cm, $f_3 = 21$ cm. $a = 42$ cm, $y' = 11,5$ cm

gesucht a'_1 a'_2 a'_3 y_1 y_2 y_1

$a'_1 = \dfrac{42 \cdot 13,5}{42 - 13,5} = 20$ cm $\quad a'_2 = \dfrac{42 \cdot 16,5}{42 - 16,5} = 27$ cm $\quad a'_1 = \dfrac{42 \cdot 21}{42 - 21} = 42$ cm $\quad y_1 = \dfrac{42 \cdot 11,5}{20} = 24,2$ cm $\quad y_2 = \dfrac{42 \cdot 11,5}{27} = 17,8$ cm $\quad y_1 = \dfrac{42 \cdot 11,5}{42} = 11,5$ cm

◀ Exercises from Theo Ballmer's photography course at the Allgemeine Gewerbeschule in Basel, 1937.

◀ 'Basic optical concepts exercise 5. The object should be photographed from the same position with lenses of different focal lengths.'
This is followed by a table showing the fields of view covered by the different lenses.

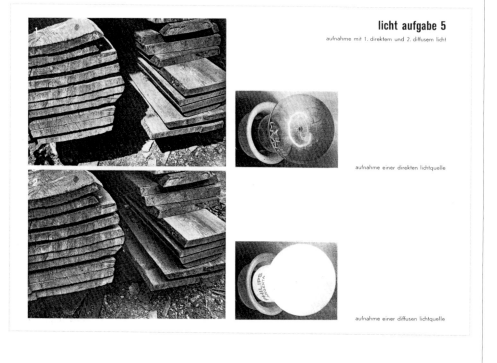

licht aufgabe 5

aufnahme mit 1. direktem und 2. diffusem licht

aufnahme einer direkten lichtquelle

aufnahme einer diffusen lichtquelle

◀ 'Lighting exercise 5. Exposures with 1. direct and 2. diffused lighting.'
The methodical examination of the subject was typical of the teaching in the schools of applied arts.

unter mitarbeil des schweizerischen photographen-verbandes

gewerbemuseum basel   ausstellung

der be**rufsphotograph**   sein werkzeug — seine arbeiten

8. mai — 6. juni

werktags		14-19	
mittwochs		14-19	19-21
sonntags	10-12	14-19	
eintritt frei			

▲ Poster for 'The Professional Photographer' exhibition in Basel, designed by Jan Tschichold, 1938. Half the size of the standard poster, printed by letterpress.

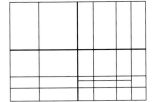

▲ The poster is organized around the central vertical and horizontal folds. The type, including the names of the printer and designer on the right-hand edge, is placed in each quarter of the rectangle, and only the main title is broken across these divisions.

Regarded as outstanding for its adherence to the principles of the New Typography, this poster is seen as the ultimate development of Tschichold's early period: asymmetrical, in Akzidenz (condensed) lowercase throughout.
◄ There is an underlying geometrical structure to the poster. Its strict horizontal and vertical alignments arise naturally from the letterpress process, where each element is rectangular in plan – type, spacing material and the frame in which it is locked up for printing.
The poster emphasizes form, yet the form depends on the meaning of the parts of the message and their relationship to the others. A clear logic has determined the size and positioning of each piece of text: a statement of hierarchies, of the priority of the parts of the message.
The requirements of an exhibition poster are to answer the viewer's questions: 'What?' (sometimes Who?'), 'Where?', 'When?', and 'How much?' But first the poster must be noticed. This need is most often met by an image.

Tschichold has chosen an image which arouses curiosity by its strangeness, yet this image as a negative expresses the central concern of the exhibition, not just *Der Berufsphotograph* (The Professional Photographer) but also *'sein werkzeug'* (his tools) and *'seine arbeiten'* (his works).
In the organization of the elements, meanings are connected. The left-hand edge of the image is on the vertical centre line of the sheet. The word-element, 'photograph', starts at the edge of the image. With the image overprinted on it, the word forms a unit of meaning which includes the first part of the subtitle, *'sein werkzeug'*. The second half, *'seine arbeiten'*, is placed after a dash. The dash bridges the image area and the white paper of the sheet, so that the works are, literally, the outcome of the process.
The rest of the text information is related by size and position according to its importance. 'Where' (the museum) is aligned horizontally with 'what' (*ausstellung*, the exhibition); this is related vertically to 'who' (the name of the collaborating organization)

at the top and to the start of the main title below. 'When' (the dates and opening times) is related, with less evident logic, by the device of reversing the dates in white out of a black rule, making a further 'negative'. Days and times are presented in a tabular form which emphasizes the Sunday morning and Wednesday evening openings.
In a vertical line of text on the right are listed the designer, photographer, blockmaker and printer. All the type except the main title is printed in black, at the same time as the photograph.
The remainder, the horizontal rules, main title and subtitle, are printed in a traditional letterpress technique, known variously as rainbow printing (in German, *Irisdruck*). This gives the effect of full colour, achieved in a single run through the press, with yellow on the inking rollers on the left, blue in the middle and red on the right.

78

Photography and Advertising

With the increasing appearance of photographs in newspapers and the widespread use of cameras for family snapshots, consumers trusted the truthfulness of photographic images.
▶ In advertising its own services, the Max Dalang agency in Zurich (see p.100) asked, 'How Are Advertisements Made?'
'The camera', they wrote, 'presented goods so attractively that everyone wanted to buy them.'

This aesthetic, formal use of the photograph contrasted with the old school of pictorial photography. In 1932 the 'International Exhibition of Artistic Photography' was held in Lucerne. It was intended to confront and oppose the New Photography. The Swiss Werkbund responded with a touring exhibition, 'Die neue Fotografie in der Schweiz' (The New Photography in Switzerland). Such a public demonstration of support for Modernism met with a violent reaction.

The photographs in the exhibition were not beautiful, nor were they artistic. There was nothing remarkable about them, they were simply appallingly ugly. That was the general assessment of visitors. [8]

Nonetheless, a selection of these 'appallingly ugly' photographs went to Milan as part of the Swiss pavilion at the 1933 Milan Triennale.

The full tonal range of photographs, thanks to the depth of ink in gravure printing, was reproduced both in popular magazines such as the *Volks Illustrierte* and *Zürcher Illustrierte* and also in an increasing number of finely produced books.

Many designers took photographs because of a fascination with the camera as a new way of seeing and of making images. Work by Cyliax and Theo Ballmer was shown in the exhibition of the New Photography in the company of the professionally expert Herbert Matter. Photographic expeditions were a favourite spare-time activity for young designers. The prints of these young enthusiasts, taken not as part of their commercial work, but for their own sake, have become part of the history of the New Photography.

▲ Press advertisement for Astra margarine by the Berne designer Frieda Meier, 1936. Frieda Meier was a graphic designer. Her commercial work is credited in the name of Allenbach, that of her architect husband, Werner Allenbach, who collaborated in her graphic work. Frieda Meier later changed her first name from Frieda to Maja.

To show consumers in the act of enjoying what they had bought, drawn illustration was the most usual graphic medium. Photographs made a more convincing endorsement, but it was extremely rare for them to be integrated into such a confident example of New Typography.

8. *Luzerner neueste Nachrichten*, 10 September 1932, quoted in catalogue, *Die neue Fotografie in der Schweiz*, Gewerbemuseum Basel, 1933, p.7.

◀ Poster for Bally shoes designed by Heiri Steiner with the photographer Ernst A. Heiniger, 1936.

Ernst A. Heiniger 1909-1993 Photographer, graphic designer and filmmaker. Apprenticeship as photographic retoucher, attended evening classes at the Zurich Kunstgewerbeschule, 1925-28. Freelance from 1929. Visit to Russia (met film director Sergei Eisenstein), 1932. Joint studio with Heiri Steiner, 1934-39. Turned to filmmaking after 1943.

▲ Photography implies an honest representation. This poster appeals to the public not with emotional suggestions or promises, but with only essential information – what the product is and what it looks like, the quality of workmanship and materials dramatized by the sharpness of detail.

The design attracts the eye by turning convention upside down: the shoes in the air, not on the ground; a hand inside them, not a foot. They are held up for our admiration. The diagonal arrangement implies that the image is the record of an emphatic gesture, and the sky-like background and carefully arranged lighting suggest the open air rather than the confines of a studio.

The poster first appeared without the slogan.

▲ Steiner's and Heiniger's design reworked by an advertising agency, 1963. Over the intervening thirty years there was a tendency to replace designers' fresh ideas with marketing concepts such as this. A banal presentation of casual and business styles – to suggest the range of Bally shoes – has replaced the original's arresting individuality.

80 ▶ This poster for Schaffhausen wool follows the lead given by Otto Baumberger's PKZ overcoat: there are no words other than those on the label. Designed by Ernst A. Heiniger and Heiri Steiner, 1936.
Photo- and handworked lithograph.

▲ The image is a literal illustration. In the background is the River Rhine and the city of Schaffhausen. In the foreground is the product, just as it is sold: a skein of wool held together by its label.

The contrast between this simple, modern image and the 19th-century graphics of the label intimates that the long-established, traditional quality of Schaffhausen wool had not been lost.

▶ 'I Combine the New Kandahar Ski Binding with the Bally Oslo Ski-boot.' Poster by Walter Herdeg, photograph by Hoek, 1932.

Walter Herdeg 1908-1995
Graphic designer and publisher. Studied at Zurich Kunstgewerbeschule under Ernst Keller, 1926-28, and in Berlin with Otto Hadank, 1929-30. Visited Paris, London and New York, 1933-37. Art director for St Moritz resort, 1932-38. Co-founder of advertising agency and publishers Amstutz & Herdeg, 1938. Co-publisher of monthly *Graphis*, 1952-86. Although the photographic posters and brochures for St Moritz are less inventive than Herbert Matter's, Herdeg was a pioneer of the full-colour photographic poster.

Herdeg has combined factual information – the diagram of the boot-fixing in the top left corner – with a photograph which, however much it is a record, tells a story.

The first-person speaker in the diagonal headline appears only as his own shadow. His approval of the boots and their fixings is made convincing by the evidence of the photograph – the snow-covered skis propped against the sunny wall.

82

Photography and Posters

▶ 'Summer in Switzerland.
Special Price Reduction 30%.'
Poster for Swiss Railways, designed by
Heinrich Schellenberg with photograph
by Ernst Mettler, 1935.
Printed in three colours by
photogravure in a smaller than
standard size.
Ernst Mettler (1903-1933) was a graphic
designer who trained at the Zurich
Kunstgewerbeschule before working
as a photojournalist for the *Zürcher
Illustrierte* weekly.

Ernst Mettler's photograph presents
Switzerland in its traditional role,
welcoming visitors to its timeless
Alpine attractions.

▶ 'We Are Collecting for the Unemployed and Their Children', poster by Gotthard Schuh for the Zurich Committee to Aid the Unemployed, 1936.

Gotthard Schuh 1897-1969
Painter, designer and photographer. Trained as painter. Photojournalist, mainly abroad, 1930s. Although his work was shown in 'The New Photography' in Basel, 1931, it was pictorial rather than 'sachlich'. Picture editor of the *Neue Zürcher Zeitung*, 1941-60.

This view of Swiss life contrasts with Ernst Mettler's image on the facing page. The effects of the economic depression of the 1930s remained. Gotthard Schuh answered Moholy-Nagy's call for the photographer's work to be 'the undistorted document of contemporary reality'. The plight of the unemployed and their families is represented not by a sentimental image but by a documentary record.

84 **Photomontage**

In graphic design the message
is conveyed by words and images.
The amount of information carried
by one or the other varies: in
a book it may be words alone.
Photography gave designers the
chance to put together messages
with images and fewer words.
Words and photograph can
carry the same message, each
reinforcing the other.

▲ 'Now Shell Summer Oil',
designed by Max Bill, 1934.
In a series of small posters, Shell
reminded motorists of their need
for a seasonal change of oil.
The idea of summer is established
by the word. The photograph of
the magnolia in flower against the
sky attracts the viewer and
illustrates the idea. Max Bill adds
a fluid, abstract shape that
suggests oil. Together, images and
words make a single integrated
idea.

▲ 'Autumn Oil-change Now.
The Shell Winter Oils Are in
Stock', 1934.
Heiri Steiner and Ernst A. Heiniger
used a more surprising expression
of the season and the product.
The bare tree represents winter,
a suggestive image on which the
objective view of the product, the
oil can, is 'pasted'. Photographs
taken separately and then
combined were at first startling;
they did not follow everyday
experience of space and time. The
viewer knows that the can of oil is
not in the tree. It remains an
image, and this visual dissonance
attracts the eye.

▶ Poster for Veralin Winter Spray and Virikupfer (copper fungicide) designed by Heiri Steiner and Ernst A. Heiniger, 1937. There are no words, except on the illustrations of the packaged products, and the manufacturer's name below.
The designers have used a more elaborate visual language than in their Shell winter oil design.
The photographs tell the whole story: what the product looks like and how it is applied. Without the curved edges of the photograph, the poster would lose its visual tension, the feeling that the image is being stretched to the corners.

Photomontage and Photogravure
The Swiss Tourist Board
(Schweizerische Verkehrszentrale –
SVZ) had printed photographic posters
in gravure since the First World War:
well produced, but in one colour, black
or sepia.
▼ 'Switzerland', an unpretentiously
elegant pictorial poster giving the
address for tourist information. The
photograph by Albert Steiner is typical
of the 'artistic' tendency which felt
itself under threat from the New
Photography.

▼ ▶ 'All Roads Lead to Switzerland,'
poster by Herbert Matter, 1935. Matter
became the master of montage. His
designs for posters were most often
reproduced by photogravure, in not
more than three colours. They were
designed to allow for overprinting with
slogans in other languages.

▶ 'Switzerland: Winter Holidays –
Double Holidays', poster designed
by Herbert Matter, 1934.
Printed by photogravure in black,
red and blue; text overprinted by
lithography in dark green.
The red appears as a slightly varied
tint on the face, and almost solid to
make the softly vignetted, airbrushed
background to the white crosses.
The diagonal tilt of the type, crosses
and head is emphasized by the
mechanical white ruling, a kind of
formalized snow which also stands
in for the knitted ribs of the woman's
absent sweater.
As is not unusual in Matter's work,
there is a surreal spirit to the design:
the head without a body, the skiers
hurtling from the tops of mountains.

Herbert Matter 1907-1984

Painter, photographer, graphic designer,
filmmaker. Studied at Ecole des Beaux-
Arts, Geneva, 1924-26. Freelance
commercial artist in Engelberg, 1926-
28. Studied with Purist painters
Fernand Léger and Amédée Ozenfant
at Académie Moderne, Paris, 1928-29.
Typographer and photographer at Paris
typefoundry of Deberny & Peignot,
worked with the poster designer
A.M. Cassandre, designed parents'
café in Engelberg, 1929-32. Returned to
Zurich, renting flat in the Zett-Haus,
1932. Freelance designer in Zurich as
member of the avant-garde, 1932-35.
Established himself in USA, 1936.
Designs for Swiss pavilion, New York
World's Fair, 1939. Photographer and
filmmaker in New York from 1940 and
art director, Knoll Furniture, 1946-66.
Professor of Graphic Design and
Photography, Yale University, 1952-76.

88

► Poster for the resort of Pontresina, designed by Emil Schulthess, 1937. Schulthess here followed the techniques developed by Herbert Matter, who had left for the USA more than a year earlier. The gravure printing is in four colours. Though not reproduced from a colour photograph, it imitates the effect. The blue is a solid blue, the red is used only on the faces, and the yellow only on the lettering.

The parts of the message – sun, snow, and healthy sport under blue skies – are unified and dramatized. Although simpler than Matter's compositions (apart from the sunglasses' odd perspective), by restricting the colour to the reflection in the lenses and leaving the background in black and white, Schulthess intensifies the effect of the vivid colour reflections.

▼ Herbert Matter's poster for the same resort, 1936 (the year he left for the USA). By the use of the low viewpoint and the up-to-date snow goggles, Matter's design transforms the single huge head into the heroic, tanned new man, the hero of the slopes. Not part of the snowy scene, the lone skier casts his shadow on the photograph of the mountain, and becomes an emblem, a reminder that the 'reality' of the image is artifice.

Emil Schulthess 1913-1996 Photographer. Trained as a graphic designer and attended classes in photography, Zurich Kunstgewerbeschule. Art director and later picture editor and contributor to *Du* magazine, 1941-57. Published books of his photographs taken on travels abroad.

PONTRESINA

▼ Herbert Matter's poster for Engelberg, the ski resort that was his home town, 1935. The design carries the usual theme of sun and snow, put together from three photographs. Without skiers, sport is suggested by the white flecks of snow on the woman's face. Again, gravure printing in black, red and blue. In other versions of the poster, the design is overlaid with irregular lines making up five-pointed stars.

▲ 'Spa and Sport: Heated Alpine Swimming Pool / 1933 Reduced Hotel Prices / Summer-happy in Engelberg.' Black-and-white press advertisement by Herbert Matter. The flatness of the rectangles contrasts with the depth suggested by the lettering and with the sunbathing figure in perspective.

Matter juggles with graphic space. The rectangle containing the text seems to float in front of the three-dimensional head; and the rectangle with the sunbather, making part of the word 'Engelberg' grey, implies by its transparency that it is in a plane close to the viewer.

back   front cover   folded inside   folded inside

▲ 'Engelberg: Summer in Switzerland.' One side of an Italian-language leaflet that folds in four. Designed by Herbert Matter, 1933.
Printed letterpress in black, red and blue.
The map, on the back when folded, shows connections to Engelberg from European cities.

The wet hair and face of the model on the front connects with the open-air pool shown in an aerial view on the inside fold and also with the photograph of water which reappears as the Mediterranean on the back of the brochure.

The striped cloud-shape behind 'engel' on the front is part of the Engelberg logo designed by Matter, but inconsistently applied.

90

**Photo-Graphic Design
and Letterpress**

▼ 'Switzerland in the Snow', 64-page
brochure for the Swiss Tourist Board,
1935. Designed by Herbert Matter, who
provided many of the photographs.

▶ The original photographs for the
cover, stuck down and fused together
by Matter with airbrushing and white
paint. When reproduced, the lightest
tone of the photographic print would
blend with the smooth whiteness of
the paper.

The brochure was printed in black only
by letterpress on glazed white paper.
The cover had the title and flag in red.
For changes of language, the black half-
tone blocks could be left in place and
a new title substituted, to print in red.
Changes could also be made in
the cut-out vertical strips on the edges
of the page which carried the page
number and headings.

front cover

L'école suisse de ski

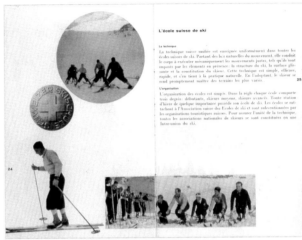

L'école suisse de ski

Le saut

La neige aux Grisons

LA SUISSE SOUS LA NEIGE

back cover

Graphic Techniques and Printing Methods

GROTESK KURSIV

▲ The Zurich printer Fretz Brothers produced this book of type specimens in 1933, designed by Walter Cyliax. As well as the type – printed letterpress – the book showed printing and reproduction processes at the factory. The photographs on this and the facing page are from this book.

▲ The photograph on the left-hand page shows the printing cylinder of a gravure press. Ink is forced into the images and type which have been etched into the plate wrapped round the cylinder. As the cylinder turns, the surface of the plate is wiped clean. The ink is drawn out of the etched hollows onto the paper surface.

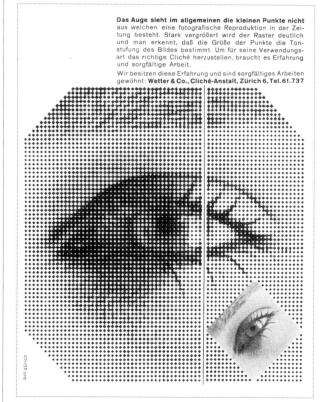

Das Auge sieht im allgemeinen die kleinen Punkte nicht aus welchen eine fotografische Reproduktion in der Zeitung besteht. Stark vergrößert wird der Raster deutlich und man erkennt, daß die Größe der Punkte die Tonstufung des Bildes bestimmt. Um für seine Verwendungsart das richtige Cliché herzustellen, braucht es Erfahrung und sorgfältige Arbeit.
Wir besitzen diese Erfahrung und sind sorgfältiges Arbeiten gewöhnt: Wetter & Co., Cliché-Anstalt, Zürich 6, Tel. 61.737

For printing by letterpress or lithography, the range of tone in a photograph was represented by dots of differing size. The original photograph, re-photographed through a finely ruled grid, appeared as a regular pattern.

▲ 'Usually the eye doesn't see the dots in a newspaper photograph.' Max Bill demonstrates the truth of this in a 1935 advertisement for a photoengraving firm. He shows the dots at a 45-degree angle, where they are much less noticeable than when horizontal and vertical.

There were few changes in methods of printing between 1920 and 1960. The full range of a large printer's activity was listed in 1928 by the Zurich company Orell Füssli: design; lithography, direct from the stone and offset from plates; letterpress; cartography: photoengraving and steel-faced blocks; gravure; share certificate and banknote printing; copperplate engraving and printing; and, finally, binding. Few printers had such a wide range.

The most common method of printing was letterpress, directly from the inked surface of metal type and photoengraved blocks. The type for text could be assembled (composed) by hand, but would normally be set by a composing machine operated from a keyboard. Type would be cast afresh for each job from molten metal. Larger type for headlines and for posters would be typeset by hand. Poster type larger than 3cm was often cut from wood.

Many posters continued to be printed by letterpress until the 1960s. Large areas were often printed from linoleum, which was cut with great skill, often in fine detail, sometimes for lettering. Illustrations, either line (black-and-white) or half-tone (in photographic shades from black through grey to white), were made as relief blocks by photoengraving, etched out of sheet zinc or copper, and mounted on wood or metal to bring them to the same height as the type. Because of the cost of blocks, they were often re-used in other publications.

The effect of light and dark in half-tone blocks was achieved by the relative size of regularly spaced dots – dark grey would result from fine white dots in a black area, light grey from fine black dots on the unprinted paper. The screen of variable-sized half-tone dots would be finer or coarser according to the surface of the paper and its absorbency. The designer would specify screen size as well as the size of the finished block.

With the development of photography, lithography and gravure became slowly more popular. It was easier to combine text with illustrations on the same printing surface, making lithography and especially gravure particularly suitable for printing magazines and posters where the quality of the illustration was important.

For the designer, whatever the printing process, there was little difference in the way finished drawings were prepared. Photographs, drawn illustrations and type had to be stuck onto a heavy white board with instructions on an overlay sheet for photoengraving or platemaking. The airbrush, producing a fine spray, most often of opaque white paint, was used to fade edges of photographs as 'vignettes', to conceal the joins in montages, and to

▲ Typesetting by hand. Individual metal letters and spaces are taken from the typecase where each letter of the alphabet is in a separate compartment. The letters are composed into words and lines in the composing stick, which is set to the measure of the column on the page. In large sizes, capitals and lowercase letters were in separate typecases, one above the other; hence the term 'lowercase'.

▲ Typesetting by machine produced type where the metal was freshly cast from moulds. The Monotype method produced individual letters, and corrections to words could be made by hand. The other systems (Linotype and Intertype) cast the type as a complete line.

▲ All typesetting, by machine or by hand, had to be locked together with spacing material and then transferred to the bed of the press for printing. Printed proofs of type could be taken to be photo-engraved, or they could be photographed to provide text on film for lithographic and gravure platemaking.

▲ Retouching photographs before reproduction was a normal practice. This was done with an airbrush which used compressed air to project a fine spray of paint or ink. Imperfections could be concealed, unwanted elements suppressed and details highlighted. The airbrush was an essential designer's tool for blending the elements of a photomontage.

▲ Photographic negatives were part of the process of reproducing half-tones by every printing method. The elements of a design – the pages of a book or a poster – were retouched and assembled at a lightbox. This was a preliminary stage in preparing plates for printing by lithography and gravure. Printing craftsmen all attended the same schools as the designers, often with the same teachers.

produce cloud effects. The designer had to paint round the outline of cut-out images which were to show no background. Advertisements to appear in letterpress-printed newspapers and magazines were supplied as a complete printing block, most often a combined line and half-tone photoengraving that included the text.

Colour half-tone printing was uncommon, even in the late 1950s. Designers were more used to their designs printed in black only, sometimes with a single second colour. This encouraged the Swiss designers' enjoyment of purely graphic contrasts of line thickness, of scale, and of white lines reversed out of black solids.

▲ Printing the second colour on a poster direct from a lithographic stone. The photographic image is printed earlier by photogravure. The finished poster, designed by Helmuth Kurtz, is illustrated overleaf.

GEBR. FRETZ A.G. ZURICH

◀ 'Autophon Radio', poster designed by Helmuth Kurtz, 1936.
As shown on the previous page, the red printing is added by lithography after the half-tone images have been printed in black by photogravure.

Helmuth Kurtz (1903-1959)
Graphic designer. Apprenticed to the printer-publishers Orell Füssli and student of Ernst Keller at the Zurich Kunstgewerbeschule. Worked in Berlin in the studio of Oskar Hadank before establishing himself as a freelance designer in Zurich, 1927. Kurtz's work for the Shell oil company shows him to be one of the pioneering Modernists in the 1930s.

▶ '5000 Years of Lettering', exhibition poster designed by Theo Ballmer, 1936. The title, in styles of handwritten and modern geometrical letterforms, is overlaid by an encoded strip. Ballmer's design has been transferred to lithographic stones — one for the red and one for the black.

▼ Cover for a special photographic issue of *Typographische Monatsblätter*, May 1933, designed by Herbert Matter. Printed by gravure in red and blue only.

▶ Eight-page A4 brochure for Fretz Brothers printers, designed by Herbert Matter, 1934. The hand on the cover shows four lines: 1, for letterpress; 2, for lithography and offset; 3, for gravure; 4, for binding. The fingers link to a globe, suggesting international connections, with Zurich at the centre, overprinted by the Fretz logotype, designed by Walter Cyliax.

▲ 1. The first left-hand page shows letterpress typesetting and printing: at the top, machine setting on the left, hand composition on the right. Below are illustrations of colour mixing, proofing, correction, and a cylinder press in action.

The right-hand page suggests the elements of visual communication: the image and the alphabet, and the eye. The photograph of a model is overlapped by the classical plaster bust, with one side chipped away and one eye replaced by the eye of the model. The reader is left to infer that the new, and a new way of seeing, are replacing the old.

The alphabet and the variety of its forms are shown by a selection of lowercase 'a's, overprinting a lowercase 'b'.
The hand on the front cover, the fusion of the two heads, and the first letters of the alphabet, imply a debt, perhaps unconscious, to Lissitzky's self-portrait and his Russian Exhibition poster.

▶ 2. Lithography from the stone and offset lithography.

The text points out that the weight of the stone makes its use less practical than the zinc plate.

The illustrations show the stone's surface being ground, the design drawn on the stone, and the damp stone rolled up with ink. Below are shown a person checking a proof, transferring the image to the plate, and an offset press.

3. To the right is the gravure process. In steps from the top: first, exposing originals to make negatives, then assembling the film before exposure to the plate and, finally, etching the plate.

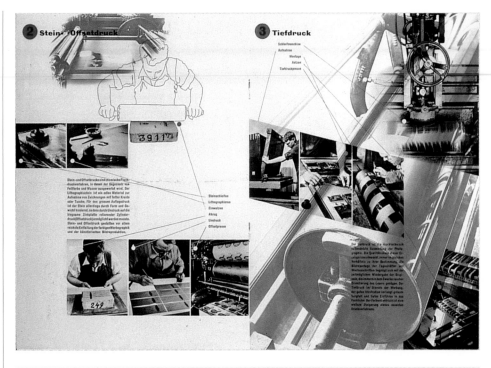

▶ 4. The bindery. This shows folding sheets, collating sections, stitching and trimming by guillotine.

▲ Matter indulges himself on the final right-hand page. The head, printed in red, black and blue, is accompanied by the statement:

'The use of colour in graphics is parallel to tone or key in music. The play of line and colour is for the designer and printer what improvisation is for the musician. Everything new is disconcerting to begin with, and everything that we are used to no longer has this effect. Printers who aren't bold are giving bad advice.'

Walter Cyliax and *Typographische Monatsblätter*

▲ Poster for Koch Opticians, designed by Walter Cyliax, 1929. Printed by gravure. The image is black and white, the flat background is yellow ochre and the letters are red with brown shadow. In spite of the much-used square as a background to the photograph, the design shows Cyliax's awkward position between avant-garde aspirations and commercial demands. Cyliax was a pioneer of the photographic poster but the mixture of lettering styles and the superfluous slogan, 'Known for Quality', ignore the New Typography's principles of economy and clarity.

Of the Swiss-based contributors to *Gefesselter Blick*, Walter Cyliax was the most established in the printing trade. Like Tschichold, he had studied in Leipzig at the Akademie der Graphischen Künste (Graphic Arts Academy). In 1924, at the age of twenty-five, he became art director of the Zurich firm of Fretz Brothers, printers of *Das Werk*. Until his return to Germany in 1936, he was an important link between the trade and the avant-garde.

In 1929 Cyliax helped to edit a special Swiss issue of the German printing magazine *Archiv für Buchgewerbe und Gebrauchsgraphik* (Book Design and Commercial Art Record). In an article on publicity, Cyliax ignores the influences which had touched his own practice – the Bauhaus and New Typography – in order to emphasize what was essentially Swiss: rather than Baumberger's PKZ overcoat, he reproduces the artist's painterly flamingoes and elephant advertising the Zurich zoo. And the reason he gives for the high standard of work in Switzerland by comparison with Germany is that most Swiss designers are painters. This was in fact a true picture of Swiss graphic design in general: well-crafted and imaginative, but aesthetically conservative. Designers such as Baumberger, with no commitment to Modernist ideology, adopted a modern idiom when it suited the job in hand. This was true also of Cyliax. Since he worked for a printer whose customers' tastes could not be ignored, he could not always indulge his avant-garde interests; when he did, he produced typography in the spirit of the Bauhaus and photomontages in the manner of John Heartfield.

Cyliax had visited the United States. This experience helped him to identify the new role of the art director as distinct from the commercial artist.

It is a matter for the education of the graphic designer to understand clearly his position at the centre of the whole apparatus of advertising, to become aware that he is one of a group in which he actually has one of the most important roles to play – but only if he plays it for the sake of an overall idea. . . this would not mean that the creative side of the advertising artist's work would be denied him. However, the development which we could not predict – of the sort of advertising which demands thousands of ideas every day, which distributes millions of items of printed matter – has gone too far for the few advertising artists with the necessary intellectual, creative and technical gifts to be able to meet its needs. A division of labour is absolutely necessary; the first and logical division was to place the creation of the advertising idea and

▼ The first two issues of *Typographische Monatsblätter*, designed by Walter Cyliax, 1933. The first shows Cyliax's uncertain judgement as a designer, and is easy to criticize from a functional standpoint. Although the right-hand down stroke of the 'M' defines the central vertical axis of the page, the letter is merely a decorative device, with no connection to the meaning of the word.

▼ The cover of the second issue shows the minimal attempt at aesthetic effect. With the title, sub-title 'For the Promotion of Professional Education' and subsidiary information all set in Akzidenz Grotesk, the design could have been a model for the graphic design of the 1960s.
Both covers are printed letterpress in black and red.

its implementation in different hands. Obviously, the advertising artist with useful ideas of his own will still have the best chance, since there will always be more need for creative heads than for busy hands.[1]

The role of art director was quickly assumed by some of the functionalist designers, including Hermann Eidenbenz, Max Bill and, in the 1950s, Fridolin Müller, Karl Gerstner and Siegfried Odermatt.

Cyliax was also a recognized exponent of the New Photography.

Photography also plays an important part in graphic design. The desire for functionalism and for clarity in modern advertising assures it of its position. Both in posters, in combination with lithography, and in small leaflets, it is used more and more as an eye-catcher and as a convincing advertising image.[2]

Working in the printing trade, Cyliax pointed out technical aspects of reproducing images.

Photogravure printing, in which Switzerland has been outstanding, has also contributed much to the development of photography in advertising. Those who still consider advertising almost entirely from an artistic point of view are inclined to prefer lithography. The latest trends, however, call for all the mechanical processes. Not simply on rational grounds but because the precision and persuasive power of photography is highly effective in advertising, where its up-to-date appeal – proved well enough by magazines and illustrated newspapers – has been a success. The modern graphic artist will use the camera more and more in combination with areas of colour and with drawing. And if this has not yet happened very extensively in Switzerland, the cause is no doubt the inhibiting effects of fine art in this respect, together with the Swiss artisan's love of craftsmanship.[3]

In the printing industry Cyliax was a true professional. As an art director he produced exemplary type specimen books for Fretz, and he brought *Das Werk* up to date. By 1926 he had introduced conventions of the New Typography in the magazine's small display advertisements. In the 1930s he was of crucial importance. His part in the launch of *Typographische Monatsblätter* (Typographic Monthly) in 1933 – a time of commercial crisis and high unemployment – was essential. This was especially true in the weight he gave to photography: the list of topics on the cover of the early issues places 'foto' before 'typo'.

Typographische Monatsblätter was published by the Schweizerischer Typographenbund (Swiss Typographic Association) in Berne. The magazine helped to introduce printers to new ideas, and encouraged them to accept designers as belonging more to the new business of commercial and industrial communications than to the printing industry. With an educational aim, reproductions of new material were balanced by illustrated historical and theoretical articles, in which Tschichold made a significant contribution over many years. Cyliax played an important part in advancing Modernist graphic design in Switzerland, especially in giving Herbert Matter the opportunity and technical support for making his unrivalled photomontage posters and brochures. He had Matter design several covers for *Typographische Monatsblätter* and gave him a very free hand in designing an A4 brochure for Fretz (illustrated on p.96-7). Its four pages, also bound into an early issue of the magazine, described the common printing methods of the 1920s and 1930s, when full-colour printing was rare. Typically with Matter's work, the brochure is printed in red, blue and black.

Over the following two decades, until the 1950s, the pages of *TM* – as the magazine came to be known – reflect the slow retreat from the revolutionary ideas of the 1920s. The text, at first set in the sanserif Erbar, soon changed to Walbaum; even folksy 'gothic' appeared and woodcut illustrations which, after the earlier emphasis the magazine had given to the New Photography, belonged to an alien visual culture and the graphic values of a pre-industrial age. But by this time Cyliax had returned to Germany.

1. 'Die Werbegraphik', *Archiv für Buchgewerbe und Gebrauchsgraphik*, special Swiss issue, Leipzig, November/December 1929, pp.24-25.

2. *Ibid.*, p.29.

3. *Ibid.*, pp.29-30.

Advertising and Graphics

▲ 'A Day in Our Circle of Clients.' The Max Dalang Agency lists the ways in which throughout the day the reader could be using one of the products or services of its clients, from getting out of bed in the morning to returning home and preparing for bed at night. The copy ends with the question, 'Don't you need us in 1932?'

▲ 'How Are Advertisements Made?', asks Dalang in its own advertisement in the *Neue Zürcher Zeitung*, 1932. The answer is, 'With, among other things, photographs and scissors, original shots, enlargements, retouching. Photomontage is only one aspect of the advertising service we provide.'

Tourism was not the only part of the economy to take a fresh approach to printed publicity. The New Typography, able to present information clearly, looking modern and business-like, soon proved its value in the design of advertisements and brochures for industry. That it did so was due to a group of designers in a Zurich advertising agency, and to the persistence of one man. The agency was Max Dalang; the man was Hans Neuburg.

Max Dalang founded his advertising agency in 1916. He had visited the United States, and brought the American scientific approach to his own management. In a 1931 advertisement Dalang demonstrated the firm's commitment across the business spectrum, its diagram like an illustration in a science textbook. 'A Day in Our Circle of Clients' shows Dalang covering a large part of the domestic economy, from toilet articles such as Pepsodent and shaving cream, via Bovril and aperitifs, to Swissair and to international companies such as Burroughs, makers of adding machines. Potential clients were encouraged to come and see the agency at work.

'How are [our] advertisements made?', asked the copy of more than one Dalang advertisement. Photography was part of the answer.

Modern advertising photography in our own studio is only one part of our advertising service. Advertising specialists, graphic designers, copywriters and photographers are ready to create good and effective advertising ideas.

The staff, at this time numbering thirty, included several of the most influential designers who laid the foundations of the Swiss style, notably Anton Stankowski, Hans Neuburg and Richard Paul Lohse.

Stankowski had been recommended to Dalang by Max Burchartz. At the end of 1929, filled with avant-garde ideas, Stankowski came to work at Dalang as a photographer. He gave an account of the studio's advanced attitudes and practice:

We needed to have direct experience of the products we were dealing with, to come to terms with them. Mostly with our camera at the factory and also through technical literature, and by talking to people. What is a diecasting? What is electricity? How is wire turned into a nail? Cement has granules. What are the by-products of coal? How is butter made out of groundnuts? To find an image for a vegetarian poster, absolutely the correct thing to do was to live for a time as a vegetarian.[1]

▲ Advertisement for Injecta Diecasting, one of the early advertisements designed by Anton Stankowski at Dalang, 1930. This endorses the claim of his fellow designer Richard Paul Lohse that Stankowski brought Constructivism to Zurich, but it also betrays Stankowski's debt to Burchartz in his treatment of the castings. Similar heavy black lines were to be a feature of Hans Neuburg's typography in the 1950s.

▼ Advertisements designed at Dalang for a diet supplement produced by a Zurich chemist, 1935. The most likely typographer was Stankowski.

Anton Stankowski 1906-1987 German painter, designer and photographer. Trained under Burchartz at the Folkwangschule in Essen, 1921-26. Worked for Johannes Canis in Bochum, then joined Dalang, 1929. Returned to Germany in 1937. Prisoner in USSR, 1941-48. Editor *Stuttgarter Illustrierte*, 1949-51. From 1951 own design practice in Stuttgart. Visiting teacher at Hochschule für Gestaltung, Ulm, 1962-63.

---

1. *Werbestil 1930-1940*, catalogue, Kunstgewerbemuseum Zurich 1981, p.78.

Hans Neuburg 1904-1983

Graphic designer and writer. From the beginning, one of the key figures and publicists of the Swiss Modernist graphic designers. Trained at the Zurich printer-publishers Orell Füssli. Worked in various firms in Basel and Zurich in late 1920s-1930s. Copywriter at Dalang agency, 1928-29. Opened his own studio in Zurich, 1936. Edited *Industrie–Werbung* (Industry–Advertising), his own magazine, 1933-37. One of the four founder-editors of the journal *Neue Grafik* (New Graphic Design), 1958. Active as a journalist and editor, and author of several important books on Swiss graphic design and advertising (see bibliography).

▲Hans Neuburg's personal newsletter, *Industrie–Werbung* (Industry–Advertising), issue 4, 1938. In an A4 format, Neuburg promoted the idea that industrial and technical advertising and catalogues should have the same practical efficiency as the goods and services they described. The cover of this issue illustrates part of the Swiss section of the 1937 Paris International Exhibition, designed by Heiri Steiner. The political development of Switzerland is represented by the ascending spiral on the left and is documented in the photographic displays on the right.

Stankowski became a key figure in a circle of young designers in Zurich. Hans Neuburg, who for a time shared a Zurich apartment with Stankowski, introduced him to Max Bill. They had interests in common: both used painting as a field for experiment. Topics that filled their evenings were listed by Stankowski as 'Bauhaus, Folkwang, Mondrian, Lissitzky, Burchartz, typography, photography, *The Threepenny Opera*, *Die Weltbühne* [a small, radical Berlin magazine], Dada'.

Richard Paul Lohse had begun an apprenticeship with Dalang in 1918, and attended Ernst Keller's classes at the Kunstgewerbeschule. Before Stankowski's arrival at the agency Lohse's work was undistinguished, typical 'commercial art'. Lohse later said that what Stankowski brought to Dalang was 'not Bauhaus, but applied Constructivism'.

Although some of Dalang's staff worked there for only a short time, for each of them it was crucial in their development as designers. Hans Trommer, for example, a lesser-known but equally radical colleague, joined the agency in 1928. After a year he left to set up his own design practice, which Lohse joined in 1931 and in which Stankowski, still at Dalang, was a third (unnamed) partner. In 1934 Stankowski's work permit was not renewed. He worked as a freelance from the German side of the border before he left for Stuttgart in 1937.

Hans Neuburg was employed for only a few months as a copywriter. He was a persistent promoter of 'industry advertising', the title of his own newsletter (*Industrie–Werbung*), published from 1933 to 1937. Not trained as an artist or designer (although he was a skilled amateur draughtsman and watercolourist), Neuburg was an advertising specialist who could write, with a good eye and a sharp mind. His style developed directly from the work of Max Burchartz and Johannes Canis, which was passed on to him by Stankowski at Dalang. To begin with, Neuburg worked as a collaborator with designers and photographers, and he knew the best and most progressive: Max Bill and Herbert Matter, as well as those at Dalang.

Neuburg's best-known early example of 'industry advertising', in cooperation with Stankowski, is his work for Sulzer, a huge engineering company. He described it in *Typographische Monatsblätter* (Typographic Monthly) in 1935. In technical advertising, he said,

> It must be clear that the means of advertising for industry are as a rule the opposite of other types of publicity, of advertisements in daily newspapers, street

▲ Outside and inside spread of Hans Trommer's and Richard Paul Lohse's 4-page promotional leaflet for their joint practice, 1931. It explains the effectiveness of typeset advertisements when they make intelligent use of printer's material, such as the crosses, bullets, arrows and rules displayed on the front. The inside spread shows examples of Trommer & Lohse's designs. They offer a remarkable service: if text copy is dictated over the telephone, within two hours they will produce a design to a given size.

Richard Paul Lohse 1902-1988

Painter, graphic designer and writer. Apprentice at Dalang, studied with Ernst Keller at Zurich Kunstgewerbeschule, 1918-22. Commercial artist at Dalang, 1922-30. Shared design office in Zurich with Hans Trommer, 1931-34. Co-founder of the Verband unabhängiger Grafiker (Association of Independent Graphic Designers), 1933. Shared flat with Trommer and Stankowski before move to apartment in Zett-Haus, 1934. Freelance designer and painter from 1934. Editor and designer *Bauen+Wohnen* architectural magazine, 1947-56. Co-founder and co-editor *Neue Grafik*, 1958-65. As with Theo Ballmer, Lohse's political concerns were integrated with his activities as a designer. He was a central figure of Swiss graphic design.

▼ 'The Living Expression of the Metal', the headline for a full-page advertisement, is justified by the illustration of the casting, as carefully photographed as a piece of sculpture. The metal casting is not what is being advertised, but the photograph's reproduction by the photoengraving firm (with the same name as Neuburg's engineering client), Sulzer.

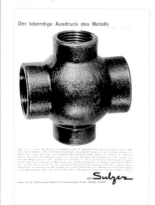

▼ The headline, 'Happy Work in the Office', explains itself in the photograph. The solution to the problem of filing, storing and retrieving business records and correspondence is presented so that the potential buyer can imagine himself in the chair with everything to hand.

posters, flysheets and so on, if they are to succeed with business professionals. And professionals have to be addressed differently . . . . They want facts, proof of performance, numbers and diagrams. They want to take in what the product is offering them when it is starkly presented.[2]

Neuburg bore all this in mind when he was given the job of designing not only the advertising material for Sulzer's central heating and ventilation department, but also the whole range of the company's forms and stationery. The items together, he wrote,

were given a contemporary, clear and above all unified look by the introduction of an extremely simple word trademark [logotype] and the consistent use of one of the cleanest and most noble grotesque types, Akzidenz (so far as this was possible, given that printing had to be split among several suppliers).[3]

Not only industry had the benefit of exactly this treatment. At the same time Neuburg undertook to modernize the publicity for Liebig stock cubes (see p.104). He was 'firmly convinced that a product bought by housewives can be presented in clean typography'. He began by transforming the spidery signature of the firm's nineteenth-century founder into a heavy script logotype. Over a period of three years, with the help of Stankowski and Heiri Steiner, he succeeded in his aims. When he discussed the work in *Typographische Monatsblätter*, Neuburg foresaw the charges of formalism which could be brought against the use of the New Typography.

Today we are convinced that we can go further in a similar way without risking the effectiveness of the advertising being sacrificed to aesthetic form. Naturally such a danger exists. . . .The graphic form must always be only the carrier of the advertising idea, never an end in itself.[4]

Hans Neuburg's work with Anton Stankowski for the Sulzer engineering company was among the first use of techniques pioneered by Burchartz for a wide range of products and services. Advertisements were dominated by the logotype and cut-out photographs of equipment or machine parts. Text was always in Akzidenz Grotesk.

▲ A central heating transformer shares the same three-dimensional space with the trademark logo – shown complete with its border – both in perspective. The photograph is anchored to the space by placing its central axis at right angles to the sides.

▼ The gas poker is shown in close-up and in use, lighting a central heating boiler.

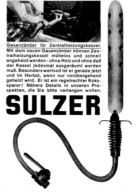

2. 'Werbung für eine Industriefirma', *Typographische Monatsblätter*, September 1935, p.281.
3. *Ibid.*, pp.281-82.
4. 'Werbung für einen Markenartikel', *Typographische Monatsblätter*, January 1935, p.7.

SULZER

Gußeiserne Warmwasser-Gliederkessel „Sulzer I"
mit Spezialendglied für den Einbau einer Ölfeuerung

Mäßige Heizflächenbelastung - Sparsamer Betrieb

Kessel	4	5	6	7	8	9
Bezeichnung	Tann	Turgi	Trogen	Tuffwil	Territet	Trutti-kon
Heizfläche . . . . m²	1,7	2,3	2,7	3,2	3,7	4,3
Normalleistung . . . . W.-E.St.	13600	17800	21600	25600	29600	33600
Inhalt Wasser . . . . . . Ltr.	37	44	51	58	65	72
Inhalt Koks . . . . . . Ltr.	34	48	62	76	90	104
Länge „L" . . . . m	0,4	0,5	0,6	0,7	0,8	0,9
Breite „B" . . . . m	0,56					
Höhe „H" (ohne Sockel) . m	0,84					
Schürzeuglänge . . . . . m	0,7	0,7	0,9	1,2	1,2	1,5
Länge des Schürstandes . m	1,0	1,0	1,3	1,5	1,5	1,8
Gewicht . . . . . zirka kg	270	320	370	420	470	520

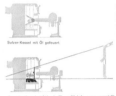

Sulzer-Kessel mit Öl gefeuert

Derselbe Kessel mit 2 Handgriffen auf Koksfeuerung umgestellt

Gegen einen bescheidenen Mehrpreis kann für diesen Kessel eine patentierte Umstell-Vorrichtung geliefert werden, um ihn in kürzester Zeit und ohne Mithilfe eines Fachmannes von Ölfeuerung auf Koksfeuerung umzustellen. Dies für den Fall, daß der Ölvorrat ausgeht oder die elektrische Stromzufuhr unterbrochen wird. Ebenso einfach ist die Wiederumstellung auf Ölfeuerung.
Die Bilder zeigen die einfache Handhabung: der Schutzdeckel wird vor die Brennermündung eingehängt.

Wenn nicht beabsichtigt wird, Ölfeuerung in absehbarer Zeit einzubauen, empfiehlt sich Anschaffung des reinen Kokskessels (siehe Rückseite).

Gebrüder Sulzer, Aktiengesellschaft, Winterthur

▲ Front cover of an A4 brochure on air conditioning, designed by Neuburg and Stankowski, 1935. According to Neuburg, the design 'expressed the result of good ventilation equipment, suggesting pure, clean and cool air by means of something non-technical, organic – a blue sky above snow-covered mountains', in which he thought that the logo, reversed out and drawn in perspective, took on the aspect and associations of 'fine-weather cumulus clouds, giving a festive look to the cover'.

▲ A4 information sheet designed by Neuburg and Stankowski, 1935. The images of the hot-water boiler are clear: a photograph shows what it looks like, with a key to the dimensions of different sizes available, and diagrammatic drawings show the boiler fuelled either by oil or by solid fuel. Complete specifications of size, capacity, fuel and water intake, etc., are given in the central table.

Liebig stock cubes, advertising campaign, art-directed by Hans Neuburg, 1933–35.

◄ The straightforward photograph, taken by Anton Stankowski, appears in the press advertisement. 'Housewives! 4 Consommé Portions 15 Pence. Liebig Super Bouillon in Cubes. Just Try It!'

▼ For the posters and showcards, Stankowski distorted and angled the image: the woman appears as a cheerful, matronly figure seen from the eye level of a child.

The signature that was the basis of the logotype can be seen on the jars in the magazine advertisement, where the square is the layout's stabilizing element.

▼ A shop-window display is backed by a showcard-sized version of the poster.

▶ Poster for Astra margarine, designed by Frieda Meier (Allenbach), 1935. The progress of the baby to the boy advancing into manhood – due to the health-giving properties of Astra – is presented with daring surrealism.
In the 1930s Allenbach did a great many designs in a Modernist style for Astra, including exhibition stands.

▲ 'Astra Margarine – Fine and Healthy', poster designed by Frieda Meier (Allenbach), 1934. Meier has repeated the Astra namestyle as the image. The word 'Erdnussfett' (ground nut fat) has been letterspaced, a method used for emphasis in German text, but counter to Modernist practice.

▲ A more straightforward commercialism in Meier's colour poster for tinned fruit and vegetables, 1938. The photograph takes the same viewpoint as Stankowski's in the Liebig poster, but without the distortion. The customer is invited to identify with the consumer's fitness, and connect it with the 'dew-fresh' fruit and the 'young and tender' vegetables.

106

The clarity of Modernist design was welcome in advertising in the building industry.

▼ An advertisement in *Das Werk* for Sichol exterior paints, credited to the Zürrer agency, 1933. It would have atracted attention by its unfamiliar use of space: the photograph of the facade under renovation is taken from below; the three painters are seen as if looking down from the scaffolding. The qualities of the paint and its cost are in the box of typography on the right.

◀ Front and inside spread of a four-page A4 leaflet, 'Practical Partitions at Last', designed by Hermann Eidenbenz, 1934. The photographs convey not only the appearance and structure of the material, but also many of its properties – that it is light, easy to cut, accepts plaster and can be nailed into.

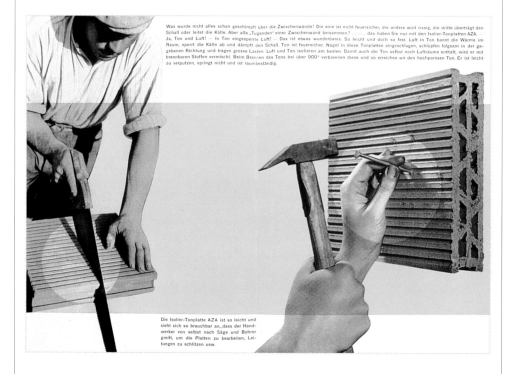

'Good Housekeeping', a publication promoting household products, designed by Anton Stankowski, 1936.
▲ The cover shows the contents as a pie-chart of activities: advice on beauty, healthcare, dressmaking and cooking, overlaid on a page of housekeeping accounts.
▶ Photographs on the inside pages, lit and cropped like cinema images, are integrated with and often superimposed on or reversed out of the text. These techniques of montage and layering were achieved by the printers in the pre-press stages of gravure printing.

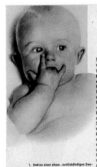
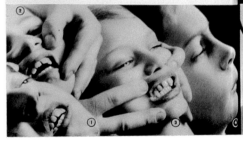

Advertising and Functionalism

▼ Pages from a brochure for medical supplies and hospital equipment, designed by Max Bill, 1934.
Bill uses double-square pages, one-third A4, to show instruments and appliances and different aspects of clinical treatment.
With black and green printing by letterpress, every variety of half-tone is employed – cut-outs, grey and black backgrounds, black type on white and on colour, type reversed white out of black and white out of colour.

▶ Bill carries out a surgical operation on the cover photograph, opening up the interior of the showrooms.

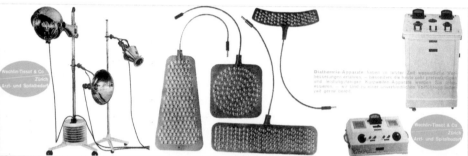

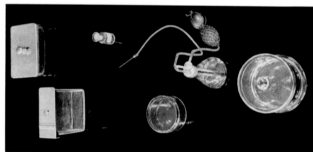
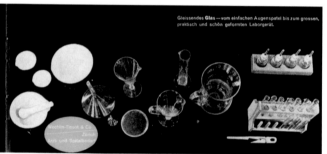

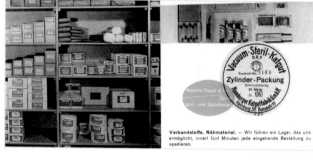
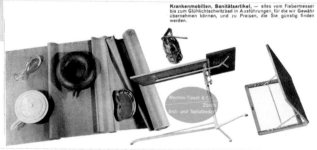

On the back, the oval trademark which has appeared on every spread indicates the exact location of the business on an aerial photograph of central Zurich.

What Hans Neuburg looked for in industrial advertising could be found in catalogues for the Wohnbedarf furniture stores. Wohnbedarf was founded in 1931 with typical Werkbund aims: to work with manufacturers to provide modern, well-designed furniture at a reasonable price. This coincided with the completion of the Werkbund's model housing estate at Neubühl, near Zurich. Like similar developments, it needed plain, modern furniture and domestic fittings in keeping with the architecture.

The Neubühl estate was among the few examples where a single enterprise was dominated by a unifying design attitude. This was the principle of functionalism. There was no rigid aesthetic aim: only that the spaces and equipment of a house should be determined by the need that they satisfied. In the case of graphic designs, the form and arrangement of words and images would meet the need to put over the message. Wohnbedarf's functionalist publicity could not be accused of the formalism which made Neuburg anxious.

Wohnbedarf's founders were an architect, an industrialist, and Sigfried Giedion. As a co-founder of the firm, Giedion took the opportunity to put Bauhaus principles into practice. Products and designs by Bauhaus staff and former students were commissioned and sold by Wohnbedarf.[1] Taking control of the firm's publicity, Giedion employed Max Bill, fresh from the Bauhaus, to design posters, leaflets and advertisements.

Bill had left the Bauhaus in 1929. He returned to Zurich intending to work as an architect, but made a living in the 1930s mainly as a typographic, graphic and exhibition designer. His work from this period made a lasting impression on Swiss graphic design.

Wohnbedarf leaflets and press advertising not only showed what the company sold, but presented it as a new 'lifestyle', and did so in a new graphic language. For a start, the type was always lowercase. Words and images are fitted together to present a message. The meaning of the words is emphasized by images, or given a more precise meaning. Two images juxtaposed express an idea which neither image alone would suggest. Max Bill's later, extensive graphics for Wohnbedarf were less playful, each piece of furniture clearly displayed in cut-out photographs, always in perspective. Folding chairs or tables are shown open and closed.

In 1932 Bill designed illuminated lettering outside the Zurich Kunstgewerbemuseum for the exhibition 'Licht in Heim Büro Werkstatt' (Light in Home, Office, Workshop),

1. Lights were designed by Hin Bredendieck, dishes and bowls by Marianne Brandt, aluminium chairs by Marcel Breuer. All were manufactured in Switzerland.

▼ Wohnbedarf's first promotional leaflet, designed by Max Bill, 1931. A double-sided sheet, approximately A4, with two horizontal folds, printed letterpress in black and red.

▲ The elements of Max Bill's leaflet are given clear priorities, as if to illustrate Hannes Meyer's idea of functional arrangement. First, the firm's logotype. Second, the unpunctuated slogan ('Through Wohnbedarf, live well cheaply, airily'). Third, the images: examples of the furniture in use, their objectivity softened by the photographs which serve as metaphors: plants in flower; acrobats with the caption, 'Today we like things fresh, clean, airy, not imitations'; and lions in the zoo juxtaposed with cast-iron lion's-head ornaments on a Zurich bridge.

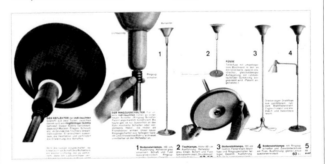

▲ Inside double-page of a leaflet describing Wohnbedarf's 'indi' light, with typography by Sigfried Giedion and photographs by Hans Finsler, 1932.

Each part of the lamp is named and each version of the lamp is numbered, as a reference to the description below.

◄ Giedion also prepared his own layouts for 'indi'-lamp advertisements, incorporating the logo designed by Max Bill.

▶ Front and back of a leaflet designed by Max Bill when Wohnbedarf exhibited its furniture in a new Le Corbusier building in Geneva, 1932. Twice the depth of A4; concertina-folded, it fitted a C6 (long, business) envelope. Printed letterpress.
The Wohnbedarf logotype appears in a French version – 'Ameublement' (furnishings).
The photographer for Wohnbedarf publicity was Max Bill's wife, Binia Bill. The illustrations show how the furniture looks in an interior, how folding tables – for use indoors or in the garden – pack away, and how the filing cabinet under the desk pulls out on castors. It is Max Bill himself standing at the folding table. The text, in lowercase Akzidenz Grotesk with emphasis in bold, is puritanical in spirit. The superiority of this furniture is not to do with luxury, but 'above all to be simple and to conform to principles of health'.

advertised by Alfred Willimann's celebrated poster (see p.70). This coincided with Wohnbedarf introducing its 'indi' (indirect) lights; Giedion concerned himself not only with the design of the lights themselves, but also designed advertisements and a brochure.

The next year, Herbert Bayer designed a catalogue of the whole Wohnbedarf range. Working from Berlin, he produced a two-colour, horizontal book. It was loose-leaf, so that new products could be added in each of the sections, which were indexed vertically in the right-hand margin: chairs, tables, beds and sofas, cupboards, bookshelves, miscellaneous. The simple layouts depended on a single, clear cut-out photograph of each item with dimensions added, identified by a number, with an occasional furnished interior and explanatory view of the way of folding a table or chair.

No less functional were the advertisements and stock lists of the firm's two chief manufacturers: Embru-Werke, which supplied tubular steel chairs, and Bronzewarenfabrik Glarus AG (BAG), which made, among other items, the 'indi' lamp. Most Embru advertisements and catalogues in the 1930s, and a logotype, were designed by Pierre Gauchat. Gauchat, one of the designers with no long-term commitment to the New Typography, nonetheless demonstrated an impeccably elegant, rational objectivity in his industrial graphics and exhibition design, and his and Bayer's formal layouts and Akzidenz typography give a powerful foretaste of the postwar Swiss style.

▲ Cover and page of the Embru catalogue, designed by Pierre Gauchat, 1935. Embru-Werke were manufacturers and suppliers of metal furniture to Wohnbedarf. The chair is clearly represented, complete with dimensions, shown with an occupant, and related to other pieces of furniture. For several years in the 1930s and 1940s Pierre Gauchat designed for Embru.

Pierre Gauchat 1902-1956
Graphic designer and illustrator. Studied under Otto Baumberger and Ernst Keller, Zurich Kunstgewerbeschule, and at Munich Kunstgewerbeschule, 1919-21. Worked at Orell Füssli printers, then freelance practice in Zurich from 1922. Drawing instructor at Zurich Kunstgewerbeschule, 1926-45. Several catalogues and posters for Wohnbedarf after 1935. On board of Verband Schweizerischer Grafiker, 1938-43; President, 1943-47. Designed Swiss banknotes, 1957.

The Profession: Organizations, Competitions, Training

The Swiss Werkbund had been spreading a message of good design through initiatives of regional groups. Members consolidated their shared interests at annual 'Werkbund Days'.

▲ Berne branch of the Swiss Werkbund: Christmas Exhibition and Fair. Small poster designed by Frieda Meier, 1932. Meier was one of the few designers outside Basel and Zurich to have made an impression by the progressive style of her work.

▲ Invitation to the Swiss Werkbund's convention, inside spread, designed by Max Bill, 1934. The ear suggests that members will have something to listen to. Bill also designed inventive pieces of ephemeral printing for the Swiss Architects Association.
The card is A4 folded to A5, printed letterpress by Fretz, whose logotype is just visible alongside Bill's credit line, bottom left.

Graphic designers had no organization of their own until 1938. Membership of the Swiss Werkbund could give them confidence that they had a professional status, but they needed a forum in which to consider their working practice, and a clear identity independent of the printing trade. Writing in 1936, Hans Neuburg saw himself as operating in a no man's land. He complained about the way the graphic designer was treated. Clients thought the fees too high, for a start.

Our profession of graphic designer and advertising consultant is not properly appreciated either in social-political terms or from a tax point of view; we are placed in between professions because we are neither obviously artists nor businessmen, neither tradesmen nor craftsmen. A graphic designer is a craftsman artist, or the other way round, and we advertising people are a colossal muddle of professions.[1]

Attempts had been made to form groups of like-minded designers. There were two local organizations, for example: the Bernese Graphic Designers Association, and the Association of Independent Designers in Zurich. In 1938 the Verband Schweizerischer Grafiker (Swiss Graphic Designers Association) was founded. Before joining the VSG (as it was referred to), members, freelance or working in a studio, were required to demonstrate their competence. Made up of designers mainly from German-speaking Switzerland, the VSG helped to establish rules to deal with such matters as plagiarism, and played a large part in establishing standards of professional practice.

A particular responsibility assumed by the VSG was the regulation of design competitions. Helped by the Swiss Werkbund, competitions for graphic design gave public services, municipal authorities and businesses an opportunity, before they gave the final commission, to clarify the aim of the proposed job, and to find a suitable designer. The museums' exhibitions and the influence of the Werkbund and the VSG, who nominated designers to serve on competition committees, encouraged a more enlightened understanding of print design.

Some competitions were limited to selected designers; others were advertised, open to all. Designs for the state postal services were in general the result of competition. For example, in 1931 a competition was held for the three Pro Juventute charity stamps. Two of the elect of Switzerland's poster designers, Otto Baumberger and Niklaus Stoecklin, were among those invited to

▲ Designs by Niklaus Stoecklin in the competition for stamps promoting the Pro Juventute charity, 1931. Asked for a landscape, Stoecklin produced the simplest, most easily reproduced design, although the full tonal possibilities of gravure printing were available. The winner produced conventional mountain scenes.

---

1. *Typographische Monatsblätter*, special Grafa issue, May 1936, p. 118.

▼ The jury competition for post office signs in 1933 recommended a remarkably modern design by Frieda Meier (Allenbach) to be made in white on bright red stove enamel.

▼ Her all-lowercase version below was rejected.

participate. It was stipulated that the charity stamps should show a Swiss view; Baumberger, like three other participants, produced painterly mountains and lakes, whereas Stoecklin, a distinguished realist painter, avoided naturalism in two of his designs, producing instead a simple linear drawing.

A competition for the standard design of the ready-stamped postcard was won by the Basel designer Ernst Mumenthaler. In 1933 Mumenthaler was also one of the chosen designers in a competition for the exterior signs of post offices. The winner was Frieda Meier, who daringly proposed lowercase lettering in grotesque. Lowercase for place names was rejected, but not the grotesque. The result was a prototype for the style of directional signs put in place around the world several decades later.

Professional training was another of the VSG's concerns. Graphic designers' education in Switzerland has traditionally taken two routes. Several of the leading designers took the earlier, and most common: by apprenticeship with a firm of printers or a commercial art studio or advertising agency, together with attendance for a specified time each week at a local school of further education. The second, and increasingly usual, professional training was by direct entrance to a foundation course, and from there to three years' specialization. Training for full-time and part-time students took place in separate classes in the same schools. Trade apprentices attended for six to eight hours a week, and those who had qualified – and this included those in printers' design studios – could extend their skills and knowledge through part-time and evening classes.

The best-known schools – those to become most associated with the Swiss style – were in Zurich and Basel, but in all the larger towns the Kunstgewerbeschulen provided a high level of training, and trade craftsmen – compositors, machine minders and process workers – all had an understanding of design. The catalogue to an exhibition in Basel in 1929 shows that full-time design students at the Allgemeine Gewerbeschule were given an all-round professional training that included posters, advertisements, letterheads and brochures, as well as illustration.[2] In both Basel and Zurich the schools made a clear distinction between 'artistic' graphics, such as printmaking, and applied graphics.

Of all teachers, Ernst Keller is the most frequently cited

▲ 'Exhibition of Student Work in the Applied Arts Department of the Zurich Gewerbeschule', poster designed by Ernst Keller, 1939.
Printed by lithography in black and red.

2. *Schülerarbeiten der Kunstgewerblichen Abteilung der Allgemeinen Gewerbeschule Basel*, catalogue, Gewerbemuseum Basel, 1929, p.17.

114

SCHÜLERARBEITEN DER
GEWERBESCHULE ZÜRICH
KUNSTGEWERBLICHE ABT.
AUSSTELLUNG IM
KUNSTGEWERBEMUSEUM
4.-31. MÄRZ EINTRITT FREI

▲ Warja Lavater's poster for an
exhibition of work by students in
the Arts and Crafts Department at
the Zurich Gewerbeschule, 1937.
The crisp drawing and geometrical
lettering show the clear
influence of Ernst Keller, head of
the Kunstgewerbeschule's graphic
department. This full-size design was
printed at the school from linoblocks
(in two parts) in black only.
Warja Lavater was a highly successful
illustrator who also worked with her
husband, Gottfried Honegger,
a designer and Concrete artist,
from 1937.

as an influence on the postwar graphic designers. He
taught at the Kunstgewerbeschule in Zurich for nearly
forty years. In 1939, Keller stated a matter-of-fact aim:

> In the specialist graphic class the aim of the teaching
> is to help the student in such a way that later he will be
> able to deal as perfectly as possible, both technically
> and artistically, with the whole range of professional
> tasks. . . . Qualified tradesmen have the opportunity
> for further education.[3]

Warja Lavater, who joined Keller's class in 1932, makes it
sound more exciting. Of twenty-eight students, seven
were women.

> What we were learning was design, and so we began
> with the most important thing, drawing. Where do you
> put a sign in a rectangle? What is the standard solution
> to this exercise? Should the strongest element be the
> sign or the drawing? How can both be distinguished at
> a distance, yet integrated in a composition?[4]

An account of the Swiss schools' teaching is given in the
special issue of the German *Archiv für Buchgewerbe* in
1929. Also included is a long text on graphic design
education by the former Bauhaus master Johannes Itten,
at this time running his own art school in Berlin; ten years
later he was to take up the post of Director of the Zurich
school. Itten insists on the importance of a *Vorkurs*, the
type of preliminary course he had pioneered at the
Bauhaus. He understood the need to balance technical
knowledge with creative ability and the necessary
professional skills of a practising designer. Photography,
even at this early date, Itten regarded as part of the
course. He realized that photographers needed special
training, and that there was more than one sort of
photographer: the studio photographer, primarily
a technician; the portrait photographer, for whom Itten
proposed a whole year of drawing as well as studying
aspects of psychology; and the press photographer, who
needed to combine the technical and the artistic.

Study abroad was not unusual. Until the 1930s many
designers, after their Swiss training, went on to further
study in the small Paris academies, such as those run by
the painter Fernand Léger or the poster artist Paul Colin.
Many went for experience to the commercial studios of
the celebrated designers of an earlier generation in Berlin
or Munich. By the early 1930s and the beginning of the
Nazi era, this option was removed.

3. Ernst Keller in *Schülerarbeiten der Kunstgewerbeschule*, catalogue,
Kunstgewerbemuseum Zurich, 1939, p.11.
4. *Werbestil 1930-1940*, catalogue, Kunstgewerbemuseum Zurich, 1981, p.82.

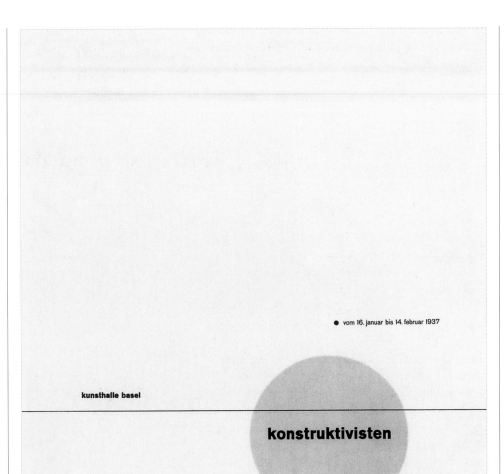

◄ 'Constructivists' exhibition poster, designed by Jan Tschichold, 1937.

The exhibition in Basel was important as a signal that, whatever the attitudes of the Fascist regime on the other side of the Rhine, Abstract, non-representational art had official approval.

In what looks like a resolutely pure example of New Typography, Tschichold reveals his interest in traditional proportions: the rectangle below the horizontal line is near the proportion of the classical Golden Section (22:34). But in common with Van Doesburg (the first on the list of exhibiting artists), the design has simple arithmetical relationships: the circle, for example, is half its width away from the right-hand edge of the poster. The circle's left-hand edge is on the vertical centre of the poster. The title and the bullet (which draws attention to the date) are aligned vertically on the centre of the circle. The type, ranged left, is aligned to the right of this axis. In this way Tschichold anticipates the mixture of symmetry and asymmetry that would be used by his young admirers in the 1960s.

Abstract Art and the Avant-Garde

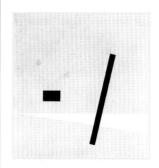

▲ Friedrich Vordemberge-Gildewart: *Composition No. 78*, 1933, illustrated by Jan Tschichold in his article, 'Non-Representational Painting and Its Relation to Present-Day Typography', 1935. Vordemberge-Gildewart exhibited in the Grafa exhibition in Basel in 1936. As a refugee from Nazi Germany, he spent a short time in Zurich in 1938, but spent the war years in the Netherlands. His painting had much in common with that of his friend, Richard Paul Lohse. From 1954 he taught at the Hochschule für Gestaltung in Ulm, founded by Max Bill.

In 1935 Jan Tschichold, exiled in Switzerland, restated his belief that 'typography and the New Architecture share common ground,' and 'without the new Abstract painting the New Architecture would have been unthinkable.'

The so-called Constructivists, to which Lissitzky belongs, and in some ways Vordemberge [-Gildewart] too, use strong geometrical forms, and it is a small step from these to typography.[1] Their works are symbols of total order made out of simple, but often strongly contrasting elements. . . . They are the finest means of teaching visual order.[2]

This was not to say that Abstract art was concerned only with form: an abstract work could be 'an instrument of spiritual influence, a symbol of harmony'.

In Zurich most of the progressive graphic designers were artists; they made Abstract paintings – Max Bill, Richard Paul Lohse, Anton Stankowski – or they were exponents of the New Photography – Walter Cyliax, Herbert Matter and Heiri Steiner. Also in Zurich, and primarily photographers, were Ernst A. Heiniger and Gotthard Schuh. (Stankowski also belonged among the avant-garde photographers.) In Basel, Theo Ballmer and Hermann Eidenbenz were among the photographers. As artists, and as photographers and graphic designers, they belonged to an avant-garde which was seen to be either stimulating or puzzling, and threatening established beliefs and values.

On the one hand the greater part of the public were unimpressed; the hostility which had met the travelling exhibition 'The New Photography in Switzerland' in 1932 was a not unusual response. And this was where the designer-photographers were well represented: for example, Ballmer, Cyliax, Heiniger and Stankowski. On the other hand, such avant-garde exhibitions demonstrated that the New had supporters, and some of the important museum curators were among them.[3] At the Zurich Kunsthaus the exhibition 'Zeitprobleme in der Schweizer Malerei und Plastik' (Problems of Our Time in Swiss Painting and Sculpture), held in 1936, included Max Bill and Richard Paul Lohse – designer-artists. Bill designed the poster and also the catalogue. The following year, the only Swiss name in the list of artists on

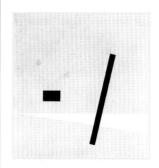

▲ Advertisement for an art gallery, designed by Jan Tschichold and reproduced with the caption: 'Comparison with the picture alongside [Vordemberge-Gildewart's *Composition*] shows the relationship between the New Typography and the New Painting.'

---

1. Friedrich Vordemberge-Gildewart (1899-1962), German painter and graphic designer, a member of De Stijl and of the Ring neuer Werbegestalter. (See side note above.)
2. *Typographische Monatsblätter*, June 1935, p. 186-87.
3. The most striking example was Georg Schmidt, curator at the Basel Gewerbemuseum and later Director of the Basel Kunstmuseum. Brother of the architect Hans Schmidt (a founding editor of *ABC*), he was a consistent supporter, as writer and curator, of the New from the 1920s onwards. Without him, many of the important exhibitions might not have taken place.

▶ 'Problems of Our Time in Swiss Painting and Sculpture', exhibition poster by Max Bill, 1936.
The design is odd: almost symmetrical except for the text, and almost a pictorial illustration, as though the round-cornered diamond at the top is a sculpture balanced on a square painting, or on a plinth. Max Bill and Richard Paul Lohse are included in the list of participating artists. Printed in black only from type and linoblock.

▲ Catalogue cover of the exhibition
'New Art in Switzerland' at the Basel
Kunsthalle, designed by Max
Sulzbachner, 1938.
Sulzbachner began his career as a
painter and was a typographer only for
a short period. Following Tschichold's
precepts, he was able to produce a
piece of irreproachable Modernism.

Tschichold's poster for the exhibition 'Konstruktivisten' (Constructivists) is Sophie Taeuber-Arp. 'Konstruktivisten' nonetheless helped in Switzerland to confirm the importance of Abstract art.

For graphic design a more significant event in 1937 was the foundation of Allianz, the association of modern Swiss artists. The first exhibition organized by the group was 'Neue Kunst in der Schweiz' (New Art in Switzerland), held at the Kunsthalle Basel the following year. The typographic poster and catalogue cover were designed in the Tschichold manner by Max Sulzbachner. Richard Paul Lohse was a founder-member of Allianz; he designed the letterhead, and for the next decade the posters and catalogues for Allianz were the purest examples of what was to become known as 'konstruktive' graphics.

The origin of the New Typography in Abstract painting had its dangers. These were foreseen by Tschichold and the other chief propagandist of the New, Hans Neuburg, neither of them artists. Neuburg, the publicity expert, had already expressed his anxiety that Neo-Constructivism, adopted as a style, might compromise any design in its role as the message carrier. Tschichold, after recommending that typographers study Abstract art, warns them: 'We must stay within the bounds of our own technology and the purpose of our work if we are to avoid crass formalism.'[4]

Whatever concerns designers may have had, they did not expect to read in the pages of *Das Werk* that Abstract art was 'an art of nihilism'. According to Peter Meyer, the editor, Abstract art added 'the intoxication of unbridled technology to the emotionalism of destruction, the sadistic enjoyment of the repressing, torturing, murdering of the individual life'.[5] Among those who signed a letter of protest were Max Bill, Sigfried Giedion, Hermann Eidenbenz and Ernst A. Heiniger: Meyer's words carried echoes of the Nazi concept of 'degenerate' art.

Although Peter Meyer had expressed doubts as early as 1926 that the Bauhaus would lead to formalism, he had earlier written sympathetically of many of the designers discussed here. Yet what might be seen as formalist tendencies in avant-garde Swiss work – the flaunting of geometry exemplified by Max Bill's 'Negerkunst' poster – was rare. Indeed, nothing could be further from the forms of Bill's painting or sculpture at the time, or from public preconceptions of the New than, for example, his poster for the Zurich Conservatoire.

▲ Small poster by Max Bill for the Zurich Conservatoire, 1934. Printed letterpress from linoblock. Bill retained the convention of lower-case lettering and type throughout his long career, but he would choose letterforms and a graphic style to suit the job in hand. The type in the white panel could change to announce new performances. Its excessively wide word spacing may have been a self-conscious experiment or an eccentricity beyond his control.

4. *Typographische Monatsblätter*, June 1935, p.187.
5. *Das Werk*, March 1938, pp.74-79.

▲ Basel City Directory, title page designed by Jan Tschichold, 1935. Tschichold departs from one of the crucial elements of the New Typography – asymmetry – making a centred layout which also demonstrated his notion that complex information could be ordered into three groupings.

The practice of the New Typography had slowly changed, and Tschichold was re-examining its principles in a stream of articles in *Typographische Monatsblätter*. In 1935 his *Typographische Gestaltung* was published in Basel, a book that was limited essentially to asymmetric typography.[6] In the same year that he extolled Abstract art and linked it to the New Architecture – which was itself asymmetrical by nature – Tschichold asked, 'How is it that the average typography now is mostly centred?' His answer is that there are subjects for which modern typography is inappropriate. The arguments are aesthetic as well as practical: short and very short lines are better arranged on a central axis, whereas asymmetrical arrangements need strong horizontals, and therefore longer lines. He even mentions a typographer's clients, who often insist on a symmetrical layout. And he adds,

> You won't be able to do a decent asymmetrical layout if you can't do a decent one symmetrically. From a formal point of view, symmetry is easier and simpler than the modern style of setting, which has the advantage of technical simplicity. But there are still not many typesetters who can design a good piece of symmetrical setting. Also it is art, or can be art. (Only it is not the art of today!)[7]

Tschichold was not turning his back on the New Typography. This was, after all, what he was teaching at the Allgemeine Gewerbeschule in Basel, and practising in the posters and catalogues he was designing for the Gewerbemuseum.

Arguments which became heated public exchanges after the war had already begun to surface. Public interest may have been stimulated by the exhibitions of Abstract art, but an instinctive conservatism, reinforced by the economic and political turbulence of the 1930s, encouraged a general suspicion of progressive tendencies. Many of the bright lights of Modernism were going out. Herbert Matter had left for the United States. Walter Cyliax and Anton Stankowski had returned to Germany. Wohnbedarf was selling antique furniture as an alternative to its types.

More than anyone, it was the artists, Bill and Lohse, and their Allianz publications which kept Modernist ideas of graphic design alive during the war years.

▲ 'New Furniture in Mountain Pine, Cherry, Walnut, Deal', poster by Pierre Gauchat, 1937. The optimistic period of selling its 'type' furniture was over. Wohnbedarf was obliged to compromise, not only by using traditional materials, but also by selling antiques.

6. 'Asymmetric Typography' was the book's title when it was translated into English more than thirty years later (see bibliography).
7. 'Vom richtigen Satz auf Mittelachse', *Typographische Monatsblätter*, March 1935, p.114.

2 The Survival of Modernism:
Conflicts and Contradictions
1939-1949

In our puritanical and critical country something beautiful is immediately seen
as a bit suspect.
Max Bill, 'Schönheit aus Funktion und als Funktion' (Beauty from Function and as Function),
Werk, August 1949, p.273.

We [graphic designers] do not determine what is the expression of the times;
but the times looks to us for an expression of itself.
Hans Neuburg, 'Die Gegenwartströmungen in der schweizerischen Zweckgraphik'
(Current Trends in Swiss Graphic Design), *Typographische Monatsblätter*, July 1946, p.237.

◀ Cover of the weekly
Zürcher Illustrierte's record of
the Landesausstellung, the Swiss
National Exhibition, in 1939.
The main entrance welcomed visitors
with a display of local banners,
culminating in the national flag.

122 ► Poster for 'Werkbundidee und Werkbundarbeit' (Werkbund Idea and Werkbund Work) an exhibition of the Basel district group of the Swiss Werkbund, held at the Basel Gewerbemuseum in winter, 1938-39. Designed by Hermann Eidenbenz, the poster shows the interlinked participants in Werkbund activity: architects, weavers, graphic designers (at the top), then furniture makers, photographers, manufacturers, goldsmiths, sculptors, salesmen and agents, and consumers.
Not all Werkbund members would have approved the exclusion of capitals in the typography.
The printing, by lithography, uses the 'rainbow' technique to give a multi-colour effect with only two printing plates.

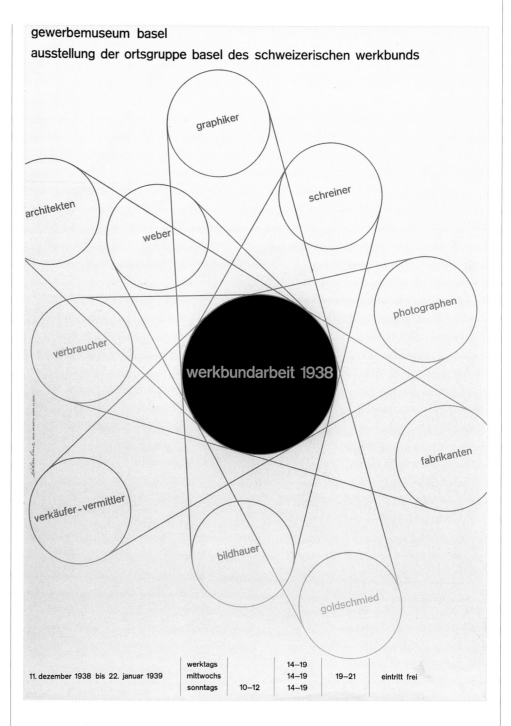

The Swiss National Exhibition 1939

▲ The exhibition in Basel designed by Eidenbenz, 'Werkbundidee und Werkbundarbeit', was a didactic exposition of Werkbund principles and practice.

Modernism was struggling for acceptance. In the winter of 1938 to 1939, the exhibition 'Werkbundidee und Werkbundarbeit' (Werkbund Idea and Werkbund Work) was held in Basel. The public was shown the 'rights' and 'wrongs' of design; ideas such as 'truth to material' were dogmatically explained; the new was exposed as not necessarily better than the old – though the Werkbund acknowledged that poster designers could legitimately respond to changes in taste. Outright Modernism, not fashion, was the essence of the exhibition's poster. Designed by Hermann Eidenbenz, its austere black-and-white diagram of the Werkbund's activities could not be more 'sachlich', its use of lowercase more uncompromising, its presentation of dates and times more rational. For Eidenbenz, style was not a matter of appearance, it was a means chosen to communicate an idea: here the New Typography had developed into functional graphics, the negation of style.

Eidenbenz was the most prodigally skilled of his generation. He began as an apprentice at the printers and publishers Orell Füssli in Zurich. At the Kunstgewerbeschule he was taught by Ernst Keller and in 1923, to complete his training, went to work in the studios of two leading Berlin designers, Wilhelm Deffke and Oskar Hadank. He stayed in Germany, and for six years taught at the art school in Magdeburg, at the time when Xanti Schawinsky was the city's graphic designer. He returned to Switzerland in 1932, opening a studio in Basel with his two brothers, Reinhold and Willi. With this wide experience, Eidenbenz had developed a facility in every style. Although he produced some of the finest works of graphic Modernism, he was not one of those designers who saw their work as steps towards a rationalist utopia.

Building a new world was, by 1939, of less consequence than the question of survival. Hitler had annexed Austria and part of Czechoslovakia, and with Fascist Italy to the south, Switzerland was vulnerable. The country's neutrality was no protection. Refugees were seeking asylum at a time when unemployment was on an unprecedented scale. The enemy, both military and ideological, was at the gates.

Switzerland now sought national solidarity by issuing a cultural call to arms. The Swiss National Exhibition, the Landesausstellung (known as the 'Landi'), which opened in May 1939, was to provide a reassuring message. The site was on both shores of Lake Zurich: 'Home and People', which included industry and culture, on the left bank; agriculture and rural life, on the right.

Design and the Landesausstellung
▼ A competition was held for a symbol for the 'Landi', the 1939 National Exhibition. Most of the designs submitted were simplified illustrations (even a cowbell), and less than a quarter, such as those below, had the graphic economy that could be described as Modernist or, later, as recognizably Swiss.

124

▶ Although the first prize in the competition for a symbol for the Swiss National Exhibition was won by Hermann Eidenbenz, Warja Honegger-Lavater's design was selected for use. The four rings were intended to represent trade, light industry, heavy industry and agriculture.

▲ Three-part full-colour poster for the Landesausstellung by Pierre Gauchat. The four women in traditional costume represent the four language groups of Switzerland: German, French, Italian and Romansch.
The exhibition itself had more Modernist design, especially in sections dealing with modern life and technology. The 'Landi-style', homely and traditional, was reserved for more essentially patriotic subjects and was in keeping with agricultural and domestic topics.
▼ Pierre Gauchat also designed the photomural in the Landi's press section. Twenty-three readers stand up to enjoy the Swiss newspapers which 'fight for freedom and social progress'.

▲ Crowds at the Landi were given information through modern graphics. The rise and fall of exports (dark line) and imports shows the growth of economic activity – at its peak in 1929, and falling to its lowest in 1932.

Competitions were held for Landi posters. The winner for the larger, three-part poster was Pierre Gauchat. It could not be described as Modernist. Uniting four women in traditional dress – the country's four language groups – under the flags of Switzerland and the cantons against a summer sky, it was effective in its colourful, defiant jollity.

Traditional folk culture was strongly represented at the exhibition. The result in some sections was a homely, so-called Landi-style. The exhibition nonetheless employed most of the progressive designers; their cool objectivity was suited to presenting the commercial and industrial aspects of Swiss life. Among them were Theo Ballmer; Max Bill; Hermann Eidenbenz and his brothers; Walter Herdeg; Gottfried Honegger and Warja Honegger-Lavater; Walter Käch; Richard Paul Lohse; Josef Müller-Brockmann; Hans Neuburg; Heiri Steiner, and Hans Trommer.

A vast pavilion was devoted to the graphic trades, where a complete printing works was installed. Reproduction techniques were demonstrated, and design, old and new, was displayed. On view in a 'hall of honour', alongside Gauchat's poster (for Wohnbedarf wooden furniture), were designs by Ernst Keller (for the Gropius exhibition and the Zurich garden show) and Alfred Willimann ('Light' exhibition). Advertising had its own section.

Photography not only had a separate space in the Landi, it was also employed throughout, as

huge enlargements to catch the eye, as photomontages to present different aspects and types of event, as added pictorial explanation of an exhibit, as substitutes for things that could not be brought to the exhibition, as effective visual statistics, as evidence and illustration of scientific and technical research, as descriptions of historical development, as portraits of important Swiss citizens, as images of popular life and customs, as the only means of portraying our industrial workshops and factories, and allowing the varied landscape of our homeland to make its own dramatic impression.[1]

Graphic designers had made a surprising contribution to the Landi. They were admired not for the expected artistic presentations but for the skills they brought to making information look interesting and understandable.

1. Ernst Rust and Hans Finsler, *Die Schweiz im Spiegel der Landesausstellung*, Zurich 1940, p.507, quoted in *Dreissiger Jahre Schweiz: Ein Jahrzehnt im Widerspruch*, catalogue, Kunsthaus Zurich, 1981, p.404.

Wartime

▲ Ration card, 1942. The war surrounding Switzerland drew on manpower and resources. Most designers served at least part time in the military, while supplies of paper and raw material for the printing industry were restricted.

▼ The general retreat from Modernism is revealed by the pages of *Typographische Monatsblätter*. The only appearance in the magazine of Akzidenz Grotesk during 1941 was on the cover of a cookery book. The title, 'Fett Sparen' (Save Fat), in homely Fraktur type, overwhelms the modest grotesque subtitle 'und doch gut kochen' (and cook well).

Neutrality did not protect Switzerland from the effects of war. Most designers spent long periods in the army. Shortages meant rationing, not only of food. 'Perhaps our fine white paper will go the same way as our white bread, which is now grey', worried the editorial of *Typographische Monatsblätter* in January 1940. The magazine illustrated a wide variety of work, mainly an anaemic, undisciplined version of New Typography. Meanwhile a few stalwarts, notably Hans Neuburg and Richard Paul Lohse, kept the Modernist flag flying.

Neuburg was tireless in pursuing and promoting the objective style of 'Industrie-Graphik' which he had acquired while working with Anton Stankowski ten years earlier. In *Das Werk* he maintained that the industrial advertiser cannot go far wrong if he lets the technical beauty of his products speak for themselves in realistic photographs with clean typography.[1] Neuburg illustrated the article with examples of his work for industrial clients – engineering firms and companies supplying services to the building industry – alongside others by Eidenbenz and Gauchat.

Allianz, the Association of Modern Swiss Artists, was crucial in keeping alive the Modernist tradition. Although its exhibitions were by no means exclusively Concrete, or even Abstract (they included Paul Klee and Le Corbusier), the group's posters and catalogues, all by either Lohse or Bill, maintained an elegant austerity, planting the mathematical systems of Concrete art more firmly in Swiss graphic design.

Lohse took part in an exhibition at the Zurich Kunstgewerbemuseum in 1943 organized by the Association of Swiss Graphic Designers, the Verband Schweizerischer Grafiker (VSG). It was simply titled 'Grafik'. Without emphasizing Modernist tendencies, the catalogue gave Lohse the opportunity to explain changes in professional practice. The conventional media of the commercial artist were paper, pencil, brush and paint, but Lohse points out that

> there are now a number of specialist 'FotoGrafiker' who have made photography an important and essential part of their graphic work . . . and with the photograph, whose use demands of the designer just as much formal skill as drawing, the question of composition is more important than the manner of representation. Working with photographs . . . rather than drawn and painted images, the designer is forced to adopt a different approach.

1. Hans Neuburg-Coray, 'Technische Graphik und Werbung', *Das Werk*, August 1943, pp.256-57.

▲ 'Almanac of New Art in Switzerland', book cover designed by Richard Paul Lohse, 1940.

▲ Poster for the 1942 Allianz group exhibition, designed by Max Bill. The all-lowercase type is ranged both left and right on the vertical axis, positioned on the 'Z' of 'Zürich'. The word 'allianz' is placed on the top of a square formed in the lower left corner, its right-hand edge ranged on the column of artists' names.

▲ Cover of the catalogue for the 'Concrete Art' exhibition at the Kunsthalle, Basel, designed by Max Bill, 1944. The all-lowercase type is ranged left on two vertical axes.

126

▶ 'Quick Load, Quick Unload, Full Load',
poster by Hans Erni for the Swiss State
Railways, 1942.
The design lacks any of the more
conventional formal elements
of Modernism. But Erni brought
the mathematical precision of his
Abstract painting to the network of
lines and arrows. They express the idea
of rail freight as urgent and efficient,
reinforced by the clean precision
of the 'sachlich' image.

Hans Erni Born 1909
Painter, graphic designer, sculptor and
stage designer. Trained as a surveying
technician and draughtsman. Studied
at Kunstgewerbeschule, Lucerne, 1927-
28, then in Paris and Berlin. Member of
the Swiss Werkbund and co-founder of
Allianz, 1937. Designed more than 150
posters, mainly as painted illustrations,
most memorably, in 1954, an anti-
nuclear design: the mushroom cloud
rising from a skull, its dome fused with
the earth's surface. Supremely facile as
a painter and draughtsman, Erni moved
from abstraction – close to Max Bill in
the 1930s – to a heightened realism,
exemplified by a 100-metre-long mural
for the Landi exhibition, 1939. He went
on to follow the Communist Party line
of Socialist Realism and to
vulgarizations of Picasso's neo-
classical style of the 1920s.

▶ 'Embru Steel-Spring Mattresses',
poster designed by Pierre Gauchat,
1940. Throughout the recession of the
1930s and restrictions imposed by the
war, Pierre Gauchat's publicity design
for Embru, furniture makers and
suppliers to Wohnbedarf, retained a
'sachlich' character rather than the
popular illustrational style he had used
for the Landi poster (p.124).

▲ Cover of a catalogue for mattresses
and sofas, designed by Pierre Gauchat,
1942.
The springing of the bed and sofa
frame gives the graphic designer
a ready-made image: a photograph
which attracts the eye and, as evidence
of first-class design and manufacture,
recommends the product.
Printed letterpress in black, with
the label in red.
▼ Gauchat has inserted the crossbow,
the official symbol of Swiss design
and manufacture, designed by the
advertising agency Steinmann and
Bolliger in the 1930s, as part of his
Embru logo.

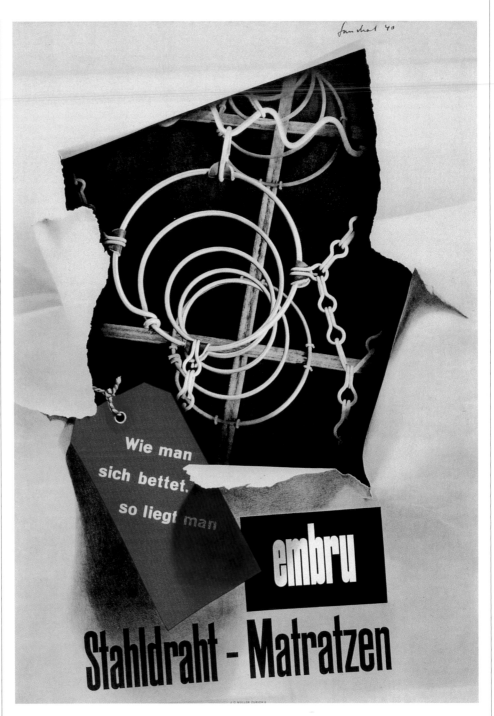

Gauchat exposes the springs as the
main selling point of the product.
The repeated red label is a sign
which links the poster with other
Embru publicity.

Although the proverb, 'As you make
your bed, so must you lie on it', is not
an essential element, it is not the kind
of meaningless claim of conventional
advertising slogans.

128

▼ Catalogue cover in red and black designed by Gérard Miedinger for the Swiss Graphic Designers Association exhibition at the Zurich Kunstgewerbemuseum, 1943. The exhibition balanced the work of its Modernist members with traditional work, and paid special attention to the training of graphic designers at the Kunstgewerbeschule.

▼ Lohse developed an unaffectedly direct language in a large number of book covers, beginning in the 1930s. The front cover and spine of a dust jacket for 'Switzerland's History of Population and Its Politics', 1947, typically combines two images by overprinting a photograph and a statistical diagram. In linking the black rectangle on the spine to the typography of the title on the front, Lohse treats the book as a three-dimensional object.

Lohse goes on to describe how the designer has to take into account the way the photograph is cropped, the variety of colouring and toning that are possible, and the opportunity for montage. And he points out that, 'previously the designer, whose medium was drawing, had little to do with typography. By comparison, typography is today a basic and essential part of the graphic designer's work.' And Lohse claimed that typography brought with it 'a shift towards constructive and measurable form'.

Only months later, when *Das Werk* produced a special issue on Swiss graphic design, there was little evidence to support Lohse's optimism.[2] In a survey of posters since the 1920s, of the sixty reproduced, Modernists such as Lohse and his colleagues are in a small and diverse minority. Few have a distinct personal style, and the only consistent use of photography appears in prewar work by Walter Herdeg and Herbert Matter.

Lohse's key position depended not only on his years as a commercial artist but also on his experience as a painter. One gave him a complete technical understanding of print and reproduction processes; the other made him expert in the use of colour and spatial organization; and from his interest in architecture came an insight into standardization and modular design. Added to his political engagement, these attributes endowed him and his work with a special authority. It was to Lohse that Wohnbedarf turned for its design when the company, after backsliding into folkish traditional furnishings, returned to its original Modernist commitment.

As well as his work for industry, there were Lohse's commissions from progressive publishers. In the ten years from 1938 Lohse designed a number of books and more than one hundred book jackets. Almost all the covers were limited to two printing ink colours, which Lohse turned to advantage, relating title to image by superimposition. Full-colour reproduction was unusual at this time. The limitation could be overcome and a rich graphic effect achieved by the common device of overprinting: not only of black on colour, but of image on image, similar to the 'dissolve' in film, where one image is gradually overlaid and supplants its predecessor. The contrast of one with another can reinforce an idea, or the combination of two images can supply a fresh, dramatic meaning.

This addition to graphic language was used by Lohse not only on book jackets but also in catalogues and

Commercial Modernism
Throughout the war period Richard Paul Lohse carried on a wide range of advertising in his Constructivist style of Modernism.

▲ The roofing materials firm Meynadier was one of Lohse's principal clients. In this advertisement for 'practical durable patio covering' in 1944, Lohse seems to pay homage to El Lissitzky. The photograph is by Ernst A. Heiniger.
▼ Lohse designed for the landscape architects and contractors Mertens over a period of twenty years. This half-page advertisement appeared in *Werk*, 1941.

2. *Das Werk*, August 1943.

As a freelance designer, Richard Paul Lohse worked for the huge engineering company Escher Wyss for thirty years. In this time he produced more than 600 items, beginning with the trademark in 1939.

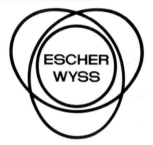

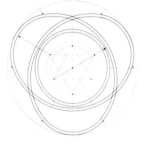

▲ Lohse's design for the Escher Wyss trademark and a diagram of its geometrical basis, 1939. The movement of the continuous looping line around a circle suggests the company's activity in the field of turbines.

▼ Original photograph of the propeller inside the Escher Wyss works, used by Lohse for the brochure cover. ▶

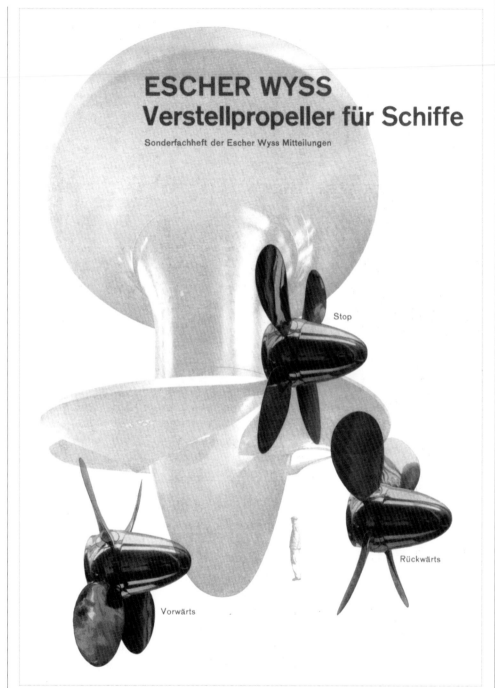

ESCHER WYSS
Verstellpropeller für Schiffe
Sonderfachheft der Escher Wyss Mitteilungen

Stop

Rückwärts

Vorwärts

▲ A4 brochure cover designed by Richard Paul Lohse for Escher Wyss, 1945. The subject is the giant variable-pitch ship's propeller shown in the photograph. Lohse has painted out the background, leaving the worker's figure – to show the relative size – and at the top has airbrushed in the missing part of the ellipse of the propeller's housing .

The three cut-out views of the propeller, labelled 'stop', 'forwards', 'backwards', show the movement of the blades on their axes.

‣ Richard Paul Lohse's small poster for the Werkbund travelling exhibition, 'Our Home', 1943. The design was seriously criticized for its unintelligible abstraction and its illegibility. The former Bauhaus teacher Johannes Itten, now director of the Zurich Kunstgewerbeschule, was co-curator. The exhibition's designer was Max Bill.

▼ Cover to an anthology, 'Outsider Poets', designed by Richard Paul Lohse, 1946, based on a square module. The typography of the book's text pages, not by Lohse, is mundane, with poor quality paper, a result of wartime restrictions.

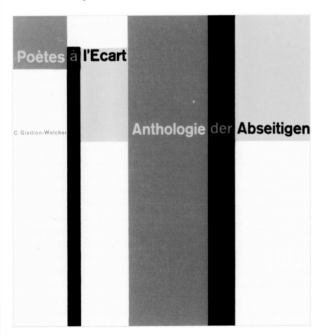

brochures for the huge engineering firm of Escher Wyss, whose trademark he had designed in 1939.

Though Swiss industry in general was slow to recognize the value of the new graphic design, the profession was publicly recognized by the government. It announced that the Department of the Interior would, with the Applied Arts Commission, make an annual selection of the best posters, beginning in 1941: the criteria would be aesthetic quality, standard of printing and effectiveness as advertising. To begin with, the commended posters were all illustrative: commercial art, rather than graphic design.

The tendency of Modernists to align with left-wing politics and commit themelves to libertarian causes continued during the war and its aftermath. In the postwar world, divisions into Eastern and Western political blocs were mirrored in the split of designers into two camps – the designers who used drawn illustration and serif typefaces – and the Modernists using photographs and grotesque type.[3]

A test case for these allegiances was Lohse's poster for the Werkbund's exhibition 'Unsere Wohnung' (Our Home). The Secretary of the Werkbund, the architect Egidius Streiff, wrote:

> The exhibition is directed exclusively towards ordinary people. It offers instruction and new ideas to workers and the lower middle class. And yet these people are encouraged to attend the exhibition by means of an abstract play of forms and with a text that can only be read from close up. . . . For our purpose we should have a completely different formal language.[4]

In other words, pictorial illustration would have made a more effective poster. Had its medium less connection with its message than with the aesthetic preferences of the artist? This was an extreme example, but it gave ammunition to the opponents of Modernism in what was becoming a battle of styles.

3. This is not to say that the illustrational designers took a more conservative or nationalistic stance. Hans Erni, for example, committedly left-wing, followed a conservative aesthetic path.
4. The Richard Paul Lohse Foundation (ed.), *Richard Paul Lohse: Graphic Design 1928-1988*, Ostfildern-Ruit 2002 (English translation), note 51, p.62.

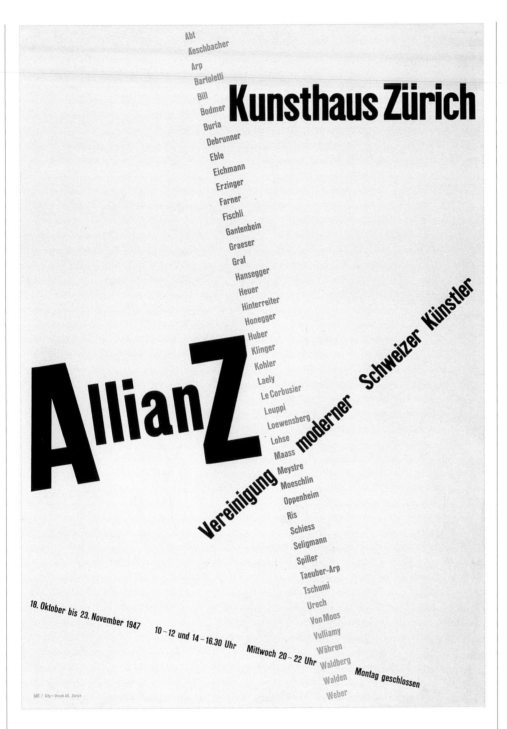

▼ Full-page magazine advertisement in *Das Werk* for fluorescent lights, designed by Hans Neuburg, 1948. There is a drawing of a fluorescent tube, but the layout refers back to the world of Constructivist utopia rather than to the everyday marketing of industrial products. It is a contradiction of Neuburg's demand that the designer should not impose style.

▲ 'Sport and Politics Magazine', cover by Jan Tschichold, 1928. The Constructivist source, common to Tschichold's and Neuburg's designs, is quite clear.

▲ Max Bill's poster for the Allianz (Association of Modern Swiss Artists) exhibition, 1947. As if in opposition to Tschichold's 'Der Berufsphotograph' poster, Bill breaks the inherent rectangularity of letterpress printing.

Angling the type, Bill has given life to the sheet. The first downstroke of the 'A' of 'Allianz', parallel with the edge of the sheet, has determined the angle of the word. By enlarging the first and last letters of Allianz, he has suggested the group's range – from A to Z.
The convention of listing the artists alphabetically in a single column could be achieved without changing the size of type by setting them at an angle.

Graphic designers in the list of artists, as well as Max Bill and Lohse, are Leo Gantenbein, Gottfried Honegger and Max Huber.

132 **Social and Humanitarian Causes**
The progressive designers made
a significant contribution to
Switzerland's tradition of charitable
aid. They were engaged in making
posters, special stamps, exhibitions
and leaflets for programmes in support
of the elderly, children in need,
the unemployed and those for whom
winter was a task of survival.

▼ 'Exhibition of the Italian Resistance',
small poster designed by Max Huber,
1946. Huber uses the simplest
elements: a photograph of Italian
resistance fighters with British soldiers,
overlaid with a flat colour. The red star
of the Italians' cap badge becomes the
dominant motif of the poster, reversed
with the lettering out of the solid red,
to show the white of the paper.

▶ One side of an unfolded exhibition
leaflet designed by Richard Paul Lohse,
c.1944. The exhibition, on the Italian
resistance to the Germans in the
Second World War, was supported by
the Centrale Sanitaire Suisse, a
medical and humanitarian organization
helping opponents and victims of
Fascism. Printed in the Italian colours,
the leaflet records the events with
facts and figures and documentary
photographs.

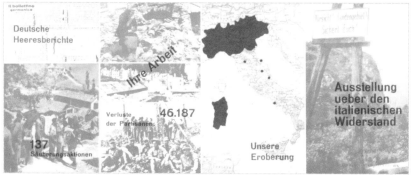

During and after the war the Red Cross, based in Geneva, could call on Swiss generosity and the willing services of Swiss designers in raising funds to help the hundreds of thousands of displaced people.
Hans Neuburg designed a Red Cross fund-raising display at the Basel Mustermesse in 1944. The following year Hermann Eidenbenz designed graphics for a travelling exhibition on prisoners of war.

▼ 'The International Committee of the Red Cross Is Helping, But It Needs Everybody's Help.' Poster designed by Hans Neuburg, 1946.
News photographs of homeless refugees and of former soldiers illustrate the problems of the time. The typewritten headline adds to the documentary nature of the images. The handwritten text, as with Eidenbenz's Red Cross poster, adds a personal element to the plea for aid.

▲ 'Help as though This Child Were One of Your Own', poster by Hermann Eidenbenz, 1946.
The handwritten message, making the appeal personal and direct, was overprinted with text in other languages.

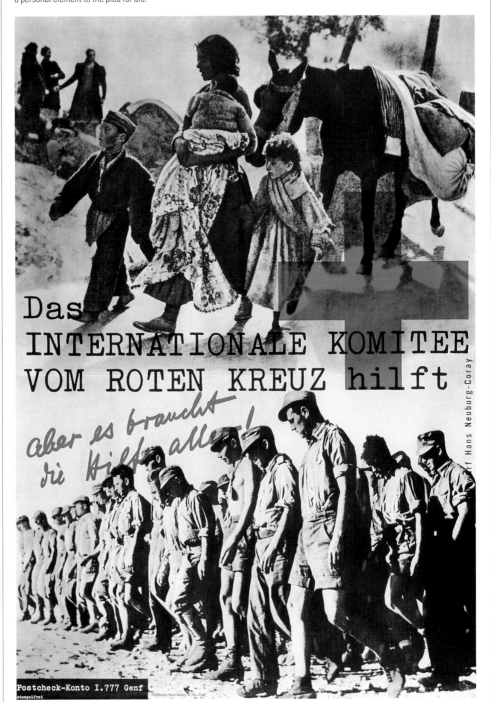

134   **Help the Aged**

▲ Poster designed by Ernst Keller, 1945.

► Poster by Carlo Vivarelli, 1949. Every year a poster was produced for this charity. Only four years separate these two designs. The verbal and iconographic content are almost the same, but they show the distance between Keller's traditional graphic design and that of his former students: a matter of style, not of effectiveness. In Vivarelli's poster, Akzidenz Grotesk replaces Keller's drawn lettering; Vivarelli employs marked asymmetry and unfilled space instead of a clear, centred design.

Both use an old woman as the symbol of need. The painted portrait, importantly, includes the hands, which suggest either prayer or patient resignation. The photograph – by Werner Bischof, one of Hans Finsler's many successful students – implies that this is a documentary record. But the low shadow dramatizes the individual and suggests simple lighting and heating – the candle and the open fire.

Für das Alter

Freiwillige Spende

The Italian Connection

▲ Cover to issue no.6 of
Abstrakt–Konkret, designed by Max
Huber with a woodcut by Hans Arp,
1945. Huber, working in Italy during the
war, was included in a survey of Italian
graphic design in *Typographische
Monatsblätter*, a rare appearance of
Modernism in 1942.
Abstrakt–Konkret ran for 12 issues,
three designed by Huber, two by Max
Bill and one by Richard Paul Lohse.

Max Huber 1919-1992

Designer, painter. Apprenticed to
advertising agency in Zurich and
studied at the Kunstgewerbeschule
under Alfred Willimann from 1935.
Worked in the Zurich printer-publishers
Conzett & Huber, 1939-40. Began
military service but left for Milan to
work at Studio Boggeri, 1940. Returned
to Zurich, as assistant at *Du* magazine
and freelance, especially for socialist
publishers, 1941-42. Member of Allianz,
1944-47. Returned to Milan, 1945.

In Fascist Italy the progressive designers were able to
establish a small avant-garde. They had absorbed the
revolutionary graphic lessons of Futurism and were not
bound by the aesthetic straightjacket imposed in
Germany. The focal point of progressive graphic design
was Studio Boggeri, where Xanti Schawinsky had worked
for a year in the early 1930s. Other Swiss designers came
to work at the Studio before, during, and for several
decades after the war. They were to make a significant
impact in their home country.

In the middle of the war, *Typographische Monatsblätter*
published an Italian issue, written by Italians, who spoke
of 'a cultural exchange' – an acknowledgement of their
debt to the Swiss designers – and they paid special
homage to Max Huber, who had begun work at Studio
Boggeri in 1940. Alongside reproductions of Huber's Italian
work is an account of the Allianz exhibition In Zurich a few
months earlier: 'Looking at the works there, many people
will ask where is the art in them.' No help is given to
answer this point, but the account notes

> many points of contact with the more recent
> developments in typography. This stands out very
> clearly with the 'Constructives'. What is surprising
> with them – and they are never able to do enough
> playing with lines and planes, circles and spirals
> and superimposition and aiming to extract the best
> from the infinite possibilities – is the clean precision
> and discipline of their work.[1]

Presumably written by Huber himself, this is not only an
explicit acknowledgement of the interrelation of Swiss
Abstract art and graphic design, but it is one of the first
instances of the use of the term 'Constructive' to describe
the Modernists.

Huber had returned to Zurich when Italy entered the
war in 1941. He was the youngest of the Swiss Concrete
artists in the Allianz exhibition and was also among
the Zurich Concrete artists who showed at the Galerie
des Eaux Vives during the war years. Huber designed
three covers for the gallery's monthly bulletin,
Abstrakt–Konkret, which appeared in 1944 and 1945.

In both artistic and political interests, Huber followed
Max Bill and Richard Paul Lohse. Like them, he worked for
left-wing publications. When he returned to Milan after
the war, he was responsible for design at the publishers
Einaudi and in 1947 he designed posters, signage and a
catalogue for the 8th Milan Triennale. Huber's work at this
period included his often-reproduced posters for the

▲ 'Abstract and Concrete Art', poster
designed by Max Huber for an
exhibition in Milan, 1947. The artists
included Huber and several of his
Zurich colleagues.
The design, typically 'concrete', is
based on the triangles produced by
tilting a square at 30° to touch the
sides of a rectangle. The left-hand
edge and bottom line of the main title
are positioned on a square in the top
right-hand corner.

---

1. *Typographische Monatsblätter*, August/September 1942, pp.177-90.

136

▶ Poster for the ski resort Flums,
designed by Carlo Vivarelli, 1940.
Lithographic printing in three colours.
The repetition of a single photograph
of a skier was a trick used by Herbert
Matter. Vivarelli, who was 21 when he
produced this design, has made the
effect of movement more cinematic; by
reversing the figure, he has suggested
the skier's turn across and down the
slope. Instead of a naturalistic image,
blue sky and sunshine are symbolized
by the yellow disc, blue lettering, and
unprinted white of the background.
▼ Page from a brochure designed by
Herbert Matter, reproduced in the
French magazine *Arts et Métiers
Graphiques*, no. 51, February 1936.

▼ A5 catalogue cover for
the 8th Milan Triennale, 1947,
designed by Max Huber.

▼ Small poster for the meeting of the
International Congresses of Modern
Architecture (CIAM), designed by Max
Huber, 1949.
Printed offset in black, red, yellow and
green.

▶ 'Monza Autodrome Grand Prix',
small poster designed by Max Huber,
1948.
Printed offset.

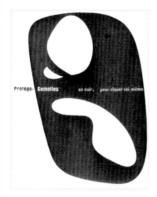

▲ Advertisement for do-it-yourself leather soles, designed by Carlo Vivarelli, 1946.
▼ Advertisement by Carlo Vivarelli for insulation material, 1947.

Monza motor races and for an exhibition of the Italian wartime resistance (see p.132). This poster's cut-out photograph, solid red background, white star and lowercase grotesque (set diagonally) exemplified the imaginative but economical two-colour graphic techniques of the next twenty years.

Modernism, it seemed, was easier to find beyond the Swiss border. In the monthly *Schweizer Graphische Mitteilungen – SGM* (Swiss Graphic News), Milanese typography appears repeatedly: four times in 1947 and 1948. Letterheads from Milan were reproduced, Max Huber's among them; they were selected by Max Bill, whose critical commentary was typewritten and, like most of the letterheads, in lowercase.[2] In 1948, *SGM* included examples of Milanese typography, among them, work by another Swiss designer, Carlo Vivarelli.

Work by Huber and Vivarelli amounted to almost half the work reproduced when the new Swiss magazine *Graphis* published Antonio Boggeri's account of Italian advertising graphics in 1947. Vivarelli worked at Studio Boggeri. Born in Zurich, he had studied at the Kunstgewerbeschule and for a short time with the poster artist Paul Colin in Paris. In 1940, aged twenty-one, he produced one of the simplest tourist posters, advertising the winter sports resort of Flums, in a simplified extension of the black-and-white photomontage technique that Herbert Matter used in letterpress brochures. In 1947 Vivarelli returned to Zurich, where he opened a design studio and was soon at work for the Züka (Zurich Canton Trade and Agricultural Exhibition). Although not a prolific designer, his standards of elegance and clarity were to make him one of the leaders of the Swiss Modernists. In 1949, his winning poster in the annual competition for the charity *Für das Alter* (Help the Aged) marked a further step in the formation of a specifically Swiss style: close-spaced bold Akzidenz Grotesk, and flat, unbroken areas, often juxtaposed with well-lit photographs, their three-dimensional depth restrained by cropping (see p.134).

▲ Symbol for twist-drill manufacturers, designed by Carlo Vivarelli, 1945.

Carlo Vivarelli 1919-1986

Graphic designer, painter and sculptor. Apprenticed in Zurich and student at Kunstgewerbeschule, 1934-39. Studied in Paris, 1939. Art director, Studio Boggeri, Milan, 1946-47. Freelance designer in Zurich from 1947.
Celebrated as winner of several design competitions, including logo for Swiss television, 1958.
Co-founder of *Neue Grafik* magazine, 1958. Concrete painter and sculptor from 1950.

2. *Schweizer Graphische Mitteilungen*, May 1947, pp.181-96.

The Magazines

The changing face of *Das Werk*
▼ In 1941 the cover of the magazine, printed on low-grade stock, had a workmanlike asymmetry suited to wartime austerity.

▼ By 1949 the magazine had dropped '*Das*' from its title, to become *Werk*. The cover forgot the lessons of New Typography to take on a hybrid and changing style. Such uncertainty reflected the general outlook of all but the most committed Modernists.

Hans Neuburg's contributions and Richard Paul Lohse's advertisements were among the rare signs of Modernism in *Das Werk*. The magazine's layout was unadventurous, its covers a muddled mixture of old and new. The main journal for advertising professionals, *Schweizer Reklame* (Swiss Advertising), paid occasional attention to design. It reappeared as an independent magazine in 1946 after a ten-year merger with the long-established monthly *Schweizer Graphische Mitteilungen – SGM* (Swiss Graphic News). *SGM* balanced printing industry news with serious professional articles on typography and design. Its editors were Hermann Strehler and Rudolf Hostettler, both expert and, in general, traditional typographers: *SGM* was impeccably typeset in Baskerville. Typical of the magazine's serious attitudes in the mid-1940s was the flow of authoritative – sometimes authoritarian – contributions from Jan Tschichold, mostly on book design. Only rarely was attention given to the kind of New Typography which Tschichold had helped to inspire only a decade earlier. For example, of the 'Best Posters of the Year' reproduced in the June 1946 issue, none was Modernist. The editors were nevertheless catholic in their allegiances; within a year Hostettler wrote knowledgeably about Modernist trademarks (designed by Herbert Bayer, Piet Zwart, Max Bill, Max Huber) and about current English typography; and he was both impresario and conciliator in some fierce debates in the mid-1940s.

Graphis, a different kind of magazine, had been launched in 1944 as a bi-monthly of 'graphic and applied art', extravagantly produced, well illustrated, and extensive in its coverage. With all kinds of graphic design, from advertising and shop window display to fine art prints, *Graphis* also included serious historical articles. The editors, Walter Amstutz and Walter Herdeg, had worked together on tourist publicity for St Moritz before the war, and had opened a joint advertising practice in Zurich in 1938.

Graphis was the official journal of the Association of Swiss Graphic Designers, the Verband Schweizerischer Graphiker (VSG). Designers and photographers were able to promote their specialist services in small illustrated advertisements. But Amstutz and Herdeg aimed at an international audience. Text and captions were printed in German and English. And they made a great effort to give graphic design the same cultural weight as painting. For covers, Herdeg sought contributions abroad from illustrious artists, always unpaid. Before 1950 he had successfuly cajoled Edvard Munch, André Derain and Picasso. Gottfried Honegger,

▲ Cover for *Typographische Monatsblätter*, January 1941, designed by Sepp Deimel. During the war the magazine lost most of its progressive attitudes. Covers were in every variation of banal good taste; Deimel's was an exception. *Typographische Monatsblätter* also held competitions for the magazine's design.
▼ Emil Ruder's unsuccessful entry in a competition for the cover design, 1946. Ruder later became an important influence as a typographer and teacher.

▲ *Graphis* cover designed by the
co-editor, Walter Herdeg, 1946.
Four-colour printing, the angled bars
in yellow, blue and red.
Most covers to the magazine were
illustrations. Herdeg's was the first,
and one of the few, to suggest the
existence of Modernism. It was
also one of the first to exploit an
oscillograph image. Such photographs
were to appear repeatedly in the work
of the progressive designers over the
next decade.

the first Swiss Modernist designer to appear on the cover
– with the fiftieth issue in 1953 – was represented by
a woodcut. When Honegger's work in partnership with
Warja Lavater was reviewed, the emphasis was on
illustration, at the expense of his graphic design.[1]

Herdeg's pioneering work with photographic posters
should have identified him as progressive. But times had
changed. When Modernist design made its appearance
in *Graphis* it did so by chance, in the stylistically random
Swiss Posters of the Year. It was at least a decade before
any tendency could be seen as uniquely Swiss.

Though the magazine carried well-illustrated historical
articles, the editors were unwilling to revive memories
of the recent, anxious years before the war. An article on
a pioneer such as Hermann Eidenbenz makes no mention
of his prewar work. Eidenbenz appears – and this was not
misleading – as a hugely skilful professional who belongs
to a tradition of engraving and calligraphy.[2] On the other
hand, in Lohse's occasional appearances, he stands out as
a consistent Modernist, even in the book designs shown
alongside those of Tschichold. Hans Neuburg took every
opportunity to introduce a Modernist perspective;
reviewing the Basel Trade Fair for the magazine in 1948,
for example, it was a simple matter for him to contrast
the often kitsch eclecticism of the best commercial stands
with his own more architectural designs.[3]

Even if it was not the kind later recognized as
'Swiss style', *Graphis* made Swiss design known to
an international readership. And at the same time the
magazine introduced the work of foreign designers to
Switzerland. Americans in particular submitted examples
of work, whose publication in *Graphis* conferred status
and demonstrated professional recognition. So the
editors became arbiters with considerable influence.

Modernism was reflected back across the Atlantic by
reports in *Graphis* of the work of émigré European avant-
garde designers such as Herbert Bayer.[4] The eclectic taste
of the *Graphis* editors gave readers a picture of graphic
design at home which gave little comfort to the
Modernists, yet which helped to internationalize graphic
design and to establish Switzerland's important
contribution.

1. *Graphis* 24, 1948, pp.372-77.
2. *Graphis* 11/12, 1945, pp.326-35.
3. *Graphis* 22, 1948, pp.156-63.
4. *Graphis* 11/12, 1945, pp.348-58.

The printer's terms

Technical terms of the printing industry
Termes techniques des industries graphiques
Fachwörter der graphischen Industrie
Termini tecnici delle industrie grafiche
Vaktermen voor de grafische industrie

▲ Written by Rudolf Hostettler,
co-editor of *Typographische
Monatsblätter*, this A6 book was first
published in 1949. Although compact,
The Printer's Terms provides a five-
language guide in 200 pages. The
practical elegance of its typography, in
varying weights of Gill type, illustrated
with line drawings and photographs,
helped to confirm Switzerland's
reputation for precision and clarity in
dealing with technical information.

▲ Advertisement for shopfitters by
Alfred Willimann, 1944. The dot on the
'i' of 'Steiner', which helps readability,
is the axis for ranging the text left and
right.
Willimann's Steiner graphics are
one of the earliest examples of
a comprehensive house style; they
extended to include the logotype on
the factory roof.

▼ Six-page A4 leaflet advertising
iron pipework, designed by Hermann
Eidenbenz, 1944.
Printed letterpress.

Overlaying the photograph of
a bathroom with the coloured diagram
of the linkage of smaller waste pipes
to the main down-pipe demonstrates
the products' range and versatility.
The photographs of the pipes in
perspective give a clear idea of their
quality, relative size and possible
combinations.

folded inside   back   front cover

inside front cover (p.2)   p.3   p.4

Printing the cut-out photographs
in a pale tone allows the black type
to be placed so that each casting
is clearly named.

142

◄ 'This Is the Way We Are Helping.'
Poster by Adolf Flückiger for an
exhibition of work sponsored by
the Swiss Fund for European
Reconstruction, 1947.
The photograph is by Werner Bischof,
one of the most popular photographers
with the Modernists in Zurich.
The coarse screen of the black
half-tone suggests the topicality
of newspaper reproduction, unifies
the surface and reinforces the vigour
of the labourers by contrast with
the gentle help given the children
in the image printed in yellow.
The yellow is as surprising a colour
as the violet printing of 'So helfen wir'.
The letterforms predict the bold
grotesque typefaces which arrived
more than a decade later.

Postwar: Coexistence and Confrontations

▲ Poster for Union solid fuel bricks, designed by Fritz Bühler, 1943. Such photorealist poster designers, mainly in Basel, were classified by Hans Neuburg as 'Naturalists'. Completely 'sachlich', objective representation of the product was a recurring technique in poster design. In the same tradition as Baumberger's PKZ overcoat (p.29), such work displayed immense skill in its drawing and, as with Baumberger, the trade name is part of the drawing. No slogan is needed. The image alone expresses the quality of the fuel.
Fritz Bühler was one of the leading Basel designers. Several of the second generation of Modernists were apprenticed in his studio.

As in art, there were many styles of graphic design. After the war *Typographische Monatsblätter* carried out a survey.[1] Members of the Association of Swiss Graphic Designers (VSG) were invited to submit examples of their recent work. Sixty out of the 140 members responded; Hans Neuburg sorted them and their work into groups.

The first was made up of 'Naturalists': those designers whose work included drawn and painted illustration. Second were the 'Classicists', the typographers and calligraphers who used serif type and scripts in symmetrical arrangements. Third were 'Illustrators'. Fourth, and largest, was a group of 'Graphic graphic designers', a title invented for the uncategorizable, 'conceptual' designers, who included Pierre Gauchat and Fritz Bühler as well as those who were merely decorative or tasteful.

A fifth batch consisted of 'Avantgardists'. Twice as many examples of their work were shown as of any other: Neuburg assigned himself to this group. He explained that the impact of the 'Avantgardists' was 'powerful in relation to their numbers'. Well-known names were included among the 'Avantgardists' – Hermann Eidenbenz, Adolf Flückiger, Gottfried Honegger, Max Huber, Gérard Miedinger – besides the designers who went on to found the magazine *Neue Grafik* (New Graphic Design) twelve years later, namely Neuburg himself, Richard Paul Lohse, Carlo Vivarelli and Josef Müller-Brockmann.

At this time there were no intimations in Müller-Brockmann's work to suggest that it could lead to his celebrated geometrical and photographic ways of designing. Indeed, of the works shown, only those by Huber, Lohse, Neuburg and Vivarelli could be termed Modernist. They were an extreme wing of the 'Avantgardist' category. At the other extreme were the conservative commercial artists, who were mystified by the Modernists' restricted visual language, their exclusive use of Grotesk type, of photographic images and asymmetry. In the middle ground, but nonetheless still thought to be Avantgardist, were the sophisticated survivors of the 1930s: the supremely able, such as Gauchat and Eidenbenz, both also masters in specialist fields – the one as a book designer and illustrator, the other as a lettering designer and calligrapher. Alongside them, between the two extremes, were Ernst Keller, Alfred Williman and Walter Käch, all former heroes of Modernism and revered as teachers at the

▲ Poster designed by Herbert Leupin, 1947. Leupin, like Otto Baumberger a master in several styles, was one of the greatest of the Swiss poster artists, best known for his hyperrealist designs. Judged only on this poster, he might have been grouped with the 'avant-garde'. He has used a grotesque style of lettering, empty space, and a geometrical basis to the design – the axis of the conductor's baton, at a precise 30° angle, passes through the top corner.

▲ Small poster for Wengen ski resort by Werner Mühlemann, 1945. Mühlemann (born 1917), later a successful exponent of 'Constructive' graphic design, clearly follows Herbert Matter in a photomontage technique that was not easy to emulate. Printed offset in three colours.

---

1. *Typographische Monatsblätter*, July 1946, pp.235-62.

▲ 'Work and Bread through Metal-Saving: House Collection Begins on 20 April 1942'. Poster designed by Ernst Keller. The signs for work and bread are negative silhouettes.

▲ 'Safe from Want with Swiss Bread', poster designed by Willi Günthart, *c.*1941.
The words 'Swiss bread' have their pictorial equivalent in the wholesome barley ingredient, drawn in colour with photographic realism against a sky-coloured background.

Kunstgewerbeschule in Zurich. Whereas the work of the radical Modernists was mechanical in its execution, theirs looked handmade, even 'artistic'.

The style of images became a point of discussion. Describing 'Trends in Swiss Poster Style', the writer Georgine Oeri identified the 'magic realism' of the 'Basel School', whose artists could, for example, reproduce the hairs on an insect with microphotographic precision; such technique, she claimed, took the soul out of what was illustrated, and left no room for the imagination.[2]

Although Basel designers supplied half the posters selected as 'Best Posters of the Year', in various styles, they were nevertheless 'not the whole of Swiss poster design'. Oeri contrasted the Basel school's gratuitously precise representation with Pierre Gauchat's Embru poster, where the photographic realism of the exposed mattress springs was intrinsic to the message (see p.127). Her five final illustrations were all from Zurich: designs by Gauchat, Willi Günthart, Ernst Keller, Gérard Miedinger and Alfred Willimann. They suggest a new style 'in that they treat the surface as a dynamic field of tension, that they convert the image into an abstract sign without surrendering its representational purpose'.

To talk of 'abstract signs' was a remarkably advanced use of critical language to discuss graphic design. In 1922 Lissitzky had asserted, 'Every flat surface is a sign – not a mystical symbol, but a concrete sketch of reality. A sign is a form through which we express reality.'[3] Such a formulation anticipates information theory of the 1950s, but it was years before this line of theoretical discussion was followed in Switzerland.[4]

The essential argument in the 1940s was about style. In *Werk*, Georgine Oeri ends her essay by quoting Van de Velde's forty-year-old view, that 'the question of style is not an art question'. Style would be imposed by the machine, it would be rational design compatible with industrial production. Modernism's natural home was industry; and it was at industry's door that Hans Neuburg was persistently knocking. In 1945 *Typographische Monatsblätter* gave him the space to illustrate his arguments for 'Industriewerbung' with his own designs.

2. Georgine Oeri, 'Tendenzen im Schweizer Plakatstil' (Trends in Swiss Poster Style), *Werk*, July 1946, pp.237-40.
3. 'New Russian Art: A Lecture', in Sophie Lissitzky-Küppers, *El Lissitzky: Life, Letters, Texts*, London 1968, p.334.
4. In the late 1950s Max Bill introduced communication theory at the Hochschule für Gestaltung at Ulm. Only in the wake of French structuralism in the 1970s did theoretical attitudes find a place in Swiss graphic design, notably introduced by Wolfgang Weingart and others in *TM*.

▲ Cover for a two-colour brochure for greenhouses and heating, designed by Hans Neuburg, 1946.
Neuburg used this illustration when he placed himself in the ranks of the 'Avantgardists'. The photograph, as a direct image of the product, is linked to the whole area of the page by geometry, both hidden and obvious. The perspective of the greenhouse has its vanishing point on the diagonal of the page. A square in the top right corner determines the position of the top of the photograph, which is aligned on its base, and the main heading and black vertical strip are ranged on its left-hand edge.

▲ Neuburg's symbol for Oertli machine tools, 1946.

▲ Hans Neuburg's postwar personal logo, 1946. Using the section of an 'I'-beam made clear that his specialism was publicity for industry. Neuburg persisted throughout the war in promoting his idea of 'Industrie-Graphik' in magazines, often using his earlier work as illustrations.

He explained that they were

the outcome of experience over many years of making graphic design for industry. From these examples it should be readily understood what industrial publicity relies on: clear description and presentation of the product or service; on catching the eye and exciting interest; in using a new type of design which excludes formalism and where the graphics are not an end in themselves. We think it justified to show our own work as the expression of a genuine interest to make graphic design serve industrial marketing.[5]

Neuburg was arguing for himself and his friends. In his concerns about formalism he is disingenuous. Like Lohse, who had been continuously busy in advertising for industry since the 1930s, his own style was loaded with formal borrowings from Constructivism.

Constructivism had been acknowledged by Tschichold as the origin of his typographic revolution. He had long ago put aside the crude decorative elements of Elemental Typography. He had refined his New Typography in the book *Typographische Gestaltung*, still advertised in *Graphis* ten years after its publication. But in the eyes of the Modernists, Tschichold had, by the end of the war, taken up a reactionary position. In December 1945 he gave a lecture in Zurich explaining his new attitude.

The substance of his views was given six months later in a single page of *Typographische Monatsblätter*.[6] They were a passionate argument on three issues: symmetry, grotesque typefaces and, more fundamentally, on the relationship between design, content and reader; the reader was important to Tschichold, since his work was mostly in book design. He made the simple distinction between the demands of book design and other types of graphic design: to be lasting, a book had to follow conventions, while commercial design was ephemeral and, in its nature, attention-seeking.

Reports of the lecture led to a famous polemic. Max Bill responded to Tschichold's assertions in *Schweizer Graphische Mitteilungen (SGM)*.[7] This was an eight-page insert, laid out by Bill himself, printed in grey and black. Its ten illustrations showed Bill's work to be an extension of Tschichold's prewar asymmetrical, sanserif typography. Describing himself as occupied 'more with the stylistic characteristics of the epoch than with ephemeral manifestations of contemporary fashions',

Bill demonstrated that the New Typography was still relevant, even for book design, the area where Tschichold considered it especially inappropriate.

Bill launched an attack on those who had retreated to the 'tried and true'. His argument was as follows:

Typography is the design of text areas in a way similar to the rhythmic organization of flat planes in modern Concrete art. These text areas consist of letters which join together as words. The proportions of the letters and their different weights and sizes are absolute, given factors. In no other kind of design are there so many precisely predetermined elements. It is the precision of this basic material that gives typography its special character.

. . . . It is not always easy to reconcile this mathematically precise medium with the arbitrariness of the written word as an image and to give it a precisely appropriate form: but this is the aim of every aesthetic-typographic endeavour. The requirements of language and legibility must be fulfilled before purely aesthetic considerations can be introduced. A text-image will always be most perfect when it combines a logical path for the eye to follow and balances typographical and aesthetic demands. Typography that is developed solely out of the given circumstances, meaning it works in an elemental manner with the basic constituents of typography, we call elemental typography ['elementare typographie']. When this typography is also directed towards designing text such that it becomes a living text organism, void of decorative trimmings and convolutions, then we would call it 'functional' or 'organic' typography. What this then means is that all requirements – technical, economic, functional and aesthetic – should be equally fulfilled and together influence the text-image.[8]

Bill pointed out that 'functional typography' was now different from the New Typography of the 1930s. Without the earlier crude decorative elements, there was greater clarity. He then came to a particular disagreement with Tschichold: over symmetry. Opponents of functional typography who claimed that centred type was essential to book typography were retreating into historicism.

Bill admitted that he was not a specialist. He was an architect and painter, politically engaged, for whom graphic design was part of a wider social picture. On the other hand, Tschichold was a professional typographer,

5. 'Industriewerbung' (Advertising for Industry), *Typographische Monatsblätter*, March/April 1945, p.74.

6. 'Graphik und Buchkunst' (Graphic Design and Book Design), *Typographische Monatsblätter*, July 1946, p.263.

7. 'Über Typografie', *Schweizer Graphische Mitteilungen*, April 1946, pp.193-200.

8. *Ibid.*, p.197.

146

▲ In defending Modernism in *Schweizer Graphische Mitteilungen* against Tschichold's attacks, Max Bill offered this A5 cover and text page to demonstrate the application of his own functional typography to book design. He points out that the title has been broken into three lines, according to the sense of the words.

trained in calligraphy and in the printing industry, widely experienced, steeped in his craft, a writer and historian of daunting erudition.

When Tschichold replied two months later, he quickly refers to Bill as 'the Zurich painter and architect'. He contrasts Bill – 'an amateur' – with his own professional status by supplying a curriculum vitae to establish his credentials, and he improves on Bill's reference to him as one of the 'well-known typographical theorists', describing himself as, 'to the best of my knowledge, the only one in German-speaking Europe'.[9]

Tschichold outlines his activities in the 1920s. He reminds readers that most print then was composed in a medley of typefaces with no sense of order. With his colleagues he had attempted a decontamination

> by returning to the simplest forms and rules. We saw aesthetic models in industrial products and, believing the sanserif to be the simplest typeface (wrongly, as it turned out), we declared it to be the modern face. . . we tried . . . to use asymmetry to oust symmetrical design, which was hardly ever employed in an intelligible manner. Everything symmetrical was . . . declared obsolete.[10]

Tschichold now thinks that this new typography as practised by Max Bill, 'conforms to the German tendency towards the absolute, its military will to regulate and its claim to omnipotence' – characteristics that brought Hitler to power and unleashed the Second World War. Tschichold seems uncomfortably aware of his earlier dogmatic tendencies and, at a time when he was anxious to acquire Swiss citizenship, he would have been keen to distance himself from his earlier political allegiances.

Bill's typography, says Tschichold, 'is marked, like my own work between 1924 and 1935, by a naïve worship of so-called technical progress'. Bill's captions had noted that his type was set by machine. But Tschichold maintains that the machine has deprived the print worker of satisfaction in his craft. Still, Tschichold was able to praise Bill's books, they all 'show great feeling for form and a sure taste', though he attacks Bill in detail for using unjustified (ragged right) setting, and for leaving a line space to indicate a new paragraph instead of indenting its first line. Bill's use of sanserif type is also questioned at length, Tschichold claiming that the revival of traditional faces is a more useful contribution to modern typography. He then reminds readers of his own rules:

▲ *Modern Swiss Architecture*, cover to the folder of loose-leaf sheets, designed by Max Bill, 1945, illustrated in his article in *Schweizer Graphische Mitteilungen*. The typography follows the design of the first part of this composite survey, which Bill carried out in 1938.

The method of typographical organization is one often previously practised by Tschichold – layouts arranged around a vertical axis, with words on the left of the axis ranged right and those to its right ranged left. Words with the same meaning or function may in this way be related vertically, as here, with the word 'Architecture' and the surnames of the contributors.

9. 'Glaube und Wirklichkeit' (Belief and Reality), *Schweizer Graphische Mitteilungen*, June 1946, pp.233-42.
10. *Ibid.*, p.234.

▶ This cover, designed by Tschichold in 1935. was reproduced in his dispute with Bill over the New Typography in 1946, for comparison with Bill's 1942 Allianz catalogue.

▼ Max Bill: Allianz exhibition catalogue cover, 1942. Type ranged right to a vertical axis, and type on the same line ranged left on the same axis, became a device of Swiss typography favoured by Bill. Such alignments gave a structure to the design without exaggerating the formal organization: the word Allianz sits on the top of an underlying square in the bottom left-hand corner; the right-hand side of the square is bordered by the list of names. Bill still follows the all-lowercase practice that he brought from the Bauhaus.

1. Fewest possible typefaces
2. Fewest possible type sizes
3. No letterspacing of lowercase (which was then still used for emphasis in German-speaking countries)
4. Emphasis by using italic or bold of the same face
5. Use of capitals only as an exception, then carefully letterspaced
6. Forming text lines into not more than three groups

Tschichold claims that Bill, without realizing it, follows these same rules. Bill, he says, is denying him the right to freedom of artistic expression. Tschichold hardly stops short of calling Bill a Nazi, as he is suppressing individual freedom, a freedom which 'perhaps a man must first lose, as I did, before he can discover its true value'.

Rudolf Hostettler, the co-editor of *SGM*, echoes Tschichold in summarizing the two distinct 'Directions in Swiss Typography'.[11] The first was design that related to the book; the second was in work related to trade, industry and advertising. Hostettler says that the majority of designers work in both ways, and among the books he illustrates are designs by Bill, Molzahn and Tschichold: all typeset in grotesque and in asymmetrical layouts.

The most reasoned response to the arguments came from the veteran German typographer Paul Renner, designer of the typeface Futura, and Tschichold's former principal at the printing school in Munich. He suggested a middle way. In the second of two *SGM* articles in 1948, with the title 'Modern Typography Will Become Functional Typography', he wrote that since symmetry was always present, asymmetry would be better described as 'ex-centric balance'.[12] Like the Werkbund, Renner found it unhelpful to assume that the 'old' is bad and that the 'new' is good. 'Modern' typography should be 'functional' in the sense that it put the reader first, as Tschichold did.

Not only those who thought of themselves as typographers were alive to the dispute. Hans Neuburg separated designers not into book designers on one side and commercial designers on the other, but into those who accept or reject drawn illustration.[13] He doubted if

▲ Typesetting on the letterheads of Jan Tschichold and Max Bill in 1945 demonstrates their standpoints. Tschichold's is set in a serif typeface (Garamond) using capitals, small capitals and upper- and lowercase, centred.
Tschichold, in the note typed on his letterhead in 1945, says that he has left off information (which was always on Modernist stationery) such as the telephone number ('I hate the telephone,' he says) and he identifies the typeface as 'the Monotype recutting of Van Dijck, a Dutch seventeenth-century design'.

The typesetting on Max Bill's letterhead is in Akzidenz Grotesk type, using lowercase only, arranged asymmetrically.
Bill stresses the importance of the exact spacing of the words, and even the space within the words. He has, for example, divided the single word of the street name into three units of meaning: 'Limmat tal strasse' – 'Limmat' (the river), 'Tal' (valley), 'Strasse' (street). The information is in two parts: who and what on the right, where and how on the left. When the A4 sheet is folded twice at right angles to fit a C6 envelope, the vertical fold is between the two horizontal rules.

11. Rudolf Hostettler, 'Typographische Strömungen in der Schweiz', *Schweizer Graphische Mitteilungen*, December 1946, pp.455-63.
12. 'Die moderne Typographie wird funktionell sein', *Schweizer Graphische Mitteilungen*, July 1948, p.312. The first article, 'Uber moderne Typographie', appeared in *SGM* in March 1948, pp.119-20. Paul Renner (1878-1956) was a German typographer, type designer, teacher, writer and painter. From 1927 to 1933 he was Director of Munich's chief printing school, Meisterschule für Deutschlands Buchdrucker. Designer of Futura typeface, 1927. Grand Prix, Milan Triennale, 1933. Harassed by the Nazis, in 1933-1934 he spent a short time in Switzerland, where he designed several booklets for the Swiss Tourist Board. (See Christopher Burke, *Paul Renner*, London 1998, pp.140-143.)
13. 'Die Gegenwartsströmungen in der Schweizerischen Zweckgraphik' (Contemporary Trends in Swiss Commercial Design), *Typographische Monatsblätter*, July 1946, pp.235-60.

148

Tschichold, from the outbreak of war, rarely returned to asymmetry. Book design was his main activity in Switzerland.
In his dispute with Max Bill, Tschichold argues that a satisfactory form for the book had been established over centuries, and there was no reason to change its conventions.

▲ Title page for a collection of Persian poetry, designed by Tschichold in 1945, reproduced as part of his response to Max Bill's Modernism. In the caption, Tschichold claims that, in his design, 'The content of the book demanded an ornamented title page.'
▼ Tschichold produced a further design for the same title page to demonstrate that a 'functional' asymmetry was unsuited to the book's content.
By the standards of Tschichold's earlier asymmetrical book typography, this looks less like a serious design than a coarse attempt to ridicule Bill's position.

'we will find our salvation in conjuring up the tried and tested.' And Pierre Gauchat was not prepared to take sides. 'Is someone unmodern', he asks, 'because, instead of being happy with the apparently pure, unsullied contemporary Grotesk typeface, they are passionately excited by the beauties of Garamond [type] . . .?'[14] Form should give a context to the content, Gauchat argued, and, as a demonstration, he set the six letters of the name Goethe in more than thirty different typefaces. 'One of these will seem the most suitable while all the others will be either less appropriate or utterly out of the question.' In choosing one rather than any of the others, he concludes: 'To stage Hamlet in evening dress is certainly original, but it is wrong and it is insensitive.'

Only when a new generation joined the ranks of designers could the Modernists win ground. The lessons of the New Typography and Constructivist attitudes had been absorbed by many of the art school teachers. But now they were history. No longer were there the powerful influences from Germany and Russia; in a war-ravaged Europe, designers were no longer able to extend their training with further study abroad.

This left those who had inherited the Constructivist tradition – the Avantgardists – to reassert the values of Modernism. It was often a bitter struggle. When Tschichold was persuaded to go to England to work for the paperback publisher Penguin Books, Bill wrote to the American designer Paul Rand: 'Tschichold is leaving Switzerland, so we will be rid of the evil that we invited in the first place.'[15] He was not gone for long. When he was back, he conceded that what was quite wrongly described as 'the style of our time' is 'not entirely useless for ephemeral pieces of print, but sterile, since it cannot create a new tradition'.[16] In book design, perhaps. But in other fields of graphic design the Swiss were to prove Tschichold wrong: they had already founded a new tradition.

---

14. *Ibid.*, p.237.
15. Letter to Paul Rand, quoted in Paul Barnes (ed.), *Jan Tschichold: Reflections and Reappraisals*, New York 1995, p.48.
16. 'Wirken sich gesellschaftliche und politische Umstände in der Typographie aus?' (Do Social and Political Circumstances Affect Typography?), *Schweizer Graphische Mitteilungen*, June 1948, p.249.

▲ Dust jacket for 'The Flight from Time', the journals of a former Dadaist in Zurich, designed by Jan Tschichold, 1945.
Tschichold believed that book jackets were discarded by the reader and, as ephemera, could have the same graphic style as advertising.
Unlike the book jackets designed by Modernists such as Lohse, the design gives no hint of the book's content or context. In his commitment to traditional forms of layout and typography, Tschichold went so far as a return to his first skill: calligraphy.

▶ *Die Farbe* (Colour), A5 catalogue for the Zurich Kunstgewerbemuseum, cover by Max Bill, 1944.
Bill also designed the poster with a similar triangulated design.
The exhibition was an example of the programme of public education carried out by the museums.
The catalogue, with an introduction by Johannes Itten, contained essays about the science and psychology of colour.

Emil Ruder 1914-1970

Graphic designer, typographer, teacher and writer. Trained as typesetter in Basel, 1929-33. Studied in Paris, 1938-39. Further printing studies at Zurich Kunstgewerbeschule, 1941-42. Typographic teaching at various levels, Basel Allgemeine Gewerbeschule, from 1942. Head of Department and finally Director of the Gewerbeschule and Gewerbemuseum from 1965. His important textbook, *Typographie,* was published in 1967.

die farbe

kunstgewerbemuseum zürich   1944

Schweizer Graphische Mitteilungen St.Gallen
Verlag Willy Verkauf, Wien

Die Farbe

Emil Ruder Kurze Farbenlehre für den Buchdrucker

▲ Cover and two inside pages of *Die Farbe: Kurze Farbenlehre für den Buchdrucker* (Colour: Short Course for Letterpress Printers), written and designed by Emil Ruder, 1948.
Ruder became one of the leading figures of Swiss typography.
▶ *Die Farbe* covers every aspect of colour in letterpress typography, including greys produced by 'rainbow' printing (on the left) and by varying thickness of rules, varying spacing of rules, and varying size of type.

150

Book Design

Asymmetrical layout and Grotesk type were the conventions adopted by Modernist designers such as Richard Paul Lohse. Their usual practice was to devise a basic modular grid, into which the text and images were fitted.
▼ ▶ Richard Paul Lohse's design of *Wir Neger in Amerika* (Us Blacks in America) 1945, a translation of Richard Wright's *Twelve Million Black Voices*.

Wir Neger in Amerika

The squares on the front cover boards imply the module of spaced squares which underly the page layouts: three squares across, four down. The white space on the page is varied to allow the photographs to appear where they relate to the text, or to make telling juxtapositions. Paragraphs are indicated by line spaces, a method disapproved of by Tschichold.

▼ *Der Film: wirtschaftlich, gesellschaftlich, künstlerisch* (The Film: Economic, Social, Artistic), a book designed by Hermann Eidenbenz, 1947.
Der Film was published four years after an exhibition on the history of cinema at the Basel Gewerbemuseum. The authors say that it is not a catalogue of the exhibition, but a reworking and enlargement of the material. 'This book is neither a picture book (although it has more than 160 pictures), nor is it a theoretical treatise (although it offers a complete "theory of film"). It is both at the same time. Image and word are so closely related that we read the words in the images and the images in the words.'
So important was Eidenbenz's contribution that his name as designer appears on the front cover.

Der Film is in A4 format. Instead of numbering each of the book's 144 pages, left- and right-hand pages of the double-page spreads are given the same number, emphasizing their interdependence.
On the cover – printed in black with text in the four orange rectangles – Eidenbenz establishes the maximum number of film stills of a practical size that would fit the format. Though this sets out the basic three-column structure, the vertical placing of images within the columns is controlled only by the demands of the verbal-visual message.
The text alongside the images is an advanced example of 'functional typography'. Sentences are broken into phrases, often attached to the image, ranged right on the left of an image, and ranged left on the right.

▼ *Kamera und Auge* (Camera and Eye), written and designed by Werner Graeff, 1942.
In 1929 Graeff's *Es Kommt der neue Fotograf!* was the pioneering book which integrated text and image. He continued these innovations in Germany, but the two textbooks Graeff produced in wartime Switzerland (the other was on designing brochures) were simple expositions of their subject. Using his own line drawings to present the basic information, the pages are exemplary in their clarity and organization.

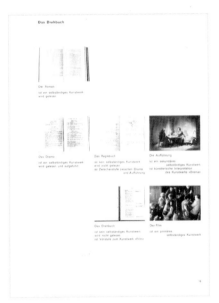

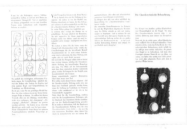

Exhibitions

▲ Full-colour poster for the Swiss Trade Fair, designed by Hermann Eidenbenz, 1944. Although superficially anti-Modernist in its symmetry, serif type, and drawn illustration rather than photography, what better symbol for Swiss precision could Eidenbenz have chosen than the builder's plumbline weight? How better to suggest the context than the sunlit streamers in the country's red and white against a summer sky?

▼ The Fair included an exhibition, 'Arbeitbeschaffung' (Job Creation), designed by Pierre Gauchat. At its centre was the plumbline.

▲ Dominoes share a simple geometry with the work of the Concrete artist-designers. Gauchat used panels like domino tiles, to show that each idea they represented was necessary to the whole, and that one falling would create the 'domino effect'.
Unusually for an exhibition space, the surrounding walls were empty, painted in primary colours, and text and images were back-projected on a single screen at the far end.

Switzerland needed to promote its business abroad, even in wartime.[1] As a neutral country it could profit from trade fairs and exhibitions in Axis or occupied countries: in Holland and Austria in 1941, in France and Czechoslovakia in 1942. These required and were given a conventional, even kitsch, presentation.

Exhibitions sponsored by local and central government, some travelling, became a significant part of designers' activity. The simplest were little more than enlarged book pages, but some, such as Gauchat's 'Arbeitbeschaffung' (Job Creation) exhibition in 1944, used the space rather as a theatre stage on which visitors were confronted by a variety of media: slogans, photographs, projected images, an architectural model.

Austerity did not restrict the Swiss Werkbund's programme of public education in design. They returned to the didactic exhibitions of the interwar years, though without 'New' as part of the title. In 1943 the Werkbund launched 'Unsere Wohnung' (Our Home) – the travelling exhibition advertised by Richard Paul Lohse's poster – to encourage people to look once more at domestic design (see p.130).

The Werkbund aim was to include Good Design in the programme for postwar reconstruction. Max Bill organized an exhibition of Swiss industrial design to tour Germany and Austria, and later published an essay which took up Henry van de Velde's concept of 'functional beauty', the criterion by which production would be judged, now and in the future.[2] Van de Velde became a partner and inspiration to the Werkbund. He was now well into his eighties, a veteran in the same fight to raise standards of design and production and against a degradation of public taste. In 1947 he addressed the Werkbund's annual meeting, when he gave an account of his own efforts earlier in the century, and proposed that the Werkbund devise a unified strategy.

The campaign opened with an exhibition two years later, in 1949, at the Swiss Trade Fair at the Basel Mustermesse. The exhibition, 'Die gute Form' (Good Design), was sponsored by the Ministry of the Interior and toured to various European cities. The design, by Max Bill, consisted of panels of text and photographs, not only of designed objects but also of natural forms and scientific images.

▲ Exhibition stand at the Basel Trade Fair for the machine parts manufacturer Oskar Rüegg, 1947. Designed by Hans Neuburg, following the house style established by Anton Stankowski more than ten years earlier (see p.39).

---

1. The Milan Triennale took place in 1940, before Italy joined the war. Eidenbenz was obliged to improvise the graphics for the Swiss pavilion on a far smaller budget in a structure crude by comparison with Bill's of 1936.
2. 'Schönheit aus Funktion und als Funktion' (Beauty from Function and as Function), *Werk*, August 1949, pp.272-75.

▶ 'Zurich Artists in the Helmhaus', poster by Richard Paul Lohse, 1950. One of the earliest large-scale examples of the structural and decorative role of basic geometry and a forerunner of the dominant 'constructive' tendency of the 1950s. Printed litho.

Geöffnet von 10-12 und 14-18 Uhr
Samstag und Sonntag bis 17 Uhr,
Montag geschlossen.
Eintritt 55 Rp., illustrierte
Ausstellungszeitung inbegriffen.
Mittwoch nachmittags, abends
und Sonntag vormittags frei.

Jeden Mittwoch 20.15 Uhr
Diskussionsabend:
Sie fragen — wir antworten!

Zürcher Künstler im Helmhaus

Zürcher Künstler im Helmhaus

Unter dem Patronat des Stadtrates von Zürich

11. November – 20. Dezember 1950

Lohse SWB Zürich / J.C. Müller A.G. Zürich 8

The design had its origin in a the masthead which Lohse designed for the Helmhaus exhibition space. The masthead lettering ran vertically, and Lohse retained this in the poster. But he thought a vertical title was not suitable for a poster, which had to be read quickly, so he repeated the title horizontally.
Red and green are overprinted to give a near black.

Lohse wrote that 'the poster made up of planes of colour demands of the designer the most extreme concentration on form and colour, and the displacement by a few centimetres is enough to have a positive or negative outcome.' (Richard Paul Lohse, *Lohse Lesen*, Zurich 2003, p.117.)

154

▶ Painted wood wall sculpture by Lohse outside a café at the 1947 Zurich Canton Trade and Agricultural Exhibition (Züka). The Concrete artists took every opportunity to bring art to the public.

▼ Poster for the 'Concrete Art' exhibition in 1944, designed by Max Bill. Printed in black from linoblock, cut by the printer from Bill's hand-drawn lettering. The exhibition included works by Max Bill, Richard P. Lohse and Max Huber, all also graphic designers. The persistence of the band of Concrete artist-designers underpinned the development of the austere Swiss style that emerged in the 1950s.

▼ The Education pavilion at the Züka. It was claimed that the 'Landi-style' had been replaced by a 'Züka-style', recognized by its 'squares, circles, triangles and other geometrical forms'. Every designer had a 45° and 60° set square to hand at their drawing board, so that the diagonals and triangles of Lohse's and Max Bill's paintings were quickly appropriated, both as motifs and as underlying structures of designs.

Van de Velde was astonished. Though he deplored the extravagance of trade fairs and their irrelevance to the objects they were intended to promote, this innovation nonetheless reminded him of his earlier struggles to bring aesthetic value to everyday objects: 'Before me stood an embryo of the Temple (a Museum of Pure Form) which I had once planned.' [3] 'Die gute Form' exhibitions became annual events, and the Werkbund awarded seals of approval to selected products.

The same year as the first 'Die gute Form' exhibition, the huge 'Zurich Canton Trade and Agriculture Exhibition' – Züka – was held on the shores of Lake Zurich. Though partly a trade show, it should have pleased Van de Velde. It certainly furthered the Modernist cause. Hans Neuburg reported that, eight years after the Landi, a 'Züka-style' had emerged: here 'squares, circles, triangles and other geometrical forms' were dominant features in the work of its architects as well as its graphic designers; and the display panels were organized on a rectangular grid.[4] This style, Neuburg claimed, was intended to give a lead to future developments. An accurate forecast: prominent among those designing for the Züka were his future co-editors of *Neue Grafik* – Lohse, Müller-Brockmann and Carlo Vivarelli.

For the future of graphic design, besides the 'Grafik' exhibition in 1943, the regular exhibitions which included Concrete art were important in carrying the spirit of Modernism. And they were uniquely Swiss. In 1944, before the war ended, with the country surrounded to the north, east and west by regimes where Abstract art was anathematized, the exhibition 'Konkrete Kunst' (Concrete Art) opened in Basel. Works which could not be moved across frontiers were represented by photographs. The organizers had no way of knowing that the only missing hero of Constructivism, Lissitzky, had died in Moscow in 1942. Twenty-two works by Max Bill were included, and seven by Lohse. With this and the annual Allianz exhibitions, Concrete art can be seen, in retrospect, as a national style.

Max Bill designed the Werkbund's 'Die gute Form' (Good Design) exhibition in 1947, which realized Van de Velde's ideas, matured over 50 years.
◄ Entrance sign with Bill's sculpture. Bill was always happy to combine symmetry and asymmetry, and to introduce Concrete art into design.
▼ Designed to tour, the exhibition was made up of square panels fixed to floor-to-ceiling wooden frames which could be arranged to suit different spaces.

◄ One of the square panels in 'Die gute Form', illustrating classic modern furniture. The demountable campaign chair (from Wohnbedarf) was included in the show with a few carefully selected domestic items.

3. 'Formes: De la pure forme utilitaire', *Werk*, August 1949, p.245.
4. 'Die Graphik an der Züka', *Werk*, March 1948, p.79.

► 'Swiss Goods', poster designed
by Carlo Vivarelli, 1951.
The design incorporates the 1930s
crossbow emblem of Swiss quality.

3

Towards a Swiss Style
1950-1957

The wish to create a Swiss typographical style was expressed three years ago. . .
So far this dream has not been realized, and it looks as though it never will be.

Rudolph Hostettler, 'Entwicklungsmöglichkeiten in der Typographie' (Possibilities of Development in Typography),
Schweizer Graphische Mitteilungen, January 1951

158

Schweiz. Foto- und Kinoausstellung

F

Kongresshaus Zürich 17.—23. Mai

Fotografie

in Industrie

Handel

Staat

Gewerbe

Medizin

Kinematografie

Geöffnet 10—22 Uhr.

◄ 'Swiss Photo and Film Exhibition', poster designed by Gottfried Honegger, 1951. The poster gives a popular view of photography, although the exhibition demonstrated its commercial applications. Honegger's versatility is shown in the way he matches his technique to the subject: he rescues professional and amateur attitudes to photography from kitsch by his jaunty montage. Honegger uses a black-and-white photograph with light colour tints. Lithoprinted.
Honegger reveals himself as being firmly in the 'anonymous' rather than the 'individualist' category, but he has ignored the doctrinaire insistence on all-lowercase typography.

Gottfried Honegger Born 1917
Graphic designer, exhibition designer,
art director and painter. Studied at
Zurich Kunstgewerbeschule, training
in shop-window display. Opened studio
with his wife, Warja Lavater, 1937.
Wartime military service. Teacher at
Kunstgewerbeschule from 1948.
Art director, Geigy, Basel, 1955-58.
Since 1960 his main activity has been
as a Concrete artist.

In 1955 the curator of the Zurich Kunstgewerbemuseum decided that the public should be given an idea of what graphic designers actually did – their everyday activity. The result was an exhibition with the title 'Grafiker: ein Berufsbild' (Graphic Designer: Picture of the Profession). Not merely a show of work, it gave a historical account of Swiss graphic design, showing the scope of designers' professional activity, and the tools and processes they used.

The exhibition indicated the vast range of designers' work: drawings and illustrations; book, newspaper and magazine design; posters; advertisements; trademarks; leaflets, brochures and catalogues; calendars; stamps; packaging; business stationery; wrapping paper, labels and carrier bags; personal stationery and announcements (such as bookplates and wedding invitations); official and security print (such as share certificates, cheques, lottery tickets, diplomas); film titling; photomontages for exhibitions; three-dimensional models, and lettering on buildings.

On show was work by designers belonging to the Association of Swiss Graphic Designers, the Verband Schweizerischer Grafiker (VSG). At this time there were five VSG branches, four representing the city centres of Basel, with 35 members; Berne, with 29; St Gallen, with 12; Zurich, with 105, and 11 in the group for French-speaking Switzerland.[1] Constituted as a professional organization in accordance with Swiss business law, the VSG took as its first commitment 'raising the status of graphic design and its promotion as an independent creative profession'. Its further interests were in training and qualifications, helping to arrange exhibitions and lectures, establishing relations with artists' groups and with other professional organizations, supervising competitions, and considering questions of copyright and plagiarism. The VSG published rules on commissioning procedure and a scale of fees, based on the type of work rather than the time taken to carry it out – which included the instruction that no work was to be undertaken without payment.

Members of the VSG were inclined to sessions of earnest self-examination. They asked such questions as, 'What is the graphic designer's task?', 'Should graphic design be educational?' and 'Is our graphic design properly contemporary?' When the VSG conducted an enquiry into the profession's aims in 1952, a preamble to the questionnaire sent to members quoted Johannes

▼ 'Graphic Designer: Picture of the Profession', an exhibition at the Zurich Kunstgewerbemuseum in 1955, organized and designed by Gottfried Honegger.

▼ Honegger's design of the catalogue cover, printed letterpress in black and lilac.

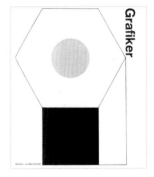

---

1. *Grafiker: ein Berufsbild*, catalogue, Kunstgewerbemuseum Zürich, 1955, pp.63-65.

160

Itten who, as long ago as 1929, had recognized the importance of 'the so-called graphic designer' as being, together with the architect, 'responsible for giving a visual character to modern life'. This was the line taken by most of the contributors to a windy debate. Emil Ruder expressed lofty aspirations for graphic design, writing that part of its function was to promote 'the good and the beautiful in word and image and to open the way to the arts'.[2]

Responses ranged from the high-flown, such as Ruder's, to the matter-of-fact banality of Carlo Vivarelli:

> The way of going about a commission and the choice of medium is largely defined by the individual task. In every case the designer should reject conventional graphic formulas – to feel his way into the nature of the task – and each time enjoy his pleasure in design and exploit his competence in design to the full.[3]

The necessary areas of professional expertise are listed in the *Grafiker* catalogue as follows: manual skill in executing a design, a knowledge of reproduction and printing techniques, and a grasp of business principles so as to understand how a design would answer the needs of the client; social sensitivity was also necessary, in order to understand how to make the message intelligible in the particular social circumstances. Finally, the catalogue explains that, as with everyone whose work impinges on the environment, designers have wider cultural responsibilities.

The catalogue also sets out the three ways that designers work – directly for the client, through an agency, or as direct employees. The sequence of a typical job is listed: client – sketches and rough designs – finalizing proposal – presenting design – negotiations and discussions – text – translations – finished drawing or artwork – photography – photomontage – retouching – lettering – typography – choosing paper – photoengraving – printing – binding – delivery – invoicing. The catalogue goes on to give an account of house styles (corporate identities), the role of graphics in education, the design of signs and symbols, the problems of plagiarism, and so on.

What *Grafiker* did not attempt was to describe various styles of design. Although differences are attributed geographically – a hyperrealist poster by Niklaus Stoecklin illustrates 'typical Basel work' – styles are said to be as individual as personal handwriting. In fact, the styles of young Swiss designers in the 1950s became simple to describe. Neuburg's classification of 'Naturalists, Classicists, Illustrators, Graphic graphic designers, and Avantgardists' was outdated. By 1957 a professional assessment in *Graphis* recognized only

> two fundamentally different lines of development: the one true to tradition – literary and illustrative – and the other progressive, with the emphasis very much on form and with a basically *anonymous* style.[4]

The first group, where 'personal traits come out more strongly', were mostly illustrators, and identified as 'individualist'. The writer, Robert S. Gessner, was Secretary of the VSG. Not only a graphic designer, but also a Concrete artist, he was naturally among the 'anonymous' designers. This group was

> at present establishing a supra-personal style closely allied to Concrete art. Its aim is the purely functional use of its media: it seeks the simplest and purest form of expression. . . . these artists are bent on bringing order, simplicity and clear formulation of the essential message into the modern flood of printed matter. They deliberately renounce the manifestation of personal artistic attributes in favour of the legitimate demands of information.[5]

Gessner had recognized no homogeneous Swiss style. Yet Johannes Itten had seen graphic designers as sharing a contemporary style with designers in other fields. At a Werkbund exhibition he identified common features:

> Fluidity, lightness, transparency, looseness, are the keynote of a new sensibility that appears in our exhibition, in the general style and in single items of household equipment, in chairs and textiles as well as in the graphic design.[6]

In the case of architects, product designers and weavers, Itten's observation might have been understandable. As far as the 'anonymous' graphic designers were concerned, it had little relevance. Indeed, fluidity and looseness were the opposite of their geometrically disciplined methods and their increasing preference for photographs over illustration. The younger designers' outlook was shared with the original Modernists, whose style was equally 'anonymous'. In practice, designers could be seen crossing the border between 'individualist' (illustrational) and 'anonymous'. The 'anonymous ' Gottfried Honegger, for example, shared a practice with his 'individualist' wife,

2. *TM,* November 1952, pp.569 *ff.*
3. *Ibid.*

4. Robert S. Gessner, 'Swiss Designers of the Younger Generation', *Graphis,* no.69, Jan/Feb 1957, p.13.
5. *Ibid.*
6. 'Die Werkbund Ausstellung in Kunstgewerbemuseum Zürich' (The Werkbund Exhibition in the Zurich Kunstgewerbemuseum), *Werk,* August 1950, p.228.

► A4 booklet for Swiss Industrial
Abrasives Ltd (SIA), designed by
Gottfried Honegger, 1956.
The basic arrangement by rectangles
contrasts with the curved forms –
side views of folded bands of abrasive
paper – and the cut-out photographs.
Printed letterpress.
The photographs are by Michael
Wolgensinger, a Werkbund member
popular with many of the Modernist
designers.

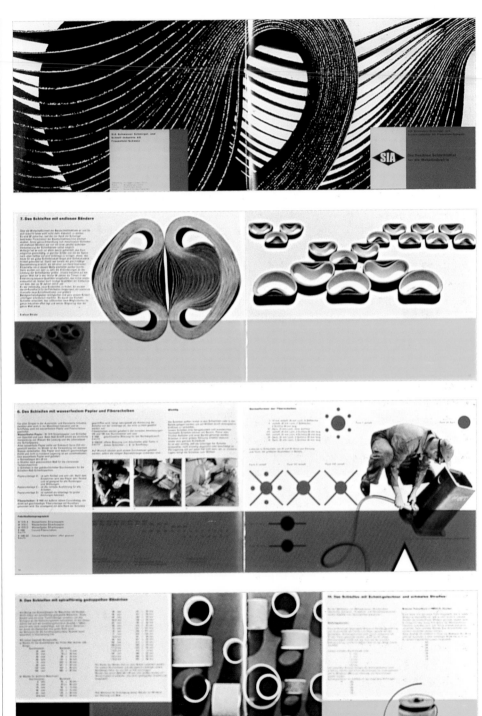

162

▲ Advertisement for a Geigy eye
ointment, designed by Armin Hofmann,
1952.
▼ Advertisement designed by Karl
Gerstner for a textile dye, 1953.
In a black-and-white advertisement,
Gerstner had little opportunity to
relate his image to dyestuffs: he used
a lithograph which he had produced
working independently – as an artist.

Irgalane Geigy

Warja Lavater, who was chiefly an illustrator. Work was
credited to 'Honegger-Lavater'. Although Gottfried
Honegger's style is inconsistent, his work around 1950
was some of the first to exemplify the complete 'Swiss'
style – the use of geometry and the formula of Akzidenz
Grotesk and photography. This was his style when
in 1955 he became art director of the huge chemical
company Geigy.

Chemical and pharmaceutical companies were
a significant part of the Swiss economy. Ciba, Geigy,
Hoffmann-La Roche, Sandoz – then international names –
were based in Basel. All kinds of print were designed to
advertise their products and activities to customers in
industry, agriculture and the medical profession.
They expected objective advertising, clear information
on products, and distinctive packaging and labelling.
The 'anonymous' style was perfectly fitted to meet
these demands.

The company to take most advantage of the style was
Geigy, producers of the enormously successful insecticide
DDT. Their products, in the form of powders, tablets and
potions, do not suggest graphic images. And yet the
company developed a style which, though essentially
'anonymous', had a free, experimental, student character.
The design team restricted themselves to a simple graphic
language; the typeface was always Berthold Akzidenz;
images were either photographs (sometimes X-rays)
or stylized drawings with a single thickness of line,
or a silhouette, identifying the part of the body at
which the treatment was directed. Photographs were
also used indirectly: a winter scene with skaters, for
example, served to recommend a product for treating
bone injuries.

In 1947 Geigy appointed Max Schmid as the firm's
publicity director. Schmid had a seven-year experience in
the studio of the versatile Fritz Bühler, who had been in
practice in Basel since 1933. But the Geigy style originated
in the teaching at the Allgemeine Gewerbeschule, where
Schmid and most of the designers employed by Geigy had
studied. By the time Schmid moved to the firm's New York
design studio in 1955, he left behind (and took with him to
the US) a Geigy style. This style, continued by his
successor Gottfried Honegger, was in fact the earliest
large-scale application of the methods of the recognizably
Swiss style.

Many of the most prominent designers of the 1950s
and 1960s were those who had worked at Geigy.
When they migrated from Basel, they helped to refresh
practice elsewhere. Nelly Rudin, for example, after three

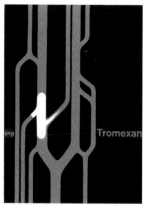

▲ Front of a brochure for an
anticoagulant drug, designed by Nelly
Rudin, 1956. After working freelance for
Geigy from 1951 to 1954, Rudin worked
in the design office shared by Ernst A.
Heiniger and Josef Müller-Brockmann
in Zurich before opening her own
practice there in 1957. In the 1960s
she turned to painting and became
a distinguished member of the group
of Zurich Concrete artists.

▲ Cover of the Italian-language
brochure advertising a hospital
disinfectant, designed by Elisabeth
Dietschi, 1956.
It was normal for designs to be adapted
for other languages. As with the bottle
here, silhouettes were a standard in
work by Basel-trained designers.

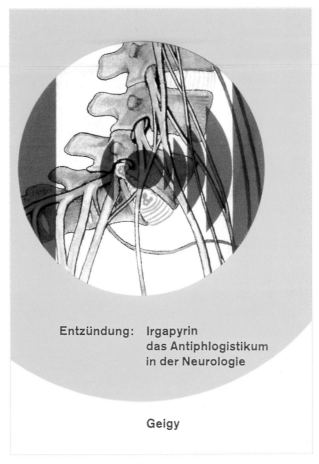

▲ Front cover of A5 leaflet for an anti-inflammatory drug, designed by Gottfried Honegger, c.1958. Printed letterpress.

▲ A5 card advertising an anti-inflammatory drug, designed by Jörg Hamburger, c.1956. The silhouette lay figure was typical of the images made by Basel students.

Hamburger left the Basel school in 1955. He worked at Geigy until 1958, when he moved as a designer to Josef Müller-Brockmann's studio in Zurich. He began freelance practice in 1960.

▲ Advertisement for Geigy infant's suppositories, designed by Jörg Hamburger, c.1956.
High contrast black-and-white photographs without grey tones became a common graphic technique much later. Popularly described as 'posterization', the technique used the methods and materials for making photoengraved line blocks (rather than the half-tone screen of graduated dots).
▼ A5 advertising card for the same Geigy product, designed by Jörg Hamburger, c.1956. The image of the child, printed in black, playing inside the glass marble, printed in red, demonstrates Hamburger's precocious skills.

▲ Packaging of suppositories for Geigy, designed by Nelly Rudin, c.1953.

▲ Labelling on detergent packaging for BP Petroleum, designed by Therese Moll in Karl Gerstner's studio, 1956. Moll, after study in Basel, was an assistant at Studio Boggeri in Milan. She returned, first to work with Gerstner, then at Geigy.

164

▲ 'If Blackmailers Are Threatening',
advertisement for police services,
designed by Josef Müller-Brockmann,
1952-53.
For a time, Müller-Brockmann's
illustrational style survived his
conversion to Modernist typography:
the text, broken into units of meaning,
is ranged left and right on a vertical
axis.

years freelancing for Geigy, was recruited by Josef
Müller-Brockmann for his studio in Zurich. Here she was
to be followed later by another from the Geigy studio,
Jörg Hamburger. Igildo Biesele came to Geigy from Paris;
Gérard Ifert went in the other direction, from Geigy to
Paris. After a short spell at Geigy, Fridolin Müller left Basel
for Zurich, where he opened his own studio in 1953.

Zurich had no focus of a consistent style such as
that provided by Geigy in Basel. On the contrary,
the varied allegiances of the city's chief designers
were illustrated in 1953 by an unusual project. The
Kunstgewerbemuseum advertised a huge international
poster exhibition and – avoiding a choice of style – invited
six designers to prepare a poster each, the principal
motif of each being a single letter of the word 'PLAKAT'
(poster). When hung together, they would make the
complete word. The remaining text was restricted to
Akzidenz Grotesk.

Designs for 'L' by Warja Honegger-Lavater and for 'K'
by Gérard Miedinger, completely geometrical, contrasted
with Hans Falk's painterly 'P'. Adolf Flückiger's 'A' was
obviously 'anonymous'. One of the six would not fit a
stylistic category, being partly 'individualist' illustrational,
partly Constructive. This was the letter 'T', with the
outline of a head in profile, drawn in the dark with a torch
and photographed as a time exposure. The designer was
Josef Müller-Brockmann.

Müller-Brockmann was a virtuoso professional
designer with a mannered style of drawing and long
experience of exhibition design. His drift from
'individualist' illustration to 'anonymous' graphics was
typical of the time. Whereas designers such as Lohse
had a longstanding, unwavering commitment to the
'anonymous' camp, for those such as Müller-Brockmann,
it was a matter of switching to the winning side in what
became a war of styles.

In 1952 Müller-Brockmann designed a series of
advertisements for the Zurich police. Their style was
hybrid: illustrations in a fashionable Paris-inspired
calligraphic manner, the text broken according to sense
into short lines of grotesque, in the best tradition of
functional typography (as practised by Max Bill in the
1930s). This shows the 'anonymous' style as being largely
a revival. Only when he was well into his thirties, and
influenced by work of the 1920s and 1930s, did Müller-
Brockmann turn from illustration, which he described as
'subjective', to photography and typography.

I avoided decorative elements and went after the
greatest objectivity [*Sachlichkeit*]. The same applied

Josef Müller-Brockmann 1914-1996

Graphic designer, illustrator, stage
designer, exhibition designer, teacher
and writer. Apprenticed as commercial
artist and studied at Zurich
Kunstgewerbeschule, 1932-34.
Freelance in Zurich from 1934.
Designed for the Landesausstellung,
1939. Army service, 1939-45. Worked
mainly in theatre and exhibition design,
and as an illustrator until 1950s.
Produced outstanding series of posters
for the Zurich Concert Hall, 1950-72.
Co-editor of *Neue Grafik* magazine,
1958-65. Succeeded Ernst Keller in
Graphic Design department at the
Kunstgewerbeschule, 1958-60. Author
of several influential books on graphic
design (see bibliography).

▶ Posters for 'Das Plakat',
the international poster exhibition
at the Zurich Kunstgewerbemuseum,
1953. Each letter of the word PLAKAT
was given to a different designer.
The result illustrates the leading
designers' wide range of styles,
from 'individualist' (illustrational) to
'anonymous'.

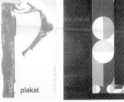

Hans Falk   Warja Honegger-   Adolf Flückiger   Gérard Miedinger   Celestino Piatti   Josef Müller-
             Lavater   Brockmann

▲ Given the letter 'A' of 'Plakat' for
the same exhibition, Adolf Flückiger
was more wholeheartedly 'anonymous'
than Müller-Brockmann, with all-
lowercase type and a photograph.
▶ Müller-Brockmann is alone in giving
both words of 'Das Plakat' an initial
capital letter. He has modernized his
style as an illustrator by drawing with
a torch in a long camera exposure.

166

▲ Poster for a Werkbund exhibition at Zurich Kunstgewerbemuseum as part of the annual June Festival, 1950. Design by Josef Müller-Brockmann, in his transitional style: image by drawn illustration, typography as practised by the 'anonymous' designers.

to photography: the subject had to appear with its own values and characteristics, straightforwardly and without any distraction [*Verfremdung*]. In purely typographic designs I tried to put the [printed] areas in contrasting tension with the blank unprinted areas.[7]

Was this a conscious re-orientation, or was Müller-Brockmann swept into the Modernist stream by the powerful personalities of the diehards, Lohse and Vivarelli?

Müller-Brockmann's conversion is recorded in the developing style of his series of posters for the Zurich Concert Hall. They have endured as one of the most distinctive contributions to Swiss graphic design. Starting in 1950, the series continued for more than twenty-five years. Müller-Brockmann began the posters using type and abstract imagery: some geometrical, some freely drawn. 'They could be taken to be an ear', Hans Neuburg said, 'or as a general symbol of the pleasures of listening' and 'to symbolize both musicality and musicianship'.[8] It was not long before Müller-Brockmann was to submit his painterly improvisations to geometrical correction.

Carlo Vivarelli, who instilled in me the fundamentals of typography and whose criticism I took seriously, commented that my use of geometrical elements was too subjective. This is what led to my making concert posters exclusively typographic. I now tried, using a dynamic organization of words and lines, to achieve a floating, transparent typography which would be able to give the effect of musical poetry.[9]

The posters looked like Concrete paintings, with words added. The source of Müller-Brockmann's images in Concrete painting is not hard to recognize. His originality lay in transforming his influences into designs that were appropriate and effective in their context.

▲ Zurich Concert Hall poster, designed by Josef Müller-Brockmann, 1951. Printed black and olive, linocut and type on cream paper.

▲ Zurich Concert Hall poster, designed as one of a series by Josef Müller-Brockmann, 1952. The abstract shapes are cut out of a lino block, printed letterpress. The same block was used for concert posters until 1954, printed in various colours and with different typographic arrangements for each concert.

7. J. Müller-Brockmann: *Mein Leben: Spielerischer Ernst und ernsthaftes Spiel*, Baden 1994, p.36.
8. 'Posters Seen from Three Angles', *Neue Grafik*, no.4, 1959, p.21.
9. J. Müller-Brockmann: *Mein Leben: Spielerischer Ernst und ernsthaftes Spiel*, Baden 1994, p.43.

▲ Zurich Concert Hall poster for
a piano performance, designed by
Josef Müller-Brockmann, 1952.
The literal representation of part of the
piano keyboard supplies the rectangles
which dominated Müller-Brockmann's
posters later in the 1950s.

▼ Zurich Concert Hall poster, designed
by Josef Müller-Brockmann, 1955.
Müller-Brockmann has become
thoroughly Modernist by this date,
even using all-lowercase for the text;
and the forms are abstract, not
illustrational.

Müller-Brockmann acknowledged his
debt to the 1920s Modernist work
(in this case, Lissitzky), and there is
a clear connection with Mary Vieira's
'Brazil Builds' poster (p.174).
Lithoprinted.

In this poster there is no evident
system to Müller-Brockmann's design:
no mathematical structure or
relationships dependent on fixed units
of measurement.

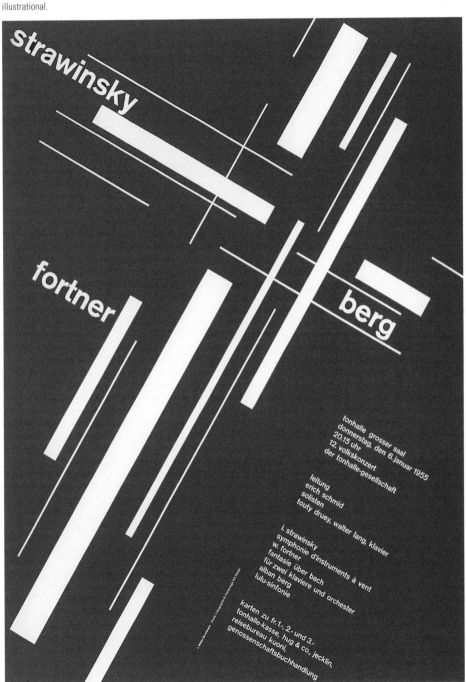

Helmhaus Zürich

Aus der Sammlung des Kunsthauses Zürich

Neuere Schweizer Kunst
18. Aug. — 13. Sept. 1953

täglich geöffnet 10—12 und 14—18 Uhr
Samstag und Sonntag bis 17 Uhr, Mittwoch auch 20—22 Uhr
Montag geschlossen

◄ 'From the Collection of the Zurich Kunsthaus: Recent Swiss Art', poster by Josef Müller-Brockmann, 1953. The exhibition included Concrete paintings. Such works present a single, usually simple, mathematical idea, and Müller-Brockmann has followed their style in applying a geometrical control to his design, the first of a series of posters using the same technique. To emphasize the works' origin in the Kunsthaus – the large state collection – rather than to make 'Recent Swiss Art' the main title, is a curious decision.

▼ Constructional drawing by Müller-Brockmann for the 'Recent Swiss Art' poster, left. The two concentric circles relate the long rectangles at the outside edges of the poster to the smaller rectangles within. The diagram does not indicate the exact centring of the smallest black rectangle between the right and left edges.

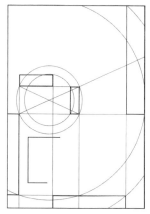

▼ Poster for 'Modern Art from the Peggy Guggenheim Collection', designed by Max Bill, 1959. The apparently casual layout is in fact disciplined by an underlying series of squares – most obviously in the top left corner.

Abstract painting, particularly geometrical abstraction, was more familiar in Switzerland than in other European countries after the war. Mondrian was celebrated in two exhibitions, in Basel in 1947 and at the Zurich Kunsthaus in 1955. The Concrete artists exhibited throughout the 1950s, and the final exhibition of Allianz was held in Zurich in 1954. As has been shown, the posters and catalogues for these events, designed by Max Bill or Richard Paul Lohse, linked high culture and the new graphic style.

Max Bill remained the single most decisive influence on the direction taken by Swiss graphic design in the 1950s. At each stage of graphic design's development in Switzerland he produced work and theoretical writing that gave a lead to other designers. In 1952 he published *Form,* subtitled 'a balance sheet of mid-twentieth-century trends in design'. This square book illustrates Bill's definition of 'form' as 'the attempt to make inert matter embody perfect suitability for a given purpose in such a way that the fusion achieves beauty'. Even so, beauty does not derive merely from satisfying the needs of function. 'When designers create new forms', he wrote,

> they are consciously or unconsciously responding to trends in contemporary art, because it is in art that the intellectual and spiritual currents of every epoch find their visible expression. Works of art may often be ridiculed or misunderstood when first produced but their almost immediate influence on every branch of design soon becomes apparent.[1]

Although Max Bill makes no reference in *Form* to graphic design or typography, the contemporary art which designers responded to was Concrete art, as practised by Bill and his colleagues. Bill's connection to the heroic days of the Modern Movement gave him special authority. On friendly terms with many of the grand names of twentieth-century art and architecture, he had edited books on Le Corbusier – an early inspiration – and on Kandinsky, one of his teachers. When he wrote for magazines, such was Bill's prestige that he could insist on making his own page layouts.

Bill's influence was at its most conspicuous in *Spirale,* an art magazine which itself aspired to be a work of art. Its embrace of progressive Swiss art and literature of the 1950s was, in principle, 'concrete'. Its aesthetic was 'minimalist' and precise. Founded in Berne in 1953 by the artist-designers Dieter Roth and Marcel Wyss, *Spirale* included Concrete poetry and articles on the arts and architecture. It also published original prints and

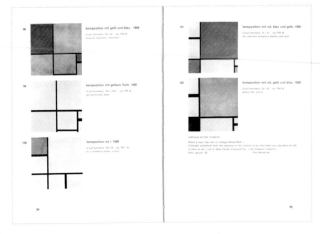

▲ Catalogue designed by Max Bill for the Mondrian exhibition at the Zurich Kunsthaus, 1955. A5 format, printed letterpress in lowercase Monotype grotesque.

▲ Max Bill owned an early Mondrian painting which he lent to the exhibition. Jan Tschichold lent no.99 in the catalogue, and the architect Alfred Roth, no.102 .

◀ ▼ Max Bill's book *Form*, published in 1952. It has a basic grid of two vertical columns for text and a narrow column for captions with left-ranging text in Monotype grotesque. The lamp and hairbrush were among the examples of Bill's own work as both industrial designer and artist.

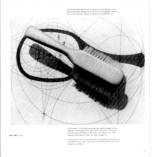

1. Max Bill, *Form*, Basel 1952, p.11.

170

▼ Advertisement insert in *Spirale*, no.3, 1953, designed by Marcel Wyss.

Following Max Bill and the Concrete ideal, *Spirale* was the movement's main vehicle, covering art, building, design and writing.
Even the advertisements, on a separate folded sheet of tinted paper, exemplified Concrete principles, designed on a systematic proportional scale,

▼ Cover of *Spirale*, no.5, 1955, designed by Marcel Wyss.

With this issue, the format of *Spirale* changed from upright to a large square. The image is made up of semicircular arcs; from the centre each successive half-circle is twice the width of its predecessor. Such simple progressions of size were typical of Concrete paintings and prints.
The image is printed letterpress in white ink on black paper.

reproduced photographs of such formal elegance as to exclude all but the barest evidence of human life. It was not only in including various media that *Spirale* followed Max Bill's many-sided activities: it adopted his lowercase typography and use of tinted paper. The advertisements, designed from the outset by Wyss himself, were early examples of the purest Swiss graphic design.

To the Concrete artists, the use of mathematically determined sizes and proportions had much wider implications, philosophical and social. For Lohse it was an article of faith.

> The essential task in art and in architecture is the creation of flexible modular systems . . . . Serial and modular structures will be the law of construction of our era, and our task will be to master these systems. Behind us is the homeland of . . . simple relationships and proportions. Before us, the field of infinite law and infinite flexibility.[2]

Lohse's painting and design work followed the same principles. As editor of the magazine *Bauen+Wohnen* (Building+Home), Lohse had a firm grasp of architectural ideas. He introduced himself to the engineer Konrad Wachsmann, famous for his modular structures, saying, 'My name is Lohse, I paint in the same way as you build.'[3]

Max Bill was principally an architect. As a student at the Bauhaus during Hannes Meyer's directorship, he had absorbed the current interest in industrialized building. The possibilities of standardization, the repetition and combination of standard-sized elements, had excited pre-war Modernists. Bill had pointed out that typography was modular design; like building, it was a matter of organizing machine-produced parts in a structure.

Architects and other groups of designers were brought together by the Werkbund and its magazine *Werk*. When Karl Gerstner (also a Concrete artist) edited *Werk*'s special graphic design issue, he reproduced a geometrical painting with the caption, 'Concrete art: a synthesis of mathematical logic and the essential means of pictorial expression. In graphics the synthesis results from the combination of function, material and design.'[4]

Gerstner analysed the construction of his colleagues' paintings in his book *Kalte Kunst?* (Cold Art?) in 1957. Almost square in format, *Kalte Kunst?* celebrated the

▲ Concert poster designed by Josef Müller-Brockmann, 1955.
In his attempts to find a visual equivalent to music for his series of concert posters, Müller-Brockmann adopted the forms of Concrete painting. He began with pencil sketches which were developed into geometrically controlled compositions into which the typography was fitted.

▲ Franz Kupka's *Composition* (1911-1930) was included in the 1944 exhibition of Concrete art in Basel, and reproduced in the catalogue designed by Max Bill.
▼ Müller-Brockmann's sketches for the Beethoven poster are clearly related to Kupka's painting.

2. 'Elementarism . Series . Modulus' in Anthony Hill (ed.), *Data: Directions in Art, Theory and Aesthetics*, London 1968, p.63.
3. Quoted in Richard Paul Lohse Foundation (ed.),*Richard Paul Lohse: Die Gebrauchsgrafik 1928-1988*, Ostfildern-Ruit 1999, p.160.
4. 'Aspekte des Standorts' (Aspects of the Current Situation), *Werk*, November 1955, p.337.

Modernist square as it had been used in the 1920s and its reappearance in Concrete art. In establishing an avant-garde lineage, Gerstner chooses as the key work a square painting by Van Doesburg from 1930. Squares were also the basis of the two paintings by Max Bill analysed by Gerstner. The subjects of both paintings are increasing numerical relationships: that is, each picture is the expression of a simple mathematical idea.

For Lohse the square was a constant resource, both in painting and in typography. It was basic to his design of the book *Wir Neger in Amerika* (p.150) and again in the layout of *Bauen+Wohnen*. And in Gerstner's work, too, the square became a recurrent feature, especially as the format of books, and often as the unit of a modular structure underlying their organization.

Müller-Brockmann was not a painter but, given a completely free hand in the design of the concert posters, he could treat the paper like an artist's canvas. His work on the Beethoven concert poster in 1955 was spread over two months.

I tried to interpret musical themes such as rhythm, transparency, weightlessness, and so on with concrete, abstract forms, which I brought together into logical relationships. I had to unify the geometrical elements – in terms of form and proportion – and the typography.[5]

According to Max Bill, music and Concrete art shared common ground: both were based on mathematical laws.[6] But when Müller-Brockmann adopted the style of Concrete art for his concert posters, he began with an image which he reconstructed according to a geometrical plan. This was to reverse the method of Concrete art, which is to proceed from an idea to its visual expression.

After Müller-Brockmann applied geometry to his posters, he saw its use for design on a smaller scale, on the book page, as a grid.

5. J. Müller-Brockmann, *Mein Leben: Spielerischer Ernst und ernsthaftes Spiel*, Baden 1994, pp.42-43.
6. Bill cited J.S. Bach's 'Goldberg Variations' as a stimulus for his work as an artist. See, Margit Staber, *Max Bill*, London 1964, n.p.

▼ In 1957 Karl Gerstner, graphic designer and artist, argued for and explained Concrete art in his small square book *Kalte Kunst?* Gerstner illustrates Van Doesburg's last great work, *Arithmetical Composition*, painted in 1930, as the immediate forerunner of the Concrete art developed in Zurich.

The painting's basis in a simple mathematical idea is the origin of Gerstner's concept of the 'programme' as a tool to generate a sequence of design solutions. The painting has four black squares angled at 45° on the diagonal. The largest is one-quarter of the total area of the canvas. The other three are each one-quarter of the area of the next larger square.

Diesen Ausführungen - wahrscheinlich allen von der Art - haftet etwas Simplifizierendes an. Der Autor ist sich des Mangels bewusst und entschuldigt sich. Natürlich ist die geschilderte Entwicklung differenzierter - die Grenzen der einzelnen Etappen sind verschwommen und entscheidende Vorgänge überschneiden sich.

Zum Beispiel muss noch erwähnt werden: was hier als ein spezifisches Anliegen Bills und seiner Altersgenossen dargestellt ist, hat noch direktere Ahnen als Mondrian. So sind bereits das Beispiel 22 auf der Basis der einfachsten, Beispiel 23 auf Grund differenzierter arithmetischer Teilungen entstanden. Und vollends nimmt Beispiel 24, das letzte grosse Werk von Doesburgs, viel von der kommenden Entwicklung vorweg.

Trotzdem: sieht man die Einzelleistungen im Verband eines grösseren Ganzen, lässt sich zusammenfassend folgendes festhalten:

Die erste Phase der Malerei unseres Jahrhunderts besteht in der Entdeckung der Elemente, sozusagen der Worte zu einer neuen Bildsprache, deren unmittelbare Harmonie zugleich Inhalt und Ausdruck ist.

Die zweite Phase gilt der Grammatik der neuen Sprache, deren Ordnung und deren universellen Gesetzmässigkeit. Hier ist die mittlere Generation massgeblich engagiert. Hier sind die Möglichkeiten gegeben und hier sind auch Resultate von in ihrer Art wieder echten Pionierleistungen entstanden.

Theo van Doesburg
1930, arithmetische Teilungen
Basel, Sammlung Felix Witzinger

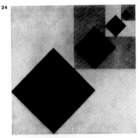

24

Damit ist der Punkt erreicht, wo wir zu dem übergehen können, um dessentwillen eigentlich diese Arbeit getan wurde: zur Kunst der unmittelbaren Gegenwart, zu den Werken der mittleren Generation. Der Altersbegriff ist dabei nicht streng wörtlich zu nehmen: Albers gehört nicht mehr zu den 50-Jährigen. Aber ist es sinnvoll, unsere Sammlung gerade mit einem Bild von ihm zu beginnen? - Nicht, weil dies bloss alphabetisch gerechtfertigt wäre; sondern vielmehr, weil er selbst schon früh zum jetzigen Stand der Entwicklung beigetragen hat. Siehe Beispiel 15.

Noch einige Worte, um Missverständnissen vorzubeugen: die Werk-Kommentare beschränken sich auf das, was effektiv und sachlich in den Bildern enthalten ist. Was mit dem Text oder nur schwer zugänglich ist, drücken die Schemata aus. Selbstverständlich ist damit noch nicht alles gesagt. Absichtlich ist zum Beispiel auf jedes Werturteil verzichtet worden: die Mühe des Urteilens möchte der Verfasser dem Leser nicht abnehmen.

Am Beispiel Bill liegen die Dinge anders. Die Darstellungsmittel sind zwar sozusagen unverändert übernommen, sie sind zur selbstverständlichen Voraussetzung geworden - deshalb die Ähnlichkeit. Aber ihren Beziehungen, ihrer Harmonie und letztlich ihrem Inhalt liegt eine neue Basis zugrunde: an Stelle oder richtiger, zu den optischen Erfahrungen des Gefühls ist die Bewusstheit des Denkens getreten. Die Bildelemente sind durch einen klaren und kontrollierbaren Gedanken zu einer umfassenden Einheit integriert. Schema 21. Nicht nur die Bildmittel an sich sind elementar und universell, sondern auch das System ihrer Beziehungen.

Damit tritt als schöpferischer Faktor nicht etwa die Mathematik selbst, aber die mathematische Denkweise in das Geschehen der Komposition. Jedes Werk ist nicht nur eine stets neu variierte Konstellation der Bildmittel, sondern durch das Gesetz ihrer Beziehungen von Grund auf original.

Bill: 'das Denken selbst scheint noch nicht direkt in der Empfindung ausdrückbar ohne das Wort, es wäre denn eben vermittelt der Kunst. Und deshalb nehme ich an, dass die Kunst das Denken vermitteln könne in einer Weise, dass es direkt wahrnehmbar ist. So kann ein Gedanke präzisiert werden, um direkt übertragen zu werden mit allen Möglichkeiten des Missverständnisses - das auch sonst nicht ausgeschlossen ist - aber mit dem Vorteil der Unveränderbarkeit des Gedankens.

Und je exakter ein Gedankengang sich fügt, je einheitlicher die Grundidee ist, desto näher findet sich der Gedanke im Einklang mit der Methode des mathematischen Denkens; desto näher kommen wir dem Urgefüge, und desto universeller wird die Kunst werden.'

Max Bill 1908*
1946, rotes Quadrat

Schema zu Abbildung 20

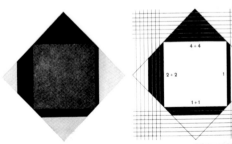

20

21

4 + 4

2 + 2

1 + 1

▲ Gerstner's diagram in *Kalte Kunst?* of the arithmetic underlying Max Bill's 1946 diagonal painting, *Red Square*.

172

Dominance of the Square

▶ 'USA Builds', exhibition poster designed by Max Bill, 1945.
An explicit forerunner of graphic designs of the 1950s and 1960s, where the square is dominant.
The square on a diagonal originated with Malevich and Lissitzky and was followed by Mondrian, Van Doesburg and Bill himself.

▼ '12 Contemporary American Painters and Sculptors', poster designed by Gottfried Honegger, 1953.

kunstgewerbemuseum zürich

USA baut

9. september – 7. oktober 1945

▼ 'Healthy Children through Swiss Holidays', poster by Emil Maurer for the Swiss Tourist Board, 1952.

kunsthaus zürich

12 amerikanische maler und bildhauer der gegenwart

25. juli bis 30. august
täglich geöffnet 10-12 und 14-17 uhr
mittwoch und donnerstag auch 20-22 uhr
montagvormittag geschlossen

honegger·hersfter · druck · buchmann zürich

Honegger has not attempted to connect the style of the American artists with the way the exhibition is advertised.
Together with the all-lowercase typography of pure European Modernism, the static square module belongs to Concrete art, and to Honegger's own painting.
Printed from linocut blocks and type, this was the economical technique also used for Müller-Brockmann's earlier concert posters.

Gesunde Kinder durch Schweizer Ferien

▲ Maurer's 'anonymous' style shows the influence of Concrete art – squares dominate the design. This stems directly from Richard Paul Lohse, and is typified in Lohse's book jackets and covers for the magazine *Bauen+Wohnen* (where Maurer later worked), which used similar overprinting of black half-tone on solid colour, and half-tones printed in colour.

▼ Book jacket by Richard Paul Lohse, 1951, a precursor of many that used the square and exploited overprinting of black and colour before the spread of economical four-colour printing.

CIAM

A Decade of New Architecture
Ein Jahrzehnt Moderner Architektur

S. Giedion

Editions Girsberger Zurich

▶ A5 booklet designed by Carlo
Vivarelli for Feller electrical equipment,
1955.
This stereotype of countless brochures
in the Swiss style has a grid structure
based on the square and the type,
Monotype grotesque, ranged left in
narrow columns.The use of red
in flat areas of colour was also typical.
There is a strict formalism: in the
photograph of the factory at night,
for example, the corner angle of
the building is in the exact centre
of the image.
By turning the firm's original
calligraphic trademark vertically,
Vivarelli converts it into an abstract
element.

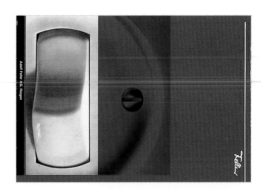

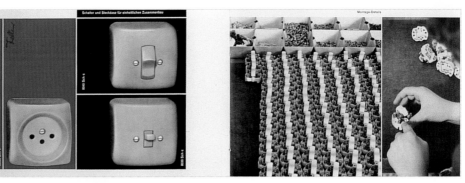

174

brasilien baut
moderne brasilianische architektur
neue brasilianische graphik
plastiken von mary vieira

kunstgewerbemuseum zürich
23. oktober bis 28. november 1954

offen: 10 bis 12, 14 bis 18, mittwoch bis 21, samstag / sonntag bis 17. montag geschlossen

With only two posters, the Concrete artist Mary Vieira made a limited but important contribution to Swiss graphic design.
◀ 'Brazil Builds', poster by Mary Vieira for an exhibition of architecture, prints and Vieira's sculpture, 1954.
▼ Outside the museum Vieira installed a painted three-dimensional relief, a version of the poster.

▶ Poster by Mary Vieira for Brazil
Airlines, 1957.
The simple application of Concrete
principles. The structure is governed
by two full-width overlapping squares.
The line of text rests on the top of
an (invisible) square at the bottom
of the poster.
The circle, suggesting movement,
aircraft propellers and the globe, is
centred on this square. (Brazil's
national flag has a globe at its centre.)
The blue square at the top implies sky
over the strip of green land below.

The Grid: From Architecture to the Page

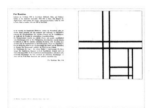

▲ The glazing bars of sliding windows, as drawn by Le Corbusier in 1925. The use of the square as a unit was to recur in the grids devised by Modernist graphic designers.

▼ The lines and planes of a painting by Mondrian are reduced to a line photo-engraving in Max Bill's design for the A5 exhibition catalogue of 'Modern Painting', 1943. The painting's proportions are intuitively arrived at, without the mathematical control of the Concrete artists or the constraints of typesetting's modular technology.

▼ Le Corbusier's Modulor man, 1948, related dimensions of the human body to the domestic environment and its equipment, so that seat and table heights, for example, were functionally determined. Such a system could help to rationalize industrial production, with various manufacturers supplying identically sized fittings or equipment. The Modulor also reduced the choice of possible dimensions – in the same way as a grid helped the graphic designer organize material on the page by limiting the variety of illustration sizes. Le Corbusier claimed that its use 'makes the bad difficult and the good easy'.

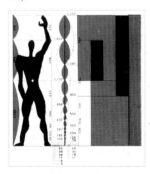

'Swiss graphic design' is a concept inseparable from the grid. In typography, the use of the grid grew from the nature of letterpress printing. As shown earlier (p.93), type metal, cast on a rectangular base, was composed in horizontal lines arranged in vertical columns, and locked in a rectangular framework. Unlike the infinite scale possible on digital systems fifty years later, type and spacing material were produced in fixed sizes: typography was a modular system.

An image of the grid is often recognized in the paintings of Piet Mondrian. His typical canvases, icons of Modernism, are composed of horizontal and vertical lines and rectangular planes. The width of the lines and the areas of the planes and their relationships were arrived at intuitively, by experiment. Whereas the 'grid' of a Mondrian painting is visually insistent, a typographical grid is an invisible armature, and a tool for assembling text and image. Such a method of putting things together had more in common with architecture – at least with industrialized buildings, whose facades can resemble page layouts in their rectangularity. The elevations of many buildings show a series of repeated dimensions, like columns of text of the same width, or lines of type of the same height. Their external appearance is frequently determined by the position of the building's structural components. (The word 'structure' is often applied loosely in discussing two-dimensional design, although the 'structure' may be represented by space – between columns, for example.)

Tschichold had stressed the relationship between painting, architecture and typography. In the development of the grid in Switzerland, architects played a significant part. Beginning with the first volume of Le Corbusier's *Oeuvre complète* in 1929, Zurich had become a centre for publications on the Modern Movement.[1] And architects, by far the largest group in the Swiss Werkbund, had been pressing since the 1920s for the standardization of the catalogues of building components and fittings which formed part of their everyday working lives (as noted on p.56). This was the very same ground on which Hans Neuburg had been campaigning for twenty years.

The Modulor, a system of arithmetical ratios, attractive not only to architects but also to the more serious young graphic designers, had been devised by Le Corbusier. It was based on human dimensions, but could be used to make related divisions of the printed sheet, the printed area, and the margins. Such questions of proportion had

▲ Yellow cloth cover of Bauhaus Book 8, Moholy-Nagy's *Malerei, Photographie, Film*, 1925. The Mondrian-like decoration, designed by the author, printed in red, is unrelated to the page layouts.

▼ By contrast, the design on the natural cloth cover of Richard Paul Lohse's *Neue Ausstellungsgestaltung* (New Design in Exhibitions), 1953, printed in black, shows elements of the grid underlying the page layout.

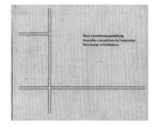

▲ The basis of the grid is a rectangle (as in the top left-hand corner of the cover), which is repeated four times across the page and four times down.

1. Max Bill edited and designed the third Le Corbusier volume in 1939.

▼ Dust jacket of Max Bill's book on the Swiss bridge designer Robert Maillart, published in 1949.
The back and front conform to the grid established for the inside pages.

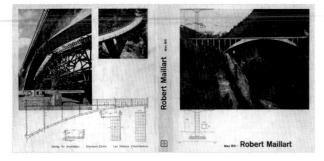

▼ In practice, while Bill was able to limit the depth of many of the illustrations to fixed dimensions, the variety of photographs made it impossible to follow a strict grid.

always interested typographers, the scholarly Tschichold predominant among them.

Two other circumstances encouraged the development of the grid. After architectural influences came the authority of the artist-designers: Max Bill, Lohse and the young Karl Gerstner. The mathematical and programmatic basis of their work as artists could be applied in typography, a field in which all three were conspicuously active. The third and essentially Swiss factor was the use of three-column text pages, to deal with three-language publications (German, French and Italian).

As a practical tool the grid was a concept that emerged only gradually. Hermann Eidenbenz's explicit use of the grid (for the book *Der Film* in 1947, p.151) was unusual. In the design of Alfred Roth's book, *The New Architecture*, in 1940, Bill introduced a partial grid, which restricts photographs to the depths and widths prescribed by a grid of nine rectangles: three across, three down.

When in 1949 Bill came to design his own book on the engineer Robert Maillart, the grid was more elaborate. With a squarer format and a grid of two columns plus a half-column, Bill provided himself with a system that allowed him to organize the photographs (some photo-engraved blocks from *The New Architecture* had to be incorporated) in several sizes and proportions, with technical drawings, text and captions.

In the case of *Neue Ausstellungsgestaltung* (New Design in Exhibitions), written and designed by Lohse in 1953, the grid is far from invisible. Lohse uses its elements as a decoration on the front cover binding. In the same format as *The New Architecture*, in the place of Max Bill's 3×3 grid, Lohse has 16 horizontal rectangles, 4 across, 4 down. It was unusual for Lohse not to use the square, commonly his basic module. When he designed *Bauen+Wohnen* in 1948, Lohse began with the text pages typeset in three columns. These form a simple vertical grid; horizontal subdivisions are varied but, as a stabilizing element, Lohse repeatedly employs the square. The square, an important feature of his painting, appears in *Bauen+Wohnen* (see p.178) as a controlling proportion in the horizontal division of printed rectangles.

Similarly devoted to the square was Karl Gerstner. In 1957, the year in which his (square) *Kalte Kunst?* was published, he used a grid of huge complexity for one of the most innovative of twentieth-century book designs: *Schiff nach Europa* (Boat to Europe), a novel. In this book the freedom and variety of column widths and sizes of type, still within the limits of metal typesetting, are used to echo the novel's changing styles of writing and the

178

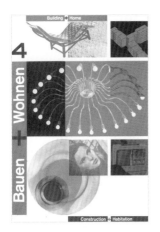

▲ Cover for *Bauen+Wohnen*
(Building+Home) designed by Richard
Paul Lohse, 1948.
Lohse was co-editor and designer of
the magazine from 1948 to 1954.
▼ A left-hand page from the previous
issue shows how the same grid
controlled the page layout: three
columns wide and five rectangles deep.

characters' way of speaking. All are mastered by an
elaborate grid. In a prefatory note the author, Gerstner's
colleague Markus Kutter, wonders why writers are not
more interested in the way their work is presented, and
says how lucky he is to have a publisher and, particularly,
a designer who understands that 'the printed letter is not
the general horse and cart onto which no matter what
kind of goods can be loaded'.[2]

Schiff nach Europa is 'a synthetic novel, a hypothetical
play', describing a boat journey from New York to the
French port of Le Havre. The book explores narrative
(and typographic) styles: the column widths vary
throughout. Beginning as a conventional novel, it
becomes a play; a traveller's night-time musings are set
out in unbroken prose. One chapter exaggerates the role
of quantity, the numbers stressed in bold type. Another
is journalistic: 'Flora's Special Edition' – in newspaper
style, set at 90 degrees, the text running up the page.

By the 1960s the grid had become a routine procedure.
Müller-Brockmann's textbook presentation of his
own methods, *Gestaltungsprobleme des Grafikers*
(The Graphic Artist and His Design Problems), first
published in 1961, introduced the grid to an international
readership of designers. The grid came to imply the style
and methods of Swiss graphic design.

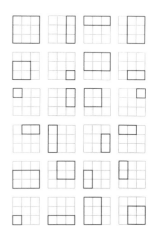

▲ The Basel typographer and teacher
Emil Ruder demonstrated a grid of nine
squares as the basis for different sizes
of image (outlined with a heavy line).
There are 24 possible positions and
shapes of image.
From Ruder's textbook, *Typographie*,
1967, p.225.

2.The original reads, '. . . dass die gedruckte Letter nicht der Allerweltskarren ist, auf
dem jede Ware gleichgemassen geschleppt werden kann'. Afterword by Markus Kutter,
Schiff nach Europa, Teufen 1957, p.213.

▼ *Schiff nach Europa* (Boat to Europe), designed by Karl Gerstner, 1957. The typography of the novel, written by Gerstner's future business partner Markus Kutter, expresses the narrative style of its characters, passengers on an ocean liner.

Gerstner explained (in *TM*, February 1972, p.33) that the grid 'provided the integration of typography and surface area: the type area is derived from [the dimensions of] this space, in other words, from the outside to the inside. So, the area is first divided into squares, 2×3; the squares into units, 7×7; the units into 3×3 units of body size, the smallest typographical measurement – type size and leading. This results in a flexible grid, in which the type area can fit with an (almost) unlimited freedom.'

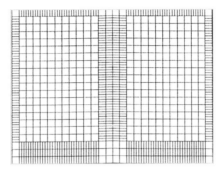

The final five double-page spreads are pastiche journalism, entitled 'Flora's Special Edition'.

◄ ▲ Advertisements for the photoengraving firm Schwitter, designed by Karl Gerstner, 1957. The designs transform Gerstner's emblem for Schwitter into enlarged half-tone dot screens similar to Max Bill's, a quarter of a century earlier. The emblem first appeared on the firm's stationery, and over the next few years its elements were reworked and reassembled in a series of advertisements.

Karl Gerstner Born 1930

Graphic designer, painter and writer. Studied on foundation course, Basel Allgemeine Gewerbeschule, 1944. Apprentice in Fritz Bühler's studio, Basel, and courses at AGS, 1944-48. Freelance for Geigy, 1949-52. Freelance designer in Basel, 1952-58. Attended Hans Finsler's photography classes, Zurich Kunstgewerbeschule, 1955-56. Redesign of *Werk*, 1955. Designer for Geigy's bicentenary, 1956. Lecture tour of USA, 1958. Opened Gerstner+Kutter advertising agency in Basel, published *Die neue Graphik* with Kutter, and 'Integral Typography' in special issue of *TM*, 1959. Gerstner+Kutter exhibition in New York, 1960. Gerstner+Kutter became GGK, 1962, and opened German branch in Düsseldorf, 1968.
Gerstner exhibited internationally. For his books, crucially important contributions to the understanding and development of Swiss graphic design, see bibliography.

The young 'anonymous' designers whose work was reproduced in *Graphis* in 1957 belonged mainly to the group of Basel-trained designers who had worked for Geigy. To these were added a few from Berne, and from French-speaking Switzerland, as well as Zurich designers such as Carl B. Graf, Gottlieb Soland and Werner Zryd.

Among the new generation it was the work of Siegfried Odermatt in Zurich and Karl Gerstner in Basel that became the best known. If Müller-Brockmann can be seen as the popularizer of the grid, it was Gerstner who gave it most thought. Indeed, Gerstner thought more creatively about graphic design than any of the Swiss designers, and he published his ideas in a series of books and articles, beginning in *Werk* in 1954. He refined, rewrote and expanded the same ideas for twenty years: about the relationship between graphic design and advertising; the practicalities of commercial design; the demands and limitations of printing and reproduction; design itself; the laws of chance; and about the aim and context of his own work, both as a designer and as an artist.

Gerstner began his design career as an apprentice in Fritz Bühler's studio in Basel, where one of his colleagues was Armin Hofmann and his supervisor was Max Schmid. Schmid left to take charge of design at Geigy, where he introduced Gerstner to his team in 1949.

Gerstner opened his own studio in Basel in 1953. He had already helped to produce pamphlets on the politics of town planning, as radical in their design as in their views. The prime movers in these publications were two students, Lucius Burckhardt, later an editor of *Werk* (as 'thinker'), and Gerstner's future partner, Markus Kutter (as 'foolish pragmatist'). They were joined by the writer and architect Max Frisch (as 'aesthetician and wordsmith').

The trio's second tract, a 60-page booklet, *Achtung: die Schweiz* (Watch Out, Switzerland), was the most widely read and discussed publication of the 1950s, prompting more than two hundred articles in the press. The authors' main proposal was to plan a new town, and to present the town itself as the next national exhibition, the Landesausstellung, due to take place in 1964. Such an idea would be a contrast to the Landi exhibition of twenty-five years earlier.

Whereas at that time there was a need for a Swiss national identity, now, for Frisch and his young collaborators, the concern was with style, an idea that included a style of life, and Gerstner matched the combative arguments of *Achtung: die Schweiz* with a bold typographic style.

Gerstner had first made his name in 1955. At a meeting

▶ 'Watch Out, Switzerland', A5 agitational booklet designed by Karl Gerstner, 1953. One of a series of 'Basel Political Texts', edited by Markus Kutter. The cover, in black on solid red, was an early stereotype of 'Swiss' design. The flap of the back cover carried a questionnaire that could be torn out as a postcard.

▼ The inside pages, typeset in bold Monotype grotesque, show Gerstner alternating paragraphs in two widths of text column.

▼ The pamphlet following *Achtung: die Schweiz*, was *Die neue Stadt* (The New Town), 1956, a three-way conversation.

The speakers are identified by large bold initials. The two shown below are **K** for Markus Kutter and **B** for Lucius Burckhardt.

► Cover of the special graphic design issue of *Werk*, designed and edited by Karl Gerstner, November 1955. Printed letterpress, the magazine's title is reversed white out of a solid red background, the text black.

▼ The text pages are based on a five-unit grid (the text column is two units wide). This allows for most vertical images to be two units (one column) wide, and the horizontal images to be three units (one column and a half). The pages below, on the left, show historical examples which relate a poster by A.M. Cassandre to a Purist painting by Amédée Ozenfant, and a Piet Zwart design to a painting by Georges Vantongerloo.

▲ Gerstner relates contemporary graphic design and art – a brochure designed by Gérard Ifert and a painting by the Zurich Concrete artist Camille Graeser.

▲ Gerstner uses two pages for a selection of trademarks, which includes his own for Schwitter engravers.

of the Werkbund, where he was the youngest member, he daringly approached Alfred Roth, the editor of *Werk*, and suggested that the magazine might publish an article on graphic design. Roth responded by commissioning Gerstner to make an entire special issue.

This special issue had little in common with *Werk*'s survey of Swiss graphic design in 1943. Instead of the large inserts of printed specimens which had disturbed the coherence of the earlier special issue, only one of the many illustrations was full-page. Not only editor and main contributor, Gerstner also gave the magazine a complete redesign. He followed the lead of Richard Paul Lohse's *Bauen+Wohnen*, which had used Monotype grotesque since 1949. But Gerstner's setting was unjustified, ranged left, a method he had used at Geigy in a calendar for farmers. This was an innovation for magazine text. The two columns were placed asymmetrically, to the right of each page. Paragraphs were indicated by a line space, without a first-line indent. Illustrations were limited to sixteen possible proportions and sizes by a horizontal and vertical grid.

Gerstner solicited articles from his expert colleagues. Armin Hofmann, writing on posters, links the changes in design to changes in technology, pointing to the disappearance of the drawn lithographic poster, and makes a case for his own method of drawn lettering. An illustrated article on trademarks by Carlo Vivarelli was followed by examples of their use; there was a report on the recent exhibition, 'Grafiker: ein Berufsbild' (Graphic Designer: Picture of a Profession); and a review of the training of graphic designers. Gerstner contributed a long illustrated article in two parts: the first, on graphic design and advertising, and the second on their future. He welcomes the opportunity of using design as part of advertising.

> The designer as an artist is not outside society, but necessarily engaged in its productive output. . . . Graphic design for advertising is not a new sort of art, nor is it on the fringe of art. Painting and graphic design are two completely different activities, with specific requirements and expressive means.[1]

It is, he writes, fruitless to discuss whether or not advertising is art, and he points out that most of the 'classic' works of advertising are not based on ideas to be found in painting: their quality rests on their use of essentially graphic media and graphic language. Gerstner's illustrations and their captions make his

1. 'Aspekte des Standorts' (Aspects of the Current Situation), *Werk*, special graphic design issue, November 1955, p.337.

message clear. On a typographic design by Piet Zwart, he comments: 'Graphics and typography are developed basically from the specific requirements of the design and the nature of the [typographic] material without consideration for the function.'[2] In the section 'Prospects for the Future', Gerstner sees the danger of a constant search for originality at any cost. However good individual pieces of graphics may be, they remain isolated. He calls for an integration of graphics into other areas – economic, technical and social. Instead of a fleeting novelty, the aim is to create something more durable.

This related to what came to be at the centre of Gerstner's thinking for years: the 'programme' (see pp.228-33). To illustrate this, he chooses three very different examples: promotional material for Geigy, where he worked; publicity by Otl Aicher in Germany for adult education courses and lectures; and the advertising in France for the aperitif St Raphaël. He provides a critical commentary to each, under three headings. First, the task; second, the given factors; third, the design. He sums up each evaluation, explaining how the work satisfies his demand for 'integration' – of the elements of the design and its purpose.

Comments of such length on contemporary graphic works were unusual. To have them as part of a sustained argument was unique. Gerstner's interest, to give graphic design not only a wider context but an intellectual basis, was developed over the next two decades. Though he distanced graphic design from painting, he was prepared to confront both with the same seriousness.

Gerstner had invited the young Zurich designer Siegfried Odermatt to contribute an essay on advertising. Alongside Gerstner, Odermatt was a leader of the new generation. He was unusual in being self-taught. He left school early, undertook various menial jobs for advertising agencies and studios before a period with a celebrated and prolific designer, Hans Falk. Despite belonging to the 'illustrational' tendency, Falk, who taught at the Kunstgewerbeschule, had a sound practical understanding of the New Typography. In 1950, after three years in advertising, Odermatt opened his own studio.

In his *Werk* essay, Odermatt points out that press advertisements (in newspapers, magazines and trade journals) are the most widely used publicity medium. And yet they are the most ephemeral. The article, written with a colleague from advertising, makes a clear, simple

▼ Bag for long-playing vinyl discs, designed by Karl Gerstner for 'Musical Box', a Basel music store, 1957.

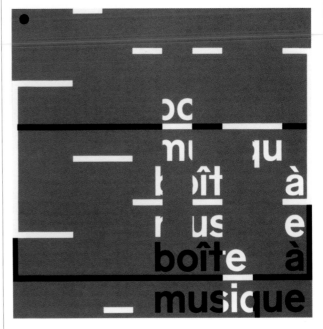

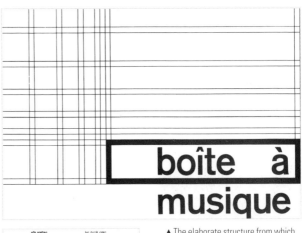

▲ The elaborate structure from which the shop's various pieces of printed matter were derived. The lettering 'boîte à' and its relation to the right-hand bottom corner of the heavy black box rule are constant. From this basic element the rules can be extended upwards and to the left in fixed increments.
◄ In designing the invoice, Gerstner allowed himself to break the system to allow for the total to appear in its conventional position at the bottom right.

2. *Ibid.*, p.336.

184

Siegfried Odermatt Born 1926

Graphic designer and editor.
Self-taught. Worked in the studio
of the painter and designer Hans Falk,
then in advertising agencies, before
opening his own studio in Zurich, 1950.
Shared practice with Rosmarie Tissi
from 1968. Became one of the
internationally known Swiss designers
and edited a book on his own
collection of Swiss posters (see
bibliography).

▲ Advertisement for the Zurich
printers City-Druck, designed by
Siegfried Odermatt, 1952.
The design advertises poster printing
using lino.
Printed in letterpress in black and blue.

▲ Double-page advertisement
for BP's special tractor oil, designed by
Siegfried Odermatt, 1955.
The design prefaced Odermatt's article
on advertising in the special graphic
design issue of *Werk*.

statement on the aims of an advertisement. It should:

1. Arouse attention
2. Present the product, service or idea clearly and objectively
3. Appeal to the customer's emotions
4. Make itself memorable [3]

Odermatt distinguishes between advertisements designed as a series and the single advertisement, which has to make its point instantly. This demands careful consideration of its design, where it is placed (which magazine or newspaper), and its size. The series (which may be a campaign) depends on appropriate design, calculating the right moments for its repetition and, most importantly, having a strong basic idea. He discusses the expected readership as a factor, makes a clear distinction between advertising for the consumer market and for trade and industry, and sees advertising, which has scarcely developed over the last twenty years, as having 'a sociological influence. The advertiser, designer and publisher are responsible for the quality of this influence.'

Odermatt was not given to theorizing. Nor was he a painter. His similarity to Gerstner was in his commitment to an 'anonymous' style and in the unique quality of his work, shaped not only by his lack of formal training but also by his natural visual gifts and intense application. More than any other designer, he depended on contrast: straight with curved, horizontal with angled, massive with delicate.

Odermatt's and Gerstner's design careers began at the same time. They had similar clients. Each worked, famously, for photoengravers and music shops, Odermatt in Zurich, Gerstner in Basel. They were not alone, but they were the most prominent of the new generation. Outside Zurich and Basel, there were a handful of 'anonymous' designers, as the example of *Spirale* demonstrates. A few posters in the streets and those displayed in exhibitions, such as the 'Swiss Exhibition of Applied Art' at the Berne Kunstmuseum in 1957, familiarized a wider public with the Modernist path being followed by a number of designers in French-speaking Switzerland (see pp.189, 237).

---

3. 'Das Inserat', *Werk*, November 1955, p.349.

▼ ▶ 24-page A5 booklet for kitchen equipment, designed by Siegfried Odermatt, 1957.
Printed in black only on the inside pages. Nearly 100 tightly packed items, including complete ranges of cutlery and glasses, are cut-out half-tone photographs. This was a formidable task for the designer in painting round them in white, ready for the process engraver's camera; and also for the engraver, who had to etch and cut away around the outside contours. The most complicated objects – the wire whisk and the vegetable rack – are reproduced by line block. Odermatt has credited the photographer, W.S. Eberle.

Back cover   Front cover

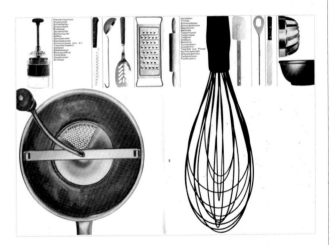

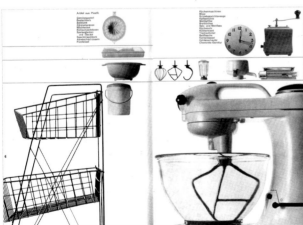

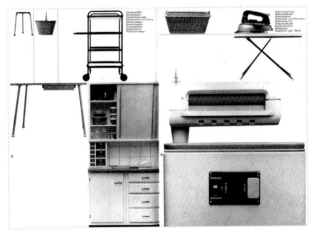

186

Odermatt completed a range of print design for this Zurich record shop, beginning with the logo.
▼ Small carrier bag for vinyl discs, designed by Siegfried Odermatt, 1959.

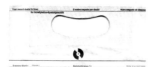

The logo on the bag kept the name style used in the smaller items, with type cut into a rectangle and the letters much more tightly spaced. Odermatt's frequent choice of closely spaced extrabold Akzidenz Grotesk would have served to illustrate a point made by Emil Ruder: 'The spaces between letters are narrow and therefore intensely bright, the white inside the [letter] "o" is somewhat weaker, while the white above the "o" is weakest.'
The drawing of the end view of the pick-up head is typical of Odermatt's contrast of fine lines with massive graphic forms.
Odermatt reinforced the logo with a symbol, a stylized drawing of a vinyl disc.
The advertisements and brochures which followed included photographs; technical, abstracted drawings of machinery; and the abstract geometrical expression of music similar to Müller-Brockmann's concert posters.

◀ Front of concertina-folded leaflet designed by Siegfried Odermatt to announce Grammo Studio's policy, 1957-58.
Printed letterpress in Monotype grotesque on rough grey paper.
As well as his own credit, Odermatt has scrupulously listed the writer and the printer.
▼ Each page of the unfolded leaflet describes a different aspect of Grammo Studio's range.
On one side, from left to right, special recordings (voice and sounds), classics and jazz; on the other, ethnic and folk music, listening equipment and light music.

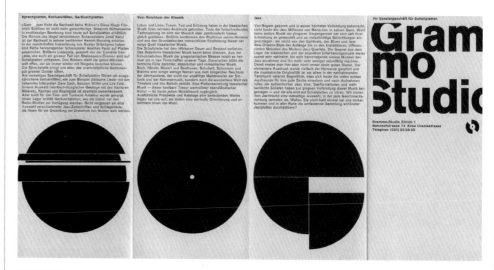

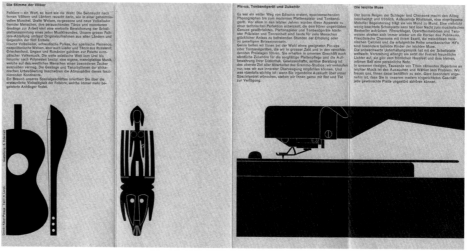

► Poster for a two-day weekend fair, designed by Rosmarie Tissi, 1956. Given that it was made for local tradespeople in a small town, Tissi's design is remarkably advanced. Lithoprinted in red and black.
Born in 1937, Tissi trained at the Zurich Kunstgewerbeschule and was a freelance designer in Zurich until her partnership with Siegfried Odermatt. Their joint practice has been celebrated in international exhibitions and publications, and in their book, *Siegfried Odermatt & Rosmarie Tissi: Graphic Design*, 1993.

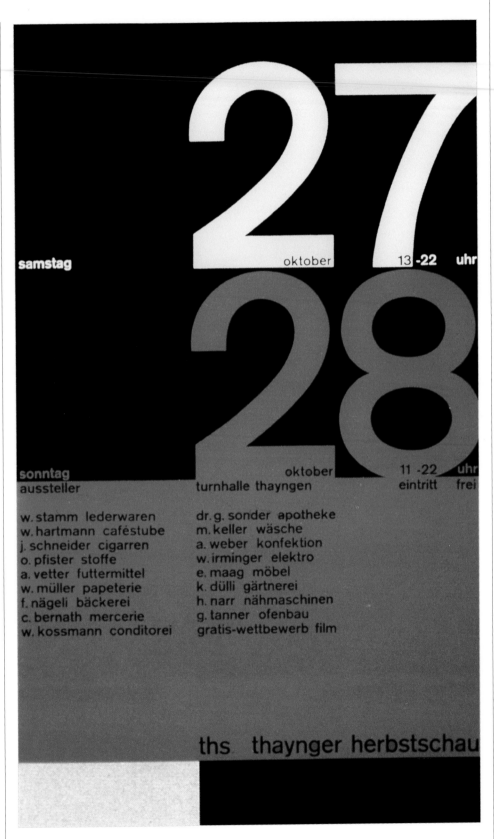

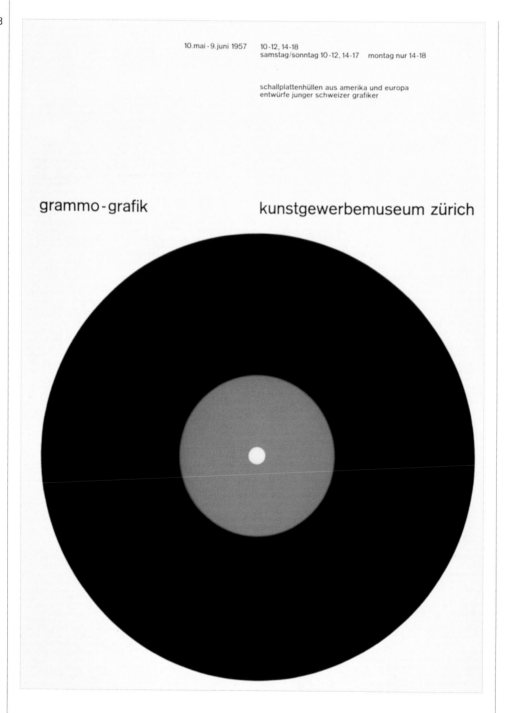

10.mai - 9.juni 1957   10 -12, 14 -18
samstag/sonntag 10 -12, 14 -17   montag nur 14 -18

schallplattenhüllen aus amerika und europa
entwürfe junger schweizer grafiker

grammo - grafik   kunstgewerbemuseum zürich

◄ 'Recorded Music Graphics',
exhibition poster designed by
Gottlieb Soland, 1957.
The minimalist geometrical austerity
of Soland's posters owes a great deal
to his experience as an assistant
in the Honegger-Lavater studio.
The disc's pure, almost two-
dimensional form was ready made
as a graphic emblem.
▼ Poster for a Bach concert by
the Zurich Chamber Orchestra,
designed by Gottlieb Soland, 1956.
The extreme formalization of
the almost indecipherable lettered
initials 'ZKO' shows the influence
of Alfred Willimann at the Zurich
Kunstgewerbeschule. The layout
has a strict geometrical control:
the top of the large geometricized
letters is on the half-way horizontal
dividing line.

Beyond Zurich and Basel
▶ 'Modern Furniture at the New
Teo Jakob Shop in Geneva', poster
designed by Alfred Hablützel, 1957.
Printed litho in black and yellow.
Extremely simple in its pure, lowercase
Modernism, the perspective is
restrained to emphasize the flat plane
of the poster surface.
Hablützel trained in Zurich and worked
mainly in the furniture industry – he
was editor and designer of the
magazine *Interieur* in the 1960s.

▲ Poster for the Lausanne Film Club,
designed by Roger Geiser, 1957.
All lowercase Akzidenz Grotesk, this
was unusually Modernist for western
Switzerland at the time.
Printed silksceen, white on black.

les meubles modernes au nouveau magasin de teo jakob à genève

le programme de meubles à utilisation
multiple comprend des créations de:
hans eichenberger · kurt thut · robert
haussmann et d'autres architectes en
europe et usa · magasin 69 rue du rhône
pl. eaux-vives. prospectus sur demande

190

Photo-Graphics

▶ 'Glass from Four Millennia',
exhibition poster designed by
Carl B. Graf, 1956.
One of the most reproduced designs of
the period, remarkable for its simplicity
and the effortless combination of
symmetry and asymmetry, text and
image. The photograph (not credited)
captures the nature of glass, a kind of
frozen movement, and its delicacy.
There is also a fortuitous pun, since
the object – glass – is described by the
same word as is used for the material.
Full colour is suggested by the duotone
black and blue, at the time a little used
technique.

▼ 'Glass', half-size exhibition poster
for the Basel Gewerbemuseum by
Emil Ruder, 1956. Printed letterpress
at the Gewerbeschule in black, with
pale blue-grey semi-transparent
overprinting.

▲ The industrial and advertising photographer Georg Vetter as he portrayed himself in *Schweizer Reklame* in 1956. In the magazine Vetter emphasizes that the more thorough the pre-planning, the better the photograph.

The judgement and skills of such well-equipped professionals, especially their understanding of lighting and choice of lens, was essential to the designers who depended on them, although the photographer often went uncredited.

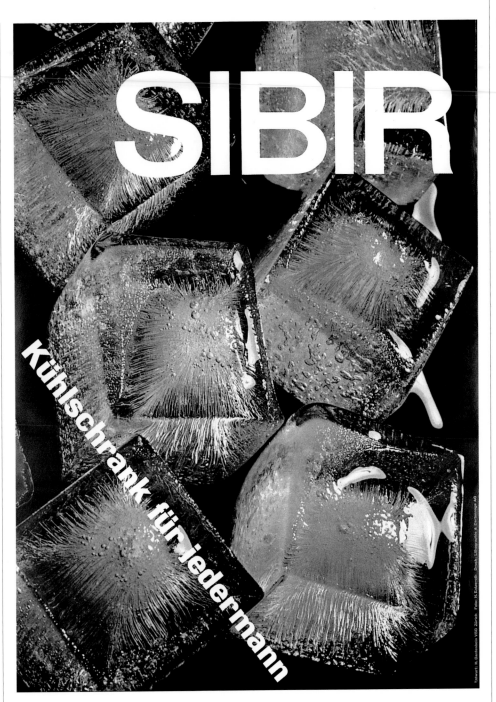

▲ 'Refrigerator for Everyone' is the slogan on this poster by Leo Gantenbein, 1957. The product is notable for its absence: represented by what it does, not what it looks like.

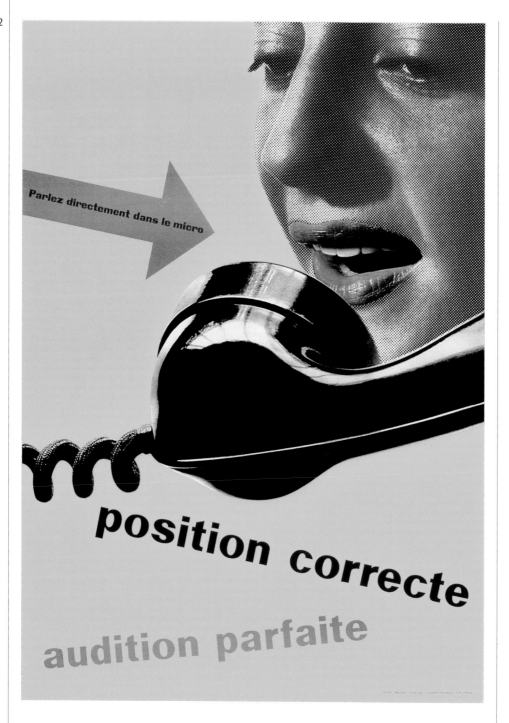

◄ 'Right Position, Perfect Hearing: Speak Directly into the Mouthpiece', poster designed by Ernst A. Heiniger, 1950.
The combination of a solid yellow background and the tint of red on the lips gives an illusion of full colour.
The large lettering is hand-drawn; the telephone handset and the face are separate photographs, montaged together.
This technique was the forerunner of Müller-Brockmann's photographic road-safety posters, which owe a great deal to Heiniger, whose studio space was shared with Müller-Brockmann.

▼ 'The Friendly Hand Signal –
Prevents Accidents', road safety poster
designed by Josef Müller-Brockmann,
1955. Photographs are by Ernst A.
Heiniger. Printed by litho.

▲ Take Care – Children', poster
designed by Hans Thöni, 1955.
Lithoprinted in black and olive green.
▼ 'Watch Out for the Child!', road
safety poster for the Swiss Automobile
Club designed by Josef Müller-
Brockmann, 1953.
With the same message, the contrast
of style with Thöni's poster above could
hardly be greater.
Printed by litho in black (for the
photographs), red (for the lettering
at the extreme top) and yellow
(for the band at the bottom).
Photographs are by Ernst A. Heiniger.

194

Initial letters and the logo

The important part that lettering played in graphic designers' training resulted in well-drawn, strong and simple name styles and trademarks.

▼ Logo designed by Gottfried Honegger for Jules Kienholz, a Zurich tailor, 1954.

▼ Logo designed by Marcel Wyss for Neuweiler rail switch engineers, 1955.

▼ Logo designed by Carl B. Graf for Certina automatic watches, 1956.

Initial letters and the poster

A simple and economical answer for a poster was to make the image with large lettering, hand drawn or using the largest size of wood poster type.

▼ Poster for exhibitions at the Zurich Kunstgewerbemuseum of 1920s German Expressionist artists associated with the journal *Der Sturm*, and work by Otto Nebel, 1955. Design by Carl B. Graf.

▲ 'Fernand Léger, Alexander Calder', exhibition poster designed by Armin Hofmann, 1957. Initial letters of the artists' surnames, geometrical and integrated with the divison of the area into four, make the image. The stencil-like forms reflect the heavy directness of Léger and the playfulness of Calder. Printed in black from linocut with text added in white letterpress.

Armin Hofmann Born 1920

Teacher, graphic designer and writer. Studied at Zurich Kunstgewerbeschule, 1937-39. Worked as lithographer until 1943. Taught at Basel Allgemeine Gewerbeschule from 1947. Opened studio in Basel, 1948. Taught at Museum School of Fine Arts, Philadelphia, 1955, and at Yale, 1956. Visiting Professor at Yale, 1956-91. Visiting adviser to the National School of Design, Ahmedabad, India, 1956. One of the outstanding personalities of Swiss graphic design and author of, among other books, *A Graphic Design Manual* (see bibliography).

▼ 'Temple and Teahouse in Japan', exhibition poster designed by Armin Hofmann, 1955.
The large letters, cut in lino, follow the rectangular forms of Japanese seals. Hofmann has daringly reversed the tradition of Western letterforms, whose verticals have more weight than horizontals.

Tempel und Teehaus
in Japan
Ausstellung im
Gewerbemuseum
Basel
täglich geöffnet
4. Mai bis 31. Mai
10-12 und 14-18 Uhr
Eintritt frei

196

▲ 'American Books', small poster designed by Gérard Ifert for the United States Information Service (USIS) in Paris, 1958.

Ifert, trained at the Allgemeine Gewerbeschule in Basel, worked for Geigy as a freelance designer before moving to Paris, where he later collaborated with Adrian Frutiger. Ifert was a skilled photographer, and also an interior and furniture designer.

▲ 'Domestic Objects', small poster for a travelling exhibition, designed by Gérard Ifert for USIS, Paris, 1958. The poster had details of time and venue added.

Ifert demonstrates the Swiss attraction to the basic forms of circle and square, and both posters combine symmetry with asymmetry in a simple geometrical structure, with a vertical, central division on which type is ranged.

Typography and Typefaces

▲ *Schweizer Graphische Mitteilungen* (*SGM*), cover, January 1951.
This special issue on the future of the printing industry had a forward-looking design. The cover, on a lemon-yellow background, has typesetting in bold Monotype Grotesque, also used for headings on the inside pages, where the text was typeset in Times Roman.
▼ The following month's cover reverted to a centred layout set in Times Roman. The chief element of the cover was this device of ornamented initials, typical of the traditional typography sometimes described as 'English' and an example of everything the New Typography planned to overturn.

The disparities of style and attitude among Swiss designers showed as clearly in typography as they did in posters. The argument between symmetry and asymmetry, beween justified text and text ranged left, between the merits of serif and grotesque, was never one that could have a conclusion. Only in part was it a dispute between two generations. Tschichold was not alone among the earlier progressive designers in withdrawing to the 'classical' position. As to the Modernists, Max Bill was now more concerned with his work as an artist and with plans for the new design school at Ulm, and so less active as a typographer.[1] But the growing impact of Modernist attitudes was evident in the annual selection of 'Best Swiss Posters' and 'Best Produced Books'.

For many years after the Bill–Tschichold dispute the trade magazines treated Modernism with caution. In 1952 *Schweizer Graphische Mitteilungen* (*SGM*) fused with *Revue Suisse de l'Imprimerie* and *Typographische Monatsblätter* into a single monthly publication known by the initials *TM*. The chief figures in the new magazine were Rudolf Hostettler, who was co-editor of *SGM*, Emil Ruder, and the typographer Robert Büchler. Ruder was a key force in typographical thinking. He had been teaching at the Allgemeine Gewerbeschule in Basel since 1942 and shared a design practice with his fellow teacher Armin Hofmann. Ruder had an instinctive as well as informed understanding of Modernism. In a series of critical reviews in *SGM*, under the rubric 'Aus der Werkstatt unserer Zeit' (From Today's Workshop), he promoted not only work designed in Basel, such as that done for Geigy, but also that of his colleagues in Zurich, such as Lohse, and he reviewed new architecture and industrial design. Three articles, in February 1952, established Ruder as a supporter of radical change. The first examined Bauhaus typography – then little known. The second, 'Tea-Drinking, Typography, Symmetry and Asymmetry', took a relaxed view at odds with Tschichold: 'I would like us to love the old things more, and copy them less.' The third article was an illustrated history of Modernism.[2]

These contributions were among many false dawns of a new, revised Modernism, *SGM* and *TM* often backsliding into 'contemporary' stylistic mannerism. In January 1952, the first issue of the combined magazines retained Times as the text typeface; for the February issue that included his Bauhaus article, Ruder introduced Monotype

---

1. Max Bill was one of the founders of the Hochschule für Gestaltung at Ulm, in Germany, in 1951. He designed the buildings and was Director of the school and head of the Architecture and Product Design departments until 1956.
2. 'Kleine Stillehre der Moderne' (Little Lesson in Modern Style), *TM*, March 1954, pp.127-28.

▲ Emil Ruder illustrated his 'Little Lesson in Modern Style' in 1954 with illustrations of 1920s German typography, typeset in facsimile by Ruder's students. One letterhead was almost a caricature of functionalism: every instruction for the placing of the address, date, references and for folding having a typographical signal in the form of a dot or rule – the mannerisms identified as unnecessary by Max Bill.

Gewerbemuseum Basel
Ausstellung «die Zeitung»
9. April bis 18. Mai 1958
Geöffnet
werktags 10-12 und 14-18
sonntags 10-12 und 14-17
Eintritt frei

die

Zeitung

◄ 'The Newspaper', exhibition poster
designed by Emil Ruder, 1958.
This was a technical tour de force,
as the intentionally coarse half-tone
screen was cut by hand in lino.
The letters of 'Die Zeitung' are the
usual wood poster type, set without
spacing.

▼ Akzidenz Bold as it appeared in the Berthold Foundry catalogue of poster types. The example shows how little space was given at the sides of the (wood) letters. The tight spacing was exploited to give a dramatic graphic contrast by several Zurich designers, most notably by Siegfried Odermatt.

Bild-Druck

Herz As

Orient

Garn

▼ Three sanserif typefaces in their medium and text weights.
The two top lines are Akzidenz Grotesk, a late 19th-century German design, the favoured font of the 'constructive' designers.
In the centre, the Neue Haas Grotesk, produced in Switzerland in 1957 as a replacement for Akzidenz Grotesk. This font, slightly redesigned and wider spaced, and available for machine typesetting, became widely popular under the name Helvetica.

ecsCSR
ecsCSR

ecsCSR
ecsCSR

ecsCSR
ecsCSR

▲ The final row of letters, less geometrical and more calligraphic, is Univers, designed by Adrian Frutiger around 1957, initially for photocomposition.

grotesque and attempted to standardize the display advertisements. In March, *TM* reverted to a text set in Times. Not until 1953, when it was designed by Robert Büchler, did the magazine look 'Swiss'.

Büchler, quick to follow Neuburg's lead in the design of industrial catalogues and technical literature, had developed a sober Modernism. He set all *TM*'s text in Monotype grotesque, despite protests from French subscribers who found the typeface difficult to read. There were three columns, with space left at the top and bottom of the page for headings and captions. The smaller advertisements, previously typeset to a more or less standardized layout in Baskerville and later in Times, now combined asymmetry with the new typeface. The change seemed to demonstrate a positively progressive attitude and when Ruder's history of Modernism appeared, the following year, in 1954, the magazine had been re-shaped again by Büchler, this time in Gill Sans. Given their geometrical interests, Swiss designers might have been expected to adopt the geometrical sanserif typefaces of the 1920s, Futura and Erbar.

When Tschichold, a few months after his clash with Max Bill, wrote a long article on 'The Use of Printing Types in Advertising', he went out of his way, in a survey of all available types, to avoid the mention of Akzidenz Grotesk.[3] Grotesques and slab-serif Egyptian typefaces he scornfully described as only 'survivals from the nineteenth century which have recently enjoyed a short-lived popularity'. But the Swiss attitude was pragmatic, not theoretical. They were committed to the old grotesque, arguing that it had essential, but almost indefinable, subtleties. The Berthold typefoundry in Berlin, advertising in *TM* in February 1956, was able to make this claim for its Akzidenz Grotesk:

> Through continuous perseverance [with Akzidenz] and in its widespread use, Swiss typographers have created a style whose consummate achievement is now generally recognized as a standard to be aimed for in other countries.

Indeed, for Berthold, Akzidenz type, marketed as 'Standard' – a name that described its role in Swiss typography – soon became an important export.

Now that the Akzidenz design was sixty years old, attention focused on smoothing out some of its irregularities. At the Haas foundry near Basel, Max Miedinger reworked the Haas version of Akzidenz. This design appeared as Neue Haas Grotesk in 1957:

3. *Publicité*, Geneva 1947, p.74.

abcdefghijklmnopqrsßtuv
wxyz äöü 123456789o
ABCDEFGHIJKLMNOP
QRSTUVWXYZÄÖÜ

abcdefghijklmnopqrsß
tuvwxyz äöü 12345678
ABCDEFGHIJKLMNO
PQRSTUVWXYZÄÖÜ

gg*g*g

▲ Jan Tschichold's typeface design for the Uhertype filmsetting machine, designed in 1933-36. Tschichold notes that it does not return to the debased grotesque forms of 19th-century grotesques. In fact it is barely distinguishable from the British Gill Sans typeface, and he comments that the lowercase 'g' needs the horizontal bar at the top (as in Gill Sans). Tschichold reproduced his Uhertype design in 'Gute Schriftformen' (Good Letterforms), booklet 3, p.15 – specimen sheets produced for the Basel City Education Department in 1941, and much reprinted.

200

▶ 'New Forms in Italy', poster
designed by Carlo Vivarelli, 1954.
The vertical arrangement of the large
type emphasizes its formal qualities.
Akzidenz Grotesk and flat colour soon
became the most widely imitated
elements of Swiss graphic design.
Printed linocut and letterpress.

the curved strokes of lowercase 'e', 'c', and 's' and the capital 'C' and 'S' terminate horizontally, parallel with the text line, and the capital 'R' has been given a curved tail. Soon Neue Haas became known as Helvetica, which was also available for Linotype machine composition.

A quite different sanserif preceded Helvetica on the market. This was Univers, produced by the Deberny & Peignot foundry in Paris for its Lumitype filmsetting machine, but which soon became available on the metal typesetting systems. The designer of Univers was Adrian Frutiger. As a former student of Alfred Willimann and Walter Käch in Zurich, Frutiger allowed calligraphic traditions to influence his typeface. The result was a more open line of type, less mechanical than Helvetica. The most surprising innovation of Univers, planned at the start, was its number of weights and widths – twenty-one in all, from light extra-condensed to extra bold extended.

Univers was successful internationally, but it lacked the impersonal neutrality which the Modernists aimed at. Their choice remained Akzidenz Grotesk for larger sizes – in posters and the headings in books – and text set in Monotype grotesque (series 215), since this could be set by machine. Some typographers ordered Monotype's alternative characters, such as the capital 'G', to conform more closely to Akzidenz, which was not available for mechanical composition until 1959 on Linotype and 1960 on Intertype. In general, Zurich typographers chose to remain with Modernist tradition – Akzidenz and Monotype grotesques and Helvetica; those in Basel welcomed Univers.

Lettering was still important in the training of typographers, designers and trade apprentices. Tschichold had produced *Gute Schriftformen* (Good Letterforms) for the Basel education authority in 1941: a portfolio of six 16-page A4 pamphlets of printed type, lettering and calligraphy, largely historical, with notes and instructions. Akzidenz Grotesk is again excluded. The sanserif example is a design made by Tschichold himself at the time of his emigration to Switzerland. In 1954 the Swiss tradition of type design and lettering inherited by such as Frutiger was displayed in the first of a series of books. With the title *Lettera,* they reproduced both historical and contemporary alphabets and type designs, many of them fanciful. Of them, the condensed grotesque, a standby for magazine headlines in the 1960s, became a further element of the Swiss style to be welcomed abroad.

▼ The variations of the Univers range of typeface. The basic normal weight font is Univers 55; the expanded version is to the left (Univers 53), the italic and condensed variations to the right (Univers 56, 57, 58, 59), the lighter weights above (Univers 45, 46, 47, 48, 49) and the heavier weights below (Univers 63 & 73 – 65 & 75, 66 & 76, 67, 68).

The widest and heaviest weight, 83, stands alone at the bottom left; at the top right is the lightest and most condensed, Univers 39.
Such rationalization exemplifies the idea of a 'programme', much discussed by Karl Gerstner.

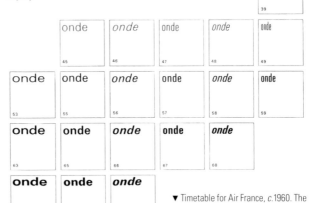

▼ Timetable for Air France, c.1960. The various weights and widths of Univers made it convenient for use in complex tabular typesetting. The timetable is filmset in a combination of extra bold, normal condensed, bold condensed, and some of the symbols designed by Frutiger.

▼ Symbols used in Air France timetables, designed to be typeset with the Univers font, c.1960.

▶ Cigarette pack designed by Jost Hochuli, 1961. The squares and lowercase Neue Haas Grotesk lettering are by this time stereotypes of Swiss design. Hochuli's design is reminiscent of Constructivist work which had been reproduced in early issues of the new journal *Neue Grafik* 'to draw attention to the fact that many of the tendencies operative in contemporary graphic design have their historical origin in the examples shown'. These examples included Lissitzky.

▼ Page from Jan Tschichold's *'Elementare Typographie'*, 1925, reproducing parts of Lissitzky's *The Story of Two Squares*.

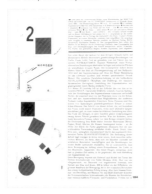

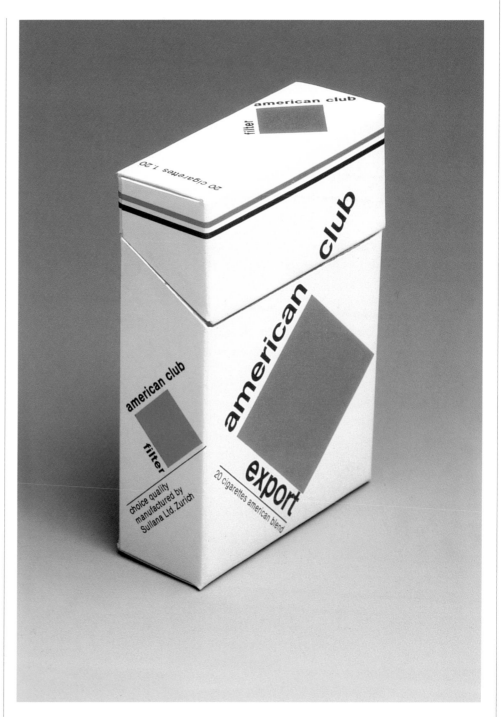

'New' Graphic Design
1958-1965

What is new in this new art is its almost mathematical clarity. Though it is striking
in its detailed design, it relies for its effect not on ornament but on the balance and tension
of form and colour. The constant change in style is a response to the subject matter or
to the product that is advertised. There are no hard and fast rules for this kind of art.
Editorial, *Neue Grafik*, no.1, 1958.

They [American designers] looked at Swiss work like they would look at paintings,
without understanding the content but admiring its formal beauty.
Aaron Burns, interview with Felix Berman, *Typographische Monatsblätter*, June 1968.

204

◀ 'Konstruktive Grafik' exhibition poster, designed by Hans Neuburg, 1958.

▲ Hans Neuburg's sketch demonstrating the structure and proportions of the 'Konstruktive Grafik' poster.
The sheet is divided into 12 squares, 3×4. The width of the remaining space (labelled 'cesura') provides the black lines typical of Neuburg's typography.

The two years 1958 and 1959 saw the Modernists realize their ambitions: they established a style and a point of view which they labelled 'Constructive', or 'neue Grafik' (new graphic design), and this was now identified abroad as 'Swiss Graphic Design'.

In 1958 Josef Müller-Brockmann took charge of the graphic design course at the Zurich Kunstgewerbeschule, and the quarterly *Neue Grafik* was launched. In the following year came three published statements which gave foreign readers their first insight into 'Swiss style' and its underlying ideas. These were Karl Gerstner and Markus Kutter's book *Die neue Graphik*; a special issue of *TM* devoted to 'Integral Typography'; and an article by Emil Ruder in *Graphis*: 'The Typography of Order'.[1]

Before the appointment of Müller-Brockmann to replace Ernst Keller at the Kunstgewerbeschule, the school's principal, Hans Fischli, announced that 'constructive graphic design, without individual affectations and without confusing playfulness, will be our guideline'.[2] Fischli was referring to the restricted visual language demonstrated in 'Konstruktive Grafik', an exhibition held at the Kunstgewerbemuseum in the Spring of 1958. Organized by Müller-Brockmann, 'Konstruktive Grafik' displayed the work of three senior designer colleagues: Hans Neuburg, Richard Paul Lohse and Carlo Vivarelli. In the catalogue Neuburg explained that 'Constructive graphics, according to us, is design that is developed out of the subject matter and is new and unique to each job.' But he admitted that

> We can recognize in most of the work on view a geometrical style of presentation which is a result of trying to compose the planes or the space so as to bring about a certain order . . .[3]

And Neuburg was ready as usual to defend the exhibitors against charges of formalism:

> Designers of Constructive graphics work from functional principles similar to those of modern architects, principles that are not in fact formalist, but constructive. . . . [These three designers] have tried to find a new stylistic basis for each task, and the careful observer will find that there are no schematic ideas dominating the finished designs . . . and between the individual solution of each of the three exhibitors there are striking differences.[4]

1. *Die neue Graphik*, Teufen 1959; *TM*, June/July, 1959; *Graphis*, no.85, October 1959. *Die neue Graphik* and Ruder's article have English texts. Gerstner's leading article in *TM* appeared in English in his book *Designing Programmes*, London 1964.
2. 'Konstruktive Grafik', exhibition catalogue, Kunstgewerbemuseum Zurich, 1958, n.p.
3. *Ibid.*
4. *Ibid.*

206

Kunstmuseum
Winterthur

Ungegenständliche
Malerei
in der Schweiz

19. Januar bis 9. März 1958
Geöffnet täglich 10–12 und 14–17 Uhr
ausser Montagvormittag

▲ Richard Paul Lohse's 1958 poster for the exhibition 'Non-Representational Painting in Switzerland' used the organizational device of the square – common to Lohse's paintings and much of his graphic design.

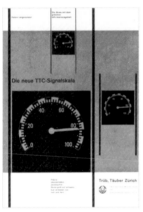

Die neue TTC-Signalskala

Trüb, Täuber Zürich

▲ Sheet from a folder advertising gauge display dials, designed by René Martinelli in Carlo Vivarelli's studio, 1955. The dial is set in a square within two vertical rules. This arrangement, repeated in three sizes, emphasizes the readability of the gauge at a distance. Martinelli came from Biel, in north-west Switzerland. He also worked for Müller-Brockmann. Like Vivarelli, Martinelli had worked at Studio Boggeri in Milan.

Yet Neuburg could not convincingly claim that examples of his own work in 'Konstruktive Grafik' were 'not in fact formalist'. On the contrary, the geometrical method of organizing the space is not only so overwhelming as to be the most conspicuous element in his designs but it is also unrelated to their subjects: the same heavy interlocking squares dominate his 'Konstruktive Grafik' poster and his advertisements for Saint-Gobain synthetic fibres.

Accusations of formalism could also be directed at Lohse's work in 'Konstruktive Grafik'. But there were of course 'striking differences' between Neuburg and Lohse. In Lohse's case the robust geometry and use of the square as an organizational device were part of an authentic personal style, carried over from his paintings. The third exhibitor, Carlo Vivarelli, was more successful in designing in a way that was 'new and unique for each job', and when the magazine *Neue Grafik* (New Graphic Design) was launched, it was he who designed the cover.

Neue Grafik was the single most important factor in establishing the international influence of Swiss graphic design. Publication was heralded, but not explicitly, in Spring 1958 by the 'Konstruktive Grafik' exhibition, although Müller-Brockmann gives a precise date and place for *Neue Grafik*'s conception: 15 February 1956 at the Seilbahn restaurant in Zurich. Müller-Brockmann, together with the exhibition's participants – Lohse, Hans Neuburg and Carlo Vivarelli – made up the editorial team. The initial proposal to include the Basel designers Armin Hofmann and Emil Ruder was put to one side, so that *Neue Grafik* came to represent the more rigid orthodoxy of Swiss graphic design as it had developed in Zurich.

Neue Grafik was a shiny, white-covered, near-square-format quarterly. It first appeared in Autumn 1958 and closed, after eighteen issues, in 1965. The page layout grid was designed by Vivarelli. Text and captions, in Monotype grotesque in German, English and French, are arranged in four columns. Apart from a few with a second flat colour, illustrations are black-and-white; most are one column wide and few wider than two columns.[5] The captions are minimal, and related to the illustrations by numbers.

The first editorial statement – signed, like much of the text, with the joint initials LMNV – has none of the declamatory style of earlier avant-garde manifestoes.[6]

---

5. There were four full-page colour illustrations in issue no.1 and several small colour illustrations to an article on 'The Physical Properties of Light' in issue 15.
6. Of the editors, Hans Neuburg, a professional writer, was by far the most active contributor, often providing two or three articles in a single issue. In the magazine's seven-year life, only two articles by Vivarelli were published, both on trademark design, and only three by Müller-Brockmann. Lohse's contributions, nine in all, covered a variety of topics.

Neue Grafik
New Graphic Design
Graphisme actuel

1

▲ Front cover of the first issue of *Neue Grafik,* designed by Carlo Vivarelli, 1958.
The four columns were the basis of the page layouts, made by Hans Neuburg.
▼ The early issues of *Neue Grafik* were sent to subscribers with a coloured identifying band.

Neue Grafik
New Graphic Design
Graphisme actuel

2

Rather than a clear programme, readers were given only hints of the magazine's aims. The editors had

examined work from all over the world which was in their opinion valid. . . . They do not prize modernity for its own sake or applaud boldness and originality at all costs, but they value the attempt at a solution by constructive methods, not an illusory solution based on emotional, representational effects. . . . The editors would like to stress the fact that the purpose of this opening number is to define their policy. The importance of design is examined from the angle of both art and industry but the editors are not content with that alone: they not only wish to exhibit certain aspects of design, they wish to stimulate discussion, to offer explanations, to give instruction and example. . . . The four editors pledge themselves to uphold the policy of reproducing only work which is absolutely contemporary in style. [7]

The overriding policy was to demonstrate first that the practice of New Graphic Design was inherently Swiss; second, that it was inevitably 'Constructive'; and third, that it was a logical development from Modernism.

The first *Neue Grafik* opens with an exhaustive presentation by Richard Paul Lohse of 'The Influence of Modern Art on Contemporary Graphic Design'. Almost thirty pages long, the essay is accompanied by 104 numbered illustrations. Lohse records the development of visual expression from Cubism to Constructivism, from German design between the two World Wars to, finally, postwar and contemporary work, all of it Swiss, and including examples by each of the editors.

To establish the predominance of the Swiss in developing a 'new' graphic design, Hans Neuburg follows Lohse's opening article with a review of what are described as 'recently designed' Swiss posters – though it looks back a quarter of a century to Max Bill's 'Negerkunst' of 1931. And Neuburg defines 'Constructive' attitudes: 'We disregard all those posters which derive only from painterly or illustrative tendencies . . . . From our point of view they are not interesting.' But among his choice of nearly fifty posters Neuburg cannot avoid some with 'illustrative tendencies'.

The editors' intention to make the magazine 'an international forum' was never achieved. In an article on graphics for industry, all thirty-five illustrations are of Swiss work – all by Zurich designers, apart from four by Karl Gerstner. The second issue of *Neue Grafik*, which

▲ In the first issue of *Neue Grafik* Richard P. Lohse's long article, 'The Influence of Modern Art on Contemporary Graphic Design', established the historical basis of Swiss New Graphic Design.

▼ One of four photographic advertisements made for Hoffmann-La Roche pharmaceuticals by René Groebli in *Neue Grafik*, no.1. Rovigon is described as a 'tonic for the middle-aged and elderly'. These were the only full-colour reproductions in the magazine until no.15, five years later.

7. Where necessary, minor amendments have been made to *Neue Grafik*'s original translations.

208

▲ Page from an article on graphic design for industry by Hans Neuburg in *Neue Grafik*, no.1. The illustrations show work by Vivarelli in the top row and at the bottom; by Sigfried Odermatt for BP in the centre; and a Philips leaflet by Neuburg, centre right.

▼ Single page of 'Catalogues of Art Exhibitions', the article written and laid out by Max Bill in *Neue Grafik*, no.2, 1959. Bill keeps to the 4-column grid devised by Carlo Vivarelli, but he places descriptive captions close to the images instead of following Neuburg's awkward means of connecting captions to illustrations by numbers.

appeared in July 1959, nearly a year after the first, introduces 'Graphic Designers of the New Generation'. Again, all are Swiss. If the editors had 'examined work from all over the world', then they were applying their criterion of 'judging it according to a quality of inevitability' with extreme rigour.

Neuburg used the magazine to continue his campaigning on behalf of 'Industriegrafik'. Though he cites the way that manufacturers have welcomed graphic design, rather than stressing its practical use in organizing information effectively, he writes that the most important demand of 'Industriegrafik' is 'without doubt the mastery of two- and three-dimensional space'. He castigates those who 'attempt a solution by inappropriate, spurious methods and contortions', but provides little careful criticism. In general, *Neue Grafik* made only an occasional analysis of work designed for a particular task, or gave space to serious critical studies.

One exception was in issue no.2, when Max Bill examined the three types of catalogue for art exhibitions. His first category is the catalogue designed like an art monograph, with the text and related illustrations followed by the list of works; the second type comprises a list, giving full details of the exhibits and a selection of illustrations; the third is a comprehensive catalogue, every work illustrated and complete details given. Bill gives each of his first two categories a double-page spread and gives the third an extra page. Several examples of each type are illustrated – Bill's own designs among them – with descriptive captions.

The editorial note states that Bill is 'responsible for the layout of his article which conforms to the style of the journal'. In reality, although he follows the grid, he implicitly criticizes Neuburg's use of the layout. By not relying on numbers to relate the illustration to the caption, Bill keeps the caption as a single unit of text, positioning it close to the image. By contrast, the article following Bill's is in the standard *Neue Grafik* style, with illustrations separated from their captions. Eighty works of young designers are dispersed over sixteen pages with only a brief introduction, no apparent sequence or structure, no commentary or extended captions, and no indication of the size of the originals.

In a rare exception to its general surveys, the fifth issue of *Neue Grafik* dealt extensively with a single comprehensive piece of design. This was a review of the book *Geigy heute* (Geigy Today) and the programmes and invitations for events celebrating Geigy's bicentenary (see p.228). Karl Gerstner, the designer chiefly responsible, provided the detailed commentary, so that the reader has the unusual opportunity of understanding the problems of the job, and how they were looked at and resolved. In this rare case, equal importance is given to the finished work and to the story of its design.

Neue Grafik took care to consider photography, both as part of Modernist practice and in its design applications. In issue no. 4 Ernst Scheidegger told readers that 'the photograph seems to approach reality more closely than the drawing', and it 'enables us to see more, to see more precisely, and to share visual experiences'.[8] Although Scheidegger stresses the 'sachlich' – 'the more documentary the photograph the better' – he also talks of its use as metaphor, 'An effectively lit ice cube represents the refrigerator' (see p.191). He points out that photography gives the designer 'a practically inexhaustible fund of creative ideas', that photography 'becomes part of design when the photograph is used as a typographical element', and he cites the lead given by Stankowski and Lohse in this method.

Neuburg introduced Stankowski's widely varied and experimental photographs in *Neue Grafik* as part of the magazine's interest in the history of photography.[9] Indeed, the historical Modernist underpinning of Swiss graphic design, initiated by Lohse, was repeatedly invoked over the six years of *Neue Grafik*'s life. When Carlo Belloli gave an account of modern Italian graphic design in the third issue, he gave special weight to its Swiss participants.[10] In the same issue Hans Neuburg describes advertising by Anton Stankowski from his time in Zurich in the 1930s. This was the moment, Neuburg comments, when

> Constructive German graphic design began to establish its own individual programme . . . . This is not a retrospective article but rather one which is to display a continuity which is still at work.
>
> We do not wish to present a biographical sketch principally but to draw attention to the fact that many of the tendencies operative in contemporary graphic design have their historical origin in the examples shown. Young graphic designers in particular will see from them that thirty years ago men were working with

▲ *Neue Grafik*, no.2, 1959, made a selection of 'Graphic Designers of the New Generation' – all Swiss. It is one of the few pages of the magazine to use flat colour to reproduce work. This page shows designs by Nelly Rudin.

▼ Illustrations to Ernst Scheidegger's article on photography in issue no.4 of *Neue Grafik*: the advertisement designed by Igildo Biesele for a Geigy product (to help leather to keep its grain) plus the original photograph. Scheidegger notes the value of 'honest and careful retouching'.

8. Ernst Scheidegger studied as a photographer and designer in Zurich with Hans Finsler and Alfred Willimann. He also studied and worked with Max Bill, worked as a designer for the Marshall Plan in Paris and as a photojournalist, and taught at the Ulm Hochschule für Gestaltung under Bill.
9. Hans Neuburg had considerable authority as a writer on photography. Editor of the monthly magazine *Camera*, 1952-53, he also organized the 1952 World Photography Exhibition in Lucerne.
10. Carlo Belloli, a Concrete poet, appears in *Spirale*, no.8, 1960, p.42. Belloli was the husband of the artist Mary Vieira, designer of the posters on pp.174 and 175.

the same imaginative power, skill and talent as now to create industrial or other styles. Drawing these parallels is the main purpose of this article.

In other words, Neuburg is quite clear that his own style derives from Stankowski's early work. [11]

A historical survey of posters undertaken by Neuburg in the fourth issue of *Neue Grafik* follows Max Bill's example of dividing the subject into three categories: 'Lettering in the Pictorial Poster', 'The Typographic Poster' and 'The Concert Poster'. But the text is disappointingly unfocused, Neuburg typically remarking that 'All the examples are representative and all give evidence of a unified, homogeneous conception of picture and text.'

First-hand accounts of work between the wars were given by two survivors of the pioneering times – Henryk Berlewi in Poland and Paul Schuitema in the Netherlands; and Lohse described *De 8 en Opbouw*, the Dutch architectural magazine of the period. [12] Paul Schuitema, a survivor from the De Stijl period, was critical of *Neue Grafik*'s attachment to history. Writing on 'New Typographical Design in 1930' he gave a warning:

> We are now especially oversophisticated and underdeveloped, technically advanced and psychologically retarded. . . . And it is not a particularly good thing that people should be interested in what was going on in the Thirties. [13]

More positively, Schuitema denies the special interest of his contemporaries' work. It has 'already become part of history. The only possibility is to go on logically from there, from those clear, definite principles.'

Social responsibility was an intermittent concern of the *Neue Grafik* contributors. Scheidegger writes that the designer 'is responsible for shaping and changing his environment; he is attempting to educate his fellows visually', and should 'contribute to culture through his use of photography, and by giving his work an ethical basis'. [14] Hans Hilfiker, designer of the famous Swiss Railways clock and now on the executive board of the domestic appliance company Therma (see pp.236, 237), argued more philosophically, that authority was given to human beings by their unique attributes of speech and inventive abilities. For this reason, the designer has authority, and with authority comes responsibility: 'To make use of this distinguishing authority without acknowledgement of the corresponding responsibility is incompatible with our innate conception of duty and justice.' [15] Such sentiments reveal the same social sensitivity as that expressed by Richard Paul Lohse, who complains that the designer is obliged to play a part in 'the ruthless combination of production, sale and profit'. On the one hand the designer is a creative artist and on the other hand a public relations specialist, but one who is still anxious to attach personal artistic aims to an alien product. Lohse nonetheless compares the designer favourably with the artist. What the designer does

> is less spectacular but often of greater profundity, shows more sense of responsibility and is more sincere despite the trivial purpose for which [the work] is intended . . .

Lohse asks,

> Is it because he is a particular type of person or is it his background which leads a young man with a certain degree of visual and intellectual sensibility to put that sensibility on the market? [16]

The education of such young men (and women) had been a recurring topic in *Neue Grafik*. The third issue carried illustrated reports on foundation courses at the Institute of Design in Chicago and at the Zurich Kunstgewerbeschule. Robert S. Gessner, who was responsible for the teaching of apprentices at the Zurich school, presents a demanding down-to-earth list of designers' educational needs – to develop a good social manner, artistic sensibility, and an ability to initiate and cooperate in research, production and sales; to be trained to deal with a variety of products used in design and its execution; to understand the aims and effect of work undertaken; to have manual and creative skills and business ability; and to be able to write and speak coherently and with a knowledge of foreign languages. But this training could be completed only by experience in a good design studio.

That professional training consists of the inculcation of 'Constructive graphics' as a *Neue Grafik* doctrine is made clear in issue no.7. Müller-Brockmann gives an account of his Zurich course with nearly two hundred illustrations. Each student spends two terms in the final year of the course designing

> all the printed matter required by a specific firm for internal and external use, all the advertising matter, the trade insignia on the facade of the building and on the delivery van, the neon sign and a small exhibition. In

11. Neuburg makes no mention of the fact that Stankowski had at the time a thriving practice in Stuttgart, which continued into the 1970s.

12. *Neue Grafik*, no.14, 1962, pp.47-49. De 8 and Opbouw were two groups of Dutch architects who designed their magazine. Mart Stam was a member of De 8.

13. *Neue Grafik*, no.11, 1961, p.19.

14. *Neue Grafik*, no.4, 1960, pp.43-44.

15. 'Design and Responsibility', *Neue Grafik*, no.15, 1963, pp.55-58.

16. 'On the Sociological Position of the Designer', *Neue Grafik*, no.3, 1959, p.59.

▲ In issue no.7 of *Neue Grafik*, Josef Müller-Brockmann illustrated work by students at the Kunstgewerbeschule in Zurich. Mathematically based foundation studies were followed by work – using exclusively Akzidenz Grotesk – that was indistinguishable from that of practising professionals.

▼ In the final issue of *Neue Grafik*, no.17/18, 1965, Fridolin Müller described the course he ran in Biel, in northwest Switzerland. After preliminary exercises very similar to Armin Hofmann's (see p.215), the students progressed to more Zurich-like design.

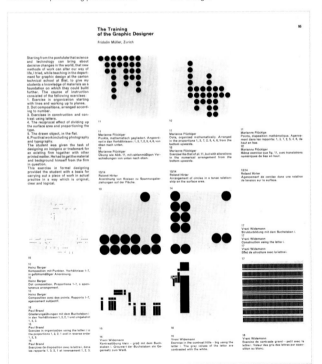

the second half of the fourth year, he has to do a similar piece of work, though for a different firm.[17]

The work has a standardized appearance, and might well have been produced in Müller-Brockmann's studio. Reprinted in his book *The Graphic Artist and his Design Problems*, within a few years such exercises became an international model not only for students, but for institutions and businesses, large and small.

The first issue described the aims of the Ulm Hochschule für Gestaltung, where each of the magazine's co-editors was at some point a visiting teacher.[18] *Neue Grafik* returned to the subject of Ulm in 1962. A member of the school's Visual Communication Department reported on a student project 'which sets out to produce not graphic designers but rather specialists who are in a position to control and put into practice the visual means of communication'.[19] Specialists in verbal communication were brought into the studios, and the heads of other departments – sociology, psychology, methodology, photography and advertising – were consulted. In other words, at Ulm there was more interest in teamwork than in the work of the individual student. Though the results were dull, it was an innovation for the magazine to consider the user's response to a design, not merely its formal aspects.

However inward-looking *Neue Grafik* appeared, however much the work it reproduced became models of a style to be imitated, the magazine showed a pattern of wide interests. They ranged from packaging and exhibition design to more theoretical subjects, such as the graphic representation of movement (no.12), the physical properties of light (no.15) and, in the final issue, the design of national flags. By this point *Neue Grafik* had achieved its aims in promoting a single 'Swiss style'.

17. 'A Training System for the Graphic Designer', *Neue Grafik*, no.7, 1960, p.19.
18. In 1958 Max Bill had recently resigned as Director of the Hochschule.
19. Dolf Sass, 'Report on the Work of a Group of Students at the Hochschule für Gestaltung Ulm', *Neue Grafik*, no.12, 1962, pp.50-57.

Flatness and Space

▶ 'Experiment in Plane and Space', exhibition poster, designed by Jörg Hamburger, 1962. Hamburger uses the simplest geometry in flat areas of colour to express the theme exactly. The design resolves the conflict between the illusion of perspective and the two-dimensional surface which the Modernists were at pains to preserve.

wohnbedarf
basel
neue möbel
von
werner blaser

ausstellung
aeschenvorstadt 43
15.– 29. märz 1958

The conventions of 'Constructive' design are all here: lowercase typography, documentary ('sachlich') photography, and geometry. The square module in the joint of the three lengths of wood is repeated in the structure of the design, based on squares.

The base of the horizontal length of wood – on the lower edge of the white band – rests on the base of a square at the top of the poster. Squares, the height of the lower red band, placed in the bottom left and right corners, leave a gap which is the width of one tongue of the joint.

The Appeal of Japan

◀ Poster by Celestino Piatti for the Basel branch of the Wohnbedarf furniture store, advertising a special display of furniture designed by the architect Werner Blaser, 1958.
▼ Photograph by Werner Blaser of a Japanese house, from his book *Struktur und Gestalt in Japan* (Structure and Form in Japan), published in 1963.

This facade has obvious similarities to both Mondrian's paintings and the graphic work of Richard Paul Lohse. Blaser's photographs reinforced the Swiss interest in rectangular and modular design and in Japanese culture, which had a special appeal for Swiss designers, whose work found some of its first admirers in Japan.
▼ 'Old and New Forms in Japan', poster by Armin Hofmann, 1959. Printed lino and letterpress, black on yellow ochre ground.

5. Sept. bis
11. Okt.
Gewerbemuseum
Basel

Alte und
neue Formen
in Japan

Celestino Piatti Born 1922
Graphic designer, illustrator and painter. Studied at Zurich Kunstgewerbeschule, 1937-38. Apprenticed at Fretz printers, 1938-42. Own studio from 1948. Best known as art director of the paperback publishers Deutscher Taschenbuch Verlag (dtv), for which he designed more than 5,000 covers. Also successful as children's book illustrator.

► Poster for a joint exhibition of the sculptor Robert Jacobsen and the painter Serge Poliakoff, designed by Armin Hofmann, 1958. With their lettering more often drawn than using ready-made type forms, and their less obvious geometry, Hofmann's designs show relative graphic freedom by comparison with their Zurich 'Constructive' counterparts. Even this geometrically based design is less stiffly elegant than, say, exhibition posters designed by Richard Paul Lohse. The almost equal areas of red and black can be read as forms, as space, or as plane surfaces.

▼ Franz Kline and Alfred Jensen, two-artist exhibition poster designed by Armin Hofmann, 1964. Black linocut overprinted with brown type.

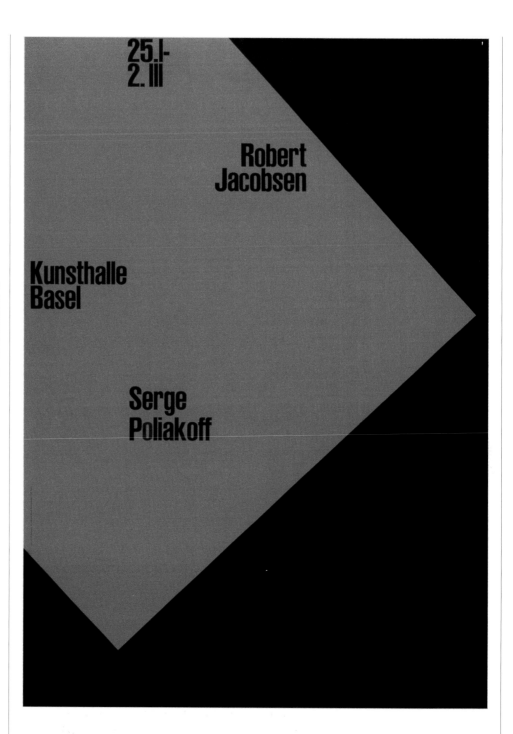

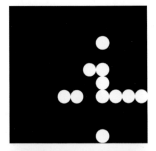

▼ Elementary exercises in Armin Hofmann's course at the Allgemeine Gewerbeschule in Basel from the early 1950s, illustrated in *Graphis*, no.80, 1958.

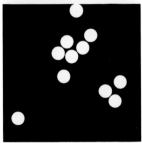

▲ On a square ground Hofmann's students make geometrical and random arrangements of discs.

▲ 'Horizontal-Vertical Endless Rhythm II', coloured relief by the Berne artist-designer Marcel Wyss, 1954. Such works demonstrate the interest in geometrical structures shared by Concrete artists and designers.

A French designer, one of a group visiting Switzerland, was depressed by the austere conformity of the Zurich style. He was shocked to find a training where Akzidenz Grotesk was the only typeface allowed and where freely drawn illustration was excluded. By contrast, the visiting designers' found the teaching in Basel to be 'exemplary, based on a tradition before it became a system, and typography not exclusively based on grotesque'.[1] The graphic design department of the Basel Allgemeine Gewerbeschule had only ten full-time students in each year of its four-year course. Design was taught by one of Basel's leading commercial artists, Donald Brun, and by Armin Hofmann; Emil Ruder was in charge of typography for trade students, and Theo Ballmer taught photography.

The training at Basel was varied. At the Gewerbeschule a class under a commercial designer such as Donald Brun was very different from one under the more aesthetically demanding Armin Hofmann, and students were sometimes confused by their contrasting requirements. As Hofmann describes in a *Graphis* article in 1958, student exercises in the four-year course begin with compositional exercises, first with lines and then with small discs, arranged both randomly and systematically.[2] Hofmann writes that, 'a distinction must be made between instinctive and mathematical procedures. These two forms of expression embody many design principles, such as repetition, intensification, contrast and dispersion.' An exercise in designing with geometrical elements familiarizes the student with 'the written character in its most primitive form', as a prelude to designing letterforms. Designs in which lettering was allied with drawn silhouettes – of keys, nuts and bolts, and spanners – demonstrated a level of visual sophistication that was unlike the work of students in other countries. Under Hofmann's uncompromising eye, contours were endlessly refined, adding black here, white there. The fact that the lettering was hand-drawn – rather than typeset in grotesque – distinguishes it from the doctrinaire uniformity of Müller-Brockmann's Zurich course.

Hofmann was inspired, charismatic and hugely influential. His ideas, set down in *A Graphic Design Manual: Principles and Practice,* first published in 1965, were introduced in design schools across the world. More importantly, Hofmann was interested in using graphics to communicate ideas.

1. Raoul Jean Moulin, 'Voyage en Helvétie', *TM*, August/September 1961, pp.553-54. The comment was made by Fernand Baudin.
2. 'A Contribution to the Education of the Commercial Artist', *Graphis*, no.80, November/December 1958, pp.504-17.

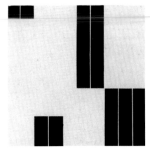

▲ Among the formal exercises on Armin Hofmann's course was the organization of vertical black bars made in lengths of fixed units to form groups within a square.
▼ The type of student illustration – refined silhouettes – which Hofmann taught became one of the defining techniques of the Geigy style.

▼ Advertisement for a Geigy product for post-dental treatment, designed by Enzo Rösli, *c.*1954. Rösli taught for a time in the mid-1950s at the Basel Allgemeine Gewerbeschule.

216

▶ Poster for an open-air ballet performance, designed by Armin Hofmann, 1959. One of the defining images of Swiss graphic design, each element contributes to its dramatic elegance. The brilliant white of the lettering is a foil to the half-tone greys of the photograph; the dancer, cut off at head and foot, is transformed into a graphic sign of movement rather than a three-dimensional pictorial image, emphasized by the round forms of the letters and further accentuated by the clean geometry of the 'i' and the two 'l's and, most ingeniously, by Hofmann's substituting a circle as the dot on the 'i' in place of the conventional square.
Printed offset.

Basler
Freilichtspiele
1959
19.-31. August
im
Rosenfeldpark

Giselle

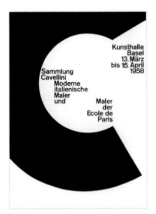

▼ Poster for an exhibition of the Cavellini Collection, designed by Armin Hofmann, 1958.
Hofmann's use of initial letters as images set a kind of house style for exhibitions at the Basel Kunsthalle. Printed letterpress and linocut in black.

▲ Poster for the promotion of cancer research, designed by Gerhard Forster, 1967. A student of Armin Hofmann, Forster adopted his teacher's enlarged initial letter.
Forster won a competition to advertise Pirelli tyres and moved to Italy in 1963, where he became one of Milan's most prominent and highly regarded graphic designers.

The student who can represent rising, falling, opposed and radiating elements with simple means has taken the first step toward the application of his art. It would be wrong to conceive the work of the designer as anything but the service of giving messages, events, ideas and values every kind of visible form.[3]

Yet Hofmann's own designs, mostly posters for cultural events, vary in style and success. His early posters rely on silhouettes and large letters, easily reproduced by linocut. In a series of posters for art exhibitions, the initial letters of artists' names are used as a pretext for formal exercises in a visual language that belongs to the designer, not to the work of the exhibited artists. With the exception of the *Giselle* poster of 1959, Hofmann's more Constructive-looking work using photographs often lacks his colleagues' confident handling of asymmetrical design. There is an almost mechanical balance between half-tone and half-tone, half-tone and solid, between white space and black, between lettering and image. In some cases this lack of graphic tension was replaced by unresolved juxtapositions, exemplified by his poster for an open-air performance of *William Tell* in 1963: each element – type, photograph and lettering – faultlessly designed, yet put together without dramatic effect. By contrast, his earlier poster for an exhibition of the artists Robert Jacobsen and Serge Poliakoff in 1958 (p.214), while it gives no idea of the character of the work on show, compels attention by its simple, dynamic composition.

Like Hofmann, Emil Ruder had studied in Zurich. One of his teachers was Walter Käch, the expert calligrapher and letterer who, like Tschichold, had renounced an early mastery of progressive typography to adopt a traditional style. From this starting point, Ruder set out on a long road of rediscovery, back to the Modernism that Käch had left behind. Ruder's early work has a light, Scandinavian aestheticism (known generally at the time as 'contemporary'), with serif type and subdued colour. His finely tuned sensibility to the printed and unprinted areas of a design, and to the shapes of letters and their relationships, was apparent in the issue of *TM* where he demonstrated the possibilities of design with the new Univers type.[4] He summed up the typographer's role thus: 'It is our job to give language a form, to give it durability and to ensure that it has a future life.'

When Ruder explained 'The Typography of Order' in *Graphis* he pointed to the role of the grid in achieving an

▲ Poster for an open-air production of *William Tell*, designed by Armin Hofmann, 1963.
The over-formalized mechanical lettering – intended to suggest the path of the crossbow-shot towards the apple – remains an abstract pattern, in a style more industrial than conventionally artistic.
Printed litho in black.

▲ 'Basel and Refugee Year', poster by Uli Schierle, a student in the graphic design class at the Allgemeine Gewerbeschule. In a Hofmann-like manner, Schierle demonstrates the effect of combining abstract forms with photography for a topic which demands a dramatic appeal. Printed litho in black and brown.

3. Armin Hofmann, *A Graphic Design Manual: Principles and Practice*, Teufen / New York 1965, p.10. A Japanese edition was published in 1968.
4. 'Die Univers in der Typographie', *TM*, January 1961, pp.18-40.

218

▲ Cover of the catalogue for the exhibition 'Typography' at the Basel Gewerbemuseum, adapted by Emil Ruder, from the poster design by Robert Büchler, 1960. The design derives its structure from the position of the vowels in the alphabet.
▼ In the 100-page A5 catalogue Emil Ruder presents an illustrated history of typography since the 19th century. To demonstrate the relationship between form and function, among more than 100 illustrations is a programme for the coronation ceremony of Queen Elizabeth II, designed by the English typographer Stanley Morison in 1953 (bottom).

integrated 'overall' design (*Durchgestaltung*).[5] In 1960 he produced a small historical survey, the catalogue to an exhibition called simply *Typographie* (like his later, much larger, textbook). Ruder filled the one hundred pages of this little book with an astonishingly complete illustrated survey of modern typography, from William Morris, via Van de Velde, Futurism, the Bauhaus and Tschichold to Max Bill and Gerstner. Ruder surprisingly demonstrates his commitment to 'fitness for purpose' – rather than style – by including American examples and, from England, the flamboyantly traditional Order of Service of the coronation of Queen Elizabeth II. However bizarre this English design looks in a Swiss context, Ruder shares the forthright attitudes of its designer, the veteran typographer Stanley Morison. 'Typography', he writes, 'like architecture and industrial design, has a clear duty; its sole purpose is communication' – words which could well have been written by Morison.

Ruder begins by listing the components of typography: movable type in restricted sizes and weights, and different styles; lines (printer's metal rules); the unprinted areas of paper (space within and around the print), and colour. After this Ruder comes to the question of form. As soon as there is a single letter on a sheet of paper, Ruder says, a series of relationships develops: first, between the black printed image of the letter and its unprinted white background; then between the unprinted white on the inside of the letter and the white space between the letters; and, finally, between the space between words and the space between lines.

> The formal quality of every piece of typography depends on the relationship between the printed and unprinted parts. To see only what is printed, to overlook the decisive contribution of the unprinted parts, is a sign of professional immaturity. The business of typography is a continual weighing up of white and black, which requires a thorough knowledge of the laws governing optical values.[6]

No other designer since Jan Tschichold was as committed as Ruder to the discipline of letterpress typography or wrote about it with such conviction.

▲ Emil Ruder's insistence that the primary aim of typography was communication did not exclude aesthetic effects. Contrast was one of his methods. Words typeset in roman (upright) letters alternate with italic in the design of wrapping paper for a Paris fashion house. The illustration is from Ruder's article on the creative possibilities of Univers (*TM,* January 1961).
▼ 'Basel Buildings for Conservation', exhibition poster designed by Emil Ruder, 1960.
Letterpress with linocut lettering.

gewerbe museum basel erhaltenswerte basler bauten

Both designs take advantage of the emphatic slope of Univers italic; Ruder adapted them as illustrations in his book, *Typography*, published in 1967.

5. *Graphis*, no.85, October 1958.
6. 'Typographie als Mitteilung und als Form' (Typography as Communication and as Form), in *Typographie*, catalogue, Gewerbemuseum Basel, 1960, n.p.

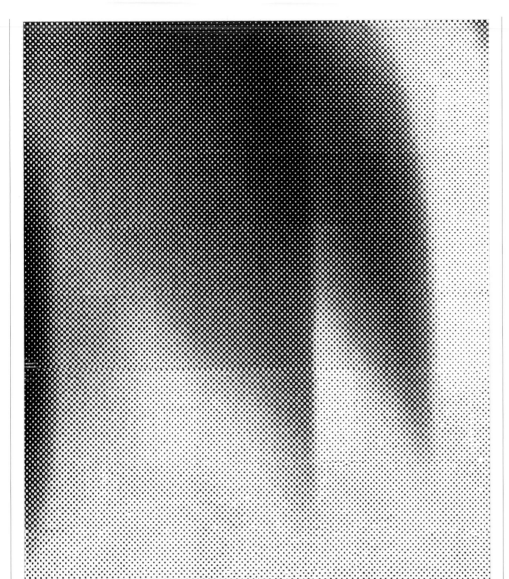

ungegenständliche Photographie

Gewerbemuseum Basel 27. Februar bis 10. April 1960   Täglich 10-12 und 14-17 Uhr Eintritt frei

◀ 'Abstract Photography', exhibition poster, designed by Emil Ruder, 1960. Ruder was essentially devoted to the craft of letterpress printing. In an astonishing work of craftsmanship, the coarse half-tone screen in this poster has been cut in lino. In the full 'Weltformat' size, the only imperfection is a scarcely visible horizontal join of the two linoleum blocks.

220

For Saffa, the Swiss Women's Exhibition in 1958, all the graphics were designed by former students of the Basel Allgemeine Gewerbeschule. In 1960 there were only ten women among the nearly 300 members of the Verband Schweizerischer Grafiker, but this was as high a proportion of practising women designers as in other advanced countries – and higher than some, despite the fact that women did not get full voting rights in Switzerland until 1971.

▲ The Saffa symbol, designed by Heidi Soland, gave a new strength and elegance to the common female sign.
▼ Voucher for the exhibition, designed by Elisabeth Dietschi.

▶ Poster designed by Nelly Rudin. The green geometrical shape, suggesting the development from early civilization to modern woman, is governed by a sequence of square units.

Saffa 1958 Zürich

17. Juli bis 15. September
Ausstellung
Die Schweizer Frau - ihr Leben - ihre Arbeit

French-speaking Switzerland

Designers in the cities of Geneva and Lausanne traditionally took their lead from Paris. They were less ready to practise the Constructive style. But there were a few notable exceptions.

▼ Poster for an insurance company by Jean and Lucien Ongaro, 1959. The Geneva-born Ongaro twins had opened a design office in the city in 1948.

▼ Poster by Roger Geiser for the Lausanne Film Club, 1960. This was one of a series designed by Geiser over several years. Although he had been a student in Basel, the design shows a marked influence of the Zurich style. Geiser was a teacher at the art school in Lausanne.

▼ Poster for the Lausanne Theatre production of the 17th-century play *Life Is a Dream* by Calderón de la Barca, designed by Aldo Poretti, 1960.

HELVETIA-ACCIDENTS
vous protège

zurich   bleicherweg 19
genève   longemalle 1

TM and 'Integral Typography'

▲ Cover of *TM*, January 1961, designed by Emil Ruder. Starting with the normal weight and width of Univers, Ruder designed covers for all the issues in 1961. They followed this layout, using the variations of Univers in roman and italic, bold and light, condensed and expanded.
The January issue included Ruder's essay on the design of Univers and his examples demonstrating the typeface's potential for the typographer.

From 1946 Emil Ruder slowly emerged in *Typographische Monatsblätter* as an exponent of Modernism. Between 1957 and 1959 he contributed a series of four articles with the title 'Wesentliches' (Fundamentals): 'The Plane', 'The Line', 'The Word' and 'Rhythm'. They formed the basis of his thinking, summed up in 1967 in the book *Typography*.

'Integral Typography', a special issue of *TM* in 1959, examined the developments of Modernism. Ruder challengingly took the title of his contribution – 'Contemporary Typography' – from an earlier article by Tschichold, who claimed the graphic designer to be

> primarily visual; a person who knows how to handle colour and form; more a painter and draughtsman than a thinker, who uses the medium for graphic fireworks so as to show off what he can do.[1]

Ruder took exception to this view. He maintained that a good designer with four years' professional training was a valuable partner of the typesetter. But his main disagreement with Tschichold was on the question of asymmetry. Tschichold now repeatedly claimed that typography was essentially symmetrical and that centring a line of type was technically simple. Ruder's view was the opposite. 'Asymmetry', he wrote,

> is technically the easiest and most logical. The line, with a fixed starting point, establishes the width which the letters and spaces take up. . . . Centring a line is less rational. In both hand and machine composition it takes more work.[2]

Ruder followed this with more technical argument, saying that although Linotype could centre a line automatically, half the Monotype machines in Switzerland could not, and that even with the latest models centring was more complicated than ranging type left.

Ruder was supported by his Basel teaching colleague Robert Büchler, who maintained that centred type had survived as a convention because the printer's main occupation until the nineteenth century was producing books. The printer's craft was now an industry, where new types of work posed problems which could not be solved with symmetry. Büchler was theoretical and aphoristic:

> Form is the outcome of function: in typography, function means to make ideas visible. Typography is exclusively in the service of communication. So its language calls for simplicity and clarity. Function here means satisfying the first demand, which we call legibility. Form is the visual expression of the thought.[3]

▲ Cover of *TM*, January 1960, designed by Yves Zimmermann. The letters spell out the title phonetically, reading the right-hand column first: te-em-1 / tip-o / gr-afise / mo-naz / bl-etr. The next five issues broke down the title in different ways, and with similar eccentricity. Zimmermann was a Basel typographer, one of Ruder's most able students. He worked in the USA and Canada before settling in Barcelona.

▲ Cover of *TM*, August / September 1960, one of a series designed by Siegfried Odermatt. The photographs, by W.S. Eberle, which showed parts of the printing process, were taken to advertise a Zurich printer.

---

1. *TM*, special issue, June / July 1959, p.363.
2. *Ibid.*, p.363-64.
3. *Ibid.*, p.351.

When Büchler added, 'A form without function is merely formalism', he was implying a criticism of the excessive rigidity of some Constructive graphics.

The antidote to formalism was suggested by Karl Gerstner. His contribution, a long illustrated essay, had also provided the special issue with its title. 'Integral Typography', reprinted in his book *Programme entwerfen* (Designing Programmes), 1964, became a key text of typographic history. Gerstner reviewed the theories of previous decades – the 'new' and 'elemental' typography of the 1920s and the 'functional' typography of the early 1940s – and he reminded readers of Moholy-Nagy's dictum, 'Legibility and communication should never suffer from a previously held aesthetic.'

Today typographers use both sanserif and roman type, set books both symmetrically and asymmetrically, use both flush left, ragged right and flush left, flush right. Today everything is stylistically allowable, allowable from the point of view of up-to-dateness.

Gerstner then arrives at his concept of 'integral'.

The designer's freedom lies not at the margin of a task but at its very centre. Only then is the typographer free to perform as an artist when he understands and considers all the parts of the job in hand. And every solution he finds on this basis will be an integral one, will achieve a unity between language and type, between content and form.[4]

What integral means is 'shaped into a whole', and typography is 'the art of making a whole out of predetermined parts'. To analyse the parts – the letters, their combinations into words and their arrangement – Gerstner takes illustrations from very disparate sources, from Schwitters's 1932 'word-sonata' (in typography by Tschichold), from Piet Zwart, a page of Mallarmé, a Concrete poem, a front page of the New York *Daily News*, a Max Bill poster and an American direct mail sheet.

The result of integral typography is 'a new unity'. . . . Unity is reached in different phases, each successor including its predecessor:

– in the integration of different signs, different letters into the word
– in the integration of different words into the sentence
– in the integration of different sentences into the 'reading-time' dimension
– in the integration of independent problems and functions.[5]

▲ Advertisements in a standardized layout typeset in Akzidenz Grotesk and Monotype grotesque, *TM*, 1960.

▲ Revision of standardized advertisements set in Univers, *TM*, 1960.

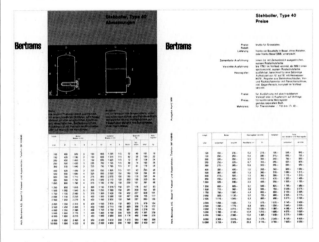

▲ Pages from a brochure for hot-water cylinders, designed by Robert Büchler, 1959, an illustration in the 'Integral Typography' issue of *TM*. Büchler's work for an industrial client keeps the conventions in the typography of tables (centred headings in the columns), but Modernist asymmetry allows him to lay out the information on the page with a clear logic.

4. *Ibid.*, p.340.
5. *Ibid.*, p.349.

Auf das Thema der integralen Typographie bezogen ist die untenstehende Abbildung, als Dokument eines einstmals neuen Beginnens, als grundsätzliches und folgenreiches Experiment interessant. Nicht so als typographische Leistung, die der Autor selber als unvollkommen bezeichnet. Eine Seite aus dem Erstdruck einer Dichtung von Stéphane Mallarmé, ‹le coup de dés›, 1897 in der Zeitschrift ‹Cosmopolis› publiziert⁴.

Paul Valéry schreibt darüber⁴: ‹Seine (Mallarmés) ganze Erfindung, abgeleitet aus jahrelang betriebenen Sprach-, Buch-, Musikanalysen, gründet sich auf der Betrachtung der Seite als visueller Einheit. Er hatte sehr sorgfältig (sogar auf den Plakaten, in den Zeitungen) die aus der Verteilung von Schwarz und Weiß resultierende Wirkung studiert, die Intensität der Typen verglichen... Er schafft ein Oberflächenlesen, das er mit dem linearen Lesen verknüpft; das war die Bereicherung der Domäne Literatur um eine zweite Dimension.› Und: ‹Ich glaube, die Komposition von ‹coup de dés› darf nicht als in zwei aufeinanderfolgenden Operationen entstanden angesehen werden: Die eine bestünde in Schreiben eines Gedichts auf die hergebrachte Weise, unabhängig von jeder Gestalt und der Größe der Zwischenräume; die andere darin, dem Text die angemessene Disposition zu geben. Der Versuch Mallarmés muß notwendigerweise tiefer gegangen sein. Er geschieht im Augenblick der Schöpfung, ist selber eine Art Schöpfung.›

Mallarmé selbst in einem Brief an André Gide: ‹Das Gedicht wurde soeben gedruckt mit der von mir gegebenen Satzanordnung, in der die ganze Wirkung beruht.› Deutlicher kann die Beziehung zwischen dem Gehalt und der Gestaltung eines Textes nicht mehr hervorgehoben werden.

Ist das Beispiel Schwitters' eine Komposition reiner Buchstaben-Kombinationen, so haben wir es hier, mit einem Blick auf Mallarmé dazu, mit einer reinen Wort-Konstellation zu tun.

Der Verfasser, Eugen Gomringer:
‹an stelle des verses tritt die konstellation: die gruppe aus worten. an stelle der syntax genügt es, zwei, drei oder mehrere worte wirken zu lassen, die äußerlich vielleicht unverbunden und mit leichter, zufälliger hand hingespielt erscheinen, bei näherer betrachtung... aber zu zentren eines kräftefelds, zu markierungen eines spielraums werden, indem der dichter diese worte findet und wählt und hinsetzt, schafft er «denkgegenstände» und überläßt das assoziieren dem leser, der mitarbeiter, ja oft vielleicht «vollender» des gedichts wird¹³.› Und: ‹das schweigen zeichnet die neue dichtung aus... dazu stützt sie sich aufs wort¹³.›

Gomringer nennt sich den ‹spielgeber, der andere zum mitspielen einlädt›. Die von ihm ‹hin-gesetzten› Worte sind nicht Worte über etwas, sondern eine Realität, begriffliche und rhythmische Werte für sich. Sie sind stets wieder aufeinander bezogene Punkte in einem leeren Raum, zwischen denen die Phantasie des Lesers spazierengeht – je nach Lust und Laune, kurz oder lang. Und je weniger Anhaltspunkte es gibt, desto präziser sind sie – auf die Typographie bezogen: desto unverrückbarer, von selbst verständlicher ist die Einheit von Wort und Wortbild. Lissitzky, zum Leser gewandt, sagt schon 1925: ‹Sie sollen von dem Schriftsteller fordern, daß er seine Schrift wirklich stellt. Denn seine Gedanken kommen zu ihnen durch das Auge und nicht durch das Ohr. Darum soll die typographische Plastik durch ihre Optik das tun, was die Stimme des Redners durch seine Gedanken schafft¹³.›

Eugen Gomringer, Konstellation, 1953¹³:

4
5

343

Auch bei Gomringer: Die Distanz des Dichters zur sogenannten Realität des täglichen Lebens ist höchstens scheinbar. Sind seine Konstellationen künstlerisch konzentrierte Konzentrate, so stehen sie bisweilen ganz in der Nähe der auf eine Sache konzentrierten Slogans, wie: Radfahrer – Achtung, Achtung – Radfahrer. Oder: Gefahr sehen – links gehen. Oder wie ein Klassiker unter den Werbesprüchen: Dubo – Dubon – Dubonnet. Zu Konstellationen von besonderer Kraft werden auch öfters die Schlagzeilen der Zeitungen¹⁴. Sie formen und reduzieren auf das Minimalste und Direkteste – nicht eine dichterische Eingebung, sondern das Tagesgeschehen.

Was zum Beispiel die vier Worte im Augenblick ihres Erscheinens alles gesagt und verschwiegen haben: moon rocket falling back, die Mondrakete – Erwartungen einer Nation und eines Erdteils sind damit verknüpft – fällt zurück! Uns interessiert hier, daß die Wirkung dieser Worte nicht nur in den Worten allein, im Gehalt ihrer sachlichen Mitteilung liegt. Zweifellos wirkten die gleichen Worte ganz anders, stünden sie zum Beispiel im Innern des Blattes irgendwo unter anderen. Wieder: Gehalt der Sprache und Darstellung ergeben zusammen, kumulativ, eine neue Einheit.

Titelblatt des Neuyorker Daily News vom 13. Oktober 1958:

Die hier angeführten Beispiele folgen keinem Plan, sind vor allem keinerlei Anthologie von Pioniertaten. Ich möchte vielmehr das Thema der integralen Typographie – der Verbindung von Sprache und Schrift – von möglichst vielen Seiten anvisieren. Dabei komme ich nicht drum herum, Dinge aufzugreifen, die aus der heutigen Sicht selbstverständlich, banal sind. Darf ich hoffen, der Leser entschuldige die Zumutung?¹⁴

Als selbstverständlich wird es etwa empfunden, daß auf dem Plakat nicht steht: ‹Im Kunsthaus Zürich findet eine Ausstellung der Allianz statt... usw.› Dabei ist das Erstaunliche: Es ist überhaupt nichts von einer Ausstellung zu lesen! Der Text ist auf das minimalste Minimum, auf Namen und Daten, reduziert, abgestuft nach ihrer Bedeutung – der Rest wird vom Beschauer ergänzt. Oder mit den Worten Gomringers: Der Beschauer vollendet das Plakat. Die Mitteilung, obwohl ausschließlich das Mittel der Schrift dafür verwendet wird, wird nicht so sehr gelesen als vielmehr ‹gesehen›.

Darin erfüllt das Plakat mit elementaren Mitteln musterhaft seine Funktion, informiert den Leser auf dem kürzesten Weg, setzt ihn buchstäblich auf den ersten Blick ins Bild – Gehalt und Form der Mitteilung entsprechen sich.

Plakat von Max Bill, Zürich, 1942:

6
7

▲ Double-page spread from Karl Gerstner's introductory article in *TM*'s 'Integral Typography' issue, 1959. To show the effect of typography on words and their meaning, he reproduces a page of Stéphane Mallarmé's poem, 'A Throw of the Dice', laid out by the author, 1897. Alongside is a Concrete poem by Eugen Gomringer, where the words are 'points of contact in the empty space occupied by the reader's wandering imagination'.

▲ On the right-hand page, Gerstner uses the front of the New York *Daily News* to show that it is not the words alone which convey meaning, but also the way they are displayed. He points out that the reader completes the message of Max Bill's poster for an Allianz exhibition from 1942: no mention of an exhibition, only the title, place and date in a descending hierarchy of importance.

Typefaces and Typesetting

► ▼ Cover and pages of a booklet designed by Hans Neuburg and Nelly Rudin for the Haas Typefoundry to promote Helvetica, originally named Neue Haas Grotesque. Photographs, taken in Josef Müller-Brockmann's studio, show the process of producing metal type.

▼ A4 brochure for the Zurich typesetters Ernst Gloor, designed by Werner Zryd, c.1960. Printed letterpress.
The left-hand page describes the reproduction department, showing positive and negative photoset type and half-tones ready for combining to make litho plates or process blocks.

▼ The right-hand page illustrates the back of a process camera.

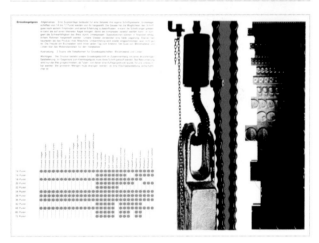

▼ The Monotype 19th-century grotesque (series 215), the grotesque used by Swiss Constructive typographers for text before the arrival of Helvetica.

► In 1960 Monotype designed these alternative characters. Like Helvetica, the ends of the curved letters are cut horizontally, the 'G' has an arrow-head termination, and the capital 'R' has a curved tail.

The Monotype Corporation Limited hat zwölf Figuren der Serie 215 neu geschnitten

Die heutige Werbegraphik verlangt eine Schrift, die unserer Zeit entspricht. Die Grotesk nähert sich diesen Anforderungen am besten; es erschienen denn auch in letzter Zeit zahlreiche Neuschöpfungen endstrichloser Schriften. Neben der ‚Monotype' Gill verfügen unsere Kunden auch über die hier gezeigte Serie 215, die sich als Akzidenz-Grotesk mehr und mehr durchsetzt. Um der modernen Typographie und ihren straffen, sauberen Formen noch besser entsprechen zu können, haben wir zwölf Figuren der Serie 215 neu geschnitten. Diese sind in der vorliegenden Nummer ‚Neue Grafik' der Grundschrift einverleibt. Mit diesen Neuschnitten wird ein Wunsch vieler führender Typographen und Graphiker erfüllt. Die neuen Matrizen stehen unsern Kunden zum normalen Matrizenpreis zur Verfügung.

The Monotype Corporation Limited
Bern, Aarbergergasse 56, Telephon 031 2 30 27
Monotype eingetragenes Warenzeichen

▲ The casting in metal of 'display' sizes of type (from 14 to 72 point). A table shows the availability of fonts, beginning with 14 variations of Univers. The right-hand page shows the bar of type metal before casting and the individual typecast letters on the far right.

226

Type and the Poster

▼ Concert poster by Josef Müller-Brockmann, 1960.

The Akzidenz letterform set in a single size, with as little word spacing as was consistent with readability, produced a vigorous, decorative texture.
The printer would have had difficulty finding enough of such large wood or plastic type to set this number of words in the same size.

Akzidenz was supplied by several manufacturers with slightly varying designs. In this poster Müller-Brockmann had to check proofs carefully to ensure that repeated letters were consistent.
Printing the names of performers and composers in a second colour has animated an otherwise starkly minimal typography.

Type as Image

▼ 'Modern French Tapestries', poster designed by Emil Ruder, 1964.
Ruder has repeated and overprinted the title to create an image which suggests weaving.
Printed letterpress.

musica viva

tonhalle, grosser saal
donnerstag, 10. märz
20.15 uhr, 1960
16. volkskonzert der
tonhalle-gesellschaft
zürich
leitung
erich schmid
solisten
annie laffra
violoncello
eva maria rogner
sopran
hans werner henze
sonata per archi
luigi dallapiccola
‹concerto per la notte
di natale dall'anno
1956› für sopran und
kammerorchester
arthur honegger
konzert für violoncello
und orchester
henri dutilleux
erste sinfonie
karten zu fr. 1.-, 2.-, 3.-
tonhalle, hug, jecklin
kuoni, dep.kasse oer-
likon, kreditanstalt

moderne
französische
knüpfteppiche

gewerbemuseum basel
25.1.-1.3.1964
geöffnet 10-12 14-17 uhr –
mittwoch auch 20-22 uhr
eintritt frei

▶ Concert poster by Josef Müller-Brockmann, 1960.
Akzidenz Grotesk set in two sizes, the larger with excessive word spacing. The result is a decorative arrangement produced at some expense of readability, though colour helps to link the words across the diagonal divide.

◀ '[Alexander] Calder Mobiles Stabiles', exhibition poster designed by Fridolin Müller, 1960.
The widely spaced letters in bold Akzidenz Grotesk placed low in the design suggest the space in and around the Calder works. Wide letter-spacing only became commonplace in work by the 'New Wave' a few years later.

Type as Image

▼ Poster for an exhibition of kinetic art, designed by Peter Megert, 1965. The effect of movement is made by shifting a typeset image on film horizontally and adjusting its focus. As lithography (offset) began to replace letterpress printing in the 1960s, phototypesetting – which by its nature suited the preparation of film for platemaking – began to compete with metal composition.
Peter Megert was trained in Berne and later in the USA, where he had a successful and influential career as a designer and teacher.

▼ '[Give] One Franc for Rheumatism Sufferers', charity poster designed by Gérard Miedinger, 1963. Distortion of lettering (by various means, which included melting photographic emulsion) was a popular technique in the 1960s. Phototypesetting simplified the very close spacing of letters.

◀ Advertisement for a machine for spooling wire, designed by R. Rothenfluh in the design offices of the advertiser Micafil, 1964. Proofs of type, wrapped round a cylinder, have been rephotographed.

Programmes as Solutions: Karl Gerstner

▼ ► *Geigy heute* (Geigy Today),
a 320-page book for the company's
200th anniversary, designed by Karl
Gerstner, 1958. The square format is
two-thirds A4, printed letterpress
in black, with occasional special
colours for diagrams and a 16-page
four-colour section.
Geigy heute was the first extensive
deployment of Swiss graphic and
typographic skills to guide the reader
through a mass of information,
showing where things were, what
they did, and how they were related.

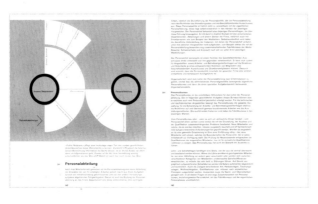

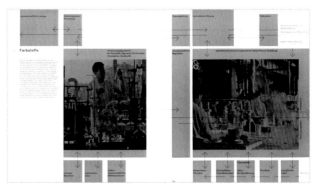

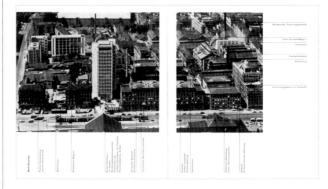

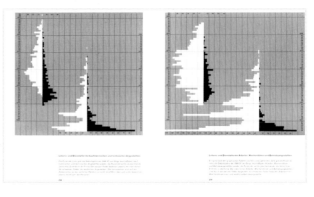

▲ 'Geigy Today', French-language advertisement for the chemical company's bicentenary in 1958, designed by Karl Gerstner. Gerstner was responsible for the complete range of publicity and printed material, which included the two books, *Geigy heute* and *Geigy 200 Jahre* (Geigy 200 Years), and items for the celebrations themselves, such as invitations and programmes for events.

Karl Gerstner's theories on 'programmes' were inseparable from his commercial practice. While designing *Schiff nach Europa* for a sophisticated, literary audience, he was also engaged in reaching a wider public. The jobs he carried out were various, but his approach was consistent.

In 1958 Geigy celebrated its 200th anniversary in two companion books: one on the company's history, the other, *Geigy heute* (Geigy Today).[1] They were designed by Gerstner and edited by the firm's advertising director Markus Kutter. *Geigy heute* not only exemplified the new Swiss book design – square format, square-backed binding, headings and text typeset in unjustified grotesque – it also set new standards for information design in its statistical charts, ingenious diagrams of management structures and departmental organization.

In 1959 Gerstner went into partnership with Markus Kutter. A brochure told clients that Gerstner+Kutter offered a complete service from print to public relations and set out its principles:

1. Publicity is neither too cheap nor too dear, it is only good or bad. Even when it seems cheap, if it is bad it is always too expensive.

2. Good publicity reaches the right people in the right place at the right time, and above all by the right means.

3. Good publicity does not add words to a given illustration, nor does it make a picture to fit a given text. Illustration and text spring from the same idea, they affect and explain each other.

4. Good publicity springs from the subject which it serves, attracts attention to it, and is harmonious with it.

5. Ideas, means and methods of good publicity should be clever but easily intelligible, because the public, while not wishing to be underrated, does not like to be forced to think too much. G+K

When the architect Paul Gredinger joined in 1962, the practice became Gerstner, Gredinger and Kutter, abbreviated to GGK. Their work for Basel enterprises, large and small, was always in the form of a 'programme', from the trademark or logotype to the advertising and brochures. With Kutter as the writer, GGK's advertisements depended as much on the headline or text as on a graphic idea. These examples of 'integral typography' could be startling. A Citroen agent was

1. In 'Publications to Celebrate an Anniversary: 200 Years of Geigy', *Neue Grafik*, no.5, 1960, pp.18-26. This was among the few works ever discussed in detail in the magazine.

▼ 'Instructions for Creative Work in the Future', and 'Readers Wanted for the Future of Creative Work', a two-sided book to be read from the front to the middle and the back to the middle. Written by Markus Kutter and designed by Karl Gerstner in 1959, the book is an experimental examination of language and the way in which typography can orchestrate and give a perfect form to the content of language.

▼ Karl Gerstner's book *Programme entwerfen* (Designing Programmes), published in 1964, was the most approachable presentation of his concept of the 'programme' as a basis not only for graphic design but for all kinds of creative activity. The English edition below was published in 1968.

230

▼ Holzäpfel furniture trademark printed from printer's metal rules, designed by Karl Gerstner, 1959.

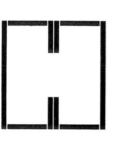

▼ The brass rules, tied up and ready for printing the Holzäpfel logotype.

▼ Back and front of an A4 brochure for Holzäpfel furniture, designed by Karl Gerstner. Perspective has been avoided by photographing the tables either from the side or from the top and combining them as a visual diagram. Printed letterpress.

▼ Inside double-page spread from a Holzäpfel catalogue with furniture photographed at table height, without perspective, like an architect's drawing, as plan and elevation. The text giving details and dimensions is printed in brown.

Exact specifications are given in technical drawings, and the complete range was shown in tabular layouts. When photographs showed furniture in an office, the wall was always hung with a Gerstner painting.

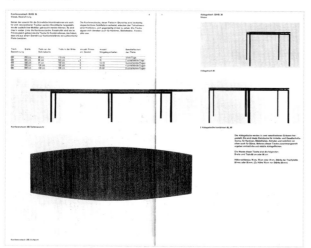

surprised to find the headline 'Don't buy this car', although the smaller text went on, 'if you don't expect something special'. Clients came to expect something special of the practice. They were rewarded with extreme professionalism, not only in advertising ideas, and in the skills to realize them with faultless photography and elegant typography, but also in the painstaking organization of product information. The design of elaborate catalogues for Holzäpfel office furniture, for example, set new standards of clarity and elegance: a balance between function and formalism.

In 1964 Gerstner brought together his critical views – on his activities as designer, as advertising consultant, as type designer and as artist – in the book *Programme entwerfen* (Designing Programmes). In English and German editions, *Designing Programmes* appeared at the dawn of the electronic revolution, when computers and their programming promised a new world of creative opportunities. His idea of the programme extends beyond modular ideas, an essential part of Modernist rationalism: it supplied a structure for possible permutations, which Gerstner investigated exhaustively for several years.[2]

The daunting complexity of Gerstner's typographic programmes, because of the small size of their basic modular units, rather than acting as a constraint on the designer, provided a paradoxical freedom. In *Designing Programmes* Gerstner cites G+K's layout for the weekly economics periodical *Capital*.

> The 'Programme as Grid' is a proportional regulator for [text] composition, tables, pictures, etc. It is a formal programme to accommodate x unknown items. The difficulty is to find the balance, the maximum conformity to a rule with the maximum of freedom: or the maximum of constants with the greatest possible variability.[3]

The central concept of 'programmes' was the repetition and development of fixed units. The programme was also implicit in the related parts of an advertising campaign, as Gerstner had intimated in his special *Werk* issue in 1955. He saw programmes as solutions for design problems. This was his most significant contribution to design. It underlies every job he undertook, and his engagement with advertising increased his interest in communication, rather than style. In this way his work moved steadily away from Modernist stereotypes.

2. See Karl Gerstner, *Kompendium für Alphabeten*, Teufen 1972, published in English as *Compendium for Literates*, New Haven / London 1974.
3. *Designing Programmes*, London 1968, p.12.

► ▼ Grid for the German weekly economics magazine *Capital*, designed in the office of GGK by Karl Gerstner and Felix Berman, 1962. Based on a square, the grid controlled text, statistical diagrams and photographs in a number of fixed relationships and proportions, but with the possibility of widely varied layouts for differing topics.

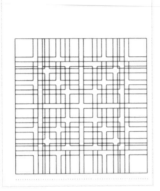

▼ The photographs in the article below on development aid are by Werner Bischof, a former student of Hans Finsler at the Zurich Kunstgewerbeschule.

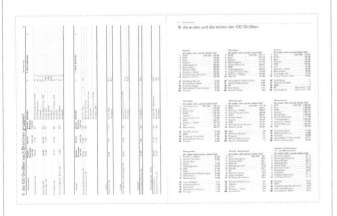

232

▲ Full-page newspaper advertisement announcing the reopening of a Basel department store after refurbishment, 1961. Gerstner+Kutter's informal layout has no headline or logo; the main text begins in lowercase, arranged like steam above the cups. The cloudy words list the innovations to be found in the store and the plus signs subtly link the elements of the added message – *Auswahl + Qualität + Preis* (Choice+Quality+Price).

The excuse for the tea-drinking image is subsidiary: 'While you're waiting for the store to reopen, have a cup of tea.'

▼ Advertisements designed by Gerstner+Kutter for the tiny Citröen 2CV, 1959: startling messages in formal arrangements. Headlines were negative instructions, 'Don't do a test-drive!' On the left, reminders of earlier parts of the campaign: 'Don't get in!' (with an elephant) and 'Don't look!' (a woman with a hotel doorman).

▲ Finally, 'Don't buy this car!' says the headline, and the text runs on in much smaller type, 'unless you want . . . ' and then lists the 2CV's advantages.

▼ Press advertisement for a dictating machine designed by Gerstner+Kutter, 1962.

The text begins with the conventional opening of a business letter – 'Dear Sirs' – then continues as if the message is being dictated, including the spelling-out in phonetics of the product name – D I C T O F A X – and ends with, 'Yours faithfully A–Köbeli', followed by a postscript with further sales information. The punctuation is typeset as words in a very small size. Gerstner's and Kutter's inventive use of language illustrates the way in which their commercial activity was fertilized by their intellectual interests – in this case, Concrete poetry.

▼ Wrappers for mailing folded copies of the newspaper *National Zeitung*, designed by Fritz Schrag for Gerstner+Kutter, 1959. Gerstner's earlier publicity for the paper had exploited the interchangeability of the letters 'N' and 'Z' when turned at 90°.part 4. p.236

▼ Two small advertisements for the *National Zeitung*, designed by Fritz Schrag. The diagonals stand out in the conventionally typeset columns of the newspaper.

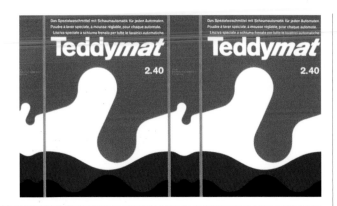

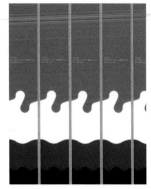

**Billig ist es.
Aber ist es auch gut?**

Das fragten wir 2500 Hausfrauen.
Und ihre Antworten bestätigten uns:
Unsere neuen Waschmittel
sind so gut wie die besten.

Aber wir wollten
sie noch besser machen.
Indem wir sie nämlich billiger machten.

Das konnten wir, weil wir
eine eigene (Co-op) Fabrik haben.
Die liefert direkt
an die 3000 (Co-op) Läden.
So verdient kein Zwischenhändler
und kein Vertreter an uns.

Nur die Kundin.
Die dann gleich doppelt profitiert:
Von der ausgezeichneten Qualität.
Und vom billigen Preis.

Zum Vorwaschen
Roby 75, ideal mit Teddy 75
auch für Automaten.
Grosspaket je Fr. 2.–
in Co-op Läden
mit je 3 Co-op Punkten.

Teddymat
speziell für Automaten.
Mit Schaumautomatik.
Das heisst:
So viel Schaum wie nötig.
So wenig Schaum wie richtig.
Grosspaket Fr. 2.40
in Co-op Läden
mit 4 Co-op Punkten.

◀ ▲ Detergents for the Co-op retail chain: packaging and advertisement designed by GGK, c.1964.
Karl Gerstner carried his concept of programmes through into the competitive commercial world.
Three types of detergent were related in their design and distinguished one from another by their colour. Placed together on the shelf, the design on the cartons fitted together like pieces of a jigsaw puzzle to make varied patterns of a foaming wave.
The advertisement headline assumes the customer's point of view: 'It's Cheap. But Is It Good?'
The Co-op logotype (on the side of the packet) was designed by Gottlieb Soland in 1958 (see p.241).

Aesthetics in Commerce

▼ Full-page newspaper advertisement for a top-loading (*obeneinfüllung*) washing machine, designed by Siegfried Odermatt, 1960.
By cropping both the photograph and the 'o' of the large bold *'oben'* (top) the word becomes an image and an active part of the illustration – it is literally loaded into the machine.

▼ Siegfried Odermatt's series of advertisements for an insurance company, 1960. They combine a single word, in German or French, with an image evoking each hazard.

Fire

Entre vous — et l'adversité —
mettez **La Neuchâteloise**
Compagnie Suisse d'Assurances Générales

Water

Für diesen Fall —
die **Neuenburger**
Schweizerische Allgemeine Versicherungs-Gesellschaft

Theft

Entre vous — et l'adversité —
mettez **La Neuchâteloise**
Compagnie Suisse d'Assurances Générales

Obeneinfüllung ist einer der ausser-gewöhnlichen Vorteile der voll-automatischen Waschmaschine Unimatic-Favorite. Zehntausende von Hausfrauen sind von diesem schweizerischen Qualitätsprodukt begeistert. Doppelseitig gelagerte Trommel und hervorragendes Material garantieren eine Lebens-dauer von Jahrzehnten. Und was jede Frau ebenso sehr schatzt: Sie weiss, dass der angegebene Trommelinhalt von 4 oder 6 kg Trockenwasche mit dem effektiven Fassungsvermogen auch überein-stimmt. Unimatic-Favorite für aller-hochste Anspruche.

Verzinkerei Zug AG   Zug

We know as graphic designers – although we are often tempted to forget it – that we are in the service of advertising, of economic life, of sales, whether it be intellectual or material. . . . But the artist sometimes allows himself to be carried away by his creative inspiration, allowing form a primary importance, giving to lines, planes, colours, and the whole composition a life of their own [and] losing sight of what is being advertised.[1]

This was how Hans Neuburg had seen things. But the new generation brought not only a refined Modernist aesthetic into the commercial world but also an intelligent understanding of how to communicate an idea. Their visual language was formal – in the sense that it was self-consciously aesthetic – without being formalistic. Designers such as Siegfried Odermatt and Fridolin Müller retained the Modernist requirement to respect the two-dimensional nature of the printed sheet, and they justified Neuburg's claim that design in the Constructive spirit could be imaginative yet remain objective.

When freelance designers and advertising agencies encouraged their clients to develop a corporate style, this was as much an aesthetic aim as it was a marketing strategy. The consistent application of trademark and typeface in printed matter, from business cards to advertisements to the painting on delivery vans, answered both Ruder's call for 'overall design' and Gerstner's aspiration to extend the life of a visual idea beyond a single use. Odermatt's work for the Sammet pharmacy in central Zurich was typical.

Odermatt's style is revealed as an original, personal extension of Stankowski's work for Dalang. His direction of photographers, who served him well, produced images that were ready designed to fit a graphic structure. The perfectly executed drawings – often the work of his partner, Rosmarie Tissi – with their contrast of fine line and black solid, are the exact counterpoint to the type. Photographs and drawings, to be comfortably located in the design area and to retain a formal abstract character, were often heavily cropped, but without losing their 'sachlich' nature as documentary records.

Odermatt's work for Remington Rand's Universal Automatic Computer (Univac), begun in 1959, typified the corporate styling introduced by many designers for Swiss companies. It exploited every possible surface which could carry a message – letterheads, forms, packaging material, leaflets, students' authorization cards, the

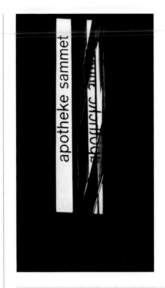

▲ From 1959, Siegfried Odermatt provided a related series of designs for the Zurich pharmacy Sammet. The logotype combines the lowercase 'a' and 's' in the weight and forms of Akzidenz bold.
◄ The lowercase of the logo is retained in the illuminated sign running up the building.
▼ Advertisements have no headline, and each text describes the preparation which Sammet would supply for certain symptoms.

The lighting of the photographs by Ferd Waldvogel makes the hands dramatically three-dimensional, but they are firmly anchored to the flat space by the tight cropping.

1. Hans Neuburg in *Publicité*, 1947, pp.23-24.

236

▼ Univac (Universal Automatic Computer) full-page newspaper advertisement, designed by Siegfried Odermatt, 1965. This diagram of a global network was made as a flat drawing. It was transferred to film, which was then stretched into a curve and rephotographed.

▼ Advertisements for Univac designed by Siegfried Odermatt, 1963 and 1965. The images draw attention to computer applications.

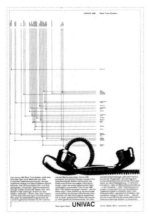

company magazine and even book matches and New Year's greeting cards.

There was nothing remarkable about the Univac logo, which was simply the name, typeset in Akzidenz capitals. What is surprising in a series of thirty-four full-page newspaper advertisements over a ten-year period is Odermatt's inventiveness, and the confidence of his client when large areas of the expensive page were kept empty.

Equally prodigal with space was Fridolin Müller. Unlike Odermatt, he had a conventional full-time training in Basel as a student of Hofmann and Ruder. After replacing Gerstner at Geigy for six months, Müller worked freelance in Zurich from 1953. While he was considering the offer of a job with a New York agency, a proposal for collaboration came from the advertising agency Erwin Halpern. Through the agency Müller worked for Therma, a company producing domestic kitchen equipment, helping to realize one of the most comprehensive 'overall' designs. Since Therma's overall design was in the hands of the engineer and industrial designer Hans Hilfiker, 'gute Form' could be exemplified not only in what they manufactured, but also in the graphics, which incorporated the logotype designed by Vivarelli – the result of a competition initiated by Hilfiker.

There is no obvious influence to be seen in Odermatt's work: it merely suggests a homage to Stankowski. Fridolin Müller's interest in the Modernist past was more explicit. He was particularly attracted to the work of Piet Zwart, the pioneering Dutch typographer of the 1920s, whom he met at a retrospective of Zwart's work in Hilversum. The result was Müller's book on Zwart, published in 1966.[2]

Such consciousness of history was the foundation of the best Constructive work. This was no longer merely a recycled avant-garde, but was both original and commercially effective.

▼ Full-page advertisements for 'Geigy's Research for Tomorrow' programme, designed by Fridolin Müller, 1962.
Müller has removed the images from the scientific to the aesthetic, locking the free, naturally random images into a square format.

Fridolin Müller Born 1926.
Graphic designer, artist.
Studied at Basel Allgemeine Gewerbeschule under Armin Hofmann and Emil Ruder, 1945-50. Worked at Geigy in Basel before moving to Zurich as freelance designer, 1953. Art director at Erwin Halpern agency, 1960-74. Taught at the National Design Institute, Ahmedabad, India, 1965, and in the US at the University College of Art, Philadelphia, 1969-70.

---

2. *Piet Zwart*, Teufen / London 1966. A second book produced by Müller celebrated the work of the Dutch typographical pioneer: *H.N. Werkman*, Teufen 1969.

Therma, makers of kitchen equipment, integrated advertising, packaging and product design.
▼ Logotype designed by Carlo Vivarelli, 1958.

▼ The letters in the logotype are linked, allowing the name to be made as a single moulding and applied to the face of a product.

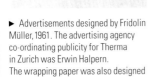

► Advertisements designed by Fridolin Müller, 1961. The advertising agency co-ordinating publicity for Therma in Zurich was Erwin Halpern.
The wrapping paper was also designed by Fridolin Müller.
▼ In 1963 a revised wrapping paper was designed by Gerhard Forster.

238

The Globus department store in Zurich organized competitions for the design of practical items for the home. The full-page newspaper announcements of the winners were designed by Siegfried Odermatt.

▶ The 1960 competition: Odermatt has laid out the information on the five designers and their designs in three constellations. First, on the left, captions in small type in three columns: one piece of information in the first column, two pieces in the second and third. The arrangement of the two sets of images – portraits of the designers and photographs of the winning objects – follows the same pattern, so that the reader can easily identify designers and their designs.

▲ The following year's announcement of winners. Odermatt has identified the designer of the table lamp by separating her from the other prizewinners. Form is illustrated by the photograph and function by the engineering drawing.

Wettbewerb

60

Form

Ideen für neue Artikel finden und sie sinnvoll entwickeln — ist unsere Aufgabe als führendes Unternehmen des Detailhandels. Ideen fabrikatorisch verwirklichen — ist Sache unserer schweizerischen Lieferanten. Im Hinblick auf die Schweizer Woche 1960 sind wir noch einen Schritt weitergegangen: als erstes schweizerisches

Warenhaus lancierte der Globus dieses Jahr einen öffentlichen Wettbewerb unter dem Titel «Form 60». Entwerfer und Hersteller wurden aufgerufen, Vorschläge für zweckmässige, sauber gestaltete Gebrauchs-Artikel einzureichen. Wir setzen also Aufgaben und fördern so die Entwicklung gut gestalteter Produkte schweizerischer Prägung.

Für 1960 beschränkte sich der Wettbewerb auf drei Themen: Aufbewahren von Schuhen/Aufbewahren von Nähzeug/Sparkassen für Kinder. Die eingereichten Modelle wurden von folgender Jury beurteilt: Gertrud Bossert, Margrit Hug, Max Bill, Hans Fischli, Rudolf Villiger. Ausgezeichnet wurden die unten gezeigten fünf besten Arbeiten.

Peter Schmid
Innenarchitekt
Uster
Mehrzweck-
Gestell für Schuhe,
Bücher etc. mit
Asbest-Tablaren

P. & A. Marghitola
Littau/Luzern
Schuh-Kasten mit
Kipp-Mechanismus

Frank Bolliger
Innenarchitekt
Zürich
Schuh-Gestell mit
Flach-Kippvorrichtung

Bruno Limberger
Innenarchitekt
Zürich
Kindersparkasse
mit pädagogisch
durchdachter
Sicherung

Robert Zumbrunn
Zürich
Kindersparkasse
in Kugelform

Globus

▲ Full-page magazine advertisement for insulating material, designed by Kurt Huber, 1961.
The product is presented so that the page resembles a Concrete painting.

Ranged right typesetting was unusual. Text could be broken to exploit the advantage of stressing the first words in the longer lines.

▼ Pages from an A4 brochure for the Swiss Industrial Abrasives Ltd (SIA), designed by Ernst and Ursula Hiestand, 1963.

Flexible Schleifmittel
eine kurze technische Orientierung

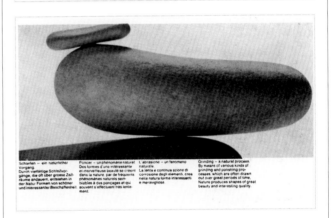

▲ The Hiestands first show that nature's grinding and polishing are a slow process which can result in 'shapes of great beauty and interesting quality'.

▼ This is contrasted with the modern industrial process of grinding and polishing a casting, carried out at speed by a machine.

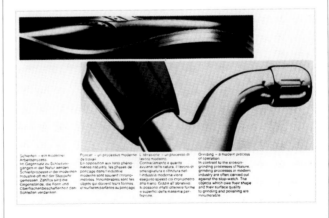

▲ Symbol for the electrical goods company Electrolux, designed by Carlo Vivarelli, 1962. The Swedish firm asked the Verband Schweizerischer Graphiker to organize a competition. Out of 200 members, 130 took part, and the jury was unable to come to a decision on the first prize. Vivarelli's was one of three finalists, each based on the square or circle.

▼ Logo for the Zurich firm Metallbau, makers of Norm metal building components, designed by Carl B. Graf, c.1964. The rectangle containing the letters becomes a structural element in the stationery and advertising.

▼ Logo for the furniture manufacturer Walter Müller by an anonymous designer, from a newspaper advertisement, 1964. Such imaginative geometrical lettering was commonplace at many levels of Swiss commercial activity.

For a nation with four languages, trading abroad in quality goods, the trademark was important. It made Swiss brands recognizable, not only by their names. As early as 1948 Graphis Press published a book on the subject by Walter Herdeg.[1] Herdeg sees the trademark as the 'symbolic expression' of an activity, its quality depending on 'the idea it incorporates and the form in which this idea is expressed'. In the nearly one hundred examples the progressive tendency is represented by Eidenbenz, Gauchat, Honegger-Lavater (Modernist in one of three designs), Helmuth Kurtz, Max and Eugen Lenz, Gérard Miedinger, Hans Neuburg and Carlo Vivarelli.

'A good trademark is in a certain sense a miniature monument', Neuburg claimed. He was one of the first to list a logo's requirements.[2] There were seven. It must typify the institution it was designed for; be unlike any other; be so simple as to be instantly recognizable; be capable of extreme enlargement and reduction; not depend on colour; be usable as both positive and negative; and it must fulfill copyright conditions so as to be registered.

Carlo Vivarelli's reputation as a trademark designer was based on his famous 1945 design for a manufacturer of twist drills (see p.138) and on his success in closed competitions, such as that for the Electrolux trademark. In *Neue Grafik*, in place of Neuburg's list, he identified trademarks as belonging to one of four possible types:

(a) the typographic, (b) the representational, (c) the symbolic, (d) the purely formal. These usually need to be combined. A simple geometrical form cannot be a trademark on its own, nor can two letters from the printer's typecase; they need special treatment.

He lists the principal combinations as a+b, a+c, a+d, c+d, d+a, and his illustrations are grouped as 'typography/form', 'typography/representation', 'typography/symbol', 'symbol/form', 'representation/form', 'factual/formal'.[3]

Vivarelli was the most notably successful designer of logotypes. And throughout Swiss business and industry it was unusual to find a company whose name or trademark had not been subjected to a designer's fastidious attention.

▲ Prizewinning trademark for a brewery, designed by Nelly Rudin, 1960. The repeated cropped lettering in a circle suggested beer's foaming transparency.

1. *Schweizer Signete, Trade Marks and Symbols*, Zurich 1948.
2. *Moderne Werbe- und Gebrauchs-Grafik*, 1960, p.76.
3. 'Principles in the Design of Trademarks', *Neue Grafik*, no.5, 1960, pp.29-33.

30   Die Prinzipien der Signetgestaltung
The principles in the Design
of Trade marks
Les principes des marques distinctives

Links
Typografisch Gegenständlich
at left
Typographical Factual
à gauche
Présentation typographique et figurative

Typografisch Symbolisch
The Typographical Symbolical Element
Typografisch Symbolisches Element
Présentation typographique et symbolique

ErpF

▲ Logotype lettering designed by Alfred Willimann for a Zurich shop, 1943.

▼ The letters adapted on a strict module when constructed in three dimensions.

▼ Advertisement for a scaffolding company, designed by Hansheini Pidoux, c.1963. The 'sachlich' approach at its minimalist extreme: one size of type, articulated only by spacing, and an image of documentary banality.

Unsere neue Vertretung:
Peiner – Rüstungsgeräte

Damit haben wir das Lieferprogramm im Dienste unserer Kunden bedeutend erweitert. Peiner-Lehrgerüste rationalisieren die Arbeit; sie erlauben schnellste Montage und Demontage mit einfacher Verbindung von Element zu Element. Verlangen Sie Prospekte oder eine unverbindliche Beratung mit detaillierten Angaben.

Conrad Kern AG

Eisengasse 6/8, Zürich 8
Telefon 051 32 12 46

▲ Page showing trademarks based on lettering, from Carlo Vivarelli's article on trademarks in *Neue Grafik*, (no.5, 1960). On the left, Vivarelli's design for Neri Pharmacy, 1943, and Hans Neuburg's personal mark. On the right, top and bottom, Neuburg's designs for Anliker, builders and excavators, and Vetroflex glass fibres; in the middle, Vivarelli's for Tenax isolators and IWS construction equipment.

▼ Typographical trademark for Zurich printer designed by Walter Käch, 1946. City-Druck used various designers for advertising, including Siegfried Odermatt (see p.184).

▲ The geometrical Co-op logotype built up of circles and bars, designed by Gottlieb Soland, 1958.

▲ Zurich Chamber Orchestra (ZKO) logo, designed by Gottlieb Soland, 1956. Without the circles and diagonals of the roman alphabet, the letterforms have an almost Japanese character.

▼ Pendt shopfitters truck with graphics designed by Gottlieb Soland, 1963. Like the orchestra logo above, Soland's trademark is more memorable for its eccentric minimalism than for its meeting the requirements listed by Hans Neuburg: that it should 'typify the institution; be unlike any other; be so simple as to be instantly recognizable', and so on.

▼ One of a series of advertisements for construction equipment, designed by Christof Gassner without margins, and with no variation of size or spacing in the lowercase text. Published in *Neue Grafik* (no.14, 1962), they were rejected by the client.

baumaschinen ag zürich
051 52 52 66
dinkum
hydraulischer grabenbagger
auswechseln
aller arbeitsgeräte
in längstens 15 minuten
motor und aggregate
leicht zugänglich
schwenkbewegung des armes
hydraulisch durch
leicht ersetzbare seile
druckschläuche mit
eingebauten drehgelenken
bewegen sich minimal

▲ Poster for City-Druck with Walter Käch's trademark as the image, designed by Emil Maurer, 1959.

▶ Advertisement for City-Druck designed by Odermatt's business partner, Rosmarie Tissi, 1958. Tissi has ignored Käch's logo and placed the 'c' and 'd' in their positions in a printer's typecase.

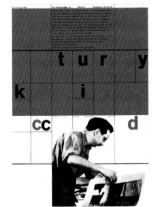

242

Sachlichkeit: Painting
▶ Poster drawn and designed
by Willi Eidenbenz, 1958.
The poster belongs to the photorealist
tradition exemplified by Otto
Baumberger's PKZ overcoat poster
of 1929 (see p.29). The image alone
carries the message: words are
superfluous.

Sachlichkeit: Drawing

▶ 'Industrial Design by Wilhelm Wagenfeld', poster for an exhibition at the Zurich Kunstgewerbemuseum, designed by Fridolin Müller, 1960. Müller has made the objective facts into a precise, elegant image. Precision is given by the measurements, elegance by the form of the casserole and by the distinct difference of the three weights of line in the drawing. The main all-lowercase lettering is ranged left on the central axis of a symmetrical object, a common device of Swiss designers.

Wihelm Wagenfeld, a former Bauhaus student, was one of the most successful in putting the school's ideas into practice, with the production of domestic items such as lights and kitchen equipment.

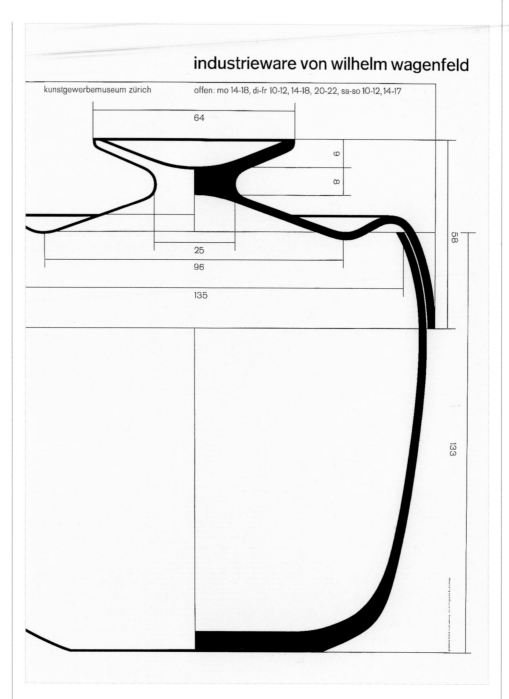

industrieware von wilhelm wagenfeld

kunstgewerbemuseum zürich   offen: mo 14-18, di-fr 10-12, 14-18, 20-22, sa-so 10-12, 14-17

die neue Graphik
the new graphic art
le nouvel art graphique

◄ Karl Gerstner and Markus Kutter's book *Die neue Graphik*, published in 1959, gave graphic design a historical position and established its role. Including American examples, it was less dogmatic than the contemporary *Neue Grafik* magazine.

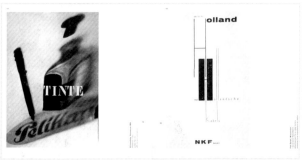

▲ Lissitzky's Pelikan ink advertisement, made when he was in Switzerland in 1924, is placed opposite Piet Zwart's Dutch Cable Factory design of 1926. Gerstner used the same typographic technique to make the 'H' logo for Holzäpfel furniture in 1959 (see p.230).

▼ In a double-page spread of US album covers, Gerstner and Kutter reproduce a design by Saul Bass (on the right). They trim away the original narrow white border, so that the design, with its regular lines and squares, resembles a painting by Richard Paul Lohse. The difference is that Bass's arrangement is intuitive: Lohse would always follow a system.

The first book which described 'Constructive' graphic design, and gave it a historical context – much as Lohse had done in the first issue of *Neue Grafik* – was *Die neue Graphik* (The New Graphic Art) by Karl Gerstner and Markus Kutter. It examined and illustrated graphic design's origins, 'its evolution, its peculiarities, its tasks, its problems, its manifestations, and its future prospects'. Published in 1959, a year after *Neue Grafik*'s first issue, the book covers a wider range than the journal. The 'new graphic art' is shown to be almost as much American as it is European – or Swiss. 'Art has no frontiers', say the authors. The illustrations, many seen for the first time, immediately established a canon of important works.

Die neue Graphik goes over some of the same ground as Gerstner's 1955 issue of *Werk*. 'Is commercial art really Art?' is the recurring question. The book suggests that this should be put in different terms: 'Are the problems set by commercial art such that they can be solved by artistic means? Is it a field of human activity in which artistic work and artistic results are possible?' These are rhetorical questions: the editors ask the reader to look for answers in the illustrations.

The examples are arranged in four groups: 'Beginnings' and 'Breakthrough' (early nineteenth and early twentieth century), 'Present' (Second World War to the 1950s) and 'Future' (contemporary work thought to touch on the problems and possibilities of a world dominated by technology). Examples in the 'Future' section

> attempt to tackle with new resources the crying problem of mass consumption and mass production of graphic art . . . we have called this method the 'integration of graphic means', and mean thereby that the resources of the art are brought together, unified and mutually coordinated. It is represented as a process extended over several stages and impossible without planning and systematic forethought.[1]

Here, recycled from his *Werk* article, are Geigy leaflets, Otl Aicher's Ulm posters, and St Raphaël publicity; but added to them are Herbert Matter's work for Knoll furniture in New York, Herbert Leupin's Salem cigarette posters, Vivarelli's advertisements for Adolf Feller electrical equipment and a German agency's series for cigarettes.[2] The final example is Gerstner's own design programme for the shop boîte à musique (p.183).

1. *Die neue Graphik,* Teufen 1959, p.214.
2. Herbert Leupin (1916-1998) was one of the most celebrated Swiss poster designers. Trained in Basel and in Hermann Eidenbenz's studio, he designed many posters in a photorealist, 'sachlich' style, without words.

▲ Cover of *Schweizer Grafiker*, the handbook of the Association of Swiss Graphic Designers, 1960. Designed by Siegfried Odermatt, the book allots a double-page spread to each of the members, who reproduce work of their choice, with a biographical note and photograph.
More than 100 members were based in Zurich and nearly 50 in Berne, 11 in St Gallen and only 17 in Basel. Of all members with work illustrated, only about 30 could be described as Modernist. The book is square-backed, 210mm wide, printed letterpress in black only, the cover pasted on the boards.

◄ Cover of Müller-Brockmann's book, *The Graphic Artist and his Design Problems*, designed by the author, 1961. Müller-Brockmann's solutions to the graphic designer's problems prescribe the formula of a grid structure and the use of Akzidenz Grotesk – there is not a single instance of serif type or a symmetrical arrangement in any of the illustrations of the work of his studio or his students.

▼ *The Graphic Artist and his Design Problems* is printed letterpress, mainly in black, in a format 225 ×255mm. There are 700 illustrations; 46 are coloured.
The final 48 pages, reprinted from *Neue Grafik*, describe the course which Müller-Brockmann directed at the Zurich Kunstgewerbeschule (see p.211).

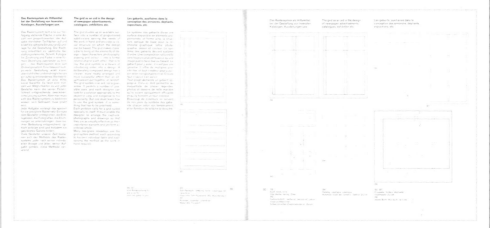

246

▶ Hans Neuburg's 1960 textbook, 'Modern Advertising and Commercial Design'.
The most comprehensive account of the business of graphic design, produced at the moment when Constructive graphic design became the dominant tendency in Switzerland. The book goes well beyond the confines of *Neue Grafik*'s outlook. The reproductions (black-and-white and in general small and of poor quality) give an unusual, broad view of Swiss design, especially in advertising.

Die neue Graphik was the first in a succession of books which demonstrated the confidence of Swiss graphic designers. Their reputation depended in a large part on the publishers Arthur Niggli, who had produced Gerstner's *Kalte Kunst?*. Müller-Brockmann's comprehensive account of his own work, *The Graphic Artist and his Design Problems,* was also a Niggli book. Much of its content, such as the influential article on the teaching at the Kunstgewerbeschule, was reprinted from *Neue Grafik*.

In creating a list of graphic design books, Niggli was not alone. In 1960 Otto Maier published both Tschichold's handbook *Erfreuliche Drucksachen durch gute Typografie* (Satisfactory Print through Good Typography) and Neuburg's overview of the whole range of graphic design activity, *Moderne Werbe- und Gebrauchs-Grafik* (Modern Advertising and Commercial Design). Straightforward, well-organized and with nearly 300 illustrations – not exclusively Constructive – the book was Neuburg's single most important work. But, unlike Niggli's editions, it was in German only, so did not reach an international public.

Four books in the 1960s, all trilingual – in German, French and English – and all reviewed internationally, celebrated the role of graphic design in the commercial and cultural life of the country. These were *Graphic Art of a Swiss Town* and *Official Graphic Art in Switzerland* by Walter Bangerter and Armin Tschanen; and Hans Neuburg's *Graphic Design in Swiss Industry* and *Publicity and Graphic Design in the Chemical Industry* – all published in Zurich by ABC Verlag. Not only the quantity of books, but also the quality of their production and the confident Modernism of their design – organization on the grid, consistent use of sanserif, square-back binding – made a lasting impact on book design in other countries.

▲ The section on publicity has examples of Neuburg's efforts to impose his black Constructivist rules on conventional drink advertisements. Several styles appear in the illustrations on the facing page.

▲ Pierre Gauchat is shown as a Modernist (Embru chair, centre) and as a commercial artist (Schuster oriental carpets, bottom left). The advertisement for skis is by Siegfried Odermatt and the design for BAG lights (bottom right) is by Gottlieb Soland.

▲ In the book's section on 'Various Graphic Tasks', Neuburg illustrates book jackets, three out of five by Müller-Brockmann's studio. At the top left, the example by the Milanese designer Albe Steiner is one of the very few non-Swiss designs in the book.

▲ The jacket for the book on the cellist Pablo Casals was designed by Otto Walter Verlag, publishers of *Neue Grafik*.

Art, Commercial Art, and Graphic Design

▲ A Zurich worker passes a signed print installed in place of commercial posters on 500 sites in the city during the first half of 1961. This was Gerstner's attempt to allow the media of commerce to carry the message of art 'for the man in the street'. Six artists took part, all of them Concrete painters. As well as Gerstner, three others were also designers: Max Bill, Richard Paul Lohse and Marcel Wyss.

▼ Quarter-page advertisement in the monthly *Schweizer Reklame* (Swiss Advertising) for the printers City-Druck by the painter-designer Nelly Rudin, 1958. Only the smallest line of type, 'city-druck ag', connects the printer to the dots of Rudin's design – although these may be intended to suggest the screen of a half-tone photoengraving. The information in the advertisement is entirely aesthetic.

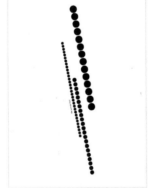

▲ Advertisement by Enzo Rösli for an anti-cancer drug manufactured by the German pharmaceutical company Merck, 1958. The design shows a typical 'Concrete' idea: the base of each triangle provides the dimensions for the next triangle in the progression.

Of all the questions that interested the Swiss Modernist designers, one was most persistent: 'Does art have a place only in painting, or can there be art in the layout of a newspaper, in an advertisement, or a poster?' This was how it was formulated by Karl Gerstner in 1961. He answered with a unique demonstration. Taking literally the old saying, 'Billboards are the art gallery of the street', he invited six Concrete artists to take part. He won the backing of printers, and the General Poster Company allotted five hundred poster sites in Zurich where the work of one artist was pasted up for a fortnight, to be followed by the five others, in turn. Gerstner was using a commercial medium for art.

Nowhere were the tensions between the 'illustrational' and the 'anonymous' designers – and between art and commercial art – more evident than in Switzerland. When the Alliance Graphique International (AGI), a self-elected, elite group of international designers, met in Austria in 1963 there had been, according to Hans Neuburg, a friendly confrontation between those representing 'the free, classic graphic artist with his inclination to drawing and painting and his Constructivist, functionally minded and intellectual counterpart. The so-called cold Swiss graphic art – as produced for instance in Zurich and Basel – came in for some particularly vigorous attacks.'[1]

In the summer of 1964 the International Council of Graphic Design Associations (ICOGRADA) chose Zurich as the venue for its first conference. By taking 'Graphic Designer or Commercial Artist' as its theme, the conference organizers prolonged the dispute. Hans Neuburg took the opportunity to defend the Constructive position. By contrast to the commercial artist

> there has grown up a new conception of graphic art based on different designing principles. In this new conception Constructive elements – for positive and practical reasons, as we shall see – have gained the upper hand, and artistic intuition and fancy have given place to a more methodical and mathematical design approach. Consequently the new graphic designers – we shall use this term to distinguish them from commercial artists – are often regarded as formalists and sectarians who have frozen the living elements of advertising art into a rigid and seemingly technical system. . . . Many works by leading graphic designers have proved, however, that an approach employing structural principles may very well yield practical

1. 'Graphic Designer or Commercial Artist', keynote address, ICOGRADA congress, Zurich 1964, typescript.

▲ *Spirale*, cover of no. 8, photograph
by Peter Keetmann, 1960. *Spirale* was
the leading vehicle for the integration
of Concrete art, writing and design.
▶ The issue devotes 14 pages to Karl
Gerstner's programmatic paintings.
▼ Also included in the issue is 'A Small
Anthology of Concrete Poetry', printed
on tinted paper. The poets include Max
Bill's secretary Eugen Gomringer.
Concrete poetry is a persistent
influence in the headlines, copywriting
and typography of advertisements
produced by Gerstner+Kutter.

▶ *Spirale*, no.9, advertisements
designed by the magazine's co-editor
and designer, Marcel Wyss, 1964.

results, in other words that advertisements, booklets
and posters designed in accordance with systematic
Constructive laws take on life, atmosphere and
advertising force.

**Neuburg provides little substantial argument to defend
the Constructive designers. Nor was he supported at the
conference by Max Bill, who spoke on 'Art and Graphic
Design – Graphic Design and Art'.[2] Asked why he chose
to address the conference, Bill said that he was 'interested
in a communication medium that represents both simple
and complicated processes in such a way that everyone
at once grasps their meaning'. Bill was convinced that
'graphic design is a formal category which easily
succumbs to the temptation to mix practical demands
with aesthetic programmes'. This was not 'the real
business of graphic art'.**

Its real business is that of visual communication –
that is, to be more precise, the communication of
a piece of information in the best possible and most
appropriate way. When this demand has been fulfilled
without restriction, an area remains where aesthetic
judgement can play its part in the arrangement of
the graphic elements.

And Bill was in favour of variety.

It would be as pointless to force graphic design to fit
one pattern of thought as it would be to free it from
the strict principles of visual organization. In graphic
design one ought to be able to find a happy medium
between Modernist aestheticism and the usual
visual noise.

**Many years earlier Bill had described works of Concrete
art as 'laboratory works for the fulfilment of pure rational
design'.[3] The limitations which Concrete artists imposed
on themselves, the exclusion of the familiar 'artistic'
gesture, of the accident, had created an aesthetic climate
of graphic restraint. Not only did their systems of
mathematical relationships coincide with the disciplines
of typography – the restriction to given sizes of type – but
also the perfection of 'sachlich' photography matched the
artist's rejection of both natural appearances and painterly
brushwork.**

2. Address at ICOGRADA Conference, Zurich 1964, typescript.
3. Quoted in Hans Frei *et al.*, *Minimal Tradition*, Baden 1996, p.136.

The Swiss National Exhibition Lausanne 1964

This huge exhibition coincided with the maturity of the 'annonymous' style. It was divided into sectors whose senior architects appointed the graphic designers.
Neuburg and Müller-Brockmann worked with Ernst Scheidegger, who was in charge of the graphic design for the 'Education and Creation' section. Among others employed were Adolf Flückiger, Emil Ruder, Jörg Hamburger, Walter Ballmer (brought from Milan), Gérard Ifert (brought from Paris) and the Zurich advertising agencies of Victor Cohen and Erwin Halpern. They were joined by other longstanding exponents of Constructive graphics from French-speaking Switzerland.

▲ Symbol for Expo 64 by Armin Hofmann, who won the competition for its design in 1961.
▶ The booklets and printed exhibition guides were in a standard vertical format, 210 × 125mm, typeset in Univers and printed letterpress. The 80-page booklet on basic scientific research celebrates the achievements of Swiss scientists as well as studies of early man and the survival of popular traditions in Switzerland. Among the illustrations to its mathematics section is a drawing by Paul Klee (bottom left). The authors might well have added Swiss Concrete artists and graphic designers to the scientists and engineers who they claim 'find fulfilment in the power and scope of maths'.

▲ 'Educate for the Future', part of a section of Expo 64, designed by Josef Müller-Brockmann. Although the exhibition's printed material used Univers, the displays used Akzidenz Grotesk.

▼ The interior of the exhibition art gallery building, designed by Max Bill.

Sculptures by Giacometti and Bill's *Endless Ribbon* dominate the room.

YOUNG SWISS GRAPHIC ARTIST

(Member of the Swiss Union of Graphic Artists)

is looking for an opening
in Canada or USA

*Talented designer for industry and commerce.
Good knowledge of English.*

GRAPHIS will pass along your enquiries

◀ Advertisement in *Graphis*, 1948.
Swiss designers were in demand
abroad. They were especially
prominent and successful in Paris.
▼ The Swiss designers Jean Widmer,
Ernst Hiestand and Adrian Frutiger,
were responsible for the signage
of the Pompidou Centre in 1970.

"in every fat man
a thin one is
wildly signalling
to be let out"

Cyril Connolly

Geigy

release him
with
Preludin®
brand of
phenmetrazine
hydrochloride

FSN
6505-853-6916
tablets of 25 mg.

Effective Appetite Suppressant
Avoids Excessive Stimulation

Precautions: Do not use in pa-
tients with severe hyperten-
sion, thyrotoxicosis or acute
coronary disease. Use with
caution in moderate hyperten-
sion and cardiac decompen-
sation. Should not be used to
overcome addiction to other
sympathomimetic drugs (ha-
bituation and psychic depend-
ence have occurred).
Side effects: Dryness or un-
pleasant taste in the mouth, ur-
ticaria, and (rarely) overstim-
ulation, insomnia, dizziness,
nausea or headache.
Under license from
Boehringer Ingelheim G.m.b.H.

Geigy Pharmaceuticals
Division of
Geigy Chemical Corporation
Ardsley, New York

▲ Leaflet advertising a drug treatment
for obesity, designed by Geigy's Swiss
art director in New York, Fred Troller,
1965.

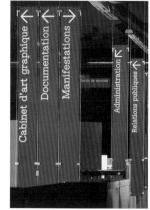

▼ One of a series of posters for
exhibitions organized by Centre de
Création Industrielle, designed by Jean
Widmer in a completely Swiss manner
of geometrical forms and lowercase
Helvetica type arranged in three
columns. Untypical of Widmer, whose
work was usually less formulaic.

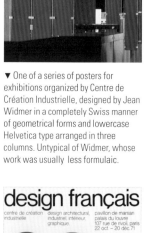

design français

centre de création
industrielle

design architectural,
industriel, intérieur,
graphique.

pavillon de marsan
palais du louvre
107 rue de rivoli, paris
22 oct – 20 déc.71

▼ Signs to indicate tourist attractions
on motorways throughout France were
devised by a team at Widmer's Paris
consultancy, Visuel Design. In white
on a brown background , the lettering
was in the typeface Frutiger, named
after its designer.

rochers de
Fontainebleau

5 An International Style

That which is internationally known as 'Swiss Typography' is at least in Switzerland in a state of radical change.

Wolfgang Weingart, *How Can One Make Swiss Typography?*, Basel 1976, p.31.

When I was first aware of what the Swiss were doing, I used to ridicule it . . . . But then I changed completely . . . there is no counterpart to Swiss design in terms of something you can describe, that you can follow, that you can systematically understand.

Paul Rand, quoted in Steven Heller, *Paul Rand*, New Haven 1999, p.158.

Exporting the Swiss Style

From abroad, in the 1950s and 1960s, Switzerland was slowly seen to be the source of a definable style. The evidence was chiefly provided by *Graphis*; but Swiss designers were active in self-promotion. In 1962 the London-based annual *Modern Publicity* recorded that more than five hundred Swiss advertising designs had been submitted for publication. The influence of Swiss designers was most strongly felt in the United States. It was heralded by Herbert Matter's arrival in New York in 1935.

After his work on the Swiss pavilion at the World Fair in 1939, Matter had become prominent as a photographer and designer. His house styles for the New Haven Railroad and Knoll furniture in the 1950s are now in the canon of graphic design history. In 1952 he began teaching at Yale. His 'Swissness' went unremarked, and his photomontages were too early to be included in the exhibition of 'Recent Swiss Posters' held at the Museum of Modern Art in New York in 1951. But when a twenty-year-old Matter tourist poster was illustrated alongside a small reproduction of a Wohnbedarf design in the US magazine *Print* in 1956, the caption added the surprisingly knowing question, 'I wonder who in America will show the first large exhibition of Max Bill?'[1]

Müller-Brockmann was the first Swiss designer of the new generation to attract special attention. In 1957 the bi-monthly *Industrial Design* praised his 'spectacular precision and clarity'. To explain his ideas, the editors gave him eight pages, which he filled with examples of his work and an earnest plea for designers to think clearly, show mental agility and have a complete understanding of type, photography, drawing and colour. He condemned common faults: too many sizes of type, poor word-spacing, and the repetition of a word, 'weakening its effect and detracting from the credibility of the statement'. And he made a special plea for the use of photography 'to show the real facts'.[2]

This was only a short time after Müller-Brockmann's conversion to the Constructive attitude. In 1953, when his work had been represented in a book on posters published in New York it was – like that of the other Swiss designers in the book – illustrative. Müller-Brockmann describes how he arrived at the drawing of a chicken to advertise egg pasta, rejecting an alternative of 'a smiling cook with a spaghetti-laden fork'.[3]

This was certainly not what *Print* magazine identified soon afterwards as the Swiss 'objectivity-conscious commercial art'. Speaking of Marcel Wyss's *Spirale* issues, *Print* commented, 'It is sad that they haven't had larger circulation in this country.' In 1958, the year after his *Industrial Design* article, Müller-Brockmann reappeared in *Print* to introduce 'Swiss Graphic Designers', a touring exhibition of work by a dozen exclusively Constructive designers.[4] Among them was Armin Hofmann, already familiar to American designers. He had given a short course at the Philadelphia Museum School of Art in 1955, and in the same year went on to Yale, where he remained a visiting lecturer until the 1990s. Whereas the Zurich school tended towards formal prescriptions, Hofmann brought from Basel the emphasis on 'the service of giving messages', clearly expressed later in his regularly reprinted *Graphic Design Manual*.

Meetings of successful designers through such organizations as the Alliance Graphique Internationale helped make a common visual vocabulary: many of its elements were derived from the Swiss model. Swiss designers abroad – those at Geigy in New York, for instance, continued in the way of working that they had acquired at home. When Ruedi Roth described his work at the corporate design practice Lippincott & Margulies in *Print*, the article, over several pages, was set in Berthold Akzidenz, ranged left, with all the appearance of having been typeset in Switzerland.[5]

Aaron Burns, the doyen of American typography, had shown an early taste for Swiss design. Burns had given a lecture in Zurich in 1959, and in his masterclass book, *Typography*, he included two works by Gerstner.[6] He later wondered if he had been responsible for importing American work into Switzerland. Swiss work, he said,

> was already looking stiff, as if in a hospital, so antiseptic.... I brought examples of Swiss work back home with me, and showed them. Strangely, Americans were as enthusiastic about Swiss work as the Swiss were about the American.[7]

Burns noticed after his trip to Zurich that 'some American designers are making the mistake of imitating design styles native to other countries'. As the head of an important New York typesetters, he must have witnessed the increasing popularity of Akzidenz Grotesk (known in the USA as Standard). In 1961 a survey asked which

1. *Print*, X:1, 1956, p.24.
2. *Industrial Design*, April 1956, pp.82-89.
3. W.H. Allner, *Posters*, New York 1953, pp.80-81.
4. *Print*, XI/2, April/May, 1957, pp.17-40.
5. 'Design Sense', *Print*, XI/4, 1957, insert after p.48.
6. Aaron Burns, *Typography*, New York 1961.
7. 'Über den lieben Gott und die Typografie' (On Dear God and Typography), interview with Felix Berman in *Typographische Monatsblätter*, June 1968, p.104. Berman was art director at GGK in Basel.

▲ Typesetters' advertisement in *Print* magazine, publicizing Berthold Akzidenz, known in the US as Standard Medium, 1957.
▼ Poster for a dance performance, designed by Rudolph De Harak, USA, 1963.

The poster shows a marked Swiss influence, especially of Armin Hofmann. De Harak had visited Zurich, and returned to the US with an admiration for Akzidenz Gotesk, which he used over several years on hundreds of paperback book covers.

typefaces were used less and which were now used more. Against the six designers who were using Standard less often, there were ninety-seven using it more.[8] This despite there being a good range of American grotesques – Franklin Gothic, News Gothic, Trade Gothic and Record Gothic. Because they all had the more ornamental lower-case 'g', Standard was a more up-to-date choice; later, Helvetica became a popular font in filmsetting and, even more, in digital typography. Rudolph De Harak, a visitor to Zurich in 1960, was converted to Standard, using it for more than 350 paperback covers. Standard and Helvetica played their part in some of the most durable corporate design, such as Paul Rand's for IBM. Among the most successful East Coast designers, Rand, art director of the international computer company IBM, later said: 'When I was first aware of what the Swiss were doing, I used to ridicule it. But then I changed completely . . . .'[9] Indeed, enough to appoint Müller-Brockmann as the company's European consultant.

Fritz Gottschalk, after a Zurich apprenticeship and a short time as a student with Emil Ruder, had formed a partnership with a Canadian designer to become Gottschalk+Ash, one of Canada's leading consultancies, with offices in Montreal and Toronto. Canada had already given Modernist graphic design public recognition when Canadian National Railways adopted a home-grown 'Swiss' house style in 1960. Gottschalk, though, was another to regret that 'more and more of the so-called American style is imitated by Swiss designers'.[10] At the same time, as in the United States, Canada was attracting Swiss teachers: among them, in the 1970s, Hans-Rudolf Lutz (see p.257).

In Japan, under US occupation after the Second World War until 1958, American influence was inevitably strong. However, a mutual recognition of the affinity between the simple black-and-white clarity of traditional Japanese symbols and the spare style of the Swiss was recognized in the pages of *Neue Grafik*.[11] When the Tokyo World Design Conference was held in 1960, Müller-Brockmann was invited to attend. The event coincided with the launch of the Japanese quarterly *Graphic Design*, whose editor, Masaru Katzumie, 'placed emphasis on the introduction of designers with a frankly constructivistic style', confessing,

8. Edward M.Gottschall (ed.), *Typographic Directions: Advertising Directions 4*, New York 1963, pp.131-32.
9. In an interview with the author in Steven Heller, *Paul Rand*, New Haven 1999, p 158
10. *TM*, March 1971, p.209.
11. Josef Müller-Brockmann reviewed recent Japanese design in the final issue of *Neue Grafik*, no.17/18, 1965.

▼ Signage for IBM plant using Standard Medium typeface design (Akzidenz), designed by Paul Rand, 1969.

Visitors & Salesmen Parking Only

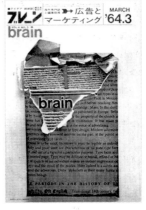

▲ Paul Rand, left, with Müller-Brockmann at an IBM seminar for European designers in the 1970s. Paul Rand was friendly with many Swiss designers through the Alliance Graphique Internationale group. His tombstone was designed by Fred Troller, the former Swiss art director of Geigy in New York.
▼ Cover of *Brain* magazine, designed by Tadashi Masuda, Japan, 1964. Helvetica became the most common typeface when the Japanese used English in graphic design.

Fridolin Müller's similar design was published in 1961 (see p.237).

▲ Advertisement for small electric motors designed by Günter and Gisela Donkowski, Germany, 1963. Swiss graphic conventions dominate the design's geometrical divisions of space, in the progressively increasing size of the elements of the 'concrete' emblem and in the use of Akzidenz Grotesk.

▲ One of the 5,000 covers designed under the art directorship of Celestino Piatti for the paperback publishers Deutscher Taschenbuch Verlag.

'I was fully aware of my lack of impartiality in this matter. Rather than Raymond Savignac, I selected Max Bill. Rather than Herbert Leupin, I chose Josef Müller-Brockmann. Instead of Hans Erni, I introduced Karl Gerstner.' [12]

Müller-Brockmann's visit led to teaching engagements in Tokyo and Osaka the following year. Also in Asia, Armin Hofmann was invited to design a course for the National Design Institute in the Indian city Ahmedabad. Inaugurated in 1965, the course was entirely European in conception. Several former Basel students were visiting tutors, including Fridolin Müller, and some Indians came as students to Basel.

In Europe, Germany was rebuilding a graphic style of timid and inconsistent Modernism. A handful of the prewar creators of the modern typography had survived as teachers: Friedrich Vordemberge-Gildewart at Ulm and Max Burchartz back at the Folkwang in Essen. For them and for many of the avant-garde, graphic design was an interlude in a creative life which began or ended with painting: they returned almost exclusively to fine art.

Anton Stankowski's time as a prisoner-of-war in Russia had not shaken his Modernist principles; he ran a successful design office in Stuttgart and continued painting in a refined Concrete idiom. One design practice that also flourished at the time of the German economic miracle, Mendell+Oberer, originated in Basel. Pierre Mendell came from Essen to study with Hofmann and set up a studio in Munich with a Swiss fellow student, Klaus Oberer.

The Swiss influence was even more evident in the Netherlands, where some design looked as if it had been carried out in Switzerland: the signage at Amsterdam's Schiphol airport, for example. Using Helvetica, Schiphol's was a model for many other sign systems. When Müller-Brockmann designed the signs at Zurich airport in the mid-1960s, they shared a 'visual language' with those in Amsterdam, and soon with every kind of transport and highway authority worldwide.

The signage in Amsterdam was by native designers. In France, on the other hand, from the 1950s to the 1980s the design of 'signalétique' – public sign systems for identifying buildings and routes – appeared as a Swiss monopoly: at both Paris airports of Orly and Charles de Gaulle, by Adrian Frutiger; at the Centre Pompidou, by Jean Widmer and Ernst and Ursula Hiestand in collaboration with Frutiger; at the Musée d'Orsay

▲ Bijenkorf (Beehive) department store, Amsterdam, 90th anniversary poster, designed by Josef Müller-Brockmann, 1960.

▲ Exhibition poster for the Van Abbe Museum in the Netherlands, designed by Wim van Sambeek, 1964. By this date imitations of the Swiss style – lowercase Akzidenz Grotesk and planes of flat colour – were commonplace. For van Sambeek this was a style acquired when he worked in Switzerland in the late 1950s.
▼ Schiphol airport, Amsterdam, signage by Benno Wissing at the Dutch design group Total Design, 1967. The Swiss style of grotesque had become the standard basis for such work.

12. *Graphic Design*, Tokyo, no.100, December 1985, p.82. Here Katzumie is quoting his contribution to issue 34, June 1969.

The influx of Swiss designers in Milan, following Max Huber in the 1940s, continued in the 1960s.

▲ Brochure for an anti-flu vaccine, designed by René Martinelli, 1957. The design, based on a grid of squares, 8×8, follows the style typical of Zurich, where Martinelli had worked with a former Boggeri designer, Carlo Vivarelli.

▼ Theatre poster designed by Massimo Vignelli, 1965.

Filmsetting allowed Vignelli to space the letters of Helvetica very tightly. This is the style – incorporating Swiss elements – which he took to the USA and employed especially for public projects over a long career.

▼ Massimo Vignelli's proposal for the New York subway signs, 1965.

by Bruno Monguzzi collaborating with Widmer. In France there had been almost no professional training in visual design offered at the country's main professional institution, the Ecole Nationale Supérieure des Arts Décoratifs (ENSAD). Widmer had given short courses there since the early 1960s and following the student agitations in 1968 he was appointed Professor, adding fellow Swiss designers to the staff. In typography, the Swiss input to Paris continued until the end of the century.

British designers working for pharmaceutical companies emulated the fresh, sober plainness in the advertising and packaging of competitors such as Geigy.[13] The 'Swiss style' was taken up enthusiastically: by the nationalized British Rail for signs and timetables, by Penguin Books, to standardize their paperback covers, by the National Theatre, for a progressive image.

In Italy it was difficult to separate what was Italian from what was imported from neighbouring Switzerland. As a leader of European graphic Modernism, Milan had benefited from its significant Swiss visitors: notably, following Xanti Schawinsky, Vivarelli (who left) and Max Huber (who stayed). There were also Walter Ballmer and Gerhard Forster from Basel, and Aldo Calabresi and, later, Bruno Monguzzi. Walter Ballmer had gone to Studio Boggeri in 1947, and worked for Olivetti from the mid-1950s, when Calabresi arrived from Zurich. When Forster moved to Milan in 1963, after studies in both Basel and Zurich, his work was not consistently 'Swiss'. From Milan many aspects of the 'Swiss' style were exported to New York by the Italian designer Massimo Vignelli – a style which he changed little over a quarter of a century, exemplified in his sign system for the New York subway.[14]

As well as signage, the Swiss had a considerable influence on the shape of books. The books on graphic design, Gerstner's and Müller-Brockmann's, carried through their ideas into the design of the books themselves: square backs, often square formats, sanserif typefaces set in more than one column. These were widely imitated.

During the 1960s the move of printing from letterpress to offset coincided with the period of 'flower power', psychedelia and graffiti. Meanwhile the letterpress-based Swiss style survived as a counterbalance.

<hr />

13. Geigy's office in Manchester, staffed by British designers, produced Swiss-style publicity material.
14. Massimo Vignelli succeeded Herbert Matter as graphic designer for the furniture firm Knoll.

▲ Exhibition poster designed by Dennis Bailey, London, 1961. Bailey, also an illustrator, worked in Zurich as an assistant editor at *Graphis* in 1957. One of the first foreign designers to work in the Swiss style, after returning to London his work was indistinguishable from the Zurich Constructive designers.

▲ London's National Theatre adopted a Swiss style, introduced by the designers Ken Briggs and Ian McLaren in the mid-1960s. This programme of events is printed in red and black.

▼ The symbol for British Rail, designed by the Design Research Unit, 1960. The design follows the Swiss use of established conventional signs, especially the arrow, and an even width of line. British Rail also adapted grotesque for its signage

Dismantling the Constructive Style

▼ Spreads from Hans Rudolf Bosshard's textbook, *Form und Farbe* (Form and Colour), setting out the basis of the typographic teaching of the Zurich Kunstgewerbeschule, 1968.

The fact that Bosshard's book was in German, and not published commercially, ensured a limited influence.

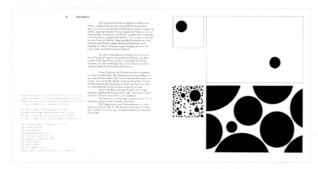

▲ The plane surface: the dot, a mark on a surface, as it is enlarged, becomes itself a plane surface rather than a mark.

▼ An increasing number of units in a grid, on the right-hand side, shows that a 16-unit grid can provide 100 possible sizes and positions of image on the page.

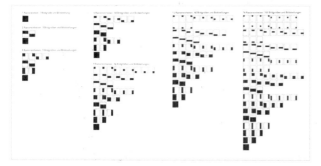

Hans Rudolf Bosshard Born 1929 Trained as typesetter, but worked as painter and printmaker, from 1960 as Concrete artist and writer, publisher of limited edition books. Teacher in various positions at the Zurich Kunstgewerbeschule, 1962-94. Author of valuable typographic textbooks (see bibliography).

▲ Poster for a John Heartfield exhibition, designed by Hans Rudolf Bosshard, 1978. The certainties of the 'Swiss' style have disappeared. Bosshard replaces them with an irrational, random typography which breaks conventional rules and has no connection with the spirit or period of Heartfield's activity. Its eccentricity competes for attention with Heartfield's simple but powerfully satirical image – 'Berlin idiom'.

However much the Swiss style was established and identified, there were still many varieties of style in Switzerland. By the mid-1960s, the selection of Best Posters of the Year was no longer dominated by designs which would have been approved by the editors of *Neue Grafik*. The discipline instilled by the schools of design ensured nonetheless that the typography in advertisements, business literature and tourist information maintained a standard that was envied and admired abroad.

In Switzerland the pioneering designers of the middle generation – Jörg Hamburger and Siegfried Odermatt, for example – introduced an expressive graphics, fresh with each job. They rediscovered and gave new life to Futura and Bodoni, typefaces only intermittently popular with Modernists in the 1930s. Of the younger designers whose work followed the Modernist tradition, the best known was Bruno Monguzzi. In the early 1960s he worked in Milan for Studio Boggeri, at first in a conventional, elegant Zurich manner, then more freely. Yet much of his work, even into the 1980s, has Modernist echoes: for example, black neo-Constructivist rules used as decorative emphasis or to make a striking image. He later marked his closeness to tradition with the publication of two studies of Piet Zwart.[1]

The theory and practice of mature Constructive typography was enshrined in a handbook (in German only) put together by a teacher of the trade typesetters at the Zurich Kunstgewerbeschule. The almost square book, *Form und Farbe* (Form and Colour), produced by Hans Rudolf Bosshard with his students in 1968, is a manual for the system and discipline of design in the final period of metal typesetting. Bosshard was to take grids to an obsessive complexity that went beyond even Gerstner's at their most elaborate.[2]

Emil Ruder's book *Typographie*, by including Ruder's own designs, was more approachable, less systematic. In a similar format and with the same topics, published in 1967 in German, English and French, *Typographie* was welcomed as a design school textbook in many countries. But designers were coming to see Swiss graphics merely as a style, and one that belonged to an earlier technology. On the other side of the Atlantic computer programmes were being prepared that would allow American designers to simulate and try to improve

---

1. 'Piet Zwart typotect' and 'Piet Zwart: L'opera tipografica', in *Rassegna* 30, Milan 1987.
2. Bosshard illustrates the grid for *Form und Farbe* in his book *Der Typographische Raster* (The Typographic Grid), Zurich 2000.

▼ English-language magazine
advertisement for Swissair, designed
by GGK, 1970s. Gerstner's 'integral
typography' finds a logical form: no
obvious aesthetic content and the
visual language subordinate to the text
message. The trademark is the only
surviving element of Modernism.

▼ Cover of the Italian printing trade
magazine *Linea Grafica*, designed by
Bruno Monguzzi, 1980. The photograph
by Antonio Boggeri is from 1934.
Monguzzi evokes the Constructivist
typography of the period of early
Modernism in the black Mondrian-like
lines – familiar in Swiss design of the
1950s as a decorative division of the
space. They exemplify the Modernist
elements which survive in much of
Monguzzi's work.

on what the Swiss had already perfected in the 1950s.

Karl Gerstner, however fascinated by mathematical
control, by systems, had for some time left the 'Swiss'
stereotypes behind. Busy mostly as an advertising
consultant, he considered his client's message, not its
form, to be his priority. The entrenchment of a style
'perfected in the 1950s' was an impediment to young
designers' ambitions. Technical innovation demanded
new attitudes, as it had with the Modernists forty years
earlier. Phototypesetting was taking over from metal,
offset litho was replacing letterpress and full-colour
printing had become economically more practical.

The chief designers to break away from the received
concept of modern Swiss typography were Hans-Rudolf
Lutz and Wolfgang Weingart. In the mid-1960s Lutz
worked for two years in Paris, where he and his employer,
Albert Hollenstein, ran an evening class together. After
his return to Switzerland in 1966, Lutz taught at the Zurich
Kunstgewerbeschule with Bosshard. He was unusual in
his concern for the social role of graphics; while Bosshard
demonstrated the fundamentals of organizing text, Lutz
examined the raw material of signs, letters and words. He
recorded the use of words as they occurred informally, on
shop fronts, as graffiti, in popular magazines: what was
referred to by designers in the 1990s as 'vernacular'.

The publication in Zurich in 1968 of *Form und Farbe*
coincided with the opening of the Advanced Course for
Graphic Design at the Allgemeine Gewerbeschule in
Basel. This was run by Armin Hofmann and Wolfgang
Weingart, a young German compositor, who had come
five years earlier as a research student to work with
Hofmann and Emil Ruder.

> Weingart took 'Swiss Typography' to be
> a sensible point of departure, and through teaching
> and experimenting to develop new design models. . . .
> It was never with the idea of throwing 'Basel or Swiss
> Typography' overboard, but instead, with an attempt
> to expand them – to enliven and change them with the
> help of intensively considered design criteria and new
> visual ideas.[3]

In spite of his claim not to be discarding 'Swiss'
typography, he deliberately broke the rules set out by
Ruder. Experience as a compositor gave him a feeling for
printing material, and hence its potential for subversion.
He records picking up a bundle of tiny metal type, tying it
up and printing from it upside down. He bent metal rules

▲ Reconstruction of a page of *Blick*
daily newspaper, made on the course
run by Hans-Rudolf Lutz at the School
of Design in Lucerne, 1976.
All the elements were taken from
a single page. Lutz's aim was to make
a literal demonstration of *Blick*'s one-
time slogan – 'Everything at a glance'
(Blick = glance)
▼ The original *Blick* page before its
reconstruction.

3. Wolfgang Weingart, *How Can One Make Swiss Typography?*, self-published
illlustrated lecture notes, Basel 1972, pp.3-4.

258

▶ Poster for an exhibition of 'The Swiss Poster', by Wolfgang Weingart, 1984. Hugely influential as teacher and polemicist, more artist than designer, Weingart broke the mould of Swiss graphics. His training as a compositor made him familiar with printing and reproduction processes and materials. He manipulated the techniques used in photolithography – photographic film and screens – to arrive at his designs.

▲ Full-colour advertisement in *Wet* magazine, designed by April Greiman, California, 1979. Before computer imaging, Greiman combined collaged elements, and she retained the orthodox typesetting – in various weights and styles of Univers – she had acquired in Basel.

From Photographic to Digital

Wolfgang Weingart was the innovator who found new forms. They were exploited by a younger generation, the first with access to the graphic fluency and speed of the personal computer.

▲ Poster for an exhibition of work submitted for scholarships in applied art, a black and white lithographic poster by Wolfgang Weingart, 1978. Weingart has superimposed film negatives and positives. The positive and negative of the photographic process enriches the surface in a way which runs counter to the spare, ordered information of a Modernist poster. Only the bold Akzidenz looks back to a Swiss tradition.

to print as snaking lines. Such improvisation was the key to his teaching, rather than the diversions into communication theory which he used to underpin his work when he presented it to lecture audiences. Weingart was carrying out Schwitters's injunction, to 'make your typography in a way no one has before'. In other words, to do the opposite of the conventional – the strategy of the *enfant terrible*.

However much Weingart's work appears as a visual hysteria, it was nonetheless a sharply exaggerated illustration of the realities of technological change. He produced his own screens on photographic film by superimposing, for example, a 20 percent dot screen and a graduated tone screen. Weingart talks of his excitement at the effect of overlapping film: 'I'd discovered the intrinsic aesthetic of a new process.' As well as his inspiration as a teacher, this was his most significant achievement, resulting in a series of posters which found an elegantly original and convincing form for their message – and in a visual language which was still 'Swiss'. The Swiss character derived partly from his preference for Akzidenz Grotesk, most often in its heavier weight. He claims to have dusted off the Akzidenz in the typecases in the composing department in Basel, where its use had been displaced by Univers.

Weingart's handcrafted work, essentially photographic, prefigured computerized graphic design. These posters initiated the 'layering' of type and image, a feature of modish 'digital art-deco' or 'cocktail graphics' – terms used to describe the mannerist typography of Weingart's most celebrated student, the American designer April Greiman. As a student at Kansas City Art Institute, Greiman had been taught by Basel designers and in 1970 she went to Switzerland with the idea of studying with Hofmann and Ruder. As for type, Greiman followed Ruder's devotion to Univers rather than Weingart's preference for the 'rugged' Akzidenz. At the time when Helvetica was regarded as more associated with design for business, Ruder's *Typographie* textbook helped popularize Univers. Ruder introduced the spacing of individual lowercase letters, which became a mannerism with those Americans who aspired to a Basel sophistication.

Greiman was not the only American designer who brought the message from Basel. Daniel Friedman, a former student of Basel and the Ulm Hochschule, began teaching at Yale in 1970. Along with the Swiss Willi Kunz (briefly a student of Weingart's), Friedman, Greiman and other former Basel students worked in the US in a style

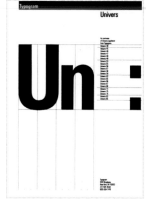

▲ Cover to a New York typesetters' brochure promoting Univers, designed by Willi Kunz, 1988. Kunz was trained as a type compositor and studied design at the Allgemeine Gewerbeschule in Basel. When he went to the US he took his enthusiasm for Univers with him, and for a time used it almost exclusively.
▼ Poster designed by Carl Zahn, 1962, following Ruder's example in exploiting the slope of Univers italic (see p.218).

▼ Advertisements calling for a 'no' vote against a proposal to expel foreign workers, conceived and designed by Jost Hochuli, 1970.

▲ The first advertisement in the series has an ironical quotation from the writer Max Frisch: 'We asked for labour – and people came.'

▲ The final advertisement cites a single example of the effect of the legislation, typeset in Times. It ends with a huge 'no' set in Gill extra bold. The mixture of symmetry and asymmetry and varied type styles typifies the relaxation of attitudes after the 1960s.

which became known as the 'new wave': typically, widely spaced condensed Univers, which might be set in curves or at an oblique angle, with fine rules in arcs or as a square grid. At the end of the 1970s Weingart wrote of

the criminalistic copy-monkeys who 'try' to find a 'new' style of typography, which reminds me very much of the Basel-Weingart-Style from the beginning of the '70s: Mr [Willi] Kunz and Mr [Wilbur] Bonnell and many others from the States.[4]

Weingart was writing to Helmut Schmid, a former Basel student working in Tokyo. Schmid was editing a 'Typography Today' issue of the Japanese magazine *Idea*. Schmid included, among the better known Swiss designers – Gerstner, Müller-Brockmann, Odermatt, Ruder and Weingart – work by Jost Hochuli who, after completing a graphic design course, trained as a typesetter and spent a short time studying with Frutiger in Paris. Hochuli made his later reputation as a book designer but, with the graphics on a flip-top cigarette pack, he produced one of the most eloquent totems of the Constructive style (see p.202).

In America, Armin Hofmann continued for many years to represent the academic aspects of Swiss graphic culture at Yale. By the 1970s, elements of 'Swiss' style could be seen all over the world. What was left after the dissolution of the 'constructive' was both a useful language for information design on the one hand, and on the other a tired formalistic cliché which had little life in it without the aesthetic and social convictions of the founding fathers. Müller-Brockmann continued refining the language of his posters with an untiring elegance. Several designers reversed the trend of the 1920s avant-garde, leaving their drawing boards to spend their time as artists, Gottfried Honegger and Nelly Rudin among them.

Each style in succession exhausts itself. It may develop from originality to orthodoxy, it may be elaborated in extreme forms, it may become fashionable. Van de Velde had witnessed this with the excesses of later Art Nouveau, and he had seen the language of Cubism transmuted into Art Deco. Yet the graphic design and typography developed in Switzerland in the middle years of the twentieth century was a template used and adapted by designers for fifty years. Its origin was pan-European. Its consummation and achievements were Swiss. But now it is justly described as an International Style.

▲ 'Architecture in France', exhibition poster designed by Carl B. Graf, 1953.
▼ 'Art Museums and Architecture', exhibition poster designed by Bruno Monguzzi, 1992, for the Museo Cantonale d'Arte, the art gallery for the Ticino province in southern Switzerland.

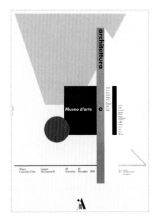

There are more than 40 years between the dates of these two posters by Graf and Monguzzi, yet they share three characteristics of Modernism. First, the Constructive aim to maintain tension between the surface plane of the paper and the depth implied by graphic perspective. Second, the use of geometrical forms. Third, text set in the movement's favoured typefaces – sanserif and Bodoni. But Monguzzi, in introducing symmetry (the black rectangle and the gallery's emblem on the central axis), exemplifies both the survival of Modernism and its assimilation in a flexible graphic language.
▶ Designed in the 1970s by Ernst Hiestand, the Zurich transport signs are a standard emulated internationally.

4. 'Typography Today' special issue of *Idea*, Tokyo 1980, p.5.

Acknowledgements

262

I have had the opportunity, over several years, of meeting several of the participants in this story, and would like to express my thanks to them for their generosity with time, with original material, and often with hospitality. They include the late Max Bill, Richard Paul Lohse, Josef Müller-Brockmann and Emil Ruder; of those happily still active, Karl Gerstner, Jörg Hamburger, Ernst Hiestand, Jost Hochuli, Armin and Dorothea Hofmann, Siegfried Odermatt and Rosmarie Tissi, Bruno Monguzzi, Fridolin Müller, Wolfgang Weingart and Shizuko Yoshikawa.

I am especially grateful for the help and kindness of others in Switzerland: Felix Studinka, curator of the Poster Collection at the Design Museum in Zurich; to Myrtha Steiner of the Graphic Collection of the School of Design in Zurich; to Dr Rolf Thalmann of the Poster Collection in Basel; to Johanna Lohse James and the late Bryn James at the Richard Paul Lohse Foundation and to Dr Jakob Bill.

The book would have been impossible without the assistance and encouragement of Paul Barnes in London and the loan over several years of a large bulk of material from his collection. Of the libraries in Zurich, at the School of Design, at the Eidgenössische Technische Hochschule and at the Zentralbibliothek, the staff have been exemplary in their courtesy and efficiency, as has the St Bride's Printing Library in London and the London Library. I have also been helped by the libraries at Central St Martins College of Art and Design, the London College of Communication and the National Art Library.

I am grateful to W.D. Jackson in Munich for some of the longer passages of translation and to Ulrike Stöpfel, translator of the Swiss edition, for putting my English right. In London I have also had invaluable help from Alan Bartram, Clive Challis, Jon Corpe, Simon Esterson, Ken Garland, the late Gordon House, Robin Kinross, Marit Münzberg, Jasmin Sieke and Brian Webb; and also from Sandro Bocola in Zurich.

The work might never have been completed without the commitment and patient encouragement of Laurence King and his staff, in particular Jo Lightfoot and Felicity Awdry; I am grateful for their patience and care at many stages of the writing and production.

Select Bibliography

Books, exhibition catalogues and journals which
have been part of the research for this book are listed here.
For a more complete bibliography readers are referred to
Christoph Bignens, 'Swiss Style', Zurich: Chronos, 2000.
Book titles have been shown in English only where there is
an English or multilingual edition.

Ades, Dawn. *The Twentieth-Century Poster,* New York: Abbeville Press, 1984

Arp, Hans. *Unsern täglichen Traum . . .,* Zurich: Der Arche, 1955

Arp, Hans, and El Lissitzky. *Die Kunstismen,* Erlenbach-Zurich, 1925; reprint Baden: Lars Müller, 1994

Bachmann, Jul, and Stanislas von Moos. *New Directions in Swiss Architecture,* London: Studio Vista / New York: George Braziller, 1969

Baljeu, Joost. *Theo van Doesburg,* London: Studio Vista, 1974

Bangerter, Walter, and Armin Tschanen. *Offizielle Schweizer Grafik / Official Graphic Art in Switzerland,* Zurich: ABC Verlag, 1964

Barnes, Paul (ed.). *Jan Tschichold: Reflections and Reappraisals,* New York: Typoscope, 1995

Bayer, Herbert, Walter Gropius and Ise Gropius (eds). *Bauhaus 1991-1928,* Boston: Charles T. Branford Company, 1959

Benton, Tim, and Charlotte Benton. *Form and Function: A Source Book for the History of Architecture and Design 1890-1939,* London: Open University Press, 1975

Berlincourt, Alain, *et al. Max Caflisch: Typographia practica,* Hamburg: Maximilian Gesellschaft, 1988

Bignens, Christoph. *'Swiss Style': Die grosse Zeit der Gebrauchsgrafik in der Schweiz 1914-1962,* Zurich: Chronos, 2000

Bill, Max. *Robert Maillart,* Erlenbach-Zurich: Verlag für Architektur, 1949

—. *Form: Eine Bilanz über die Formentwicklung um die Mitte des XX. Jahrhunderts : A Balance Sheet of Mid-Twentieth-Century Trends in Design,* Basel: Verlag Karl Werner, 1952

—. *Robert Maillart,* Erlenbach-Zurich: Verlag für Architektur, 1949

Bircher, Urs. *Vom langsamen Wachsen eines Zorns: Max Frisch 1911-1955,* Zurich: Limmat, 1997

Blaser, Werner. *Struktur und Gestalt in Japan (Structure and Form in Japan),* Zurich: Artemis / Verlag für Architektur, 1963

Bonjour, E., *et al. A Short History of Switzerland,* Oxford: Oxford University Press, 1952

Bosman, Josef, and Sokratis Georgiadis. *Sigfried Giedion 1888-1968: Der Entwurf einer modernen Tradition,* Zurich: Ammann, 1989

Bosshard, Hans Rudolf. *Mathemathische Grundlagen der Satzherstellung,* Basel: BST, 1985

—. *Typografie, Schrift, Lesbarkeit. Sechs Essays,* Sulgen: Niggli, 1996

—. *Rastersysteme: Gesetzmässigkeit und Intuition,* Sulgen: Niggli, 1999

Brüning, Ute. *Das A und O des Bauhauses,* Berlin: Bauhaus-Archiv, 1995

Bucher, Annemarie. *Spirale: Eine Künstlerzeitschrift 1953-1964,* Baden: Lars Müller, 1990

Burchartz, Max. *Typographische Arbeiten 1924-1931,* (facsimiles) Baden: Lars Müller, 1993

Burckhardt, Lucius, Max Frisch and Markus Kutter. *Achtung die Schweiz,* Basel: Verlag F. Handschin, 1955

—. *Die neue Stadt,* Basel: Verlag F. Handschin, 1956

Bürkle, J. Christoph et al. *Jost Hochuli: Drucksachen, vor allem Bücher,* Sulgen / Zurich: Niggli, 2002

Burns, Aaron. *Typography,* New York: Reinhold, 1961

Carter, Rob. *American Typography Today,* New York: Van Nostrand Reinhold, 1989

Diethelm, Walter. *Signet Signal Symbol,* Zurich: ABC Verlag, 1970

—. *Form+Communication,* Zurich: ABC Verlag, 1974

—. *Visual Transformation,* Zurich: ABC Verlag, 1982

264

Finkeldey, Bernd, *et al* (eds). *Konstruktivistische Internationale Schöpferische Gemeinschaft 1922-1927,* Dusseldorf: Kunstsammlung Nordrhein-Westfalen/ Stuttgart: Gerd Hatje, 1992

Fleischmann, Gerd (ed.). *Bauhaus, Drucksachen, Typografie, Reklame,* Dusseldorf: Marzona, 1984

Fleischmann, Gerd, Hans Rudolf Bosshard and Christoph Bignens. *Max Bill: Typografie, Reklame, Buchgestaltung,* Zurich: Niggli, 1999

Frei, Hans. *Konkrete Architektur?,* Baden: Lars Müller, 1991

Frisch, Max. *Schweiz als Heimat? Versuche über 50 Jahre,* Frankfurt/Main: Suhrkamp, 1990

Geigy heute, Basel: J.R. Geigy AG,1958

Georgiadis, Sokratis. *Sigfried Giedion: An Intellectual Biography,* (tr. Colin Hall), Edinburgh: Edinburgh University Press, 1995

Gerstner, Karl. *Kalte Kunst?: zur Standort der heutigen Malerei,* Teufen: Niggli, 1957

—. *Programme entwerfen,* Teufen: Niggli, 1964 ; tr. as *Designing Programmes,* London: Tiranti, 1968

—. *Kompendium für Alphabeten,* Teufen: Niggli, 1972; tr. as *Compendium for Literates,* New Haven: Yale University Press/ London: Tiranti, 1974

Gerstner, Karl, and Markus Kutter. *Die neue Graphik,* Teufen: Niggli, 1959

Gerstner, Gredinger + Kutter 1962, Basel: Gerstner, Gredinger+ Kutter Werbeagentur, 1962

Giedion, Sigfried (ed.). *Befreites Wohnen,* Zürich and Leipzig: Orell Füssli, 1929

—. *Walter Gropius: Work and Teamwork,* London: Architectural Press/ New York: Reinhold,1954

Giedion, Sigfried, *et al* (eds). *Moderne Schweizer Architektur,* Basel: Verlag Karl Werner, 1939

Gottschall, Edward M. (ed.). *Typographic Directions: Advertising Directions 4,* New York: Art Directions Book Co., 1963

—. *Typographic Communications Today,* Cambridge, Mass./ London: MIT Press, 1989

Graeff, Werner. *Es kommt der neue Fotograf!,* Berlin: Hermann Reckendorf, 1929

—. *Prospekte wirksam gestalten,* Zurich: Verlag Organisator, 1950

Greiman, April. *Hybrid Imagery,* London: Architecture Design and Technology Press, 1990

Haab, Armin and Alex Stocker. *Lettera: A standard book of fine lettering,* Teufen: Niggli 1954

Hans Neuburg, Teufen: Niggli, 1964

Hans Neuburg: 50 anni di grafica costruttiva, Milan: Electa, 1982

Herdeg, Walter. *Schweizer Signete.Trademarks and Symbols,* Zurich: Graphis Press, 1948

Hernandez, Antonio. *Emil Ruder: Lehrer und Typograph,* Basel: Gewerbemuseum im Pharos Verlag, 1971

Hight, Eleanor M. *Picturing Modernism: Moholy-Nagy and Photography in Weimar Germany,* Cambridge, Mass./ London: MIT Press, 1995

Hill, Anthony (ed.) *DATA: Directions in Art, Theory and Aesthetics,* London: Faber & Faber, 1968

Hochuli, Jost. *Buchgestaltung in der Schweiz;* tr. as *Book Design in Switzerland,* both Zurich: Pro Helvetia, 1993

Hofmann, Armin. *Methodik der Form- und Bildgestaltung: Aufbau/ Synthese/Anwendung,* trilingual edition, Teufen: Niggli 1965; tr. as *A Graphic Design Manual: Principles and Practice,* New York: Van Nostrand Reinhold, 1965

Holz, Hans Heinz. *Xanti Schawinsky,* Zurich: ABC Verlag, 1981

Holz, Hans Heinz, et al. *Lohse lesen: Texte von Richard Paul Lohse,* Zurich: Offizin, 2002

Horat, Heinz (ed.). *1000 Years of Swiss Art,* New York: Hudson Hills, 1992

Huber, Max, *et al. Due Dimensioni,* Milan: Editype, 1964

Ingberman, Sima. *ABC: International Constructivist Architecture, 1922-1929,* Cambridge, Mass/London: MIT Press, 1994

Isaacs, Reginald R. *Walter Gropius: Der Mensch und sein Werk,* Berlin: Gebr. Mann, 1983

Jost, Karl, and Peter Münger. *Richard Paul Lohse: Concrete Artist,* Zurich: Artists Video Documentation, 1999

Kappeler, Suzanne (ed.). *Carlo Vivarelli: Plastik, Malerei, Gebrauchsgraphik,* Zurich: ABC Verlag, 1988

Kinross, Robin. *Modern Typography: An Essay in Critical History,* London: Hyphen Press, 1992; 2nd edition, London 2004

Kostelanetz, Richard (ed.). *Moholy-Nagy,* New York: Praeger, 1970/ London: Allen Lane, 1971

Kulturpolitik in der Schweiz, Zurich: Stiftung Pro Helvetia, 1954

Kunstgewerbemuseum der Stadt Zurich. *Gründung und Entwicklung 1878-1978: 100 Jahre Kunstgewerbeschule der Stadt Zurich,* Zurich: Schule für Gestaltung, 1975

Kutter, Markus. *Schiff nach Europa,* Teufen: Niggli, 1957

—.*Werbung in der Schweiz: Geschichte einer unbekannten Branche,* Zofingen: Ringler, 1983

Le Corbusier. *Vers une Architecture,* Paris: Vincent, Fréal, 1923; new enlarged edition, 1958

Lemoine, Serge (ed.). *Piet Mondrian/Alfred Roth: Correspondance,* Paris: Gallimard, 1994

—. *Art Concret,* Mouans-Sartoux: Espace de l'Art Concret, Réunion des Musées Nationaux, 2000

Lissitzky-Küppers, Sophie. *El Lissitzky: Life, Letters, Texts,* London: Thames & Hudson, 1968

Lohse, Richard P. *Neue Ausstellungsgestaltung/New Design in Exhibitions,* Erlenbach/Zurich: Verlag für Architectur,1953

Lohse, Richard P. , Josef Müller-Brockmann and Carlo Vivarelli. *Hans Neuburg: der Jubilar, der Zeichner, der Kunstkritiker, der Publizist, der Grafiker,* Teufen: Niggli, 1964

McLean, Ruari. *Jan Tschichold: Typographer,* London: Lund Humphries, 1975

Margadant, Bruno. *'Für das Volk – Gegen das Kapital': Plakate der Schweizerischen Arbeiterbewegung von 1919 bis 1973,* Zurich: Verlagsgenossenschaft, 1973

—. *Das Schweizer Plakat/The Swiss Poster,* Basel: Birkhäuser, 1983

Mehlau-Wiebking, Friedericke, *et al. Schweizer Typenmöbel 1925-1935: Sigfried Giedion und die Wohnbedarf AG,* Zurich: gta Verlag, 1989

Mühlemann, Louis. *Wappen und Fahnen der Schweiz,* Luzern: Reich Verlag, 1977

Moholy-Nagy, László. *Malerei, Photographie, Film,* Munich: Albert Langen, 1925; reprint Mainz: Florian Kupferberg Verlag, 1967; tr. as *Painting, Photography, Film,* London: Lund Humphries, 1969

Molins, Patricia. *Suiza constructiva,* Madrid: Museo Nacional Centro de Arte Reina Sofia, 2003

Müller, Lars. *Josef Müller-Brockmann: Pioneer of Swiss Graphic Design,* Baden: Lars Müller, 1995

Müller-Brockmann, Josef. *Gestaltungsprobleme des Graphikers/ The Graphic Designer and his Design Problems,* Teufen: Niggli / London: Tiranti, 1961

—. *Geschichte der visuellen Kommunikation/A History of Visual Communication,* Teufen: Niggli, 1971

—. *Mein Leben: Spielerischer Ernst und ernsthaftes Spiel,* Baden: Lars Müller, 1994

Müller-Brockmann, Josef, and Shizuko Müller-Brockmann. *Geschichte des Plakates/History of the Poster,* Zurich: ABC Verlag, 1971

Müller-Brockmann, Josef, and Karl Wobmann. *Photoplakate: von den Anfängen bis zur Gegenwart,* Aarau/Stuttgart: AT Verlag, 1989

Neuburg, Hans. *Moderne Werbe- und Gebrauchs-grafik,* Ravensburg: Otto Meier Verlag, 1960

—. *Schweizer Industrie Grafik/Graphic Design in Swiss Industry,* Zurich: ABC Verlag, 1965

Nunoo-Quarcoo, Franc. *Bruno Monguzzi: A Designer's Perspective,* Baltimore: University of Maryland, 1998

Odermatt, Siegfried, and Rosmarie Tissi. *Siegfried Odermatt & Rosmarie Tissi: Graphic Design,* Zurich: Jack Waser and Werner M. Wolf, 1993

Odermatt, Siegfried (ed.). *100+3 Schweizer Plakate,* Zurich: Waser Verlag, 1998

Rasch, Heinz, and Bodo Rasch. *Gefesselter Blick,* Stuttgart: Wissenschaftlicher Verlag Dr. Zaugg & Co., 1930 (reprint Zurich: Lars Müller, 1996)

Richard Paul Lohse Foundation (ed.). *Richard Paul Lohse: Die Gebrauchsgrafik 1928-1988,* Ostfildern-Ruit: Hatje Cantz, 1999; texts tr. as *Richard Paul Lohse: Graphic Design 1928-1988,* Ostfildern-Ruit: Hatje Cantz, 2002

Roth, Alfred (ed.). *La nouvelle Architecture/Die neue Architektur/ The New Architecture,* Erlenbach-Zurich, Les Editions d'Architecture, 1946

Rotzler, Willy, *et al. Das Plakat in der Schweiz,* Schaffhausen: Stemmle, 1990

—. *Constructive Concepts,* Zurich: ABC Verlag, 1977; 2nd revised edition, 1988

Ruder, Emil. *Die Farbe : Kurze Farbenlehrer für den Buchdrucker,* Vienna: Willy Verkauf, 1948

—. *Typographie,* Teufen: Niggli, 1967

Schmid, Helmut. *Der Weg nach Basel/The Road to Basel,* Tokyo: Helmut Schmid Design, 1997

Schnaidt, Claude. *Hannes Meyer: Bauten, Projekte, Schriften/ Buildings, Projects and Writings,* Teufen: Niggli/London: Tiranti, 1965

Schwarz, Frederic J. *The Werkbund: Design Theory and Mass Culture before the First World War,* New Haven/London: Yale University Press, 1996

Schweizer Grafiker: Handbuch VSG, Zurich: Käser Presse, 1960

Spencer, Herbert. *Pioneers of Modern Typography,* London: Lund Humphries, 1969

Stankowski, Anton. *Visual Presentation of Invisible Processes,* Teufen: Niggli, n.d.

Studinka, Felix, and Christina Reble. *Poster Collection: Armin Hofmann,* Zurich: Museum für Gestaltung/Baden: Lars Müller, 2003

Stürzebecher, Jörg. *'Max ist endlich auf dem richtigen Weg': Max Burchartz 1887-1961,* Frankfurt: Deutscher Werkbund, 1993 (also published with *Max Burchartz 1887-1961: Typographische Arbeiten 1924-1931),* Baden: Lars Müller, 1996

Tschanen, Armin, and Walter Bangerter. *Grafik einer Schweizer Stadt/Graphic Art of a Swiss Town,* Zurich: ABC Verlag, 1963

Tschichold, Jan. *Die neue Typographie: ein Handbuch für zeitgemäss Schaffende,* Berlin 1928; reprint, Berlin: Brinkmann und Bose, 1987; tr. as *The New Typography: A Handbook for Modern Designers,* Berkeley: University of California Press, 1995

—. *Typographische Entwurfstechnik,* Stuttgart, 1932 (tr. as *How to Draw Layouts,* Edinburgh: Merchiston Publishing, 1995)

—. *Typographische Gestaltung,* Basel: Benno Schwabe & Co, 1935 (revised tr. as *Asymmetric Typography,* London: Faber & Faber, 1967)

—. *Gute Schriftformen,* Basel: Allg. Gewerbeschule/Erziehungs- Departement Basel-Stadt, 1941

Tupitsyn, Margarita. *The Soviet Photograph 1924-1937,* New Haven/London: Yale University Press, 1996

— *El Lissitzky: Beyond the Abstract Cabinet,* New Haven/London: Yale University Press, 1999

Van de Velde, Henry. *Die Renaissance im modernen Kunstgewerbe,* Berlin: H.Seemann, 1903

—. *Zum neuen Stil,* Munich: Piper, 1955

—. *Geschichte meines Lebens,* Munich: Rowohlt, 1961

—. *Déblaiement d'art,* Brussels: Archives d'Architecture Moderne, 1979

Wagner, Julius (ed.). *Das Goldene Buch der Landesausstellung 1939,* Zurich: Verkehrsverlag, 1939

Webster, Gwendolen. *Kurt Merz Schwitters: A Biographical Study,* Cardiff: University of Wales Press, 1997

Weingart, Wolfgang. *How Can One make Swiss Typography,* Basel: 1972

—. *Wege zur Typographie/My Way to Typography,* Baden: Lars Müller, 2000

Wichmann, Hans (ed.). *Armin Hofmann: His Work, Quest, Philosophy/Werk, Erkundung, Lehre,* Basel/Boston/Berlin: Birkhäuser, 1989

Willett, John. *The New Sobriety: Art and Politics in the Weimar Period 1917-33,* London: Thames & Hudson, 1978

Wrede, Stuart. *The Modern Poster,* New York: Museum of Modern Art, 1988

Exhibition catalogues

Aargauer Kunsthaus, Aarau:
Dreissiger Jahre Schweiz: 1936 – Eine Konfrontation (The Thirties in Switzerland: 1936 – A Confrontation), 1981

Gewerbemuseum, Basel:
Neue Typographie (New Typography), 1927
Neue Werbegrafik (New Advertising Design), 1930
Die neue Fotografie (The New Photography), 1931
Basler Plakat Kunst (Basel Poster Art), 1933
Die neue Fotografie in der Schweiz (The New Photography in Switzerland), 1933
Planvolles Werben: vom Briefkopf bis zum Werbefilm (Functional Advertising: From Letterhead to Advertising Film), 1934
Der Berufsphotograph (The Professional Photographer), 1938
Werkbundarbeit (Werkbund Work), 1938
Photographie in der Schweiz: Heute (Photography in Switzerland Today), 1949
Typographie (Typography), 1960

Kunsthalle Basel:
Konstruktivisten (Constructivists), 1937
Neue Kunst in der Schweiz (New Art in Switzerland), 1938
Konkrete Kunst (Concrete Art), 1944

Kunstmuseum Berne:
Schweizerische Ausstellung Angewandter Kunst (Swiss Exhibition of Applied Art), 1957

Kunstmuseum Lucerne:
These Anithese Synthese (Thesis Antithesis Synthesis),

266

international modern art, 1935
Skulpturenmuseum der Stadt Marl:
Werner Graeff: ein Pionier der Zwanziger Jahre (Werner Graeff:
A Pioneer of the Twenties), 1979
Kunstverein St. Gallen:
Konkrete, Abstrakte, Surrealistische Malerei in der Schweiz
(Concrete, Abstract, Surrealist Painting in Switzerland), 1947
Gewerbemuseum Winterthur:
VSG-Grafiker zeichnen, malen, formen 1915–1945
(Graphic Designers of the VSG Draw, Paint, Design
1915–1945), 1964
Kunstmuseum Winterthur:
Ungegenständliche Malerei in der Schweiz (Non-Figurative
Painting in Switzerland), 1958
Neue Sachlichkeit und Surrealismus in der Schweiz 1915–1940
(New Objectivity and Surrealism in Switzerland 1915–1940),
1979
Konstruktive Kunst (Constructive Art), 1981
Helmhaus Zurich:
Der Berufsfotograf (The Professional Photographer), 1944
Allianz (final exhibition), 1954
Pierre Gauchat, der Grafiker (Pierre Gauchat, Graphic
Designer), 1960
Kunstgewerbemuseum Zurich:
Das neue Heim (The New Home), 1926
Neues Bauen (New Building), 1928 (toured to Basel)
Das neue Heim (2nd exhibition), 1928
Film und Foto (Deutscher Werkbund touring exhibition), 1929
Russische Ausstellung (Russian Exhibition), 1929
Bauhaus Dessau, 1930
Die neue Fotografie in der Schweiz (The New Photography in
Switzerland), Swiss Werkbund touring exhibition, 1932
Internationale Plakat Ausstellung (International Poster
Exhibition), 1933
Schweizer Architektur und Werkkunst 1920-1936 (Swiss
Architecture and Design 1920-1936), 1936
Unsere Wohnung (Our Home), 1943
Grafik: Ausstellung des Verbandes Schweizerischer Grafiker
(Graphic Design: Exhibition of the Association of Swiss
Graphic Designers), 1943
SWB Ortsgruppe Zurich des Schweizerischen Werbundes
(SWB: Zurich Section of the Swiss Werkbund), 1950
Grafiker: ein Berufsbild (Graphic Designer: Picture of the
Profession), 1955
Konstruktive Grafik (Constructive Graphic Design), 1958
Henry van de Velde 1863-1957: Persönlichkeit und Werk (Henry
van de Velde 1863-1957: The Man and His Work), 1958
Meister der Plakatkunst (Masters of Poster Art), 1959
Die zwanziger Jahre: Kontraste eines Jahrzehnts
(The Nineteen-Twenties: Contrasts of a Decade), 1973
Kulturelle Plakate der Schweiz (Swiss Cultural Posters), 1974
Jan Tschichold: Typograph und Schriftentwerfer
(Jan Tschichold: Typographer and Letter Designer), 1976
Ernst Keller: Graphiker 1891-1968: Gesamtwerk (Ernst Keller:
Graphic Artist 1891-1968: The Complete Work), 1976
*Um 1930 in Zurich: Neues Denken Neues Wohnen Neues
Bauen* (Around 1930 in Zurich: New Thinking New Homes
New Building), 1977
*Dreissiger Jahre Schweiz: Werbestil 1930–1940: Die alltägliche
Bildersprache eines Jahrzehnts* (The Thirties in Switzerland:
Advertising Style 1930-1940: Visual Language of
a Decade), 1981

Kunsthaus Zurich:
Zeitprobleme in der Schweizer Malerei und Plastik
(Contemporary Problems in Swiss Painting and
Sculpture), 1936
Allianz, group exhibition, 1947
Albers, Glarner, Vordemberge-Gildewart, paintings, 1956
Dreissiger Jahre Schweiz: Ein Jahrzehnt im Widerspruch
(The Thirties: A Decade in Conflict), 1981

Journal special issues

Archiv für Buchgewerbe und Gebrauchsgraphik, Leipzig
Sonderheft Schweiz (special Swiss issue), no. 11/12, 1929
The Journal of Propaganda and Decorative Arts, Miami,
Swiss issue, no. 19, 1993
Octavo, London, Ring neuer Werbegestalter issue, no. 7, 1990
TM (*Typographische Monatsblätter / Schweizer Graphische
Mitteilungen / Revue suisse de l'Imprimerie*), St Gallen
El Lissitzky (edited by Jan Tschichold), December 1970
Emil Ruder, March 1971
Karl Gerstner: Typographisches Memorandum (Typographical
Memorandum, with English translation), February 1972
Jan Tschichold (designed by Tschichold), April 1972
Wolfgang Weingart, November 1974
Robert Büchler, November 1974
Odermatt & Tissi, January 1979
Armin Hofmann, March 1983
Typography Papers, Department of Typography, University
of Reading, UK (includes complete translations of Max Bill–
Tschichold dispute, 1946), no. 4, 2000
Werk, Zurich
Schweizer Grafik (Swiss Graphic Design), no. 8, August 1943
Sonderheft Grafik (Graphic Design issue), no. 11, November
1955

Journals

Ciba Zeitschrift, Basel
Die Form, Frankfurt
Du, Zurich
Format, Stuttgart
Gebrauchsgraphik, Munich
Graphic Design, Tokyo
Graphis, Zurich
Idea, Tokyo
Neue Grafik, Olten (Zurich)
Schweizer Graphische Mitteilungen, Basel
Schweizer Reklame, Zurich
Spirale, Berne
Typographica, London
Typographische Monatsblätter, Basel
(Das) Werk, Zurich

Annuals

Die Schönsten Schweizer Bücher, Berne: Eidgenössische
Departement des Innern
Graphis Annual, Zurich: Graphis Press
Modern Publicity, London: Studio Books
International Poster Annual, St Gall: Zollikofer

Picture Credits

Illustrations are identified by designer's name and page number. Full-page and colour illustrations are indicated by pages numbers in **bold grey** type.
Page numbers in brackets indicate a copyright image within a larger illustration or a detail.
The author is grateful to Jörg Hamburger, Jost Hochuli, Fridolin Müller, Siegfried Odermatt and Rosmarie Tissi, who have kindly lent original works or supplied photographs or scans for reproduction.

The marginal illustrations are reproduced mainly from various collections in London, in particular that of Paul Barnes.

Copyright © DACS London 2005

Arp, Hans/Jean: **14**, (135)
Baumberger, Otto: **29**, (30), **35**, 45, **58**
Bayer, Herbert: 24
Bill, Max: (45), 49 (all), 54(both), 55 (all), **59**, 59 (all), 69 (both), **84**, 92, **108**, 109 (both top), 110 (both), 112, **117**, 118, 125 (right margin, centre and bottom, 125, **131**, 146 (all), 147 (both, centre), **149**, 154, 155 (all), 168, 169 (all), (171), 172, 176, 177 (all)
Burchartz, Max: 21 (both), 28 (both)
Huber, Max: **132**, 135 (both), **137**, 137 (all)
Kandinsky, Wassily: 42
Lavater, Warja: 114
Le Corbusier: 39, 170
Lissitzky, El: pp.26, 27, **57**,
Lohse, Richard Paul: 11, **12**, 101, 119, 125, 128, 129 (all), **130** (both), **132**, 150 (all), **153**, 154, 172, 176, 178, , 206, 248
Moholy-Nagy, László: 20, 176
Müller-Brockmann, Josef: 6, 7, 17, 164, **165**, 166 (all), **167**, 167, **168**, 168, 170 (2), **193**, 205
Schmidt, Joost: 17
Stoecklin, Niklaus: 11, 64, 75, 112
Van Doesburg, Theo: 24, 25, 52

Illustrations from books by
Le Corbusier, 41, 176
and
Kandinsky, Wassily: 44
are © FLC / ADAGP Paris and DACS, London 2005

Reproduced by courtesy of the Poster Collection, School of Design, Zurich

Ballmer, Theo: **23**, **34**, 50
50 (bottom and margin)
Baumberger, Otto: **35**
Bill, Max: **59**, **84**, **131**
Cyliax, Walter: 32
Diggelmann, Alex: **33**
Eidenbenz, Hermann: **67**, 45 (bottom left and top centre left), **122**, 133
Erni, Hans: **126**
Flückiger, Adolf: **142**, 165
Gantenbein, Leo: **191**
Gauchat, Pierre: 119, **127**
Geiser, Roger: 221
Graf, Carl B.: **190**, **194**
Gunthard, Willi: 144
Haasbauer-Wallrath, Helene: **61**
Hamburger, Jörg, **212**
Heiniger, Ernst A.: **192**, **193**
Heiniger, Ernst and Steiner, Heiri: **80**, **84**, **85**
Herdeg, Walter: **81**
Hofmann, Armin: **195**, **214**, **216**
Honegger, Gottfried: **158**, 172
Huber, Max: **132**, **137**
Käch, Walter: **63**, **71**
Keller, Ernst: **46**, **52**, 113, 144
Kurtz, Helmuth: **94**
Lissitzky, El: 26, 27, **57**,
Lohse, Richard Paul: 11, **153**
Matter, Herbert: **87**
Meier (Allenbach), Frieda: **105**, 105 (both), 112
Megert, Peter: **227**
Miedinger, Gérard: **65**, **227**
Mühlemann, Werner: 143
Müller, Fridolin: **243**
Müller-Brockmann, Josef: 164, 166 (top left), **168**, 226 (bottom)
Neuburg, Hans: **104**, **133**, **204**
Rudin, Nelly: **220**
Ongaro, Jean and Lucien: 221
Schellenberg, Heinrich and Mettler, Ernst: **82**
Schuh, Gotthard: **83**
Schulthess, Emil: **88**
Soland, Gottlieb: **188**, 188
Stoecklin, Niklaus: 11,11
Thöni, Hans: 193
Trommer, Hans: **51**
Vieira, Mary: **174**, **175**
Vivarelli, Carlo: **134**, **156**, 200
Willimann, Alfred: **70**

Reproduced by courtesy of the Graphic Collection, Museum of Design, Zurich

Bill, Max: 49 (top)
Eidenbenz, Hermann: **66**, **106** , **141**
Honegger, Gottfried: **161**, **163**
Lohse, Richard Paul: **130** (both)
Matter, Herbert: 67, **89**, 90-91, **96-97**
Neuburg, Hans: 101
Stankowski, Anton: **107**
Vivarelli, Carlo: 138 (portrait), **173**
Zryd, Werner: **225**

Reproduced by courtesy of the Poster Collection, School of Design, Basel

Anon: 74 (both, right margin), 79
Arp, Hans and Cyliax, Walter: **14**
Ballmer, Theo:10, **48**, **50** (both), 70, **72**, **95**
Baumberger, Otto: **29**, **58**
Diggelmann, Alex: 65
Eidenbenz, Willi: **242**
Hablützel, Alfred: **189**
Heiniger, Ernst and Steiner, Heiri: 79
Lohse, Richard Paul: **12**
Matter, Herbert: **86**
Maurer, Emil: 172
Müller, Fridolin: 226
Müller-Brockmann, Josef: **165**, **167**, 226 (top)
Mumenthaler, Ernst: 18, **19**, **62**
Piatti, Celestino: **213**
Ruder, Emil: 190, **198**, 218 (bottom right), 219, 226
Schierle, Uli: 217
Steiner, Heiri: 74
Stoecklin, Niklaus: 11 (bottom), 64
Trauffer, Paul: 9
Tschichold, Jan: **77**, 115
Vivarelli, Carlo: **136**, **200**

Index